The Absence of Soulware
in Higher Education

Scrivener Publishing
100 Cummings Center, Suite 541J
Beverly, MA 01915-6106

Publishers at Scrivener
Martin Scrivener (martin@scrivenerpublishing.com)
Phillip Carmical (pcarmical@scrivenerpublishing.com)

The Absence of Soulware in Higher Education

Way Kuo

Senior Fellow, Hong Kong Institute for Advanced Study
President Emeritus, City University of Hong Kong

This edition first published in 2023 by John Wiley & Sons, Inc., 111 River Street, Hoboken, NJ 07030, USA and Scrivener Publishing LLC, 100 Cummings Center, Suite 541J, Beverly, MA 01915, USA
© 2023 Scrivener Publishing LLC
For more information about Scrivener publications please visit www.scrivenerpublishing.com.

All rights reserved. No part of this publication may be reproduced, stored in a retrieval system, or transmitted, in any form or by any means, electronic, mechanical, photocopying, recording, or otherwise, except as permitted by law. Advice on how to obtain permission to reuse material from this title is available at http://www.wiley.com/go/permissions.

Wiley Global Headquarters
111 River Street, Hoboken, NJ 07030, USA

For details of our global editorial offices, customer services, and more information about Wiley products visit us at www.wiley.com.

Limit of Liability/Disclaimer of Warranty
While the publisher and authors have used their best efforts in preparing this work, they make no representations or warranties with respect to the accuracy or completeness of the contents of this work and specifically disclaim all warranties, including without limitation any implied warranties of merchantability or fitness for a particular purpose. No warranty may be created or extended by sales representatives, written sales materials, or promotional statements for this work. The fact that an organization, website, or product is referred to in this work as a citation and/or potential source of further information does not mean that the publisher and authors endorse the information or services the organization, website, or product may provide or recommendations it may make. This work is sold with the understanding that the publisher is not engaged in rendering professional services. The advice and strategies contained herein may not be suitable for your situation. You should consult with a specialist where appropriate. Neither the publisher nor authors shall be liable for any loss of profit or any other commercial damages, including but not limited to special, incidental, consequential, or other damages. Further, readers should be aware that websites listed in this work may have changed or disappeared between when this work was written and when it is read.

Library of Congress Cataloging-in-Publication Data

ISBN 978-1-394-17474-4

Cover image: Pixabay.Com
Cover design by Russell Richardson

Set in size of 11pt and Minion Pro by Manila Typesetting Company, Makati, Philippines

Printed in the USA

10 9 8 7 6 5 4 3 2 1

Contents

Preface	ix
List of Figures and Tables	xxi
Acknowledgments	xxiii
Introduction	xxvii

Part I: Internationalization of Higher Education — 1

1	Internationalization without Soulware	5
2	Higher Education in the UK	19
3	On Universities across the Strait	25
4	Simplicity is the Ultimate Sophistication	55
5	Blind Spots and Loss of Scholarship	69
6	Communicating Rigorously	79

Part II: Integration of Teaching and Research — 101

7	The Essence of University	103
8	University Positioning	113
9	Pitfalls of Misaligning Whole-Person Education	123
10	Strategies for Nurturing Generalists and Specialists	137
11	The Successful Evergreen Tree	149
12	Students and I	161

Part III: Separation of Politics and Education — 169

13	External Forces that Interfere with Soulware	175

14	Stains in Academic Freedom and Campus Autonomy	193
15	Mechanism of the Separation of Politics and Education	205
16	University: The Seedbed of Social Movements?	219
17	Populism: The Stumbling Block of Academic Progress	231

Part IV: Quality and Evaluation — 251

18	Review is the Father of Success	255
19	Rankings in the Humanities and Liberal Arts	273
20	Tuition, Salary Comparisons of Professors and Graduates	281
21	Course Design and Choice of Majors	293
22	Accomplished Hermits behind Unprepossessing Gates	303

Part V: Creativity and Innovation — 311

23	Creativity Depends on Asking Questions	315
24	How to Promote Innovative Technology?	323
25	Where Is the Innovative Talent?	339
26	Creativity in Higher Education and Risk-Taking	351
27	Setting Policy Direction and Avoiding Nano-Management	365

Epilogue: How Does a University Set the Trend?	371
References to Tables and Figures	377
Appendix: Basic Principle of Academic Governance	385
About the Author	387
Index	389

Keep Distance from Empty Talk

Money comes and goes like endless traffic in and out of a tunnel;
It is nothing compared to the knowledge that enriches thinking.

A degree gives only a temporary pride of owning a certificate,
Not worth holding on to and relying upon.

Give full play to one's potential throughout one's life,
For the promotion of the sustained development of society.

Effectiveness must be reviewed and assessed;
If we really care for education, keep your distance from empty talk.

Preface

The Chinese and English editions of *The Absence of Soulware in Higher Education* are simultaneously published by Linking (聯經) in Taipei and Wiley in New Jersey. The book reflects the momentous changes taking place in higher education in Taiwan, Hong Kong and Mainland China as well as globally in the past five years and analyzes strengths and weaknesses with concrete examples.

Reasons for Publishing

Before I took over the presidency at City University of Hong Kong (CityU) in 2008, I had been engaged in teaching and research in the US and Europe for 34 years, starting as a graduate student and progressing through the ranks to assistant professor, associate professor, professor, chair professor and university distinguished professor. During my tenure in the US, I also had progressive responsibilities in academic leadership, starting from being appointed the head of department to dean of engineering and associate vice-chancellor for engineering at Texas A&M University System. I was a Fulbright scholar during that period and was elected director of the Council of Industrial Engineering Academic Department Heads. I have also been an ABET (Accreditation Board for Engineering and Technology) member for ten years.

I have been personally involved in scientific research and innovation in the US, heading scientific research administration at national laboratories and serving as a high-tech and government consultant for over 40 years and as editor-in-chief for *IEEE Transactions on Reliability* for 16 years. Therefore, as I have access to and have provided first-hand higher education and research, I have a legitimate voice in this matter.

The English version of *Soulware: The American Way in China's Higher Education*, published by Wiley-Scrivener in New Jersey, 2019, highlighted the importance of separating politics from education. In the last four years, while tremendous changes have occurred in higher education across the Taiwan Strait (the Strait) including Taiwan, Hong Kong and Mainland China, political conflicts, street politics and populism have swept through campuses. Much worse, some media organizations have often acted as go-betweens for those entangling politics with education, a phenomenon hardly seen in the US. This is why significantly revising and updating the English version and publishing the Chinese version are required.

I endeavor to be as factual as possible in all these versions when I make my arguments. In several instances, my arguments are critical of what I perceive as serious mistakes in higher education, if not outright failures.

Soulware

Before moving on to higher education, it is necessary to define the terms I will be using. Borrowing from the verbiage of computer science, I will reference the hardware and software found in higher education.

By hardware, I mean a university's infrastructure or physical facilities, such as buildings, libraries, internet, laboratories, and so forth, which provide an environment conducive to good teaching and research. By software, I mean human resources, government policy, society's attitudes, strategic plans, the research abilities of faculty, and the sound educational background and preparedness of students. People often say grandmasters can be categorized as software and can be more important than grand buildings.

Whereas the hardware and the software are both essential for success in higher education, a third element is even more critical. It is essential for achieving greatness at a university and is related to education efficiency and internationalization.

In Chinese culture, people with great talent and ability are referred to as "1,000 *li* horses (supposedly able to gallop 1,000 *li*, approximately 400 kilometers, in a single day), while Bo Le (伯樂) is the legendary person who could judge a horse's qualities from appearance. While there may be 1,000 *li* horses here and there, finding the right judge of horses or Bo Le is hard. Here, 1,000 *li* horses refer to academic masters, and Bo Le is the recognition of soulware, the subject of this book.

Education calls for efficiency. The Chinese ancestors believed that education could not only enlighten our minds and cultivate our moral self so that we could learn to manage our families, govern our state and be a "gentleman" but also serve as a stepping stone for obtaining government positions at the imperial court. Today, for anyone receiving an education, we need to assess the results of education: the capability to pursue a personal career, give back as a citizen, advance social harmony, and maintain the sustainable development of the world. Internationalization is a commonly discussed topic among university administrators and governmental officials. It demands the presence of a certain mindset that goes beyond the hardware and the software of a university. This mindset enables better communication and coordination toward achieving greatness in education and research.

"Go ahead setting a high moral standard and advocating noble ideas, and don't overthink the rest, be it east or west, past or present." This mindset is what I have labeled soulware. So what exactly is soulware for a university?

At a more abstract level, I see soulware as a vision, as the crucial bringing together (or fusion) of technical virtuosity and humanistic cum spiritual engagements. Soulware entails a commitment to enable our hearts and souls to embrace due processes, follow international norms in all our educational endeavors, and devote ourselves truly to learning from our studies and research. Soulware can refer to moral character and *Bildung* (cultivation of self or formation of one's character).

Su Shi, a Chinese Song dynasty poet, once wrote, "With straw sandals and a bamboo staff, I am better suited than riding a horse / And fear not / The wind and storm in life though clad only in a palm-leaf plaited cape." If we keep our goals in sight and let them be, we can travel light no matter what happens. At the operational level, we need to make the best use of the hardware and software at our disposal and spearhead innovation, the combination of teaching and research, and the separation of politics and education for the betterment of society. Conceptually, I envision hardware, software, and soulware working and communicating in concert as the three constituting parts of a university, with soulware as an internal cosmic force, as shown in Figure 0.1.

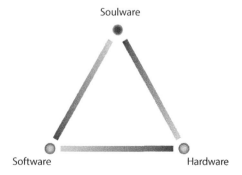

Figure 0.1 Elements of university composition.

An ideal university has the pursuit of excellence in producing and disseminating knowledge as its goal. The soulware concept elaborated in this book encompasses anti-discrimination, openness and transparency, fair competition, equal treatment, and accountability applied to all stakeholders, including universities, government, and society. These principles provide a conducive environment for achieving the goal with significant opportunities for students' enlightenment. It sharpens both the pen and the sword, whereas the reverse might see them coerced by politics and politicians, making such students more like subcontractors who survive only by following trends. Achieving such goals depends on implementing healthy soulware in higher education, free from politics, government interference and the babbling of populists.

Simply put, the separation of politics and education, academic freedom, and campus autonomy constitute the ideal combination of higher education soulware and the three pillars that drive a great university forward. As shown in Figure 0.2, we can only guarantee academic freedom and campus autonomy by ensuring the separation of politics and education. With clear guidelines, universities should play a leadership role in integrating industry, education and research. To promote innovation, academics should refrain from holding positions simultaneously in industry, government and universities, and neither should the community encourage such practices. Instead, they should seek industry-university-research collaboration.

Higher education across the Strait

For the most part, the higher education system in the US has been the most advanced over the past century, and therefore it deserves to be studied and benchmarked.

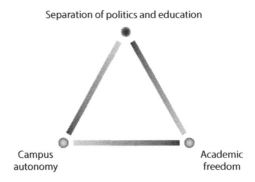

Figure 0.2 Three wisdom pillars of higher education soulware.

Much of this book concerns higher education systems, in Taiwan, Hong Kong and Mainland China. Though I have somewhat less personal experience in the Mainland than in Taiwan and Hong Kong, my observations via my visits and other sources and data help provide sufficient evidence for the analysis presented in this book. Compared with the US, the observations and analysis made in this book regarding higher education across the Strait are equally applicable elsewhere, especially in universities in Europe, South Korea and Japan.

Ironically, some people in Taiwan and Hong Kong dissociate themselves politically and even economically from Mainland China. Some think of themselves as not Chinese; however, they turn out to be more Chinese and retain more traits of traditional Chinese culture than they may have realized or are willing to admit. Culturally speaking, they may be more Chinese than people on the Mainland because they did not experience the Cultural Revolution (1966–1976) when educational institutions from primary schools to universities were closed and intellectuals were targeted for ideological critique and physical abuse. The Mainland Chinese of that generation were subject to physical and spiritual distortion, the influence of which is deeply rooted. As a result, "uncultured intellectuals" can be seen everywhere.

More objectively, however, there are many similarities among universities across the Strait because they share similar cultural roots. For example, on a somewhat negative side, people in Taiwan, Hong Kong and Mainland China—not only students but also perhaps their parents, and especially our society—fetishize academic degrees, believing that the more the better. They often possess an obsequious admiration for Westerners and Western things, and yet they may not learn from others' strong points or avoid others' shortcomings. As a result, the value of academic degrees becomes diluted, people fail to find jobs despite their elevated level of education, and degrees do not reflect actual learning. They may be well-disciplined, but often they lack the spirit of innovation and creativity. They are primarily diligent, energetic, peace-loving, interested in learning, and highly respectful of those with knowledge, degrees, or power. These phenomena, whether positive or negative, are the result of the influence of what happened in modern China and its historical heritage.

One common criticism of Mainland Chinese students is that many need more humanistic literacy. Such students may seem like robots with mechanical memories and lots of skills but with insufficient education in the arts and humanities. On the other hand, students from Hong Kong tend to be too particular about trifles, write poorly in both English and Chinese, and need to be taught about Chinese and world history. In recent years, the youth in Taiwan, confused by history re-written out of political concerns, do not know what to believe anymore, which may be the implications of the entanglement of politics and education, with the most serious situation being in the Mainland, followed by Taiwan and then Hong Kong.

I do not subscribe to a universal way of educating people, given that employment must be the ultimate aim. Therefore, general education, which is promoted in many universities, must be modulated for university students from different disciplines. In some cases, general education may be unwarranted for professional education at the university level and could even backfire.

On the other hand, the primary purpose of education is for students to learn how to serve society rather than just to benefit from what society offers, "dancing around under the moonlight, oblivious of time and place." (Su Shi, 蘇軾) However, it is common to find people in Hong Kong and Taiwan who are self-centered and keep asking for favors. Universities across the Strait are encouraged to inculcate humanistic literacy studies at college, but it might be too late by then because the students may have already formed their patterns of behavior.

So how do we learn the lessons going forward?

The Absence of Soulware

In Hong Kong or Mainland China, names in official documents are often recorded according to the local romanization system, and sometimes the first and last names are reversed. During my many years in the US, such errors were seldom seen. Americans don't know the meaning of Chinese names, yet they don't mix things up because they regard it as impolite to misspell others' names. In the US, there are all kinds of given names and family names. Such matters are always dealt with carefully. This is *Bildung*, a manifestation of soulware.

What's outrageous is that not only is a person's name or an overseas university's name misspelled, some people who have communicated with us multiple times and have letterheaded paper at hand that spells CityU, short for City University of Hong Kong, as CUHK (short for The Chinese University of Hong Kong) or even worse, simply as the University of Hong Kong (HKU), crediting the papers written by CityU professors to The University of Hong Kong or The Chinese University of Hong Kong. Sometimes, such mistakes are made by people from a government's education departments. In the US, people are taught to respect others, while people across the Strait tend to only care about sweeping the snow from their own doorstep, i.e., minding their own business or being more concerned about their own feelings. Due to their poor upbringing, they are more interested in tricks than in seeking justice. This might epitomize some of the reality across the Strait.

In addition to a lack of respect for others, universities in societies across the Strait are incorrectly viewed as political assets to be manipulated and utilized. Even in Taiwan, which has experienced a baptism of democracy and the impact of political disputes, young people still feel lost and disoriented. The Western democratic system may not be perfect, but it offers people ways to secure power for the betterment of society. Unfortunately, the benefits of democratic practices for the people have been overlooked by many across the Strait when they use universities and their students as a platform for promoting political propaganda. More or less controlled by politics, people in societies across the Strait put forward empty slogans and advocate populist actions. What the superior loves, his inferiors will be found to love exceedingly. It is, therefore, not surprising to see young people, knowingly or unknowingly, fall into a cheap cycle of political disputes, willing to be pawns or the hands behind the action.

As a result, they are almost always imitators when dealing with academic issues and major decisions; instead of dealing with genuine concerns, staying busy responding to those issues experienced by local communities or outside practices, when ideally, universities should be leaders for the betterment of society. Among others, using the internet in the classroom is an example; establishing big data research is another. Both were standard industry practices before universities started to pay attention to them.

Many universities lag behind others because they possess poor mindsets. They should stay away from empty talk and, while following academic autonomy and ethics, implement internationalization wholeheartedly from the outset.

According to Wang Chuanshan (王船山), a Chinese essayist, historian, and philosopher of the late Ming and early Qing dynasties, "If we put knowledge first, respecting knowledge at the cost of ability, then our ability will be lost." But the truth is, we don't know, either! Curing the blindness of the mind and promoting a healthy soul and spirit are the essential points of this book.

With the right soulware and dedication to excellence, what counts is not the number of texts studied, the breadth of books read, the degrees obtained, or the depth of the research carried out. Everything can be overcome in higher education if we adhere to the integration of teaching and research and the separation of politics and education.

Publication of the Book

The Absence of Soulware in Higher Education provides an analysis for promoting healthy soulware in the higher education sectors in Taiwan, Hong Kong and Mainland China from five angles: internationalization of higher education, integration of teaching and research, separation of politics and education, quality and evaluation, and creativity and innovation. In addition to the Introduction, titled "How Should Universities Be Run?", I offer an analytical account of higher education in Taiwan, Hong Kong and Mainland China in 27 chapters, with examples of best practices from higher education in the US for guidance. We must uphold the four basic requirements in higher education: adhering to procedures, simplifying administration, adopting good advice from all quarters, and leadership accountability. Otherwise, nothing is left but castles in the sky.

The book ends with an Epilogue: "How Does a University Set the Trend?"

The tables and figures were prepared based on the materials listed in "References to Tables and Figures". Due to time constraints, there may be errors.

Included in the Appendix is "Basic Principle of Academic Governance," which states that the separation of politics and education is the foundation of academic freedom and campus autonomy.

A previous book was published in Taipei in 2015 under the Chinese title 《高等教育怎麼辦》, which was my first attempt to explore the soulware concept. In 2017, a slightly modified version was published by The Commercial Press in Hong Kong, and a version printed in simplified Chinese by Citic Press Group in Beijing under the title 《高等教育的心件》 and 《心件－大學校長說教育》, respectively. What's more, the concept of soulware attracted attention in Japan. A Japanese edition under the title 《高等教育とはいかにあるへぎか　両岸　の大学における「心件（ハートウェア）」の探求》 was published by Josai University in Tokyo in 2018. After a lot of updates and enrichments to the 2019 Wiley-Scrivener version, *Soulware: The American Way in China's Higher Education*, the new version in Chinese titled 《高等教育的心盲》 was published to serve as a witness to history.

The Absence of Soulware in Higher Education is written as a reference for the higher education sector. All royalties will be donated to scholarships for university students.

PREFACE xvii

Video Clips of Interviews with Academic Leaders

I have interviewed the presidents of 32 universities worldwide and the principals of six high schools across the Strait and France since 2019 for a video series "Beyond Boundaries: Dialogue with Presidents of World's Leading Educational Institutions." We have recorded 36 episodes in total. A 22-minute condensed and a 40-minute full version of each of these high-quality programs have been broadcast each Friday, except during leave breaks, on the CityU website since March 2022 and then at Master-Insight.com. From January 2023, Hong Kong Cable Television has broadcast ten edited interview episodes, each featuring conversations with two university presidents. These interviews caught the attention of Times Higher Education (THE), which uniquely introduced each episode with quite an exceptional treatment. As of May 1, 2023, THE has generated over 2.2 million social media impressions and attracted more than 13,000 visits to the microsite across all 32 episodes. THE has leveraged the reach of its e-newsletters to showcase the series to a global audience of over 135,000 academics and administrators.

The university presidents and high school principals invited for the interviews come from institutions either with a long history and having passed through many setbacks or leading institutions known for their outstanding achievements, or both. Not only do these pioneering interviews in the higher education circle allow us to witness the teaching, research and management philosophy of top universities in the East and West, but they also represent the prevailing concepts of teaching and research as well as governance and reinforce the points illustrated in this book, for example, the "integration of teaching and research" and the "separation of politics and education", thereby enriching the content of this book and endorsing its arguments.

Figure 0.3 shows the universities and schools in South Asia, East Asia, the Caucasus, Europe, North America, the Middle East, South Africa, Australia and other places whose presidents or principals have been interviewed. Most of the talks were conducted face-to-face, and a few were conducted on Zoom due to quarantine restrictions during the COVID-19 pandemic. Higher education must keep pace with the times. The interviews elaborate on the arguments presented in this book and can be used as a reference

Please browse the CityU website, through the QR code in Figure 0.4, to access the video series "Beyond Boundaries" for my interviews with 36 presidents and principals.

xviii PREFACE

1. Tohoku University
   Hideo Ohno
   President (2018-)
2. Taipei First Girls School
   Yang Shih Ruey
   Principal (2014-2019)
3. Taipei Municipal Jianguo School
   Chien-Kuo Hsu
   Principal (2015-2022)
4. Shanghai Jiao Tong University
   Zhang Jie
   President (2006-2017)
5. Beijing No.4 High School
   Ma Jinglin
   Principal (2017-)
6. Diocesan Girls' School
   Stella Lau Kun Lai-kuen
   Headmistress (1999-)
7. Pui Ching Middle School
   Ho Lik Ko
   Principal (2018-)
8. National University of Singapore
   Tan Eng Chye
   President (2018-)
9. Indian Institute of Technology, Delhi
   V. Ramgopal Rao
   Director (2016-2022)
10. University of Delhi
    Yogesh K Tyagi
    Vice Chancellor (2016-2020)
11. Ivane Javakhishvili Tbilisi State University
    George Sharvashidze
    Rector (2016-2022)
12. Cherkasy National University
    Oleksandr Cherevko
    Rector (2015-)
13. Tel Aviv University
    Ariel Porat
    President (2019-)
14. Technion-Israel Institute of Technology
    Uri Sivan
    President (2019-)
15. PBC of the Council of Higher Education, Israel
    Yoseph A. Mekori
    Chair (2021-)
16. University of Vienna
    Heinz W Engl
    Reactor (2011-2022)
17. Humboldt University of Berlin
    Sabine Kunst*
    President (2016-2021)
18. Ludwig Maximilian University of Munich
    Bernd Huber
    President (2002-)
19. University of Stuttgart
    Wolfram Ressel
    Rector (2006-)
20. Catholic University of Leuven, KU Leuven
    Luc Sels
    Rector (2017-)
21. University of Louvain (UC Louvain)
    Vincent Blondel
    Rector (2014-)
22. Lycée Louis-le-Grand, Paris
    Joël Bianco
    Principal (2020-)
23. Le College de France
    Serge Haroche
    President (2012-2015)
24. Université PSL
    Alain Fuchs
    President (2017-)
25. Institut d'Optique Graduate School
    Alain Aspect
    Director (1992-)
26. École Polytechnique
    Eric Labaye
    President (2018-)
27. Institut Polytechnique de Paris
    Eric Labaye
    President (2019-)
28. University of Bologna
    Giovanni Molari
    Rector (2021-)
29. University of Cape Town
    Mamokgethi Phakeng
    Vice Chancellor (2018-)
30. Cornell Tech
    Juliet Rothschild Weissman
    Chief Administrative Officer (2015-)
31. George Washington University
    Mark S Wrighton
    President (2022-)
32. U of Illinois at Urbana-Champaign
    Robert J Jones, Chancellor (2016-)
    U of Minnesota, Senior VP (2004-2013)
33. Washington University in St. Louis
    Mark S Wrighton
    Chancellor (1995-2019)
34. The University of British Columbia
    Santa J Ono
    President and Vice Chancellor (2016-2022)
35. Simon Fraser University
    Joy Johnson
    President and Vice Chancellor (2020-)
36. The University of Queensland
    Deborah Terry
    Vice Chancellor & President (2020-)
37. Epilogue, City University of Hong Kong
    Way Kuo
    President & University Distinguished Professor (2008-2023)

*In October 2021, shortly after the interview, Kunst announced her resignation as president to protest the parliamentary amendment to the "Berlin Higher Education Act" in which the government mandates that all university professors be awarded tenure. This is an effort to separate politics and education.

Figure 0.3 Geographical locations of the 36 universities and high schools whose presidents and principals were featured in the videos.

(a) (b)

Figure 0.4 The QR codes to access (a) the video series "Beyond Boundaries", featuring interviews with university presidents and high school principals; (b) ten edited interview episodes broadcast by Hong Kong Cable Television.

Due to COVID-19 and my own health, the project was not completed by the end of 2022 or before my retirement as CityU president in spring 2023 as scheduled. It was especially disappointing not to conduct interviews with the presidents of the following well-regarded institutions: the University of Helsinki, Korea Advanced Institute of Science and Technology, McGill University, National Taiwan University, Seoul National University, the University of Sydney and Tsinghua University.

The Right Way

"Some things are essential, and others are incidental. For every issue, there are an end and a beginning. Knowing what is first and what is last, we will be close to the Way" *(Great Learning)*. There is no Way without the soul; there is no soul without the Way. Both the "integration of teaching and research" and the "separation of politics and education" are the right Way for higher education. If you still feel perplexed about the Way, then soulware is absent.

Way Kuo
City University of Hong Kong
Hong Kong Institute for Advanced Study
June 2023

List of Figures and Tables

Figures

Figure 0.1	Elements of university composition.
Figure 0.2	Three wisdom pillars of higher education soulware.
Figure 0.3	Geographical locations of the 36 universities and high schools whose presidents and principals were featured in the videos.
Figure 0.4	The QR codes to access (a) the video series "Beyond Boundaries", featuring interviews with university presidents and high school principals; (b) ten edited interview episodes broadcast by Hong Kong Cable Television.
Figure 3.1	University enrollment rate in the US, Mainland China, Japan, Singapore, South Korea, Taiwan and Hong Kong.
Figure 3.2	Number of newborn babies in Taiwan, Hong Kong and Mainland China (1950 to 2021).
Figure 3.3	Birth rates in Taiwan, Hong Kong and Mainland China (1950 to 2021).
Figure 20.1	Percentage of starting salary of university graduates to GDP per capita.
Figure 20.2	Percentage of the typical annual salary of assistant professors to GDP per capita.
Figure 20.3	Percentage of student tuition to GDP per capita.
Figure V.1	R&D investment in the US, Mainland China, Taiwan, Hong Kong, Singapore, South Korea and Japan.
Figure 23.1	The One Health concept.

Tables

Table 0.1	Students from Mainland China studying in the US (2009–2020).
Table 17.1	Annual fatalities in Taiwan, Hong Kong, Mainland China and the US over the indicated years.

Table 18.1	Number of universities ranked in top 100 in the US, the UK, Mainland China, Japan, Singapore, South Korea, Hong Kong, Taiwan, Israel and Others.
Table 18.2	Number of universities in the world's top 100 with the top 2% of scholars in the US, the UK, Japan, Mainland China, Singapore, South Korea, Hong Kong, Taiwan, Israel and others; and number of universities in the world's top 100 with "the ratio of top 2% to total number of professors in the university."
Table 20.1	Comparison of four Asian Tigers.
Table 24.1	Number of US utility patents granted to universities in the US, the UK, Mainland China, Japan, Singapore, South Korea, Hong Kong, Taiwan and others.
Table 25.1	Academic background of CEOs in the US, Mainland China, Hong Kong and Taiwan.

Acknowledgments

The Forewords for *Soulware: The American Way in China's Higher Education* were written by G. P. "Bud" Peterson, President of Georgia Institute of Technology (2009–2019); Yong Qiu, President of Tsinghua University in Beijing (2015–2022); and Frank H. Shu, President of National Tsing Hua University at Hsinchu (2002–2006).

The book has been reviewed by Mr. Longgen Chen, Mr. Michael Gibb, Dr. Eva Lui, Dr. K F Tam and Dr. Kevin Downing of CityU.

I am indebted to Professor Loren Crabtree, former Chancellor of the University of Tennessee; Professor Mike Crow, President of Arizona State University; Professor Mike Kotlikoff, Provost of Cornell University; and Professor Chin-Chuan Lee and Professor Longxi Zhang of CityU for their input during the writing process.

A 40-minute video clip of each of the interviews that I conducted with university presidents and high school principals between 2019 and 2022 was produced by a team of five led by Professor Joe He of CityU, who traveled a long distance with me, designing, editing, and completing the final production, with coordination handled by Ms. Pauline Chan of CityU. The ten edited interview excerpts were produced by him and his team. The final product confirmed that if there is a will guided by the right soulware, there is a way.

In addition, I have been invited in the last few years to deliver speeches on education and science and technology by over 100 universities, high schools and academic institutions across the Strait, as well as by international forums in the US, Japan, Australia and Europe. These include:

Universities: The Chinese University of Hong Kong, CityU, The Hong Kong Polytechnic University, The Hong Kong University of Science and Technology; National Taiwan University, National Tsing Hua University, National Chiao Tung University, National Cheng Kung University, National Chengchi University, Asia University, China Medical University, National Sun Yat-sen University, Tamkang University; Peking University, Tsinghua University, Zhejiang University, Shanghai Jiaotong University, Northwest University, Northwestern Polytechnical University, Fudan University,

Beihang University, Xi'an Jiaotong University, Harbin Institute of Technology, University of Chinese Academy of Sciences;

High schools: Several dozen high schools in Hong Kong; Taipei Municipal Chiankuo High School, Taipei First Girls' High School, Tainan First Senior High School, Taichung First Senior High School, Municipal Kaohsiung Girls' Senior High School, Taipei Jingmei Girls High School, St. Viator Catholic High School, National Hualien Girls' Senior High School; Beijing No. 4 High School, Hengshui High School, Hebei, Yanyuan Nationality Middle School, Sichuan; Robert College in Turkey;

Professional organizations: Ministry of Education, Taiwan, Republic of China, National Science and Technology Museum, Chinese Institute of Industrial Engineers, Chinese Management Association, Institute of Engineering Education Taiwan; The Hong Kong Jockey Club, The Hong Kong Federation of Youth Groups, Master Insight Media, University of Chicago Centre in Hong Kong, CityU Eminence Society, Hong Kong Professionals and Senior Executives Association, Hong Kong College of Radiologists, Tsinghua Alumni Association of Hong Kong, The Federation of Hong Kong Writers, Asia Pacific Taiwan Federation of Industry and Commerce, Rotary International, Global Institute For Tomorrow (GIFT), 2021 Hong Kong Book Fair; Chinese Academy of Engineering, Chinese Academy of Sciences, The Forum by Phoenix TV, China Association for Quality, Systems Engineering Society of China, Annual Meeting of Institute of Quality & Reliability of Tsinghua University; Asia-Pacific International Symposium on Advanced Reliability and Maintenance, Eurasian Conference RISK.

Organizations outside the areas across the Strait: The Russian Presidential Academy of National Economy and Public Administration; Iowa State University, DIALOGUE360 live TV in San Francisco, Texas A&M University, The Institute for Operations Research and the Management Sciences, The Electrochemical Society Meeting in New Orleans, US; Tsing Hua Entrepreneur Network; North America Federation of Tsinghua Alumni Associations; PARIS VI (University of Pierre & Marie Curie), Paris, France; Indian Institute of Technology Bombay; IEEE NSW Section held at The University of Sydney, Australia; Atomic Energy Society of Japan, Yokohama, Japan; Cross-Strait University President Forum 2015 in Macau.

This book was partially written by adapting speeches delivered on the above occasions. Some of my views were reported in newspapers and magazines, such as *Hong Kong Economic Journal, Ming Pao Daily, Sing Tao Daily, Hong Kong Economic Journal Monthly, Ming Pao Monthly, Yazhou Zhoukan, East Week, Hong Kong Economic Times, Master Insight* and *South China Morning Post* in Hong Kong; *Global Views Monthly, China*

Times, United Daily News, Economic Daily News, Management Science Newsletter and *The Storm Media* in Taiwan; and in internal publications of universities and institutions in Mainland China; as well as editorials for *IEEE Transactions on Reliability*. Interviews have been conducted by US, Taiwan, Hong Kong and Mainland China media corporations such as TVB, Bloomberg, Evaluation Bimonthly by TWAEA, *Journal of General Education, Business Weekly*, iFeng Century Forum, NetEase, *Sohu, People's Daily Online*, Asia-Pacific Satellite TV, *The New York Times, The Chronicle of Higher Education*, and *Times Higher Education*, among others.

The above-mentioned people, interviews, professional societies, schools and institutions have provided me with precious opportunities and assisted me in authoring the book. I would like to express my gratitude to them all.

Introduction

How Should Universities Be Run?

It is well acknowledged that Chinese culture pays special attention to education. But how has education been viewed and how modern is the current practice of education in Chinese societies? How is it going to develop further? And to what extent has the modernization of Chinese higher education been developed?

In ancient times, "Chinese" was more of a cultural concept than a racially or ethnically defined notion, but at the same time, there was the differentiation of *hua*, meaning civilized Chinese, and *yi*, meaning barbarians outside central China and a different race. Such differentiation between *hua* and *yi* has been embedded in the mind of the Chinese for a long time, even when China was economically and politically weak. Even today, we still hear people in Hong Kong use the slang *gweilo* and *gweipo* (meaning literally "ghost/devil men or women") to refer to white men and women, respectively. In Taiwan, in addition to a small sub-group of the non-Han population of Taiwanese native inhabitants who have inhabited the island for millennia, there are the ethnic Hoklo or Hakka immigrants from southern Fujian province and people who migrated to Taiwan after 1949 from Mainland China and their descendants, and the newly naturalized residents in recent years.

In addition to the southern culture in Hong Kong and Taiwan that discriminates against people from specific provinces, there are all kinds of discrimination cases on their campuses. Since they are not serious enough to be considered violations of the law, little attention has been paid to them, or they have simply been ignored. Discrimination is common in the US as well, but racial, sex and age discrimination are strictly prohibited. If similar cases should happen at American universities, they are dealt with as serious matters, and the responsible party will face dire consequences.

In this part of the world, however, it is not rare to see people poking fun at foreigners, mocking foreign customs, or joking about foreign names or faces. There was once even a university president in Hong Kong who laughed at someone's foreign-sounding name. Because it was not viewed as a big issue, no one demanded an apology. This not only shows bad taste and a lack of sensitivity among the Chinese but also a lack of respect for other people and their identities.

People of the world hope to learn from advanced civilizations, understand multiple cultures, make effective use of or update their cultural resources and, at the same time, create their own brand. Measured by higher education standards, on many occasions, the United States seems to be *hua* (or the civilized Chinese), while the three territories across the Strait become *yi* (or barbarians)! How did this happen?

Current Status of American Higher Education

Campus autonomy is the essence of American higher education. With respect to the professional management of higher education, any improvements needed in teaching and research at universities should be left to the professors rather than outsiders, with strategic measures that encourage healthy and open competition so that universities can make contributions to society through academic research.

American colleges and universities excel; American citizens enjoy opportunities to receive a high-quality education. They have been at the top for many years, which is unprecedented in human history. Nowadays, even some European universities with a long history are trying to imitate the successful practice of American universities. But the popularization of higher education should not be achieved at the cost of reducing the quality of higher education and degrees. Even though everyone can be educated, success depends on personal effort. There is no guarantee of getting a degree. In this regard, the American higher education system is the best and worth emulating. In addition to the elite private educational institutions widely known to the public across the Strait, the state universities and colleges in the US may be more admirable, but they are often neglected by people worldwide.

Of course, American higher education is not perfect and is continuously adjusting and improving. Although American universities adopt strict quality assurance when granting degrees, higher education has been under general attack due to cuts to state-funded public universities, expensive tuition and fees of private universities, and regular tuition increases, which are different from the practice at European universities. Moreover, there are many success stories concerning people around the world, including those in the US, who never went to college or only had limited further education. This shows that global higher education is still inadequate, and so we should consider more adaptable, inclusive and innovative solutions.

In recent years, US college enrollments have declined due to fewer high school graduates. Increasingly four-year universities actively recruit overseas students to offset falling numbers of domestic students. However, with fierce competition from the UK, Australia and New Zealand, as well as from educational institutions in Mainland China, the enrollment of overseas students in the US also started dropping.

According to a research report by the National Student Clearinghouse Research Center, American colleges and universities experienced the largest drop in enrollments in half a century in 2021. The number of undergraduate enrollments declined for two consecutive years. The number of freshmen in 2021 was down 6.6% from 2020. International undergraduate enrollments continued to decline as well. The 8.2% drop in 2021 followed the previous year's 12% year-over-year decline. The number of international graduate students grew by 13.1% after a 7.8% decline in the fall of 2020. Under the influence of free-market competition and the COVID-19 pandemic, some small private universities are on the brink of bankruptcy.

Trump, Roosevelt vs Biden: A Historical Overview

Trump

According to a report on *CNN*, former US President Donald Trump characterized Chinese students in the US as spies during a private dinner with corporate executives in New Jersey on August 7, 2018. Apart from the impact on international unity and historical perspectives, such careless words, if they were in fact uttered, endanger both Chinese students and US society at large, which is lamentable.

Whether or not influenced by Trump, Mainland China was no longer on the list of countries for the 2018/19 admission cycle, during which an optional interview program was offered by Stanford University, after Massachusetts Institute of Technology (MIT). That means applicants from the Chinese Mainland interested in applying to these two universities did not have an interview opportunity.

Developments in the US-China trade war, and the investigation of researchers affiliated with the Thousand Talents plan, a scheme to attract Chinese scientists and entrepreneurs back to Mainland China mostly for part-time appointments, have slowed academic advancement and technological modernization in China and ultimately hurt China-US scientific cooperation. This is based on news published in *Nature* on October 24, 2018, in an article titled "China hides identities of top scientific recruits amidst growing US scrutiny." By the same token, Taiwan's Yushan Talents scheme, like Mainland China's Thousand Talents scheme, could be in jeopardy because it was being questioned by the US.

Upon hearing all these news stories, people might wonder why Chinese students go to study in America in the first place and what they have brought to these societies over the years. Do we know what has happened historically in Sino-American student exchange?

Roosevelt
In 1906, Edmund J. James, the fifth president of the University of Illinois, proposed that the US establish scholarships enabling Chinese students to study in America. "The nation which succeeds in educating the young Chinese of the present generation will be the nation which for a given expenditure of effort will reap the largest possible returns in moral, intellectual and commercial influence," James wrote to US President Theodore Roosevelt at the time.[1]

Instead of mimicking those 19th-century imperialists, who reaped huge financial gains from old China, Roosevelt's administration accepted the idea of establishing the Boxer Indemnity Scholarship Program. Roosevelt believed such a program could maximize American profits by bridging China with American culture and traditions. In 1908, the US Congress passed a bill endorsing Roosevelt's vision, which led to the establishment in 1911 of a preparatory school in Beijing for young Chinese who would later pursue studies at American universities. The school was named Tsinghua College (Tsinghua Xuetang) and would use half of the Boxer Indemnity to support Chinese students studying in the United States.

The Boxer Indemnity Scholarship Program was a milestone for Chinese students wishing to study at US institutions of higher learning, and it set the scene for *The American Way in China's Higher Education*. Other than during the war years in the 20th century, studying in the US has been the mainstream for Chinese students going overseas. The number of Chinese students in the US set an all-time high in the 2019/20 academic year, reaching 372,532. Among them, 55,661 were PhD students and 28,779 high school students. China also remained the largest source of international

---

[1] Mary Timmins, "Enter the Dragon", *Illinois Alumni*, December 15, 2011.

students in the US for the tenth consecutive year. Table 0.1 outlines the number of Chinese students studying in the US over the last 12 years.

In addition to bringing back to China the American way in education and technology development, Mainland Chinese students, as well as students from the three territories across the Strait, add value to American campuses and societies through the diversity of their perspectives, which American high-tech industries and national laboratories know full well. The impact of the Tsinghua program and other extended programs on China and the US has been much greater than either James or Roosevelt could have imagined.

The history of Chinese immigration to the US can be traced to as early as over 170 years ago, from the railway workers who contributed to building the first railway on the North American continent in the mid-19th century to the government-sponsored overseas students around the 19th

Table 0.1 Students from Mainland China studying in the US (2009–2020).

Year	Students from China studying in the US	% change over the previous year
2020/21	317,299	-14.8
2019/20	372,532	0.8
2018/19	369,548	1.7
2017/18	363,341	3.6
2016/17	350,755	6.8
2015/16	328,547	8.1
2014/15	304,040	10.8
2013/14	274,439	16.5
2012/13	235,597	21.4
2011/12	194,029	23.1
2010/11	157,558	23.5
2009/10	127,628	---

Note: According to the *Wall Street Journal*, the number of student visas issued by the US to Mainland citizens in the first half of 2022 was reduced by 50% compared to the same period in 2019 due to US-China tensions and the COVID-19 pandemic.

and 20th centuries, and the university, high school and primary school students studying in the US, investors, high-tech talents or people who choose to retire in the US because of their naturalized children. By 2021, there were approximately 5.5 million ethnic Chinese in the US (including those from Hong Kong, Macau, Taiwan and Southeast Asia). Among them, 54% had at least a bachelor's degree, 51% were engaged in professional and managerial work, 27% had a master's degree, whereas only around 13% of immigrants from other countries had a master's degree. Among the local residents, 12% had a master's degree.

Chinese students also bring honor and pride to America. One such example is that eight Chinese-American Nobel laureates in physics and chemistry studied and did their research in the States. In addition, about 200 Chinese Americans are members of the National Academy of Sciences, the National Academy of Engineering and the National Academy of Medicine. Numerous Chinese Americans who work in national laboratories, high-tech companies and higher education institutions have contributed economically, technologically, and scientifically over the past few decades, promoting those American values cherished in China and elsewhere in the world. The top three regions with the largest distribution of prominent Chinese scientific and technological talents in the US are Silicon Valley in California, Greater New York, and Greater Boston. Of course, we should also include the outstanding Chinese in arts, sports, and so forth who add to the brilliance of the US.

Chinese culture has enriched, and will continue to enrich, life in America, helping to make the US a more internationalized country. Disparaging an entire population or any ethnic group is wrong-headed and un-American. James' remarks about educating young Chinese in America had held true for more than 100 years until the Trump period when he complicated the matter. An overall view of the situation for the US and China shows that the world benefits when it is united; it suffers when divided. For that reason, Roosevelt's vision to bridge China with American culture and traditions should be enhanced instead of diminished. We should also bridge the US with Chinese culture and traditions to make this a better world.

Biden

Trump lost the election and was succeeded by Joe Biden, and yet the American policy towards China has not changed. On March 18, 2021, top American and Chinese diplomats held high-level in-person talks in Alaska, where both sides exchanged sharp rebukes. US-China relations were degraded from "contact" to "confrontation." The sharp conflict gradually evolved into a geopolitical war in which the US tried to contain China, challenging US hegemony. Biden seemed to be following in Trump's footsteps and was going to launch a "new cold war" with China.

A US-China confrontation will produce no winners. It is detrimental to the development of the world economy and the realization of the goal of sustainable development for humankind. In September 2015, the United Nations, involving 193 member states, approved the 2030 Agenda for Sustainable Development and officially introduced 17 Sustainable Development Goals, ranging from poverty, inequality, climate change, diseases, and environmental degradation in 2016.

The general understanding of US-China relations after 2021 is that there will be both confrontation and competition. And at the same time, there will be room for cooperation. The 2030 Agenda for Sustainable Development depends on the US-China partnership. However, the fundamental problem is that it will be difficult to achieve these goals if there is no international higher education cooperation in research and education. In this regard, there is so much for the Chinese Mainland, Hong Kong and Taiwan to learn from American higher education.

First Encounter with Hong Kong

My first encounter with Hong Kong was an eye-opening experience. I had studied and worked in North American higher education institutions and the science and technology sector for 34 years. Apart from short-term visits to universities in Hong Kong, I knew truly little about the city when I took over the presidency at CityU on May 14, 2008; and Hong Kong knew nothing about me.

Somehow, it was destiny that brought me to Hong Kong, in a zigzag kind of way. Prior to 2008, I had frequently visited universities and research institutions in Taiwan, my birthplace, maintaining a keen interest in education reforms. I was aware of university reforms on the Chinese Mainland and the rigid education system there. I had visited South Korea many times, having supervised a number of South Korean doctoral students and having enjoyed discussing higher education, science, technology, and innovation with South Korean academics. I had also had close contact with scientific research institutions under the Ministry of Economy, Trade and Industry (METI, originally MITI) in Japan. Therefore, I had a good understanding of higher education and research in Northeast Asia.

How Should Universities Be Run?

Higher education has three important components: universities, government and society. The soulware of higher education refers to the mindset of universities, the government and society at large. Due to the influence of traditional Chinese culture, governments and the external communities in Taiwan, Hong Kong and Mainland China are often the bottlenecks for achieving the ideal soulware. Government funding and promotion are not results-oriented. They are biased toward specific well-established local universities, and they fail to achieve the maximum marginal utility of investment, a phenomenon that our society is accustomed to ignoring.

Relying on universities alone to uphold the right soulware can only get half the result with double the effort. There are also non-academic factors from the external community exerting influence on campus, for example, numerous cases of students engaged in high-profile movements, faculty with an uneven teaching and research performance, staff members who take university jobs as an "iron rice bowl" (with guaranteed job security or a job for life), media organizations with ulterior motives, and the long-arm of governments meddling in university affairs. Compared with universities in the US, such factors are particularly prominent in universities in Taiwan, Hong Kong and the Mainland. They cannot be ignored and are extremely troublesome. I refer to all of these factors and phenomena as blindness of the soul.

This book has evolved from my exposure to East Asia and my experience in the US, as well as my observations and reflections on higher education across the Strait.

The book has a total of 27 chapters. In addition to the Preface and Introduction, the text is divided into Five Parts, plus an Epilogue, outlining my observations, views and expectations of higher education on both sides of the Strait. This book will take the American higher education system and practice as a benchmark to measure higher education across the Strait. Overall, more on the governments and society at large are discussed. Areas that are worth narrating and analyzing regarding universities in the region are introduced in each of the following chapters. I hope these analyses will serve as a reference for the higher education sector in other parts of the world.

Internationalization of Higher Education

Officials and universities across the Strait often talk about internationalization, by which they mean nothing other than an emphasis on English, adopting the American system and expanding universities. At the same time, we see laypeople micro-managing universities, undue emphasis on credentials, the separation of teaching and research, mixing politics and education, and indulgence in populism. In fact, the internationalization of higher education simply means governance by professionals, an emphasis on quality, respecting procedures and walking the walk rather than talking the talk. This is the moment to strengthen the morale of your officers. It is not the time to listen to bad advice or close your ears to the suggestions of loyal men.

As an ethnically non-mainstream resident in the US, I held various academic leadership positions over many years. I was familiar with the widespread practice in academia of going by the rules, be it in teaching and research, or administration and management, or discussions and debates. Therefore, I was taken aback when, soon after my arrival in Hong Kong, I witnessed how the entire CityU campus was thrown into chaos over a decision taken by a vice-president not to renew several instructors' contracts. It was incredible that a legal and reasonable decision could trigger heated reactions and interference by outsiders who tried to disrupt the normal functioning of a university. Where did the anger come from? And where did it go? Regrettably, this was the work of just a few who refused to play by the rules or who tried to make some personal gains by politicizing the issue.

Another uncommon example was related to a student's thesis. Shortly before my arrival at CityU, a PhD student from the Mainland failed his final examination and was asked by his study committee to amend his thesis. But the student insisted he was correct and claimed that he was more qualified than the committee members. He asked CityU to overrule the committee's decision. After my refusal to alter an academic decision, he started to make all kinds of noises, including bringing in street politics and suing the university for delaying his graduation. He requested the court to order CityU to pay for the losses associated with the delay after he had already entered and passed a second examination. Such an absurd violation of the academic regulations of the committee on research degree candidature was unthinkable. It was severely refuted by the judge who imposed a huge fine. And yet, the student ignored the fine and simply disappeared into thin air.

The lack of a soul can be seen in this student, perhaps as a result of a lack of moral quality and poor family education. Why did this student repudiate the academic judgment of his committee? What would be the use of forcing his way through an academic degree? Would he behave this way if he were in the Mainland, the US or Taiwan?

It has been 15 years since I came to Hong Kong, yet rumors and slander still pervade university campuses; street politics have infiltrated university campuses under the guise of democracy; students who advocate taking the lead in university governance get cheered. The non-responsible internet culture floods society, and the government intrudes and instigates education. The trend of sending anonymous letters and mounting anonymous personal attacks goes from bad to worse. Several cases of abnormal and non-sensical behavior, like the above-mentioned doctoral student, have surfaced in recent years. Such stories were highly uncommon until relatively recently.

Hong Kong is an Asian metropolis where English is a major language and claims to be one the most internationalized cities in the world. There are many good things to be said about this great city, but even a cosmopolitan hub like Hong Kong is plagued by the increasingly unhealthy entanglement of outside politics interfering in higher education and a failure to achieve an advanced level of higher education. How can the modernization of education in Taiwan or Mainland China fare any better, given the shared cultural roots?

What is internationalization anyway? Could it be that people in higher education across the Strait are barking up the wrong tree by promoting issues not central to higher education?

Integration of Teaching and Research

The second phenomenon I noticed after arriving in Hong Kong was treating teaching and research as two distinct and unrelated activities. Lecturers were only involved with teaching, while professors mainly did research. Not only that, during my visits to Taiwan, I learned that the so-called research universities prioritized research activities while the so-called teaching universities undertook no research at all. What puzzled me was why anyone interested in learning would want to choose to study in so-called research universities that do not care much about teaching and why teaching-oriented universities would be involved in granting PhD degrees. What kind of research universities are they if they do not teach, and what kind of teaching universities are they if they do not conduct research at all and yet grant doctoral degrees?

Later, when I revisited Mainland universities that I was familiar with, I realized that university teachers on either side of the Strait who had not done any research tended to classify universities that emphasized teaching as teaching universities. As a result, professors involved in research were classified as professors of research universities.

The underlying assumption is that those who do research do not know how to teach and therefore have no teaching duty, while teaching staff concentrate on their teaching and do not engage in research and, as a result, do not know how to discover or create new knowledge through research. But how valid is this assumption that those who are not engaged in research do indeed know how to teach and that those who are engaged in doing research do not really know how to teach?

How can anyone be healthy by consuming nutritious food but not exercising or by exercising but not consuming nutritious food?

Limited innovation and the segregation of teaching and research also exist in North American and European institutions of higher education; however, the situation is seemingly worse among universities across the Strait. The ability to foster innovation with a good balance between teaching and research is what really separates modern universities from the rest. High-sounding empty talk, which originates from a Chinese tradition, exists in the political sector and society at large across the Strait, the only difference being a difference in degrees. If we fail to adopt the right mindset and do away with empty talk, the higher education system may be reduced to a platform for cultivating many degree stars at most substandard schools.

Separation of Politics and Education

To maintain accountability, universities must evaluate student learning, graduate employability, faculty productivity, alumni contribution to society and social responsibility. They reflect economic and non-economic influence. However, the above are only some of the prerequisites for a university to achieve excellence.

If we want a university to function normally under a sound education system, we need to lead and govern with the right mindset rather than relying on mechanical control. The operation of a university is also a business, an intellectual business related to learning, not a business for making profits, even less a platform for political confrontations.

Professors exercise academic freedom in teaching and research. They should not use universities as a platform to deal with non-academic issues or use teaching and research as an excuse for making profits and even worse for seeking political power. This is a universal truth, no matter where the universities are located. To ensure that universities enjoy autonomy and academic freedom, universities should adhere to the separation of politics and education, both on and outside the campus. Students shouldn't use the free academic environment to engage in political rebellion, governments should leave university operations alone, and faculty and staff must avoid the tradition of holding positions simultaneously in industry, government and universities.

In the past few decades, academic exchanges between US and Mainland China scholars have been extremely active. However, due to policy changes during the later period of Trump's presidency, Gang Chen, an MIT professor, was accused of concealing his ties with China and obtaining US federal government research funding. He was arrested and imprisoned in 2021. Soon after the incident, the university president L. Rafael Reif issued an open letter clarifying the cooperation project between MIT and Mainland China and the university offered to pay for his legal defense.

While we may find someone like the MIT president who stood up and defended fundamental principles in the US, such cases may not be tolerated in Taiwan, Hong Kong or Mainland China, where it is impossible for high-and-mighty governments to accept such responses!

Universities, governments, societies, and traditional cultures should be responsible for ensuring the separation of politics and education, especially the government because it has the most power.

Quality and Evaluation

At one time, due to various excuses, university faculty and staff were wary of evaluations of their teaching and research, regarding them as a violation of academic freedom. But how can anyone make progress in the absence of feedback from evaluation? How can one groom oneself without checking in front of the mirror? In any case, academic freedom refers to the freedom to engage in academic studies. How can someone demand academic freedom when what they do is unrelated to academic pursuits? Why is it that people who are not directly involved in academic activities keep talking about academic freedom when in fact people who are directly engaged in academic pursuits do not necessarily lack freedom?

It is obvious that quality assurance should be prioritized within a clearly defined assessment framework. No stone should be left unturned in the pursuit of excellence and efficiency. Nowadays, recognition for the importance of the design, evaluation, and enhancement of quality has been extended from manufacturing to the service, medical, government, education and legal sectors.

It must be pointed out that the average graduation rate for four-year colleges in the US is only 56%. There is no guarantee that every college student can graduate. Generally speaking, the graduation rate in top American universities (i.e., top-ranked universities) is fairly high. The worse the university, the lower the graduation rate. However, for university students across the Strait, almost everyone can successfully graduate as long as they are admitted. This is very different when it comes to the US. It is reasonable to say that anyone who can graduate from any American university must have a certain amount of knowledge. As for graduates from universities across the Strait, their ability varies. God knows whose degree is genuine and whose is fake.

The lack of a sound and healthy development turns out to be one of the key reasons why higher education across the Strait lags behind other global leaders. With the promotion of quality assurance, universities have made rapid progress, having made a tremendous investment in hardware and software. It is time to evaluate the investment in soulware. Additionally, all individual organic entities closely related to higher education, such as the government and society, should be evaluated.

Creativity and Innovation

Creativity may be spontaneous, but innovation has to be built on quality. Creativity becomes innovation only when original ideas spontaneously conceived are implemented systematically. Innovation is tomorrow's quality yardstick, which is why quality improvement and enhancement are considered innovation. After all, the purpose of innovation that spurs entrepreneurship is to improve the quality of life. Like internationalization, innovation is often a goal that universities aspire to, yet it is also the most puzzling concept and difficult to achieve. Innovation is not given due attention in Chinese traditional culture. Therefore, there is a lack of creativity in higher education in Taiwan, Hong Kong and Mainland China.

Higher education depends on government investment in resources and policy guidance, but operations should be left to academic professionals, free from bureaucratic micro-management and meddling by government agencies. Society should respect higher learning as a profession. University is likely the best platform for creating and innovating. Therefore, professors should be committed to pursuing innovation, knowledge creation, and knowledge transfer to provide quality education for students and for academic advancement. They must observe professional ethics and be willing to accept peer evaluation.

The government encourages innovation, yet it is bureaucratic and conservative, mixing politics with education. Whom should we believe?

Learning and Questioning: Ancient Chinese Wisdom

Some visionary scholars, aiming high in ancient China, wished to devote themselves to contributing to society, either as a doctor saving lives or as the prime minister ensuring security and prosperity for the state. That was the ideal for knowledge seekers. Today we refer to such aspirations as social responsibility. The aspirations ought to make innovation accessible to all; they go far beyond localization or one-way learning.

To enhance the soulware of internationalization, we should emphasize teamwork and collaboration among industry, university and research institutions and avoid being trapped in the entanglement of the academe-industry-government relationship. Creativity is meaningful for humankind, and innovation offers hope for a better future as long as these basic requirements are met and we remain committed to solving real problems instead of chanting lofty slogans and propagating high-sounding rhetoric.

An essay entitled *On Teaching*, written by the well-known Tang dynasty scholar and writer Han Yue (韓愈, 768–824), exemplifies the traditional idea of learning and education for the Chinese. For more than 1,000 years, the idea expressed in that essay has remained powerfully influential even today. It defines the teacher as one who transmits knowledge, imparts skills, and dispels perplexities. From the perspective of modern education, that essay, with its deeply rooted ideas, may be partial and outdated, but Han Yue's open-minded ethos remains vitally relevant.

The essence of learning lies in questioning and doing research. As early as the Song dynasty, some 1,000 years ago, scholars argued for the importance of investigation as the way to understand all phenomena, seek new knowledge and challenge existing knowledge. This ignored and often forgotten Chinese learning mode promoted by Zhu Xi (朱熹, 1130–1200) suggested *ge zhi* (格致) or investigating natural phenomena to acquire new knowledge. Only knowledge acquired by investigating and understanding phenomena thoroughly can be called scientific knowledge. We should promote the scientific spirit of Zhu Xi by incorporating learning and investigating into higher education and even in the primary and high school curriculum.

No one can accomplish anything without studying, nor can one understand anything without questioning. Traditionally, the Chinese emphasize studying more than questioning. Our higher education today has the same problem. For example, are there any sociological theories and sublime views worth discussing in Taiwan, Hong Kong and the Mainland in our narcissistic environment?

How should universities be run? What should be done, and what should not be done? By whom should it be done? The following chapters are a collection of my reflections over the years on these questions.

Part I
INTERNATIONALIZATION OF HIGHER EDUCATION

Meeting people you do not know
'Tis futile to talk about your aspirations;

Whereas internationalization of higher education
Is forever blossoming in the verdant garden.

Internationalization is a hot topic in universities and society at large among people responsible for the implementation of education policies. But what is internationalization? Why are people so interested in talking about it?

Internationalization Enriches World Civilization

Looking around, we notice how in every way, the cultural diversity of our global society is juxtaposed with a trend for homogenization. Crises follow one another. Internationalization has captured our attention, more so than financial globalization. It has been a driving force for progress in education, especially higher education, which in turn has accelerated the development of internationalization by playing a leading role in promoting global communication and exchange in a comprehensive way. Higher education is closely related to internationalization, and its ramifications reach everywhere.

One of the reasons that the US dominated the 20th century is that graduates from its universities are scattered all over the world, playing a crucial role in politics, the economy, culture, education, and society.

New York may be the most important metropolis in the world today, a point-of-view widely acknowledged, but the biggest city in the world 1,000 years ago was China's Kaifeng, while Italy's Florence was the most influential city in the world 500 years ago. Further back in history, Chang'an, today's Xi'an, the capital city of China's Tang dynasty in its prime, was an international metropolis and the first choice for high officials and young students from neighboring countries as a place to visit or study. Some 2,500 years ago, Confucius led his disciples on study tours from one feudal state to another. I believe the civilization of the 25th century will be somewhere else, just as diverse and colorful, with its own specific features.

Back in my childhood, I was told the 21st century would be the century for the Chinese to contribute to the world. Whether China or not China, as a latecomer, can live up to that expectation will depend on how universities across the Strait fulfill the responsibility of nurturing the necessary talent, understanding the forms of government and taking the thriving and governing of the world. With the rapid rise of China's economy, many well-known international institutions, including the World Bank, have concluded that China is likely to surpass the US by around 2040. The BBC Chinese website pointed out on March 26, 2020, quoting "The World in 2050" report prepared by PricewaterhouseCoopers, an international professional services company, that 30 years later, six of the world's top seven economies would be emerging countries. In addition to China, India would rise rapidly, replacing the US as second, and Japan's ranking would fall from fourth to eighth.

In addition, there is one difference between today's higher education and the 1950s' higher education. The popularization of science and technology and the development of the internet have promoted international exchanges, which has never happened before. The mass production brought about after the industrial revolution has now evolved into mass customization. The personalized development caused by this does not conflict with internationalization, because advancing the world through science, technology and quality has no borders. High inventory, which was once considered a flaw, is all of a sudden found to be necessary. Individualized production, online distribution and other concepts have become popular and been enriched through internationalization and have also broadened the scope of higher education with more diverse and more convenient information for reference.

We live in a rapidly changing society where the information flow is swift and convenient, and communication between people, which is made up of diverse instruments and voices, is no longer restricted to local regions or time zones. In 2008, the financial turmoil in the US engulfed the world like a tsunami, illustrating how small today's world really is and how the forces of reciprocal influence have grown exponentially. In 2018, the US started a trade war against China, rallying its allies to counter China, while China exemplified its tough "equal footing" stance in response. With both countries raising tariffs on goods, global trade is in for a bumpy ride.

The rapid flow of information and personnel has also caused other sequelae. In the midst of the US-China confrontation, which has adversely impacted global supply chains, a new coronavirus emerged in January 2020, together with several mutated variants, in pace with internationalization.

Zero-case and Blindness of the Soul

The virus swept the world since 2019 for three years, resulting in almost 800 million cases of infection and about 7 million deaths as of June 2023. From the onset till mid-2022, only Taiwan, Hong Kong and the Mainland, plus Macau, all four places sharing the same language, being of the same race and taking the same steps, took a different approach from the rest of the world, insisting on eliminating cases, which means striking down on infections even if it inconveniences people. The "zero case" policy did have a short-term effect.

"*The autumn wind blows from the Wei River / And fallen leaves cover the streets in Chang'an.*" In 2022, part of the global community achieved herd immunity, with the 27 EU countries reopening from February 1, 2022, and relaxing COVID-19 rules and restrictions in a bid to salvage their economies. But societies across the Strait stubbornly dismissed the practice in Singapore of "coexisting with the virus" and then saw the pandemic get worse. Taiwan, Hong Kong and Mainland China saw a surge of new cases from March. They continued to adhere to implementing a quarantine policy for incoming travelers, which was hardly seen elsewhere in the world.

The new term "dynamic zero-case" began to appear in the Chinese world, proving that wishful localized thinking may not work sometimes. Disregarding whether the "zero-case" policy was appropriate or a success, I am afraid that, throughout the world, only the three places across the Strait adopted this approach to the pandemic. A wonderful coincidence! Obviously, whichever party or government is in power doesn't make any difference.

In December 2022, they eventually said goodbye to their zero-COVID strategy.

Hong Kong and Taiwan have one thing in common in the handling of the pandemic, that is, the anti-pandemic campaign was not led by a cross-disciplinary and multi-function team including members such as doctors, public health experts, biostatisticians, engineers, safety and reliability professionals, social workers, financial practitioners and policymakers. For almost three years, at least 20 people have appeared to speak, explain, analyze, direct, and predict the pandemic. After the Chinese New

Year holiday in 2022, the coronavirus pandemic in Hong Kong grew worse, though still insignificant initially compared with the situation in Europe, America, South Korea and Japan. In March, some patients had to weather the cold and wind in tents while waiting for hospital beds as if they were in a less-developed country or region. Taiwan faced the same embarrassment, which was staggering. Mainland China was proud of its record in growing the economy and improving people's livelihoods, but nothing else. It was such a speed demon carrying out its zero-COVID policy that people lived a Kafkaesque life in the anti-foreign spirit of the Boxers in late 19th century China. What's left for China to boast about after economic growth dropped sharply in 2022?

Like cupping water with filter paper, shutting down the borders and quarantining people may have isolated the virus temporarily, but the impact was short-term. Rather, we witnessed collective psychological breakdown due to seclusion before the virus beat us.

Beyond the new coronavirus pandemic, Taiwan, Hong Kong and the Mainland seem to share unique advantages and blind spots in higher education as well.

Internationalization provides a sustainable operating environment, but the current excessive consumption of natural resources has caused environmental damage, and the Earth's ecology has lost its balance due to unlimited expansion. Universities should take the lead in dealing with global warming, energy, and environmental protection challenges. In this regard, universities in Taiwan, Hong Kong and the Mainland are lagging behind and slow in response.

Some say that meeting someone in person builds rapport; others say doing so may be worse than not meeting in person. In reality, people who know each other may not be able to meet, but we meet new people in other circumstances. What is important is sincerity. If there is sincerity, knowing someone is better than meeting them in person; if there is dedication, meeting people one knows may not be necessary. In promoting internationalization, we must have sincerity before we can achieve actual results, which may not be accomplished simply by a visit or an exchange. Without sincerity, meeting in person may be a futile gesture.

1
Internationalization without Soulware

American higher education has been a role model for universities around the world. The academic atmosphere is mostly free from political interference. American universities emphasize both teaching and research and promote the integration of learning and enterprise, diversity, meritocracy, accountability at all levels, and peer review, among others. Academic affairs are led by professors. Its strong industry-university-research collaboration relies on the strong research capabilities of its universities. It has had the highest number of international students in the past fifty years. The accomplishments of American higher education can be reflected in the number of Nobel laureates, their outstanding faculty, high academic rankings and their inventions, among others.

Several decades ago, internationalization became highly popular in US universities. In addition to promoting American culture, there was unprecedented enthusiasm for the Chinese language and anything related to China. Hong Kong may have overlooked the trend partly because it was preoccupied with the approaching 1997 sovereignty transfer from British colonial rule; or perhaps because Hong Kong already thought of itself as a cosmopolitan city. Taiwan, on the other hand, was busy pushing for localization, and the whole of society was brimming with schemes for implementing four official languages—Mandarin, Hokkien, Hakka Chinese, and Indigenous language(s)—that it lacked the energy to consider the rationale for internationalization. On the Mainland, higher education was at a crossroads and faced a major overhaul when English replaced Russian as the major foreign language. Some English grammar books even became bestsellers in Mainland China.

About 30 years later, when internationalization was finally on the table for discussion, universities across the Strait lacked the confidence to parade their own culture and instead promoted English as a common consensus, believing that an ability to speak English qualified them to be modern.

International Branch Campuses around the World

Although setting up international branch campuses is considered a contemporary phenomenon, the practice was commonplace during the colonial era in the 19th century. For example, the American University of Beirut was founded in 1866. In 1954, the Catholic University of Leuven in Belgium established a branch in Congo, which merged with two other universities in 1960 after independence. As of 2020, 81 countries or regions hosted branch campuses from 33 originating countries. Most hosting countries are anxious to be westernized. Among them, Temple University, Japan campus, is Japan's oldest and largest foreign university.

There are around 308 international branch campuses, with the US being the biggest originating country with 86.[1] Many of these are located in the Persian Gulf and, increasingly, in Asia. Moreover, quite a few Russian universities have set up branch campuses in Ulaanbaatar, the capital of Mongolia. The UK led the way in Europe. It set up 44 of the 128 outposts listed. British universities are doing well despite the conservative establishment of branch campuses. The University of Nottingham's campuses in Malaysia and the Mainland account for 90% of the UK's overseas campus enrollments. With both the US and the UK leading the way in setting up such campuses, English became the international language in the 20th century.

By July 2022, there were 42 international branch campuses of Australian, European and North American universities offering degree programs in Mainland China and Hong Kong, such as the University of Nottingham Ningbo, Duke Kushan University, Xi'an Jiaotong-Liverpool University, University of Michigan-Shanghai Jiao Tong University Joint Institute, Guangdong Technion-Israel Institute of Technology, UOW (University of Wollongong) College Hong Kong, and The University of Chicago Booth School of Business in Hong Kong. Lately, as an indication of the determination to enhance higher education in China, many first-class universities like New York University and even Harvard Medical School have been invited to open campuses in China. They provide an opportunity for students who decide to stay home to get exposure to a diverse classroom, a global perspective, and an international teaching and research environment.

In February 2019, the Chinese government released the Outline Development Plan for the Guangdong-Hong Kong-Macao Greater Bay

---

[1] January 2020 C-BERT database (http://cbert.org/? page_id=34).

Area, aiming to build the region into a vibrant economic hub by developing modern technologies and enterprises. In response to the requirements of the plan, universities in Hong Kong started to establish branch campuses in the Pearl River Delta in collaboration with local universities. The Mainland government strictly controls universities while promoting the establishment of universities through international collaboration. Though such international collaborations may have attracted Mainland students, their academic performance is often lacking.

At the same time, universities in Mainland China have opened campuses abroad as well. For example, Shenzhen University announced the possibility of establishing a branch campus in Hong Kong. Peking University opened a campus in Oxford, UK, in 2018, and Tsinghua University and the University of Washington launched a master's degree program seeded by Microsoft near Seattle. Fudan University planned to build its branch campus in Budapest, Hungary, in 2024. This proposal has been temporarily shelved due to objections from the local community. If it goes well, this will be the first Mainland university branch campus established in the European Union.

In parallel with globalization, transnational education has become a trend. Branch campuses are beneficial to transnational education in the host country for the following reasons:

1. They provide additional learning paths for individuals who want to receive a high-quality university education. Many students seek overseas study experiences, hoping to satisfy employers who value skilled students who can solve problems of common concern across institutions, national boundaries and disciplines. Domestic students who decide to stay in the same place will have more opportunities to access diversified classrooms, global perspectives, and an international teaching and research environment through branch schools.
2. Foreign universities can accelerate the modernization of local universities through short-distance exchanges. Foreign influence and the modernization of the host country are closely related to the progress of the host country's society.
3. For certain universities, a successful international branch campus can generate the necessary revenue to sustain their internationalization efforts and even revitalize the local city's economy.

However, based on the work of Anna Kosmützky, a professor in methodology for higher education and science studies in Hanover, Germany, setting up international branch campuses started only in the late 1990s when Australian, British and American universities established branch campuses in countries with policy priority on attracting international campuses such as Qatar, Singapore and the United Arab Emirates.[2]

There have been tremendous difficulties in implementing these initiatives; therefore, there were numerous closures even if there was an increase in branch campus activities. According to Kosmützky, five of the 26 branch campus openings within Dubai International Academic City have closed. According to a *YaleNews* report on August 26, 2021, the Yale-NUS College, established by Yale University and the National University of Singapore, will close in 2025. So far, the performance of many European, American and Hong Kong branch schools in Mainland China has not been satisfactory.

Establishing overseas branch campuses can broaden the brand name of parent universities and increase the influence of their country of origin. According to an *ICEF Monitor* article published on October 4, 2015[3], establishing overseas branches for many universities is not primarily for revenue generation but more for "broadening their brand footprint and increasing their prestige over the long run in international markets. Many universities would like to pursue these goals, but relatively few can afford to sustain and support such efforts to the extent required". Other major international initiatives are considered more effective, such as strategic partnerships, international research and innovation, staff exchange (outgoing and incoming), and internationalizing the curriculum. However, the establishment of overseas branch campuses is often met with resistance from university professors in the source countries and the residents of the region where the branch campuses are to be located, out of concerns over funding allocation, lack of personnel, and damage to the school's reputation. Many doubt the justification for establishing branch campuses because there is no spare capacity for such endeavors.

In some rare cases, students from Europe and the US can choose to study at the international branch campuses of their own country and obtain a home university degree with international experience.

In addition to setting up overseas branch schools, universities have worked together to issue tens of thousands of online undergraduate,

---

[2] See Elizabeth Redden in her *Inside Higher Ed* article titled "The Branch Campus Boom(s)" on March 16, 2015.
[3] https://monitor.icef.com/2015/10/a-more-cautious-outlook-for-international-branch-campuses/

master's, doctoral degrees and short-term course completion certificates every year. According to an announcement by the Chinese Ministry of Education in August 2021, as reported in the *South China Morning Post* in Hong Kong, as many as 286 cooperative programs have been officially suspended between Chinese and foreign universities. Programs discontinued include a master's degree in economics and finance between Peking University and the University of Hong Kong, and social work courses offered by East China Normal University in Shanghai and New York University. It is widely believed that this is an extension of the rectification of off-campus training. All these pose challenges to internationalization of higher education.

Essence of Internationalization

Internationalization is not merely a ritual involving different universities signing agreements on cooperation and exchanging scholars and students. The essence of internationalization is realized by institutions of higher learning pursuing modernized programs and advanced research studies, adopting evidence-based teaching methods, and nurturing talented people to acquire an international perspective and innovative spirit. In addition, internationalization is a process and a mode of thinking. In promoting internationalization, universities and societies across the Strait should recognize the necessity of integrating teaching and research and use it as a benchmark to evaluate the quality of education in pursuing excellence as the ultimate goal. Progressive multinational corporations and non-profit organizations provide teachers and students with internships and attachments that foster understanding and experience of the operation and the success of an industry or organization from an internal perspective. These are also ways to realize internationalization.

For universities across the Strait, the essence of internationalization lies in demonstrating respect for institutional integrity, strong research and work ethics; an emphasis on quality; attention to efficiency, conservation of energy and the environment; a readiness to pursue marginal benefits and a commitment to evidence-based and outcome-oriented teaching and research using data science in response to societal needs.

Universities should be a stabilizing force in today's world of conflict and uncertainty. Ideally, an internationalized university promotes diversity, emphasizes sustainability, respects political, religious and cultural differences as well as differences of opinion and thought, and does not discriminate on the basis of age, language, nationality, gender or race.

As such, internationalization carries the consequence of promoting mutual understanding and interaction between a range of societies and economic systems. At the operational level, we should be considerate of others, abide by rules and promote interaction between students and teachers. In terms of content, we should be inclusive and aim to benefit society through academics and education.

Hardware and Software

To be exact, internationalized higher education can create an eye-opening effect, leading to an advancing society. Has the higher education sector across the Strait fulfilled its role when judged against such a standard?

For the promotion of internationalization, sufficient funds must be provided to support teaching and research, purchase books, software and equipment, enhance faculty quality, recruit international scholars and excellent teaching and research personnel, attract high-caliber students, and build collaboration and exchanges with globally advanced universities and research institutions that will result in advanced teaching, cutting-edge studies and innovation and entrepreneurship.

It is known to many that regulations and mechanisms in concert with international standards must also be established for quality assurance and good governance. For convenience, equipment-related objects are referred to as universities' hardware, and people- or procedure-related matters, including recruitment, administrative systems and policies, as software.

Soulware and Absence of Soulware

As the *Flower Ornament Sutra* says, "The soul is like a painter, able to paint all worlds."

However, internationalization requires the presence of a certain mindset. After all, hardware and software need to be operated by human beings from different departments and ranks. They must share the same mindset to communicate, coordinate, and apply the hardware and software effectively to achieve a common goal. Such a mindset is the soulware of higher education.

With the will to solve issues, solutions are identified. Soulware is a professional spirit and culture, a behavioral habit and mode of thinking, and an educational temperament that requires learning, reflection and precipitation. Universities should not be places for seeking fame. The traditional culture found in Taiwan, Hong Kong and Mainland China places degrees first, which makes degree-seeking people flock to university campuses, losing sight of their direction and individual niche. Without the right soulware, a college is bound to be of limited value.

Universities discover new knowledge and educate students, but the public increasingly expects the faculty at the best institutions to impact society positively. This can be achieved by impacting students and what they do for society after graduation; through direct outreach to society; or by the university, partners or faculty applying research to create start-ups.

Universities across the Strait may have caught up with international standards in hardware and software, and hence the recent improvement in international academic rankings in Hong Kong and Mainland China. But in terms of the mindset of higher education, including governments and society, progress still lags far behind, and the barriers are formidable.

For example, imitating practices in US and European universities, Hong Kong and Taiwan universities have set up numerous committees that, theoretically, should be adept at generating collective wisdom and identifying solutions, especially since they tend to be much bigger than their Western counterparts. But in practice, they often perform poorly in terms of both the quality of decisions reached and the efficiency of executing them because they are frequently handicapped by rules and regulations made at a different time under different conditions and with hugely different considerations of which a major one seems to be avoiding controversy and conflict.

The prevalence of such a phenomenon reflects serious flaws in an institution. Because it is difficult to eliminate fraud and selfishness, members are appointed to ensure others do not seek private gain. However, those unwilling to join forces avoid joining and ensure the avoidance of personal responsibility. Any mishap in a committee can be glossed over as a collective decision rather than a personal mistake.

Western universities set up committees and appoint people from various backgrounds in a balanced way, with the understanding that members are trusted to exercise the authority granted to them to perform their tasks. The committees rarely have many members and are held responsible for specific outcomes that constitute their performance indicators; that is, how the system of accountability has evolved. A committee's resolutions are not entirely binding, serving instead as a reference for the executives under many circumstances, an approach that differs from how committees function across the Strait.

The Hong Kong government and universities are fond of hiring business and overseas consultants and, in some cases, even influential politicians to deal with higher education issues. Generally speaking, these external consultants lack an understanding of the higher education culture, and their suggestions are sometimes off the mark. During the consultation process, they need to be coached by the universities. Academic staff must first explain the relevant issues and even the way a university is run. In one case, a university was asked to explain what "postdoc" meant, while their recommendations are often used to endorse administrative directives designed to implement pre-set government policies. In fact, I once joked that these lay consultants should pay the universities for instruction or consultation rather than the other way around.

The practice of seeking outside consulting firms to endorse education and research policies in one's home place is out of style and detrimental to progress. At least in other places, or in the US with its world-leading higher education, such practices are rare. Committees in the US are set up with simple yet broad representation to look for collective wisdom, and members express their opinions honestly. In Hong Kong and Taiwan universities, committees are set up under super complicated rules, which are more for preventing the misconduct of others. Additionally, the membership of many committees is not always representative, and there is little consideration for diversity. Student unions at Hong Kong universities in which only local students participate exemplify this issue; similar phenomena are found in government committees. Without the right mindset from the very beginning, committees set up only to fulfill certain regulatory requirements will never function effectively or be convincing, despite the rituals of holding meetings properly. The blind spots of soulware in the above cases are collectively referred to as the absence of soulware.

Anonymous Letters and Surreptitious Whispers

Social responsibility is an ethical principle for higher education that suggests that universities have an obligation to act for the benefit of society at large.

Despite the prevalence of setting up committees to solve problems, we still tend to see a growing number of problems in opposition to solutions. In Mainland China, where few such committees exist, problems are even more apparent, while in Hong Kong and Taiwan, where these committees proliferate, a breach of confidentiality often arouses great public concern. In universities across the Strait, anonymous letters accusing committee of personal misconduct or mishandling committee matters are common. Such allegations are difficult to verify. Anonymous allegations reflect an irresponsible mindset. In contrast, Americans prefer to argue out openly, even vehemently, but generally avoid putting accusations behind people.

I once received an anonymous letter from a mother requesting that her son be admitted to the university. But the letter was not signed, and her son's name was not mentioned, making it impossible for anyone to follow up on the case. It is alarming that writing anonymous letters is becoming more prevalent among the young generation. In recent years, with the convenience of free internet, Google, YouTube, etc., anonymous allegations have become rampant in Hong Kong and Taiwan. In addition, individuals are seen secretly recording or video-taping during meetings or conversations, particularly so in meetings with student associations. The internet media with such backgrounds often seek personal gains and gather personal political energy under the pretense of freedom of the press. The media's rampant arrogance can hardly be categorized simply as disgusting.

In comparison, Westerners tend to follow resolutions and have an open mind. When I was Dean of Engineering at the University of Tennessee, an American colleague who handed me an anonymous letter said apologetically, "I am sorry I didn't sign it." Though unsigned, I at least knew who had written it. According to common Western practice, anonymous letters are not to be handled. Even letters from whistleblowers have to be signed to show accountability.

Universities should resist outside forces that undermine professionalism or interfere with the quest for truth. Hong Kong has a fairly comprehensive system of rules and regulations, while Taiwan is proud of its transparent democracy. What then is the justification for anonymous letters and surreptitious whispers, even when decisions or resolutions are not considered acceptable or agreeable?

One may argue that Eastern and Western history and culture are basically different and that the habit of violating a confidentiality agreement, informing someone or sending anonymous letters is deeply rooted in the Chinese tradition. There is another reason for the lack of mutual trust in society. In many cases, bad habits such as reporting on others and sending anonymous letters were led by the government or political parties to demonstrate their authority. Such an inability of the government to convince the public is a bottleneck in the internationalization of higher education and a manifestation of the blindness of the soul. In this new era of internationalization in the higher education sector on both sides of the Strait, it is imperative to relinquish outmoded behavior and regenerate modern standards. Our higher education sector must cultivate a willingness to comply with modern standards and rules. Otherwise, internationalization will remain a lofty, empty slogan even if some relatively high-profile universities are associated with this region.

Societies in Taiwan and Hong Kong have made noteworthy progress in democracy and science since the May Fourth Movement 100 years ago in Beijing, but the development of higher education still leaves much to be desired. People from all walks of life should learn to respect the rule of law and abide by regulations and practices to avoid harming society. Failing to do so will lead us to fall short of international standards for another 100 years.

Localization

Internationalization, not necessarily excluding the local culture, goes beyond investment in hardware and software, and building a first-class university goes beyond the recruitment of grandmasters, highly cited researchers or popular media speakers. Though no higher education system is perfect, those across the Strait, particularly those in Taiwan and Mainland China, are less international. This is partly because they lack the kind of mindset that prevents them from adopting modern governance standards, exercising anti-discrimination practices, integrating teaching with research, adhering to quality assurance for graduates, respecting campus autonomy and academic freedom, and promoting innovation for better human welfare.

In addition, attracting more international students is only a palliative if the right kind of soulware is present. While many emphasize a diverse cultural experience and globalization, universities tend to emphasize the importance of English as the communication medium and provide an educational experience more geared towards career development. But internationalization encompasses more than simply language learning. Taiwan discriminates against foreign brides, and Hong Kong discriminates against foreign domestic helpers. All these, including Taiwan and Hong Kong governments' "inbreeding" practice of recruiting mainly local people, are worth reviewing and improving, yet no university students care about or probe into the issues.

Ironically, although government officials across the Strait claim they are immensely proud of their local universities, many send their children, at any expense, to North America, Australia or Europe to study at expensive, cash-strapped colleges instead. So despite the progress that dedicated faculty at universities across the Strait are making, higher education systems there seem more localized than internationalized.

> *Without the right soulware,*
> *'Tis impossible to cure illness of the mind.*
> *A frog at the bottom of the well,*
> *Wastes its breath bragging about internationalization.*

People should be judged by their deeds rather than their words. However, the inconsistency between what one says and does is extremely serious, especially in Hong Kong where English is widely spoken.

Thoughts at Taipei Marathon

In 2012, I went to Taipei with close to 100 CityU staff members, students and alumni for an international marathon held on December 16 where I ran the 9K race. During my Taipei visit, I encountered three incidents.

The night before the event, I realized I had forgotten to pack a pair of running shorts. I asked a staff member at the Health and Leisure section of the Far Eastern Shangri-La Hotel if there was a place nearby where I could buy a pair. To my delight, a young staff member, upon learning that I needed the shorts as a stop-gap measure, offered to lend me a clean pair of sweatpants. I wonder if a similar incident would happen in Hong Kong or Mainland China!

In addition, the taxi fares were fairly reasonable and the drivers tended to chat amiably with passengers. But I noticed on several occasions that the drivers were watching South Korean TV dramas on a small screen by the side of the steering wheel while driving. To think they would allow themselves to be distracted is enough to wreck anyone's nerves.

On the day of the race, I witnessed a scene that could only be described as shocking. Along the route, local people were pushing their bicycles through the stream of runners. Further along, I saw quite a few taxis waiting at the side of the road, ready to cut across the road packed with runners. I pointed out to the volunteer police officers monitoring the traffic what was happening, only to be told that there was nothing to worry about and that I should just run my race. At that very instant, one taxi took off, wove its way through the crowd and drove away. I guess the volunteer cop might have thought to himself complacently, "See, everything is fine!"

But more hair-raising scenes were in store for me. As we headed back to the starting point about forty-five minutes into the race and about one kilometer away from the municipal government building, the traffic police stopped thousands of runners in order to give way to several vehicles. I am sure such chaotic scenes would not occur at international marathons elsewhere.

These three incidents tell us something about present-day Taiwan, a peaceful, politically democratic society with a strong middle class and a strong communitarian ethos. There is, unfortunately, a lack of effective exercise of public authority and public safety, and that should be a grave concern. Hong Kong, on the other hand, is different. The rule of law is strong, and society is orderly, though somewhat apathetic. The gap between the rich and the poor is, however, very distinct. Nevertheless, law enforcement is effective, and it is a relatively safe working and living environment. Comparing Taiwan and Hong Kong, one can say with some exaggeration that the former allows one to lead a happy life but to be exposed to potentially more industrial and other hazards. One could die even without knowing the cause. At the same time, the other place is the kingdom of food, where bureaucracy rules and people are used to going by the book and where feasting and revelry go side by side with frugality and simple living. There, many are oblivious to the sufferings of the world.

There have been a number of bizarre accidents in Taiwan in the last ten years, such as the gas explosion in Kaohsiung on July 31, 2014, that killed 32 people; the dust explosion in Taipei's Baxian Paradise that resulted in nearly 500 casualties on June 27, 2015; the collision on April 2, 2021, of the Taroko Express train of Taiwan Railway with a construction vehicle that rolled down a slope onto the track, killing 49 people and injuring 247 others. As I was writing, a fire broke out in the early hours of October 14, 2021, in a residential building in the Yancheng district of the southern Taiwanese city of Kaohsiung, killing 46 people. Government officials did nothing other than bow and apologize to the public for the disaster and announce that they would give the family of each victim who died NT$10,000 (approximately US$330) as condolence money, which is a cheap way to deal with a severe disaster. Anyways, no one has learned the lesson. After a few days the public's attention shifted to another story and politicians again took the lead in chanting "We Love Taiwan" as if nothing had happened. When the next accident happens, they will bow again, assuming themselves to be good officials, wear a fake smile and give some money away to get rid of the matter.

Hong Kong enjoys a safer transportation than other places in the region. Comparing the number of traffic accident deaths per 100,000 people, the death rate from traffic accidents in Taiwan over the years is, on average, eight times that of Hong Kong (see Table 17.1). Hong Kong was also a more orderly society before 2019. People are generally law-abiding though not necessarily better-mannered, and those who are affluent are not necessarily happier. According to statistics from the last decade or so, members of Hong Kong's disadvantaged communities are getting poorer every day. Since 2021, Hong Kong people become panicky and many have started leaving the city. Putting politics aside, Hong Kong is more like a society shaped by legalistic ideology, yet people are distant from one another.

In contrast, Taiwan seems more like a moderately prosperous society shaped by Confucian humanistic values.

In his address on December 16 before the 2012 marathon, the Mayor of Taipei gave a little display of his English to demonstrate internationalization. In Hong Kong, many people are similarly proud of using English as their native language, and some even take special pride in speaking with an Oxford accent, reminiscent of the days of post-war Taiwan when some people saw it as an honor to be able to speak Japanese. Hong Kong and Taiwan preach internationalization and pay special attention to English. Language is a communication tool. In international communication, you can speak and write English when necessary. However, the key lies in what you want to accomplish with the use of the language and what the purpose is. When we talk about internationalization, we should adhere to adopting best international practices to meet lofty standards. The many problems we find across the Strait today, such as the disparities in wealth, the failure of the public authority to assert itself, the lack of commitment to workplace safety, and an unwillingness to address genuine issues, have little to do with English proficiency. When gauged by advanced international standards, we have some catching up to do.

My visit to Taipei and my participation in the marathon was another informative experience. Obsession with English ability is a blind spot in our pursuit of internationalization. Instead of focusing on ill-informed priorities, we should strengthen the regulation of workplace safety, invest more in the development of the middle class, and talk less and do more in our everyday life in order to deal with practical problems. There is no shortage of smart people in Taiwan, Hong Kong and the Mainland. Rather, there is an oversupply that makes mistakes. Whatever we do, we should start with the basics if we want education to achieve high quality and lead the world.

Internationalization is not just promoting an international language or signing agreements with non-local partners. Learning from the best practice is key. Only with soulware can university management spot the gaps in their institution and address issues through internationalization.

2
Higher Education in the UK

When people think about the UK higher education system, the 800-year-old University of Cambridge and the 900-year-old University of Oxford often come to mind. UK-style universities were once considered role models. Even now, people in Taiwan and Hong Kong still like to follow the British system and encourage the establishment of UK-style colleges that focus on liberal arts education.

The UK universities discussed below do not include those in Scotland, as Scotland determines its own education policies and systems.

From Elite to Mass Higher Education

Until the establishment of Girton College in Cambridge in 1869, only males could receive higher education in the UK. Subsequently, for the first time in history, females at Girton College were allowed to participate in college graduation examinations, although they were still barred from enjoying equal status in many areas. In fact, a substantial number of British universities had unequal admission criteria for female students until 1948.

The terms post-80s (Generation Y) or post-90s (Generation Z), commonly used now in Chinese society to refer to young people, remind me of the polytechnics that were given university status in the 1980s and 1990s. These universities seem to share the same development trajectory as universities established in the 1990s in Taiwan, albeit with distinct characteristics.

Until the early 1980s, elite higher education was the norm in England, Wales and Northern Ireland. There were only 38 universities for a national population of over 55 million, and one in seven eligible students between 18 and 21 had the opportunity to attend. In 1979, Margaret Thatcher became prime minister after the Conservative Party won the general election. Until 1990, when she lost office, Thatcher implemented a series of measures, known as Thatcherism, in support of a smaller state and free markets. These policies were continued by her successor, John Major, and his cabinet and were considered to have helped to improve primary and high school education and the expansion of higher education.

Universities that were established in the UK after the publication of the Robbins Report in the 1960s are called "plate glass universities," as are all the former polytechnics and higher education institutions that were granted university status under the Further and Higher Education Act, which was enacted by John Major's government in 1992. The number doubled overnight when all 35 polytechnics were upgraded. Between 1980 and 2000, the number of university students in the UK jumped from 800,000 to 1.7 million.

By 2000, one in three graduating high school students could be admitted into higher education institutions. By 2008, the number of universities reached 91. The total number of higher education institutions, including university colleges and other tertiary institutions, grew to 132. The traditional elite universities continue to excel, and among the new universities, many were formed by the conversion of polytechnics or the amalgamation of established institutes. Imperial College London, which became an independent university in 2007, was ranked 7th in the world in the 2023 Quacquarelli Symonds (QS) World University Rankings, while the University of Manchester, which was re-invigorated in 2004 by the amalgamation of the Victoria University of Manchester and the University of Manchester Institute of Science and Technology, is known for having 25 Nobel laureates among its current and former staff and students.

The rapid development of higher education has had its advantages and disadvantages. Traditional university education has nurtured many successful elites, most of whom, however, come from upper-class families, arousing concerns about social discrimination and injustice. To some extent, these concerns were addressed by the emergence of post-80s universities, opening up opportunities for young people from ordinary families. It also helped to significantly increase the talent pool entering science and technology, information and communication, business and finance, and many other sectors that support social and economic progress.

Thatcherism lies at the heart of the emergence of these new universities. Related measures included public spending cuts, reduced social welfare bills and greater privatization. One of the first negative impacts of a rapid increase in universities was a shortfall in higher education funding. Between 1989 and 1999, government funding for each university student dropped by 40%, from an average of a little over US$8,800 per student to less than US$5,700. Universities had to cope with the shortage by asking teachers to increase the number of students they tutored.

Teachers at polytechnics used to teach only. Once converted to university status, they had to conduct research. Some of the older teachers could not adapt and had to vacate their positions. On the other hand, with a much larger number of teachers involved in research, applications for research funding increased tremendously, thus significantly decreasing the availability of funding support for research.

Increase in Tuition Fees

In October 2010, the UK government announced more plans to cut funding for university teaching and research. At the same time, it allowed universities to increase tuition fees substantially from a maximum cap of US$4,200 to up to US$11,400, an increase of close to 300%, effective fall of 2012, breaking away from the low tuition practice in Europe. As a result, 50,000 students and teachers took to the streets, protesting that such measures would deprive young people from less wealthy families of the right to higher education.

As it turned out, the previous year's cuts were not just a temporary measure to help cope with the 2007/08 economic crisis. Rather, the cuts signaled attempts to introduce market-led reforms into higher education to promote competition. This was evident from the white paper titled *Higher Education: Students at the Heart of the System* that the UK government published the following June. In parallel with funding cuts and the rise in tuition fees, the UK government increased student loans and made use of tuition payments as an incentive to drive improvements in the quality of teaching and research in more than 100 public-funded universities.

A low tuition fees policy is rarely a primary consideration for those committed to quality. In fact, such a policy in higher education is unfair to society as a whole because the public has to pay for the subsidy, while the subsidy may not be deeply appreciated by those who receive it. A related problem is that low tuition policies often go hand-in-hand with low philanthropy and endowments. On the other hand, higher tuition strategies can be coupled with need-blind admissions and aggressive financial aid, or at least the availability of subsidized loans. That way, tuition is not a barrier to entry. Raising tuition fees by the UK government in much the same way as US universities initially attracted international attention, but eventually society began to accept the policy and consider it a rational decision.

Notwithstanding the emergence of many post-80s universities, the UK higher education sector was able to uphold quality as the primary principle of education, demanding that universities engage in research and enjoy a significant level of academic autonomy. To ascertain whether these reforms were delivering the promised benefits, from 1986, the government worked with the higher education sector to develop bench-marking tools and assessment systems for evaluating university performance. These tools have since become standard practice, and vigorous evaluative assessments and strict adherence to the quality principle have resulted in improved overall quality. Traditional top-notch universities continue to maintain their leading position while new and progressive universities can compete and exert pressure on the older ones. This is similar to the recent phenomenon in Hong Kong where new and dynamic universities like CityU and The Hong Kong University of Science and Technology (HKUST) can create a new impetus in the local higher education sector and spur innovation and progress.

Financing

The UK established the Higher Education Funding Council for England (HEFCE) in 1992 to fund higher education teaching and research. HEFCE was reorganized into the Office for Students and UK Research and Innovation on April 1, 2018. The Office for Students is an independent regulator of higher education in England. It aims to enrich the education of students at all levels and help students progress into employment. UK Research and Innovation provides funding for university research, innovation, and knowledge exchange, including the management of US$1.1 billion research fund and the British Higher Education Innovation Fund.

Higher education is an expensive business. Increasing tuition fees itself is not sufficient for universities to excel. For example, UK universities have received US$13 billion from Horizon 2020, a European Union research and innovation program since it began in 2014. On January 4, 2019, university presidents in the UK as well as higher education organizations such as Universities UK, University Alliance and the Russell Group warned that Brexit, a portmanteau of "Britain exit" from the European Union, would pose "the gravest threat" to UK's higher education sector. The bottom line is that, after Brexit, the UK government needs to finance higher education for research and teaching and to provide support for students in the UK from both the UK and the EU and students in the EU from the UK.

Adoption of the American Way of Higher Education

In some ways, the higher education movement in the UK since the 1980s is an adoption of the American way of higher education. "The floating clouds in the sky are like a white dress / Which suddenly takes the shape of a grey dog." (Du Fu, 杜甫) Yet some people in the Hong Kong government, while reminiscing about the old colonial days, were frantically intent on following British-style universities even though the UK was migrating towards the American way of higher education in terms of funding management and operations. This was confirmed in my conversations with Nancy Rothwell, President and Vice-Chancellor of the University of Manchester, on November 18, 2011, and with Sir Keith O'Nions, President and Rector of Imperial College London, on November 22 of the same year.

Marconi's Contribution

Marconi Road, adjacent to the CityU campus in Kowloon Tong, commemorates the pioneering contributions of Guglielmo Marconi to wireless telegraph communication and the assistance that Marconi's Wireless Telegraph Company offered Hong Kong in developing ultra-short-wave broadcasting in 1962. Marconi was awarded the 1909 Nobel Prize in Physics for developing the wireless telegraph, one of the few engineers to win this award.

Marconi was born in Italy in 1874 and attended the University of Bologna, the oldest university in the world. In 1894, Marconi became intrigued by Heinrich Hertz's experiments that validated James Clerk Maxwell's theory concerning electromagnetic waves traveling through the air at the speed of light. Marconi wanted to use electromagnetic waves to send signals, and in 1895, after repeated setbacks, he succeeded in creating a wireless device for the long-distance transmission of signals. He failed in his request to secure funding from the Italian government, but he succeeded in obtaining a patent from the British government.

The radio signals crossed the English Channel and the Atlantic Ocean. When the RMS Titanic hit an iceberg in the North Atlantic in 1912, the crew used his device to send out a distress call to an operator in New York.

Marconi studied in Italy, was recognized in the UK, and succeeded in the Americas. His research benefited from international exchange, and in turn, his wireless communication technologies benefited the world. He is one of the top 100 most influential people in history.

3
On Universities across the Strait

Higher education in Taiwan, Hong Kong and the Mainland has developed rapidly. The governments of these three places have invested an average of 1% of their Gross Domestic Product (GDP) in higher education over the years, which helps promote social progress and economic development. According to data as of 2021, in terms of the percentage of the population with tertiary education who are aged 15 years and over, Taiwan stands at 49%, Hong Kong at 35% (including the 2-year degrees), and Mainland China at 19%. While Taiwan has the highest number of university and college students majoring in "engineering, manufacturing and construction", it is "business" for Hong Kong students and "engineering and industrial science" for the Mainland, which aligns with the current mode of development in all three places.

Looking to the future, humankind faces increasingly critical challenges posed by the energy shortage, environmental pollution, aging, sustainable development, epidemics, artificial intelligence (AI), and global political and economic instability. Solutions requiring cross-disciplinary research and collaboration between academics from universities around the world are needed.

Do university teachers devote enough time and effort to conducting related research, supervising their students, communicating with society, and leading the world to a better future? Do students understand why they enter university, have expectations, and plan to contribute to society? Are graduates' certifications quality assured? Do governments and society respect universities, collaborate with them wholeheartedly, maintain university autonomy, and support the progress of higher education on these issues?

The higher education reforms in England, Wales and Northern Ireland in the 1980s outlined in Chapter 2 may serve as a useful pivot for universities across the Strait to guide their adjustments when necessary.

Universities in America and across the Strait

What is the difference between American universities and universities in the three places across the Strait? This question can be viewed from different perspectives. In short, a semester is 14 to 16 weeks long in Hong Kong, 18 to 19 weeks in Taiwan, and 21 to 22 weeks in Mainland China. In the US, an academic year is either divided into two semesters, with each semester being 13 to 15 weeks long, or three semesters, with each semester being 9 to 10 weeks long. On the surface, campus life for American college students seems less intense.

Students across the Strait overestimate the ability of those teachers who excel at giving lectures. The more eloquent teachers in Taiwan, Hong Kong and Mainland China tend to attract attention, especially in the media, which is rarely the case in the US. Such teachers may not be valued in America because students must take many project-oriented courses and spend less time in class. Chinese students take more courses than American students, but American universities revolve around the principle that students are required to master the knowledge they have learned. From the perspective of teaching attitudes, American professors emphasize clarity, Hong Kong professors value simplicity, while Taiwan and Mainland professors present complexity.

College students in the three places across the Strait work hard to complete the courses and homework, but afterwards, according to the prescribed pattern, they don't seem to have much interest in exploring further. Most university teachers across the Strait are committed to their duties, propagating the doctrine and imparting professional knowledge. However, their American colleagues' teaching style differs. While they want students to respect their knowledge and opinions, they generally expect students to ask open questions and try their best to answer questions. At the same time, they focus on conducting research on related phenomena to achieve the mission of broadening knowledge. Those who cannot get academic research funding find it difficult to gain a foothold in universities. Many universities in Hong Kong employ lecturers with different titles who specialize in teaching. They do nothing else other than give lectures.

Universities in Taiwan, Hong Kong and the Mainland have been influenced by the American way to varying degrees and, therefore, with varying effects. American universities are highly autonomous while universities in Taiwan, Hong Kong and Mainland China are often required to be obedient and take the cue from the government.

Higher Education in Macau

Portugal established a stronghold in Macau in the middle of the 16th century. This Chinese territory became a colony of the Portuguese Empire in 1849. From then on, Portugal governed Macau until it was returned to the People's Republic of China in 1999 and became a special administrative region. The Higher Education Bureau (restructured from the Macau Higher Education Auxiliary Office in 2019) is a government department in charge of local higher education affairs. It was established about 30 years ago. This shows that the previous government paid little attention to education.

With a population of 687,000, Macau has a per capita GDP that ranks among the top in the world and is highly dependent on the gaming and tourism industries. Macau has 10 higher education institutions, of which four are public. Compared with Taiwan, Hong Kong and the Mainland, the scale and influence of Macau's higher education system are limited despite its rapid development. For that reason, this topic won't be discussed here, though the discussion in this book can be used as a reference for the future development of higher education in Macau.

Higher Education in Hong Kong

Over the past 30 years, Hong Kong's higher education system has made steady progress. In 1962, Hong Kong had only one university for a population of 3 million. By 1990, the population had grown to more than 5 million, and there were only two universities and a few small polytechnics and colleges. The development trajectory of universities in Hong Kong is almost identical to that of England, Wales and Northern Ireland. Today, Hong Kong has a population of over 7.5 million, and the number of universities has expanded to eight government-funded universities and several non-government-funded universities. Among the government-funded universities, six can be considered universities of the "post-90s." Although the percentage of Form Six (grade 12 in the US system) graduating students entering universities in Hong Kong is not as high as in Taiwan, the Mainland and the UK, and many high school graduates passing their exams every year still cannot enter local universities, at least university education has spread to the children of ordinary people. In recent years, the interaction between universities and the recruitment of outstanding Taiwan, Mainland and other non-local students into local universities have boosted the quality of higher education in Hong Kong. Even so, the city still does not have many universities, and their scale is relatively diminutive.

Funding is a real issue for contemporary higher education. The tuition fees of university students in Hong Kong have not been adjusted for 20 years. Today, government subvention for the eight government-funded universities constitutes approximately 52% of the total operating budget of each university. In 2003, university staff salaries in Hong Kong were delinked from those of civil servants to allow for greater flexibility in resource utilization and to reflect market value. So far, however, only CityU has adopted the American way of salary adjustment, which is 100% based on performance in teaching, research and professional service.

A milestone for higher education development in Hong Kong was reached in 2012. The three-year UK-modeled undergraduate curriculum was converted to the American four-year curriculum, and accordingly, the primary and high school system was changed from 13 years to 12 years. Universities in Hong Kong finally had the opportunity to expand and diversify their education responsibilities. But unfortunately, the government, following the precedent set by its predecessor, hung on to the old practices under the British higher education system.

It is standard practice in Hong Kong that universities are supervised by a university council (equivalent to the Board of Regents or similar boards in the US). In between the Education Bureau and the university council, the university is also under the oversight of the University Grants Committee (UGC), which has already been phased out in the UK. Despite the education reform, the UGC sees itself as the universities' superior, classifies them into categories and funds them according to rules established during the colonial era (see *HK01* October 26, 2022).

Despite access to sufficient resources, there are minimal meaningful long-term plans in Hong Kong aimed at responding to changes in higher education. As far as practice is concerned, Hong Kong doesn't have a proper understanding of the concept of the integration of teaching and research and leaves much to be desired in terms of operation, innovative thinking and academic culture.

The success of higher education depends on the academic autonomy that faculty enjoys when engaging in teaching and research. Within this broad framework, there is also the obligation not to violate academic ethics and to refrain from self-serving, non-academic activities for the pursuit of personal interests. These norms are highly respected and rarely breached in progressive universities.

The success of higher education lies in the adoption of ambitious standards to seek truth and propel society forward. In 2021, the government of the Hong Kong Special Administration Region (HKSAR) decided to adjust the 2023 Hong Kong Diploma of Secondary Education (HKDSE) core subjects and related examination requirements, including the cancelation of the school-based assessment for Liberal Studies and replacing it with a pass/fail grade in the renamed subject, Civil and Social Development. It was correct to amend the superficially designed Liberal Studies subject, as I have pointed out in my speeches over the years. However, the reason for the cancelation seems to be politically motivated. It is rather absurd, and funny even, that a wrong reason seems to have achieved the correct result.

Hong Kong used to be able to attract scholars from all over the world with appealing remuneration packages and a highly liberal environment. University faculty and staff were much better paid than those in Taiwan and the Mainland. Today, the remuneration packages are not as competitive any more due to changes in the academic environment and the government's incapability. It will be a challenge to continue to secure sufficient resources to sustain such an advantage, especially since some universities on the Mainland are already providing their professors with far higher packages than those supplied in Hong Kong.

Education Reforms in Taiwan

After Japan invaded China, the corrupt and weakened Qing government was forced to sign the Treaty of Shimonoseki on April 17, 1895, and ceded Taiwan and the Penghu Islands. Before 1945, under colonial rule, the higher education model was based on that of Japan.

Although literacy levels among local Taiwanese increased between 1895 and 1945, and thus raised the standard of skilled workers, the enrollment rate for local Taiwanese school-age children was only 60% compared with the higher rate for Japanese children. During the Japanese occupation, National Taiwan University (NTU, formerly Taihoku Imperial University) was one of the Japanese militarist government's most important "southward move" bases.

According to official Japanese data, local Taiwanese were treated as second-class citizens. The best high schools in Taiwan during the Japanese occupation period, such as Taipei Municipal Jianguo High School (called No. 1 Taihoku High School), were designed mainly for Japanese families. Local Taiwanese were not allowed to apply for studies in social sciences or law, and hence many studied medicine, engineering and agriculture.

After 1945, Taiwan followed the American system, with 12 years for primary and high school education and four years for university education.

Except for compulsory primary education in the early days and the implementation of nine-year compulsory education in 1968, access to education was highly competitive and the quality of certifications was guaranteed.

Since 1990, Taiwan has undergone a series of distorted reforms, changing the rules and curriculum dramatically. By 2002, the Joint College Entrance Examination was abolished after 48 years of implementation and was replaced by the Diversified College Enrollment Scheme. The original purpose of the reforms was to create multiple entrance routes to provide a fair opportunity for young people to receive education and to eliminate excessive drilling. But what happened, in reality, was the almost unlimited mushrooming of universities, which in many cases was driven by an aim to win local votes. These education reforms have had a far-reaching impact on all aspects of society, including the severe loss of control over quality and the generation of endless social conflicts and disputes.

In 1994, there were 50 tertiary institutions with a total of 250,000 college students, an appropriate size for a population of 21 million. Under popular demand, the education ministry relaxed the threshold for upgrading vocational schools and technical institutions to university status, greatly increasing the number of national universities. By 2012, the number of universities skyrocketed to 165, with an undergraduate student population of more than a million, plus 180,000 graduate students and over 30,000 doctoral students. Rapid growth created an unexpected failure to produce an appropriate name for universities. For lack of a better option, some universities simply adopted almost the same name as existing universities on the Mainland. The university enrollment quota far exceeded the number of graduating high school students, but many universities failed to recruit enough students, with several graduate schools at national universities failing to attract any applicants.

The new universities in Taiwan emerged against a background of political transition and the opening of society to democratization after the lifting of martial law. The post-90s universities, established under the call for more universities, provided more university degrees than education opportunities for young people. But the rapid development of universities had unintended consequences given its less than half of the UK population but more universities. For example, the establishment of an additional 50-odd national universities further diluted limited resources. Today, a typical Taiwan university gets a fifth of the funding that universities of comparable size and nature in Hong Kong receive, thus adversely affecting infrastructural, teaching and research.

In addition, vocational schools and technical institutions were upgraded quickly to university status without proper facilities or adequate equipment, reducing their technical niche and instigating a further decline in the overall quality of higher education.

As early as 1995, I advised against the decision to establish many additional universities. Introducing the American higher education system to Taiwan in such a crude way was poorly executed by the amateur leadership at that time. Taiwan's self-certified rulers have distorted the American higher education system, boning up frantically to the detriment of fair education and paying a high fee for filling out the "learning history file." As a result, the extra-low starting salaries for university graduates have remained unchanged for over a decade. Taiwan became, in some ways, a low-class socialist state hampered by serious resource constraints. The value of academic degrees has depreciated. Many PhD holders are used as master's degree holders; master's degree holders are used as bachelor's degree holders; and bachelor's degree holders end up unfit for a higher post but are unwilling to take a lower one. They complain all the time, idling away their time, and subsequently, society suffers.

It was quite popular for Taiwan college graduates between the 1960s and the 1990s to pursue graduate studies in the US or Canada. Many returned to Taiwan after graduating. Universities in Taiwan during that period were at the forefront of higher education, ahead of universities in Hong Kong and Mainland China, priding themselves on strong faculty, outstanding students and a progressive American curriculum. But the education reforms hindered higher education development, and Taiwan began to lag behind South Korea, which once followed closely behind. University closure and amalgamation were hot news in Taiwan's higher education in 2023 and subsequent years. Mistakes in higher education policy not only affect the higher education sector but account for the low level of innovation in science and technology, the lack of vibrancy in culture and the arts, as well as in political and economic developments.

Higher education was blinded, as indeed were those in charge!

A Tale of Two Territories

From 1842 to 1898, coerced by British forces, the Qing government signed three inequitable treaties, ceding Hong Kong Island and Kowloon Peninsula and leasing the New Territories. Under the British oligarchy, Hong Kong adopted an elite higher education system, and British English became the medium for communication. Society became hierarchical and laws were respected. What was lacking, though, was the cultivation of a foundation for teaching and research. Perhaps that was deliberate so as to facilitate the command and management of the British Hong Kong government. Interestingly, the Hong Kong people were fairly compliant under British rule.

Around the same time Hong Kong became a British colony, Japan implemented epoch-making reforms between 1860 and 1880. The government established by the Restoration patriots promoted democracy and Westernization. This is the well-known Meiji Restoration. Building on the ancient culture of the Han and Tang dynasties, it introduced the Western education system and ideologies and brought the country to new heights, enabling Japan to become a world power.

After the Sino-Japanese War of 1895, the Qing government signed the Shimonoseki Treaty, ceding Taiwan and other places to Japan. Japanese occupation lasted until World War II ended in 1945. In the early days of its rule, Japan adopted somewhat different colonial policies from Western countries and failed to engage in large-scale capital activities in Taiwan. Later, in response to the needs of war, Japan fully implemented the *Kominka* policy and only then began to promote the modernization of Taiwan's education and agriculture.

Hong Kong and Japan both adopted Western-style laws and institutions. However, prior to 1990, there was only a very small number of elite universities in Hong Kong. Because of their monopoly, they enjoyed a high status, and their graduates occupied high-paying government positions. They were socially influential but not academically prominent. In contrast, higher education institutions in Japan, where English was not as commonly used as in Hong Kong, were the region's most innovative and academically renowned, producing 28 locally educated Nobel Prize winners, the most in Asia. In the 21st century, there was almost one Japanese Nobel Prize winner annually, the most in Asia.

Comparing Hong Kong with Japan suggests that success in higher education is not related to using English or any language. Building on the foundation laid by the Japanese, the government of the Republic of China vigorously promoted education, and in those 30 to 40 years, higher education in Taiwan was far more advanced than in Hong Kong. Taiwan achieved a great deal in scientific research, innovation and advanced manufacturing, whereas Hong Kong's performance continues to be lackluster. Higher education in Hong Kong was never treated equally by the UK, which explains why it didn't flourish.

Second Rise of Mainland Universities

In the late Ming dynasty, St. Paul's College, Macau, was the first Western-style university established on Chinese soil. The college closed down after a series of fires. Around 145 years ago, China already had some fairly advanced private universities, such as Yenching University in Beijing and St. John's University in Shanghai. The latter is the earliest Chinese university, established in 1879 by American missionaries, two years after Japan's earliest university, Tokyo University, but earlier than Kyoto University, which was founded in 1897.

Thereafter, no public universities existed in China until the end of the 19th century, when the first government-run university, National Peiyang University, the predecessor to Tianjin University, was established in 1895 with the approval of Emperor Guangxu of the Qing dynasty. The Imperial University of Peking founded in 1898 was renamed Peking University during the Beiyang government period.

In the 1950s, however, not only did Yenching, Fu Jen Catholic and St. John's disappear during the overhaul of universities in Mainland China, but even national universities like Peking University and Tsinghua University were also divided into several smaller, more specialized colleges or universities in imitation of the Soviet model. During the 1966–76 Cultural Revolution, the development of China's higher education system came to a standstill, creating an enormous talent deprivation.

Between 1949 and the 1990s, universities in Mainland China were handicapped by a lack of sound educational philosophy, quality teaching and research, high-caliber faculty, and supportive higher education investments and policies. Higher education administration was basically very weak. Over an extended period, Mainland China adopted a 9-, 10- or 11-year primary and high school system. Only a few universities, Tsinghua University, for example, offered a five- or six-year undergraduate curriculum as if to make up for the deficiency in primary and high school education.

Following the economic rise of China in the 1990s, the wheel of fortune turned. China's higher education system switched back to the American-style system for a second time, but it was already over half a century behind world development.

On May 5, 1998, on the occasion of the 100th anniversary of the founding of Peking University, the Mainland Chinese government announced the launch of Project 985, which aimed at creating 39 world-class universities in the 21st century. Especially worth mentioning is the C9 League, a subgroup of the top universities under Project 985, which includes Tsinghua University, Peking University and seven others. The institutions on the Project 985 list, particularly the C9 League, received preferential treatment and funding from the central government. For example, Tsinghua University enjoyed an annual expenditure exceeding US$4 billion in 2022, larger than the total annual funding promised for the top 12 national universities, including NTU in Taiwan, supported by the Taiwanese government.

The Mainland has repeatedly shown its ambition to reinforce higher education. On September 21, 2017, the Chinese Ministry of Education released a list of 42 designated world-class universities and 95 world-class academic subjects participating in the country's higher education plan. Also known as the "Double First Class" initiative, the plan is to build a number of world-class universities and disciplines in China by the end of 2050, transforming the country into a global higher education power. In February 2022, further adjustment was made for the "Double First Class" university goal based on academic subjects. The outcome of such an initiative remains uncertain because we know that implementation and results do not always match the level of official ambition and high-sounding rhetoric found on the Mainland.

In recent years, infrastructure and student recruitment at Mainland universities have expanded rapidly, and attractive packages are deployed to recruit talented faculty. With the increase in funding, China's research into the natural sciences has yielded fruitful results. According to "Science and Technology Indicators 2020" published by the Japan Science and Technology Academic Policy Research Institute on August 7, 2020, the Mainland surpassed the United States for the first time in the number of annual papers published in the field of natural sciences from 2016 to 2018, ranking first in the world. Third and fourth places went to Germany and Japan, respectively.

This result is consistent with the "Thirteenth Five-Year" development plan issued by the National Natural Science Foundation of China (NSFC) in June 2016. According to the plan, the Mainland's scientific research investment would reach US$4 billion in 2016 and US$6 billion in 2020, basically the same as the total scientific research investment of the US. At the same time, according to the plan of the NSFC, China's basic research would achieve "three parallels" in the next 35 years, namely: "total parallelism", which would be achieved in 2020, that is, the total volume of academic output and resource input is equivalent to that of developed countries in science and technology; "contributions in parallel", which would be achieved by 2030, that is, Chinese scientists would strive to make many milestone contributions to the world's scientific development that are comparable to powerful countries in science and technology; "parallel sources" which would be achieved in 2050, that is, to have major original innovations that contribute to the world's scientific development. However, despite the mentioned contributions, the effects are uneven; the Mainland may not significantly contribute to the humanities and social sciences unless academic freedom can be tolerated.

Nowadays, there are all kinds of tertiary institutions on the Mainland. If one just wants to get a degree, it is not difficult. Tuition fees are low and the quality of teaching and research is uneven, following the steps of many universities in Taiwan. A disparity between universities in Hong Kong and Taiwan and those on the Mainland is that Mainland universities seem to be more capitalistic under the one-party rule. The faculty's salaries and research funds fluctuate and are adjusted according to market value.

Many new university campuses on the Mainland are spacious, well-landscaped and fully equipped with advanced teaching and research hardware. They are catching up with universities elsewhere in terms of software. Driven by strong ambition, higher education on the Mainland is full of vitality. However, it is hampered by a lack of transparency in governance, the predominance of local norms in administration, insufficient diversity, a lack of integration of teaching and research, an emphasis on formality over substance, didactic teaching, too much emphasis on degree exploration in the classroom, and the absence of the fundamental relationship between investment and return in education.

The party-state status in the Mainland defines the agenda for higher education and generously finances education while at the same time spoiling the soil for creativity through the imposition of regimented control mechanisms. Yet students from major universities in Mainland China are enthusiastic, dynamic, and eager to discuss academic issues, to some extent more so than those in Hong Kong and Taiwan.

Common Characteristics of Higher Education across the Strait

Whenever I travel, I like to chat with taxi drivers. Education is usually one of the most common topics. Many taxi drivers consider themselves experts, often voicing their opinions even on education. It is no wonder that unsolicited comments on higher education resound everywhere. People are just parroting each other. As a general phenomenon, the government tightly controls the budget; officials explain complicated rules and regulations; members of the public criticize government policies as they please; the media interpret public opinion as they wish; parents express their feelings as they like; and even students do not shy away from offering their share of criticisms directed towards teaching and research and university governance.

The emphasis on education in Chinese culture is a virtue to be proud of. Over the years, higher education across the Strait has followed dissimilar trajectories propelled by societal changes, resulting in vastly varied developments. Today, Hong Kong as a society can be said to have a high IQ (Intelligence Quotient), but is lacking in innovation; Taiwan has the resources but lacks management; Mainland China has impeccable human resources but lacks skills. Under close scrutiny, all these deficiencies share a common cultural factor.

Firstly, higher education development is more under the direction of laypeople instead of professional experts. On the surface, higher education appears to be a job that requires no specialized knowledge or expertise. Many people in power have the same mentality as taxi drivers and consider themselves sufficiently informed to make relevant comments and suggestions. They fail to appreciate that higher education has its own culture; one has to participate in the culture to appreciate what really needs to be done and how it is done. Even with some teaching experience, people may not be up to the task. This is as simple to appreciate as asking who you should consult when you get sick: a doctor or a neighbor?

Secondly, higher education is entangled with politics, but the aim of education is not to serve politics. Neither should higher education be used as a political bargaining chip. Unfortunately, the education system and policies in societies across the Strait often get changed for non-academic reasons, with their direction shifting under the manipulation of influential political figures. Politics and academics should serve different purposes and separate functions, but regrettably, they are deeply intertwined on both sides of the Strait; their entanglements are like weeds in wheat fields. It's outrageous not only that officials put themselves at the top of the universities but also that the universities follow suit, which is recognized by the media and society as the norm.

Thirdly, universities lack sufficient autonomy. In addition to policies that are determined by politicians, academic governance in universities is impeded by bureaucratic rules and an emotional society. Universities in North America enjoy higher autonomy. Academic issues are left to academics. Rarely have alumni, students, the media, board members, legislators or government officials tried to direct the academic administration of universities. Nor do they meddle with the teaching curriculum and research agenda.

Many people like to emphasize the young history of some universities. While universities across the Strait may be young compared with some European counterparts, they have more or less the same history as Japanese universities or an even longer history than some much-admired universities in the US, such as Stanford University or Caltech that were established in 1891. Compared with world-renowned Asian universities such as Seoul National University in South Korea, established in 1946, Tel Aviv University in Israel, established in 1956, and the National University of Singapore, converted from a medical school in 1980, some universities across the Strait can hardly be called young.

Taiwan's universities, having been surpassed by the universities of its neighbors for good reasons, will continue to be ranked at the bottom. It is unreasonable and lamentable to be narcissistic or to want to compare the ages of universities. Although Mainland China has launched its ambitious Project 985 and "Double First Class" plans, the overall level of higher education, despite heavy investment in several universities, is similar to that in Taiwan due to a considerable gap between reality and soulware standards.

Higher education across the Strait is undergoing tremendous growth, but it should be noted that a university's primary role is to create an intellectual environment where faculty are free to expose students to novel, unfamiliar and even potentially dangerous ideas while guiding them to seek solutions and remaining free to propose sometimes opposite hypotheses in the pursuit of truth. That's what a university education is all about.

We would do well to remember the remarkable exchange between Dwight D. Eisenhower as President of Columbia University and Isidor Isaac Rabi, a Nobel laureate in physics. Eisenhower, in a speech, addressed the faculty as "employees of the university." Rabi then stood up and said, "Mr. President, we are not employees of the university. We are the university." Such an exchange would be hard to imagine in a Chinese university.

In essence, the higher education sector across the Strait is plagued by administrative complexity, too many checks and balances, and too little trust due to cultural reasons.

Low Tuition Policy in Universities across the Strait

Universities across the Strait have generally adopted a low tuition policy because societies traditionally lack a conception of education in terms of investment and return. The tuition for national universities in Taiwan, the UGC-funded universities in Hong Kong, and the band-one cut-off point universities on the Mainland is about one-seventh, one-third and one-twentieth of the tuition of state universities in the US, respectively. There is no such thing as a free lunch. Low tuition fails to reflect the full cost of education, adversely affecting quality and competitiveness. In Mainland China where tuition is the lowest in absolute value, the government has to spend copious amounts to help balance budgets and diffuse administrators' complaints.

People actually value high quality education and are willing to pay for it. The fact that the number of children sent to study at respected universities in Europe, the US, Canada and Australia at much higher tuition by officials and middle-class families across the Strait has increased so much in recent years clearly indicates that the low tuition policy is not attractive at all. It reveals a lack of confidence and trust in local higher education.

Compared with Hong Kong and Mainland China, Taiwan's higher education resources have been so depleted over the years that the government lacks a long-term vision or plan. Society at large remains happy with its meager benefits, not worrying how a low tuition policy is hindering university development. If there is no clear funding source, low tuition harms the quality and competitiveness of teaching and research; on the other hand, because of low tuition fees, students and parents fail to appreciate the value of education. The result is low faculty salaries, which encourages moonlighting, which in turn leads to a further decline in education, the erosion of quality and rising social discontent, until eventually a vicious closed loop is formed, encroaching on the fundamental interests of both the students and society.

With unemployment at less than 4% for years, a high percentage of Taiwan's youth, like "the green and lush sunflowers in the garden, waiting for the rising sun to dry the dew on their leaves", chose to postpone graduation, enjoying their time on campus or content to be a member of the NEETs (not in education, employment or training) generation, and further imposed on much-reduced education resources. This is really a consequence of the low tuition fee policy. Postponing graduation, an emerging culture of self-indulgence and willfully fabricated nonsense, is a challenge facing Taiwan today. Made in Taiwan for Taiwan.

In fact, resources can be made available by the government or the private sector to subsidize the higher education of children from middle- and low-income families. Hence, family income should have little or no bearing on setting tuition fee levels. The real beneficiaries of the current low tuition fee policy are a small number of upper-middle-income families who can afford the actual cost of university education for their children. The low tuition policy means that the huge cost differentials will have to be borne unfairly by society, with the government serving as the intermediary. It results in an unfair reality.

It is a rather common phenomenon to find outstanding US universities charging high tuition fees. The average tuition for a first-rate private university is usually two to four times more than that of a first-rate state university, which in turn charges higher tuition than an average state university. In Taiwan, Hong Kong and Mainland China, it is the other way around, as the tuition for UGC-funded universities in Hong Kong is lower than the tuition for community colleges that take in students who cannot enter university. The tuition for outstanding universities in Taiwan is more than 50% lower than the tuition for second-rate private universities. In comparison, the tuition for band-one cut-off point and band-two cut-off point universities in Mainland China is much lower than band-three cut-off point universities. How can one understand the logic of a low price for high quality and a high price for low quality?

A low tuition policy is reasonable in a poor society, with a few people receiving education to improve literacy. But it is inappropriate for a developed society with a relatively advanced economy. Proposals for raising tuition fees were broached by universities in Taiwan, the UGC in Hong Kong, and university presidents on the Mainland, but they have met with a lukewarm response in their respective societies. Provinces in the Mainland settled on fee rises for the 2023 academic year, with drastic increases as high as 54% at some public universities.

Comparing Students Studying Abroad

In 1847, Huang Kuan and Rong Hong, both from Guangdong, left Hong Kong for advanced studies in America. They were the first Chinese students across the Strait in recorded history to study overseas.

In 1850, Huang Kuan entered the University of Edinburgh in Scotland after graduating from Monson Academy in the US and got his PhD in medicine in 1857, while Rong Hong went to study at Yale College and got his BA in 1854. Rong was also the first Chinese student to graduate from a US university. After returning to China, Rong Hong promoted the benefits of overseas study and persuaded the Qing government to encourage more young Chinese students to study abroad. Between 1872 and 1875, 120 young Chinese students went to study in the US. Among them were leading figures in modern Chinese history, such as the railway engineer Zhan Tianyou, a Yale graduate, and Tang Shaoyi, who briefly served as the first Premier of the Republic of China.

In addition to students sent to study in the US through the Boxer Indemnity Scholarship Program in 1909, high school graduates from Hong Kong started to go to Europe and the US in 1950. And the trend has never stopped. Hong Kong has the highest percentage of its student population studying abroad compared with Taiwan and Mainland China. There are a number of reasons for this. One is the extremely limited enrollment quota at local universities. From 2009, the UGC in Hong Kong only allocated 15,000 first-year places to eight universities each year. In 2017, as many as 4,500 high school graduates, or Form Six students as they are known in Hong Kong, went to study overseas for college degrees. This number constituted 8.6% of the total graduating population of 52,300 students. The number of Hong Kong high school graduates studying abroad for college degrees is about two times the number of non-local students studying in Hong Kong. In 2020, the number of Hong Kong high school graduates studying abroad for college degrees hit a new high at over 6,000. Based on student numbers, the most popular countries and regions where Hong Kong students study are Mainland China, Taiwan, the UK, Australia and Canada.

In addition, under the impact of emigration and the COVID-19 pandemic, a total of 2,643 students who had enrolled in the associate degree, bachelor's and postgraduate courses in the eight UGC universities in the 2020/21 academic year dropped out, of which more than 85% were undergraduates, accounting for about 2.9% of the total student population of 87,294.

Among students from Mainland China studying overseas in 2016/17, about 64%, or close to 350,755, went to study in American universities. Among all students studying in the US, 142,851 pursued undergraduate degrees, constituting 1.8% of 7,923,500 high school graduates in Mainland China in that year. It is an indication that overseas universities were fairly attractive to Mainland Chinese parents.

Comparatively speaking, the number of Taiwanese students studying abroad has never been remarkably high. It has been relatively rare in the past for outstanding high school students to opt to study overseas. Nowadays, essentially 100% of high school graduates can go to college in Taiwan. But a college degree does not hold the same value as before. As a result, the number of graduates studying abroad increased from 551 in 2010 to 1422 in 2015. A considerable number of outstanding students with a high or even a maximum General Scholastic Ability Test score would rather dismiss the offer of low tuition education in Taiwan, give up a place at the best-regarded universities in Taiwan and opt for overseas universities.

Exchanges of Cross-Strait Students

Hong Kong students began to study on the Mainland during the early Republican period. Universities were closed down on the Mainland during the Cultural Revolution, and when college entrance exams resumed in 1977, a small number of Hong Kong students participated. It was 2017 that saw a significant increase in the number of Hong Kong Form Six students, about 760, going to Mainland China for undergraduate studies.

With the rise of China, degrees granted by Mainland Chinese universities are beginning to get recognized worldwide. Chinese is becoming the second most important international language, next only to English. Some transnational corporations have even started recruiting employees conversant in Putonghua, i.e., Mandarin Chinese. For Hong Kong students, getting a university degree from Mainland China helps them to understand Mainland culture, establish social networks and build a foundation for future career development. In the second half of 2019, Hong Kong experienced a tumultuous time as people protested against the plan to allow extradition to Mainland China, and consequently, the number of Hong Kong students going to the Mainland to pursue undergraduate study decreased. However, with the rapid progress of the Mainland economy and increasing international recognition of its universities, the number of Hong Kong students applying for undergraduate study at Mainland universities in 2020 increased significantly to 3,999. The number of HKDSE applicants for Mainland universities in 2022 reached 4,890, a 21.1% increase over 2020.

In Hong Kong, Mainland Chinese students are referred to as *Neidisheng* (Inland Students). There were hardly any Inland Students in Hong Kong universities before 1997. In 2014, 1,646 Inland Students were newly enrolled in undergraduate study in Hong Kong, and this number has remained roughly the same. However, Mainland postgraduates studying for doctoral and master's degrees in Hong Kong universities account for most non-local students in these universities. At present, Hong Kong has become the first choice for Mainland students to study outside Mainland China. From January to July 2021, the number of Mainland students enquiring about studying in Hong Kong increased sharply, with a year-on-year increase of 126%. In 2022, the number of Mainland students studying for a degree in Hong Kong continued to grow, compared with 2021.

In 2011, Taiwan universities opened up to students from Mainland China. Mainland students studying in Taiwan are referred to as *Lusheng* (Mainland Students). But until today, only private universities and an extremely limited number of national universities could take Mainland students. In 2015, 2,553 freshmen from Mainland China were admitted by 115 universities in Taiwan. The children of Mainland-Chinese married to Taiwanese citizens face many restrictions if they live with their parents in Taiwan. Even though the restrictions were relaxed in 2012, such children aged below 20 and without permanent resident status would still be forced to deregister from the university and be sent back to Mainland China.

In 2020, the tenth year since Taiwan started to enroll Mainland students, the number of Mainland students who actually registered to go to Taiwan hit a record low, at 576 only, as a result of the pandemic and the Mainland Chinese government's decision in the previous year to allow only Mainland students already studying for their bachelor's and master's programs in Taiwan to further their studies.

According to reports, only 706 Mainland students were admitted in 2021, which accounted for 28% of the 2,523 admitted in 2019. This situation was even more prominent in the enrollment of doctoral students. In the past three years, more than 300 people could have been recruited during the preliminary assignment stage, accounting for 80 to 90% of the total enrollment. In 2021, only 20% of the enrollment quota for doctoral students was taken. Mainland Chinese students were once the largest source of overseas students in Taiwan. The Ministry of Education announced that following the amendments to Three Laws providing Mainland Chinese students access to Taiwanese colleges, the number of mainland students studying in Taiwan reached 41,981 in 2016, accounting for almost one-third of the total number of overseas students. Due to the deterioration of cross-strait relations, the Mainland banned their students from studying in Taiwan. In 2021, only 4,293 Mainland students were left and in 2023, almost no student. With reduced overseas students from the Mainland, the rapidly expanded universities, especially private ones, face operational difficulties.

From the time of the Japanese occupation until 1985, there were individual Taiwanese who went to the Mainland to study at universities, but there is no complete record on hand. In 1985, however, Mainland universities started to enroll students from Taiwan for undergraduate study. In 1989, there were only a dozen students admitted. Since 2008, the number of Taiwanese students studying on the Mainland has been growing annually following the increase in cross-strait exchanges, even though degrees granted by Mainland universities were initially not recognized by the Taiwan authorities. In 2017 alone, about 1,600 Taiwanese students were admitted to Mainland Chinese universities. Since 2018, significant numbers of graduates from among the most elite high schools in Taiwan have applied for the prestigious C9 League universities on the Mainland. By 2020, this number had increased to over 10,000. The number decreases in 2023.

Hong Kong students studying in Taiwan are considered overseas Chinese students. They started to go to Taiwan for post-secondary education as early as the 1950s, and that trend kept growing over the years with offers of preferential admission. In 2017, as many as 1,209 Hong Kong freshmen studied in Taiwan universities, national or private. Since 2019, there has been a substantial increase in Hong Kong students studying in Taiwan because of the lack of students going to college in Taiwan and the high anti-China sentiment in Hong Kong. With limited places in Hong Kong's universities and low tuition fees and living expenses in Taiwan, studying in Taiwan has become an alternative. In 2021, this number reached 3,093, an increase of 26% compared to 2020.

However, few Taiwanese students studied in any of the Hong Kong universities, except for some rare cases, before 2008. In 2009, one year after I came to Hong Kong, CityU took the lead in reaching out to recruit Taiwanese students. In 2018, 232 Taiwanese freshmen were enrolled in the eight UGC-funded universities in Hong Kong. Until today, there is still no official record of Taiwanese students enrolled in graduate studies in Hong Kong, except for a few individual cases. The number of Hong Kong students registered for postgraduate or doctoral studies in Taiwan is also believed to be limited. In 2020, the number of Taiwanese freshmen pursuing undergraduate study in Hong Kong dropped to fewer than 50 due to political factors as well as COVID-19. In 2021, about 90 Taiwanese students were enrolled.

Since 2019, the Taiwan government strongly discourages students to study in Hong Kond and the Mainland. Due to the discriminatory admission policies set by the Taiwan government, its universities have little appeal to outstanding Mainland students. The consequence is that the academic scores of Mainland students admitted to Taiwan universities are rarely as good as university freshmen admitted to band-one universities on the Mainland. There is also preferential treatment for overseas Chinese students studying in Taiwan or Taiwanese/Hong Kong students on the Mainland. They usually come from less privileged backgrounds and their academic performance tends to be uneven. In contrast, universities in Hong Kong set a high standard for Taiwan and Mainland students even though the tuition is much higher in Hong Kong than in Taiwan and the Mainland. They are mostly elite students from affluent families and have commendable academic records. They perform outstandingly after admission.

From the performance of non-local students in Hong Kong, one can understand the degree of external recognition of higher education in Hong Kong. Except for CityU's implementation in 2021 of the graduation honor system used at American universities, all universities in Hong Kong employ the British graduation honor system. About 14% of graduates are estimated to be awarded first-class honors each year. In recent years, about one-tenth of local students in Hong Kong have been awarded first-class honors, about 50% of Mainland students have received this honor, and one-third of other non-local students (from Taiwan, South Korea, India, Malaysia, Europe, etc.) have got this honor. Obviously, the performance of non-local students in Hong Kong, especially Mainland students, is much better than that of local Hong Kong students.

There are some differences between the universities established in Taiwan in the 1990s and those established in the UK (other than Scotland) in the 1980s and 1990s. From the very beginning, the expansion in the number of senior high schools and universities in Taiwan was driven by a kind of misconceived egalitarianism. This kind of thought invaded the campus and brought many negative effects. Unlike in Hong Kong, the performance of non-local students in Taiwan is much worse than that of local Taiwanese students. This should be related to the quality of the enrolled non-local students. Taiwan society has now begun to seriously weigh the actual costs and benefits of establishing those new universities in the 1990s.

Undergraduate Degrees Granted by Universities across the Strait

The enrollment rate of high school graduates entering four-year universities in the US and major Asian countries and regions in 2010–2020 is presented in Figure 3.1. To better understand the proportion of undergraduate degrees granted by universities across the Strait, the enrollment figures are measured by the percentage of the number of freshmen to the number of high school graduates between 1990 and 2020. Universities included are from across the Strait, Singapore, Japan, South Korea and the US.

As shown in Figure 3.1, Taiwan's high school graduates have the highest chance to enter local universities, more than twice that of high school graduates in Hong Kong. Therefore, it is conceivable that there are far more university degrees awarded in Taiwan than in Hong Kong.

In 2017, Hong Kong, Taiwan and Mainland universities granted 21,204, 228,793 and 3,391,586 bachelor's degrees, respectively, constituting 0.26% (or 0.35% if non-UGC funded students are included), 0.95% and 0.29% of the total local population, respectively. In comparison, a total of about 1,840,000 bachelor's degrees were granted by US universities in the same year, constituting 0.56% of the American population. Approximately the same respective number of degrees were awarded in 2022.

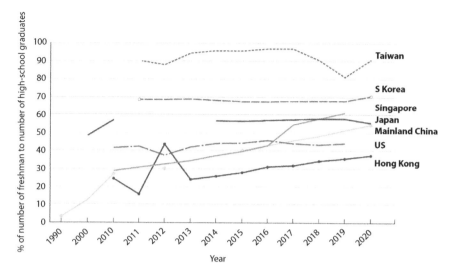

Figure 3.1 University enrollment rate in the US, Mainland China, Japan, Singapore, South Korea, Taiwan and Hong Kong.

Two extremes between Hong Kong and Taiwan are revealed when taking into consideration the number of outbound and inbound students and the local population, as well as when comparing the ratio of bachelor's degrees granted against the total population in each place. Judging by the degrees granted against the total population, Hong Kong is only one-third of Taiwan. In other words, the former grants too few degrees, while the latter grants too many. While the enrollment rate at primary and high schools is not much different between Hong Kong and Taiwan, Hong Kong seems to be stringent in granting college degrees, whereas Taiwan seems to be dishing them out at a low cost. This difference is consistent with political development in these two societies.

Taiwan has established so many universities, essentially allowing all high school graduates to pursue degrees at four-year universities. The main reason is the influence of the political environment on the development of education. In Hong Kong, one's career advances with age. Government bureaucrats generally lack the incentive to seek advancement by taking initiatives or pioneering changes. Maintaining the status quo by following the government book is politically correct. In Taiwan, however, one's career advances with social networking through wining and dining, by aligning with public opinion and popular sentiments, and letting laypeople take charge. Both cases in Hong Kong and Taiwan illustrate how the political environment can exert influence on education development.

Learning from Global Experience

The American model, where universities, among many good practices, enjoy high autonomy and adopt the beneficiaries-pay principle, has become a role model for other universities.

During my second visit to Imperial College London at the end of 2011, Sir Keith O'Nions, then president and rector, commented that the UK should revitalize its higher education by simplifying its administrative procedures and emphasizing research. He holds the view that UK universities should lean towards the American way, raising tuition fees under the principle that education beneficiaries pay for their education. It has already become a reality.

Higher education in Finland has also moved toward the American way in recent years. For example, Aalto University, established in 2010 as a merger of three major Finnish German-style single-topic universities, adopted the tenure system and formed an independent university governing board, leading the university to be internationalized.

During my visit to the Collège de France in Paris in 2009, I learned that France was planning to copy the American system, modernize university operations and amalgamate and re-organize universities in order to enhance functionality and efficiency. The grandes écoles of France are known for cultivating professional talent. As members of the Top Industrial Managers for Europe network, they maintain close ties with industry. Even though it is already a scientifically and technologically advanced nation, France has refused to be complacent. It rolled out a comprehensive plan for the amalgamation and reorganization of universities in 2011, led by two leading universities with a proud history of more than 200 years, in order to revitalize its higher education system.

In April 2022, I visited the Collège de France again. Ten years ago, I drank to the peach and plum blossoms in the soft spring breeze; ten years later, I returned to Paris amid the spring rain. How higher education in France has changed with each passing day!

First of all, the Paris Sciences et Lettres University (PSL), which was merged and established as a university in 2019, quickly climbed international rankings and attracted international attention. PSL's core components are École Normale Supérieure, which has 14 Nobel Prizes and the world's largest number of 12 Fields Medal alumni, unmatched by any university; and several other outstanding universities and research institutes located in Paris, such as École des Mines de Paris. In the QS World University Rankings 2023, PSL is ranked 26th.

In addition, the Institut Polytechnique de Paris was formed around the École Polytechnique, one of the most respected and selective grandes écoles in France, in May 2019, together with four other top-tier French engineering schools: the Superior National School of Advanced Techniques, the National School of Statistics and Economic Administration, Télécom Paris and Télécom Sud Paris. The Institut Polytechnique, which welcomes 8,500 new students each year, hopes to establish itself as France's MIT. Among its alumni are four Nobel Prize winners, one Fields Medalist, three French presidents and many CEOs of French and international companies. In the QS 2023 World University Rankings, the Institut Polytechnique ranked 48th.

The university system in Germany is public and its professors and researchers enjoy complete freedom to engage in scientific research. Since the arts and sciences are under the authority of the state rather than the federal government, academic freedom is further protected and its diversity can be maintained. However, the cost of independence from the federal government is that universities do not receive state funding. There is, therefore, a huge gap between rich and poor universities. Those universities in affluent regions such as the Ludwig-Maximilians-Universität München (University of Munich), the Technical University of Munich, Heidelberg University and the Karlsruhe Institute of Technology tend to get more resources.

In addition to constitutional guarantees for research and education and the authority of the state governments, some research institutions are fully funded by the federal government, for example, Max Planck Gesellschaft. Funding for university research projects comes from federal agencies such as the Federal Ministry of Education and Research, the Federal Ministry for Economic Affairs and Climate Action or from the independent German Research Foundation. In the past 20 years, Germany has adopted the American "Excellent Initiative", hoping to improve university rankings. Researchers are first sent to the US for postdoctoral research before they return to Germany to contribute to their home country.

I had the opportunity to interview Professor Mamokgethi Phakeng, Vice-Chancellor at the University of Cape Town, on July 18, 2019, while Hong Kong was in turmoil following opposition to the proposed amendments to the city's extradition law. She was very analytical and her explication of the issue was quick and to the point. The University of Cape Town has five Nobel Prize-winning alumni and is the alma mater of Christiaan Barnard, the surgeon who performed the first-ever human heart transplant. For most of the 20th century, South Africa was under apartheid. In the fall of 2015, students there demonstrated against tuition fee increases that made it more difficult for poor minority students to enter university. Funding is an important factor in successful higher education. No matter when and where, the operation of a university relies on a stable source of finance. What the right level of tuition fee is, and the pros and cons of tuition fees are issues worth discussing.

During several visits to Saint Petersburg State University in Russia, I noticed that, as a leading university in Russia, it adopted extensive academic practices and connections with universities in North America. The Skolkovo Institute of Science and Technology (SIST), founded in 2011 in collaboration with MIT, is a good example. MIT has assisted in building SIST as a unique, world-class graduate university with a strong emphasis on innovation and entrepreneurship, but it terminated the collaboration after the Russian invasion of Ukraine in February 2022.

In modern higher education, it is common for the East, including Japan, to learn from the West, particularly from the US experience in the past half-century. The representative reformer of the Qing dynasty, Zhang Zhidong (張之洞), once advocated "Chinese learning for fundamental principles and Western learning for practical application" to simultaneously emphasize education and the development of heavy industry in China. This approach was in the right direction at least even though it followed the Meiji Restoration in Japan and achieved far fewer effective results. The story of the once famous Chinese aeronautical engineer Wong Tsu is a case in point. Although Wong helped design the Boeing Model C, which was purchased by the US Navy, he was largely forgotten after his return to the Mainland. In 1949, he came to stay in Hong Kong for a short while and then went to Taiwan, apparently failing to find a permanent anchor in Taiwan, Hong Kong or the Mainland.

In spite of their aspirations and expertise, both Zhang Zhidong and Wong Tsu were unable to fully realize their visions and ambitions due to the lack of a conducive environment, reminding us that talent alone is not enough. Universities across the Strait followed different models. Mainland Chinese universities converted to the late Soviet model in 1949, even though they were first established on European and American models back in the late Qing dynasty and early Republican years. Hong Kong universities followed the UK tradition; universities in Taiwan, on the other hand, were more like universities in the Japanese and American systems.

These different education systems across the Strait have become closely intertwined in recent years as they increasingly turn to the American system as the guiding model. At the same time, universities in Taiwan and the Mainland have expanded in terms of numbers, size and scale and now look to form a distinct block on an equal footing with their counterparts in Europe and North America.

Universities around the world have each mapped out their own distinct trajectory in response to the impact of globalization. Universities across the Strait are still at the beginning stage of globalization and need to learn from more advanced societies, understand the diversity of world cultures, adjust their policies, exploit opportunities that can revitalize Chinese culture through higher education, and create a brand name.

The essence of campus autonomy can be summarized as one showing respect for professional management in the higher education system and redressing some of the deficiencies by leaving education and research to be managed by teachers and scholars. In terms of strategy, promoting positive competition can revitalize higher education, and only by doing this can higher education contribute to society. Popularizing higher education should not lead to a reduction in the quality of universities or in the quality of university students.

We should learn from overseas experience; and universities across the Strait should try to avoid the same pitfalls.

Declining Birth Rate Problem in Taiwan, Hong Kong and the Mainland

Figure 3.2 shows the number of births from 1950 to 2021 in Taiwan, Hong Kong and Mainland China. From the 1950s to the 1970s, Taiwan and Hong Kong experienced a peak fertility period, and people born during this era belong to the baby boomer generation. In Taiwan, this era lasted until the number of births gradually declined in the mid-1980s. In Hong Kong, the number rose after falling in the 1960s and then dropped sharply in the mid-2010s. In Mainland China, population growth slowed after the number of births reached a high point in the late 1960s but peaked slightly again in the 1990s. Following the introduction of economic reform and the one-child policy in 1979, the number of births has declined steadily since the 1990s and has dropped sharply since the late 2010s.

Until about 1995, the pattern of births in Hong Kong and Mainland China ran in opposite directions but converged from then on, while Taiwan had its own trend. Since 2017, a decline has been observed across the Taiwan Strait that may last for many years, as indicated in Figure 3.2.

The rise and fall in the number of newborn babies directly impact the birth rate. Birth rates in Taiwan, Hong Kong and Mainland China from

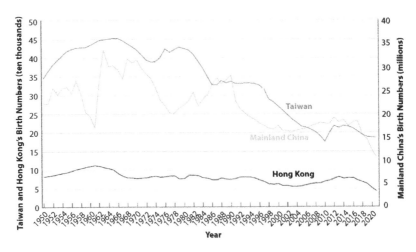

Figure 3.2 Number of newborn babies in Taiwan, Hong Kong and Mainland China (1950 to 2021).

1950 to 2021 are shown in Figure 3.3. Taiwan's birth rate has been declining steadily since the 1950s; Hong Kong's birth rate has been decreasing year by year except for a slight rise in the early 2000s; Mainland China maintained a high birth rate in the 1960s and then reached a peak in the 1990s after a temporary decline. The one-child policy has lowered the birth rate since the 1990s.

The number of births in Taiwan has declined since 1997 and is worsening. With the current low number of births in Hong Kong and Mainland China, severe drops in the number of high school graduates are expected in 2035 and 2037, respectively. University enrollment is likely to suffer, and the situation in Mainland China should be more critical. The impact of the low number of births on Taiwan's higher education has emerged 15 to 17 years earlier than in Hong Kong and Mainland China.

The number of newborn babies in Taiwan in 2015 was 213,598, the second highest in the last 10 years, after the record of 229,481 babies born in 2012, the Year of the Dragon. If one looks at the availability of the 2015 freshman enrollment places of 230,000 at the four-year and technical universities, it is easy to predict the issue of over-supply and less-demand, notwithstanding the ever-increasing number of young people seeking overseas study opportunities. In 2021, Taiwan had one of the lowest birth rates among countries/regions in the world, and the natural increase rate was -1.27/1000. The declining birth rate, which partly accounts for the imbalance, further compounds student recruitment challenges for universities

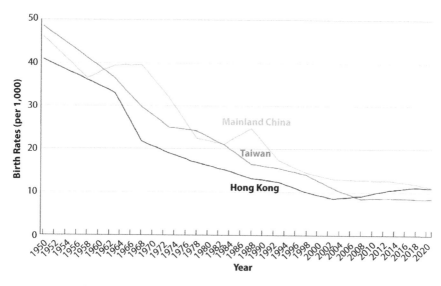

Figure 3.3 Birth rates in Taiwan, Hong Kong and Mainland China (1950 to 2021).

and the government. Not only will the number of college and graduate students decrease, but colleges and universities may also have to weather salary cuts, layoffs, and transfers of faculty and staff. There were early signs of a drop in newborns in Taiwan, but the government failed to respond adequately.

Under the education reform in Taiwan, universities face enrollment shortfalls at both undergraduate and graduate levels, while graduates are poorly paid when they are employed. Under the impact of the low birth rate, we see sharp falls in the number of vocational school students on the one hand; on the other, outstanding students may not value local degrees and choose to study abroad, which further worsens the enrollment situation. More than half of the students have barely made their way into universities, ending up having a degree only. What is the root cause for all this? Is it because there are too many university places, or is it due to the inadequate quality of our universities, the outdated higher education policy or the low birth rate?

Taiwan's population in 1950 was six million, reaching 16 million by 1972. The current population of 23 million does not seem small, yet society is troubled by the low birth rate. The fact that we have more schools than students results from nothing but a lack of planning.

The configuration of the four widely acknowledged ethnic groups in Taiwan — the Hoklos, Hakkas, Mainland Chinese and Indigenous people — is undergoing fundamental changes. Newly arrived residents in the past 20 years and children of migrant mothers are gradually becoming the third largest social group. It is expected that they will help to alleviate the impact of the declining birth rate, trigger new issues and bring new vitality to junior and high schools as well as universities in Taiwan.

The post-90s in Taiwan are a feel-good, pampered generation, but society needs an outstanding talent pool capable of facing the challenges in the higher education system. Therefore, it's not surprising that the education system in Taiwan faces confusion. South Korea, Japan, Hong Kong and Singapore are trying to attract gifted overseas students, not to mention that Western Europe, the US, Australia, Canada and Russia are recruiting enormous numbers of Mainland students. Taiwan alone is adhering to a strict localization policy, which accounts for its lack of international students. Along with Taiwan's limited recruitment quota for students from Mainland China, the practice of excluding the best talent and employment restrictions, Taiwan is not an attractive destination for Mainland students.

In Hong Kong, the number of high school graduates has decreased yearly due to the long-term decline in the birth rate. Coupled with the continually increasing number of students studying abroad, the ratio of high school graduates enrolled in local universities has hit a new high. In 2021, only about 35% of high school graduates were enrolled in the eight government-funded universities. As shown in Figure 3.1, this number is relatively small compared with any other developed country or region, and yet some government officials indicated their concern over the increase in this ratio caused by the constant decline in the birth rate. But the fact remains that the administration has provided a large number of publicly funded senior-year places on degree programs for sub-degree holders. Even if the enrollment for four-year degree university programs is doubled, the ratio remains low compared to other developed nations and regions.

The birth rate in Hong Kong is less than 7 per 1,000, and the natural population growth rate is negative. Like Taiwan, the declining birth rate in Hong Kong does not necessarily mean a decrease in the number of high school students since many other factors impact the population's size, including new immigrants from the Mainland.

China's National Bureau of Statistics announced that China's birth rate in 2021 was 7.52 per 1,000, and the natural population growth rate was 0.34 per 1,000, both record lows. Faced with a faster-than-expected aging population, China is expected to see a rapid decline in its total population after peaking between 2025 and 2030. With a decrease in the number of people taking higher education entrance examinations and the increase in enrollment numbers in Mainland China, the national university enrollment ratio for high school graduates increased from 29% in 2005 to 40% in 2022. In some provinces and municipalities, the enrollment ratio is even higher. In the next few years, students applying for entrance examinations will have at least a 50% chance of being admitted. In Northeastern China, enrollment rates are even higher. An exaggerated comment was that it may *not* be easy for high school graduates to fail to enter university in some areas. The excessiveness of university places seems to be catching up with the situation in Taiwan.

In the US, 68% of high school graduates were admitted to universities and community colleges. Considering also factors such as the graduating rate, at 56% in the US and almost 100% in Taiwan, Hong Kong and Mainland China, one can say that the ratio of Mainland China high school graduates enrolled at universities and the ratio of their graduation have exceeded those of US high school graduates.

Some say that to fill the gap caused by the declining birth rate and the excessive number of university places, universities started to recruit international students. If true, such universities distorted the aim of internationalization to enrich the development of universities and society. The Chinese idiom *xue zu shi lü* ("to cut one's feet to fit the shoes") tells the story of a foolish person who tries to cut his feet in order to fit shoes that are too small, satirizing those who look without considering the real problem and rigidly adhere to unsuitable rules. What should we do then when the shoes are too big today?

Does the problem that perplexes the higher education sector in Taiwan, Hong Kong and the Mainland stem from the declining birth rate or other factors such as mismanagement? Is the high graduation rate or the lack of quality assurance over university degrees the problem? Are the shoes too big or the feet too small? Or the shoes too small and the feet too big?

4
Simplicity is the Ultimate Sophistication

Many believe that the American way is the most advanced for many countries and universities to follow. Considering that Taiwan has been the front runner in Asia in adopting the American way in almost every direction of higher education, including using textbooks written by American professors, adopting the American educational infrastructure, and lecturing and doing research by the most qualified American-trained faculty members, why then is Taiwan's higher education lagging behind other major Asian universities? What has gone wrong? Whose fault is it? Why?

Ralph Evans, my predecessor as editor-in-chief at *IEEE Transactions on Reliability*, and I shared the following credos in selecting and editing papers for publishing. They can explain the plight of Taiwan's higher education today and help make Hong Kong and the Mainland more vigilant. These ideas are worth mentioning as they are principles that governments should understand and follow while shedding light on our daily lives.

First: A Good System Should Make It Easy to Do the Right Thing and Hard to Do the Wrong Thing

This principle applies to the setting up of engineering systems and rules for social affairs such as civil proceedings, legal procedures, etc. An ideal system should be clear in its goals and easy to operate, explain and execute. However, "simplicity" and "clarity" do not always co-exist. More often than not, we have systems that are designed neither to be simple nor amenable to a clear explanation.

For example, complicated lighting systems designed to convey a sense of status are often installed in hotel rooms. But the design often makes it easier for guests to press the wrong button, and sometimes they may even fail to locate the plug sockets. The toilet signs in some restaurants are so confusing that customers cannot distinguish which is for female and male use. Some signs are under dim lighting or placed in hard-to-find corners as if the designers bear a grudge against the guests. Today's cars are the same. In spite of their multiple fancy features, I am certain high-heeled footwear is incompatible with safe driving because of the design of the pedals.

Explaining the details of overly complex systems and functions within a heterogeneous society is hard, but a lack of simplicity is the source of unreliability and error.

Take mobile phones as an example. Most of the dazzling functions are rarely used. The keyboard is so complicated that it is easy to make a mistake and tough to find the right key when you want to select a particular function. Mobile phones are changing with their increased popularity for most users; so simplicity and reliability should be the primary considerations. Inconveniencing others by misusing the phone should be minimized unless it is for meeting some special needs.

In personnel management, under the influence of a strong culture of mistrust in the East, complex rules and regulations are often preferred to monitor others, but none takes the responsibility. These complex systems discourage initiatives and inhibit risk-taking, thus avoiding failure or making wrong decisions. This is one of the barriers to innovation in societies across the Strait.

In an ideal environment, it is easy for good people to shine and difficult for bad guys to succeed. In other words, an effective system should minimize both types of errors. Consider problems in society such as food safety, illegal lobbying, corruption, unauthorized building works, deaths from bullying in the military, gas explosions, and Taiwan train accidents, among others. The causes are as overwhelming as their post-disaster management. But one common causal factor is an abundance of complicated rules and regulations, which are incomprehensible and subject to arbitrary interpretation, besides often being self-contradictory. In the Taiwan railway case, unnecessary attention was given to the garish decorations in the carriages and low ticket prices instead of quality and safety. Low fares and losses from old pension plans have caused long-term losses for Taiwan railways. Under such a heavy burden, the ultimate victims are the passengers.

Under the sway of populism, perpetrators take advantage of these flaws, paying little heed to the law, while innocent people get implicated without any hope for redress. Law enforcement agents are kept running around but accomplish very little. In the wake of these complications, the populace generally offers its judgments freely, regardless of whether they understand the rules or regulations, have any direct involvement or are politically motivated. They are all delighted to participate in the public trial, distorting the truth, wasting social resources and creating additional and unnecessary confusion.

Campus autonomy is a prominent example.

The promotion or recruitment of professors is relatively straightforward in the US and causes few disputes. If the rules and procedures for promoting and recruiting professors are complex and there is any dispute, it is extremely hard to decide who is right and who is wrong. Often at meetings held by the governments in Taiwan and Hong Kong, I hear people saying: "It is so hard to do anything these days. No matter what decisions you make, society simply doesn't trust you. In fact, who will trust who in this day and age?"

Setting up a complicated system to keep one another in check from multiple angles is little more than cocooning oneself. As a result, talented people become risk averse and choose to stay away, while those without abilities try to boss others around, ready to seize every opportunity. Mindset is the key factor. Systems must be simple and well-defined if we want fair-minded people to embrace them. A system that is reasonable and easy to understand will enable those with the right mindset to deal with issues effectively. A complicated system, on the other hand, will only paralyze law-abiding citizens and reward politicians and opportunists. When one is young, it is easy to be happy and hopeful; when one is old, simplicity becomes the source of happiness.

Unbelievably, simplicity is the ultimate sophistication!

Second: Avoid Using the Right Solution for the Wrong Problem

Decision-makers often make two types of errors. They may reject something that is right by mistakenly judging it to be wrong, or they may accept something that is wrong by mistakenly judging it to be right. These errors are common in engineering manufacturing, scientific explorations and judicial decisions. In the everyday world of social interactions, it is often our petty-mindedness that gives rise to suspicion and misjudgment about something right as wrong; alternatively, it is our hypocrisy that causes the acceptance of something wrong as right. In a healthy society, both petty people and hypocrites are rare. In an unhealthy society, they are everywhere.

But there is a third type of error that is even more serious, i.e., finding the right solution with the correct method, but it turns out to be for the wrong problem. Therefore, even though a solution is found, it is irrelevant to the problem. Treating symptoms without dealing with the root cause offers only temporary relief. It will not serve as a cure. To really solve a problem, we must have the wisdom and the determination to get to the root cause.

A case in point is that promoting the learning of English as a way to internationalization is like "climbing a tree to look for fish". It is a futile activity.

Simply by strengthening English proficiency but failing to adopt advanced norms and modifying an outdated mindset (e.g., implementing systems that make it easy to do the right thing and hard to do the wrong thing), we will not be able to achieve internationalization. Conversely, by following advanced norms and standards and making substantial progress, we can keep abreast of modernization even if there is a lack of English proficiency in society. From another point of view, if we really want to emphasize the importance of language, people across the Strait should prioritize Chinese, which is the fad today and their strong suit. The fact that the MBA/EMBA program jointly offered by Cornell University and the PBC School of Finance (Wudaokou) at Tsinghua University uses Chinese rather than English as the language of instruction provides a new interpretation of internationalization.

Establishing a vast number of universities in Taiwan to increase employment and enhance the quality of society is another example of finding the right solution for the wrong problem. After all, we have examples of Filipino university graduates who are proficient in English working as foreign domestic workers, which reflects a bigger issue.

In the cultivation of talent, substance is the top priority. I learned recently that a high school graduate in Taiwan was finally admitted to his first choice, the School of Medicine at NTU, after sitting for the College Entrance Examinations four times in a row. The celebration party held at his alma mater in his honor was widely reported in the media. It turned out that the student in question had been admitted by NTU when he first graduated from high school, but it was not his first-choice program. So he took another exam after studying for six months.

This time he was accepted by the College of Medicine at Kaohsiung Medical University, which he was also not happy about. Therefore, he sat for another exam the next year and was admitted to the School of Medicine at Taipei Medical University, where he studied for two years before taking yet another exam, which finally got him accepted at NTU's School of Medicine. It was reported that he was driven by "an inexplicable persistence" to study at NTU's School of Medicine and nowhere else. In the end, he spent an extra five years trying to realize his dream.

While it is understandable that he had decided to take another exam when he was not admitted by his top choice medical school, the repeated exams in the following years were rather ridiculous. This story is yet another example of trying to get the right solution for a misconceived problem. Such examples of re-examinations have been common in Taiwan for quite some time.

Come to think about it, are other medical schools so bad that they are not worth attending? Or is he really suitable to study at NTU's School of Medicine? What reasons does he have for holding such an assumption, wasting his own time and social resources, other than simply his vanity? And yet this case was widely reported in the media, sending a wrong message. What is really going on? No wonder a high-achieving medical student was heard wondering whether she was but a designer handbag for her mother to show off to others. It turned out that her mother's proud wish was to see her daughter enter a medical school.

Looking for the root cause is a prerequisite for problem-solving. Good research starts with having a worthwhile topic, and raising the right question is half the way to the right solution; effective administration, on the other hand, begins with a proper understanding of the problem before working on a solution. Looking around, we often find people who have raised misconceived problems based on self-serving interests and offered some taken-for-granted solutions that they justify as correct. These people are either ignorant or driven by ulterior motives.

The following is another erroneous development. The Chinese academies have decided to deprive academicians over 80 years old of the right to vote. It is claimed that malpractice in selecting academicians is one reason for this decision, which makes one feel that senior academicians must be the culprits. Notwithstanding the fact that academicians over 80 are old, are we sure there will be fewer malpractice cases with younger academicians? Apparently, the answer by many is: "Not true!" In that case, aren't we again looking for an answer to the problem from the wrong direction?

Hong Kong is not known for having a robust innovation culture, and the locals know it. Therefore, it has been at the top of the government's agenda over the years. The next thing is to establish advisory committees composed of mainly locals and westerners. But unfortunately, they found the wrong people and knocked on the wrong doors. The difference in the profession makes one feel worlds apart. The people involved have had no innovative experience themselves other than some superficial qualifications. They don't understand either that you cannot find innovative solutions from rules and regulations. A *square* peg cannot fit into a *round* hole. No wonder it did not work!

In an Asian society, there is a tendency to extol those who have read a few books and refer to them as scholars, so much so that the word has become abused and who show themselves off as wise guys while slighting the importance of experience and practical learning. The ignorance of these wise guys becomes fully exposed when they fail to discern the root cause behind problems and cannot produce appropriate solutions, notwithstanding the many books they have read. Applying oneself to doing more research is more useful than learning to recite the dictionary, and developing a critical mind is more helpful than just having a good memory. Reading books uncritically may make a person act like an ostrich burying its head in the sand, failing to see where the problem lies.

Third: Models are not to be Trusted Completely, but are Useful for Reference

Models are based on assumptions and therefore are not perfect. However, if we have a huge problem involving complex operations with far-reaching but unpredictable consequences, the use of simulation is necessary.

Modeling is useful to the extent that it helps us understand and solve problems. For example, it is impossible to achieve perfect urban transport management, a statement based on theoretical and mathematical grounds. Therefore, computer models are often used to optimize solutions. Even though computer models are not perfect, they are still useful as a reference for urban transportation control if they are managed properly.

Modeling is a useful method for avoiding mere speculation to understand complex phenomena. Simulations are often used in tactical training for the military and enhancing a sense of crisis. Such simulations are a kind of modeling.

Before planning its education reforms, Taiwan had no resources to plan the needed supporting measures. High school joint admissions were replaced with multiple and complicated exams; more changes introduced made the situation messier. After implementing the reforms, there was no mechanism for market adjustment. The American system was introduced in haste, without properly understanding its spirit and system of teaching and research, but it brought about an unprecedented expansion of universities and a proliferation of student enrollment. Almost everyone can graduate regardless of quality. When questioned about this at the time, officials in charge of education told me not to worry.

Nowadays, higher education in Taiwan is plagued with problems. Why was no simulation modeling conducted at that time to explore the many likely scenarios and impacts ensuing from adopting such a policy of rapid expansion so that some of the adverse consequences could have been prevented? Now cronies and laypeople are in charge of higher education. The derived problems were all self-inflicted.

According to my observations, Mainland China seems to be following in Taiwan's footsteps with a surge in the number of universities and students. Why do I say that? Because the process of higher education development in Taiwan can be regarded as a simulation for the development of higher education on the Mainland, and it is a free simulation, one that can be used to learn lessons from others' mistakes.

Such problems are not limited to education. In recent years, many areas in Taiwan and Mainland China have suffered from a severe shortage of water in the springtime, causing widespread complaints. In the summer, on the other hand, typhoons and rainstorms destroy roads and embankments, precipitating flooding and mudslides that cause a high number of casualties and considerable damage to property. People denounce the public works departments for their deficiencies. As usual, on sunny days, no one bothers getting prepared for rainy days; but when a disaster falls, everyone complains about insufficient funds, sub-standard designs, sloppy infrastructure, uneven quality, and so forth. Why are people so good at holding celebrations and squandering money on fireworks to bloat their success and pollute the environment but not at considering the importance of constructing basic infrastructure for effective water control?

Over the past few years, 80% of the world's electricity has come from fossil fuels, which has resulted in a bitter experience for coal miners and their families, at the same time damaging the ecological system, creating air and soil pollution, and spawning widespread diseases and other disastrous consequences. Thermal power generation, which accounts for 70% of Taiwan's electricity, contributed to a certain extent to the bitter century-long history of coal mining families and neighboring residents in Taiwan (see the statistics from the Taiwan Mining Bureau). We are still hearing about the catastrophic consequences ranging from the destruction of the ecology (The first batch of a vast number of trees was cut down in Fenglin to build a photovoltaic field in 2022. Nothing could be more saddening[1].), air and soil pollution and the spread of diseases, and reading about their stories from sources such as the database for Taiwan's Ministry of Health and Welfare. But most people have become oblivious, rarely bothering to predict the direct or indirect disasters that will befall the world as a result of environmental degradation, climate change and smog. Taiwan's air pollution has seriously harmed the earth's ecology; it does not put itself in others' shoes, harming people like coal miners and their families in other countries.

---

[1] *United Daily*, May 24, 2023.

The world's major industrial countries have reached a consensus on reducing carbon emissions. In September 2021, a feature article in *Forbes*[2] reported on the popularization of nuclear power and the reduction in plant construction costs. The International Atomic Energy Agency has raised its forecast for future growth in nuclear power generation capacity. This is the most obvious sign of a nuclear energy revival since the accident at the Fukushima Daiichi Nuclear Power Plant twelve years ago; and, according to a survey in July 2022, a majority of Germans now express their support for their country to maintain its nuclear energy capacity, which has helped to reverse the previous decision to phase out all nuclear power plants in Germany. However, Taiwan's NT$300 billion (US$10 billion) No 4 nuclear power plant was replaced with highly polluting natural gas. The construction of a port for receiving liquefied natural gas may damage a unique algae reef ecosystem built up over thousands of years along Taoyuan's coastline. At the same time, much more than another US$10 billion will be spent on building coastal and offshore wind turbines, which may destroy the ecosystem and have a high mechanical failure rate and unstable wind. Why do they import Fukushima's nuclear-contaminated food, which Taiwan doesn't lack, if they are opposing nuclear power? Today, lung cancer in Taiwan has replaced liver cancer as the most common form of the disease, a result of not conducting simulation exercises.

Cities and districts that tend to flood whenever there is heavy rain usually have not conducted any simulation excises to evaluate the reliability of their drainage systems or the safety of their geological structure. Taiwan Taoyuan International Airport suffers from leaks during heavy rain. Such leaks are inexcusable, especially when the airport prides itself on its exquisite interior decoration, sophisticated English broadcasting and signage systems, indigenous cultural designs, and convenient and friendly services. Because no modeling or simulations were conducted for testing a range of scenarios during the design stage, the misuse and abuse of resources have occurred, and society, in turn, has to endure the constant fear of flooding, leakages and shortage of water. Prevention is always more important than cure. The key lies in thoroughly assessing our systems using modeling and simulations to enhance environmental protection and effective disaster prevention.

Modeling involves more than mounting a few slogans or postings. Modeling as an analytical tool is a highly professional skill that has to be conducted by qualified individuals; otherwise, there would be problems,

---

[2] "Is Nuclear Power Ready At Last For Its 'Model T' Moment?" by Michael Lynch, September 20, 2021, *Forbes*.

and big ones at that. Under the coronavirus pandemic, was the impact of the zero-COVID policy across the Strait simulated beforehand? Have the following been considered: people's livelihoods and the economy, key product supply, medical supply and demand, service transportation, education, international exchange, and industrial manufacturing, among others? Also, will the zero-COVID policy guarantee that lives will be saved?

Chaos is often created by too many laypeople trying to influence the pre-event analysis and the post-factum conclusion of an event or a phenomenon in a pre-emptive bid to steal the show from professionals. Such individuals create noise with their amateurish views, forestalling any possibility for problem-solving while confusion and fear are further aggravated. The many problems we see today, whether in transportation, energy, environmental protection, work safety and soil and water conservation, among others, have a common root cause: the predominance of lay opinion over professional judgment. This explains why nothing gets done while collective anxiety mounts!

The lack of simulation exercises by professional experts is why mistakes in higher education are easily made. Indeed, many successful American practices are copied in a half-baked way, without a simple adaptive simulation for the local environment.

Is a Low Birth Rate a Real Problem?

Taiwan, Hong Kong and the Mainland each has its respective strengths. To promote social progress, one should value other people's assets and learn from them. There is no point in getting agitated and finding excuses to make yourself feel good. Social equality and the quality of higher education can improve if the three principles disclosed above are followed.

When we analyze problems, we should specify the corresponding time and place indicators and find the crux of the problem through simulations. Otherwise, like seeing the trees without seeing the woods, rashly conceived solutions may not solve the predicament. For example, do Taiwan, Hong Kong and the Mainland really have a declining birth-rate problem? Don't we have other matters that deserve more attention?

The world's population was about 2.6 billion in 1950, 6 billion in 1999 and over 8 billion by the end of 2022. Overpopulation is a major cause of many global problems. Without recognizing that population growth and welfare are likely to collide, there is a reasonable chance that floods of people will trek around the world, polluting the earth and creating unthinkable issues. Over the past half-century, the two sides of the Strait have been racing to grow, and the excessively swelling population consumes a great deal of resources and energy, burdening the environment. Ironically, the declining birth rate is becoming a common concern for communities across the Strait even though populations there are already reaching historical highs.

Around 30 to 40, or perhaps even more, universities and higher education institutions in Taiwan have had to lay off employees, merge to form conglomerates, downsize operations, reduce salaries, lower quality control and even close down. Even a minor adjustment in tuition fees in the last few years, far from adequate for making a significant difference, was met with such resistance that it was not implemented. Problems involving students, faculty, campuses and facilities need to be dealt with urgently, added to which are issues of public welfare, private interest and legal concerns, all looking like a hot potato, but the government has no idea what to do except play political tricks driven by its own interest. The declining birth rate issue is not the cause, nor is it unique to Taiwan. Hong Kong, Japan, South Korea and even the Mainland face the same problem. The only difference is that, dominated by populist sentiment, Taiwan hasn't devised any plans for tackling the situation. It has suffered the most from the deep involvement of non-professionals in the process and has ended up receiving the most complaints and criticisms.

Due to a lack of resources, university faculty and staff face low pay, which has been seldom adjusted over the years (See Chapter 20). As a result, teachers are lost under the market mechanism. With its closed-door policy, too many universities and insufficient applicants, Taiwan fails to attract overseas students, is unwilling to allow Mainland students to study in Taiwan, and refuses to accept Mainland academic qualifications. It is like aggravating today's problem and then leaving it for tomorrow.

According to some superficial thinking, the declining birth rate can have a massive impact on higher education in Taiwan and the Mainland, but the effect on student enrollment in Hong Kong should be limited. People fail to realize that the unbalanced thinking about the declining birth rate has already directly hit higher education across the Strait. It's like the flu, drifting from Taiwan to Hong Kong and then spreading to the Mainland.

Hong Kong's historically low enrollment rate is the result of inaction (not taking much action). A slight increase in the enrollment rate now makes people panic. In fact, the vast majority of Hong Kong residents are new immigrants who came to Hong Kong around 1949 or during the late 1980s and their offspring. Strictly speaking, Hong Kong has always been a low-birth-rate paradise. The problem with Hong Kong is a lack of a forward-looking and marco-oriented thinking. If there are concerns about a declining population, Hong Kong should formulate an appropriate immigration policy, coupled with allowing the enrollment of non-locals. Hong Kong's self-assumed concerns about the low birth rate are groundless. Perhaps it is because the HKSAR government, happy to rest on its laurels and complacent about the status quo, feels baffled about changes in society, even when the changes are positive, and is uncertain about what to do.

As for the Mainland, which has a huge population, why bother adding more human resources? Small is beautiful. Slimming down is the right way. There is no need to have more births for the sake of economic growth. Besides, at the height of the US-China trade war and the war between Russia and Ukraine, the energy crisis has exacerbated inflation, and the world is in deep recession. A reduction in investment in the US and China due to COVID-19 has impacted economic activities, while unemployment for young people in Mainland China remains high. So who worries about the low birth rate? To quote a line from an ancient Chinese poem, we are all "melons that grow on the same vine beneath Huangtai." Aren't we afraid that a similar crisis may occur again?

Whether it is true or not, due to a lack of planning, the vague narrative of a declining birth rate has undoubtedly become a social problem in the three territories on both sides of the Strait, impacting higher education in Taiwan, Hong Kong and the Mainland. Also, its chain reaction affects the UK and the US because British and American universities recruit overseas students, and high school graduates from both sides of the Strait are important to their education industry.

There are quite a few young people who might be able to find their way to success by routes other than an academic degree. But unfortunately, they tend to follow the crowd no matter what or are sometimes misled by the decision-makers. Even though they manage in the end to squeeze their way through the narrow alley of university education, they are simply drifting, which is a personal loss as well as a loss for society. The malfunctioning of universities and high schools has drawn complaints from all occupations, and education investment is out of balance at both the high and low ends in the chain of the education system. (See Chapter 11 for numerous examples of successful people who do not have a degree.)

Is a "declining birth rate" a real issue? At this time when university degrees depreciate in value and human expertise is wasted, there is a strong need to reposition university and high school education and incorporate the declining vocational and technical education into the overall planning of secondary and tertiary education. More young people are looking for opportunities to study abroad, and the imbalance of human resources planning has exacerbated the difficulties in college admissions and calls for improving the declining birth rate. Therefore, universities must run simulations on student admission and the arrangements for exchange students and graduates as early as possible to implement measures step by step.

How to Deal with a Low Birth Rate?

South Korea's birth rate in 2021 was 0.81, the lowest in the world, according to an announcement by Statistics Korea in August 2022. A survey by Gallup Korea in October 2021 indicated that 58% of the respondents believed that the major reason for the low birth rate was "economic burden." Respondents from Taiwan, Hong Kong and Mainland China expressed similar views on their respective low birth rates.

However, various reports point out that the vast majority of countries with high birth rates are in Africa, which is less economically advantaged than much of the rest of the world and has poorer living conditions. The top 10 countries with the highest birth rates are in Africa, with an average of 5 to 7 births per woman. Data also show that the UK, France, Germany and other advanced countries with a high living index have higher birth rates than the three places across the Taiwan Strait. Even within the same society, the higher the income of the family, the lower the birth rate; families with higher education levels and better living conditions usually have smaller households. Therefore, it is questionable that "economic burden" is the main factor.

However, "economic burden" was indeed the reason given, which could have been a result of inaccurate questionnaire surveys, questionnaire designers failing to grasp the main points, respondents not telling the truth, or respondents' other considerations such as "the definition of economic burden is too vague, and the standards are too high," and so on. With individualism heavily influencing the present generation, other than exceptional circumstances, perhaps most people feel that having kids is a matter of personal choice. Therefore, it is futile to dig out the root issues.

Instead, what is strange is that people in power continue to make the same mistakes. To please the public, they find ways to subsidize young couples assuming that "economic burden" is the root issue and are not interested in evaluating the effectiveness of the subsidies. Why is it that no one wants to locate the root cause and solve the birth rate issue?

The reason for finding solutions to the wrong propositions, I'm afraid, is the desire for power and probably due to incompetency, too. What is left is only the desire to cater to populism to attract some votes. Every day counts, and one vote is one vote.

Examples that violate the three principles introduced in this chapter are found everywhere. The usual approach in dealing with a low birth rate is another example of "finding the right solution for the wrong problem." On reflection in life, one finds that everything vanishes into nothingness in an instant. Could it be that the real crisis for our society is nothing but complacency and absent-mindedness?

To measure the progress of a society, we must consider the human impact on the environment, pollution and the interdependence and co-prosperity between human beings and the earth. In addition, a large population is by no means the same as strong productivity. We should not only focus on the quantity of the people but also on the quality; not only pay attention to the size of the population, but also to the education, living conditions and cultivation of talents and their diversity.

"Declining birth rate" may not be a worrying concern. What calls for our attention is the rapid expansion of higher education in Taiwan and the Mainland, with so many universities, strong ambitions, plus easy graduation, diverse subjects, and no guarantee of quality. Planning for excellence in higher education requires optimizing human resources, optimizing the performance of universities, and optimizing learning effectiveness. It is particularly important to streamline the university's scale and determine its mission or position.

Stress Relief

There are some simple and clear "buttons" on the soda caps at McDonald's and other fast food restaurants. These buttons can be used as codes for the staff to tell the difference between different drinks and facilitate the unique needs of their customers. For example, press the small round button on the left to indicate it is Coke, the middle button for another soft drink, and the right button for juice. In addition, the circle of rectangular buttons on the lid fits the bottom of the cup perfectly and can sometimes be used as a coaster, collecting any water dripping from the cup. The button design is an example of a simple and effective simulation for taking orders.

After finishing your Coke, you can while away your time pressing the buttons, which may help you relax. If you don't believe me, just look at the customers around you next time you go to a McDonald's or any other fast-food restaurant and see what they are doing other than drinking their beverages.

5
Blind Spots and Loss of Scholarship

Higher education is a distinct field of professional practice involving complex issues that should be overseen with competence specific to the profession, whether these are issues of university governance or promoting university education.

Compared with North American universities, those in Hong Kong usually have small campuses but have much more intense issues, which can originate from the outside, be created inside, be a collusion between inside and outside forces, or even be fabricated. All these intertwined viruses have harmed the principles that universities should uphold and should be eliminated as soon as possible.

Selection of University Leaders

University is the place where faculty and students come together in the quest for truth, virtue and beauty. We should not allow the dogma of populism to distort our academic discourse on education, research and development and dictate the selection of university presidents. Otherwise, it confuses academia with politics, confounding the selection of academic leaders with the election of political leaders. Unfortunately, such politicization in the selection process for a university president by external intervention is often found in many places and is at its worst in Taiwan, a result of the spread of populism into higher education. The parties involved often form cliques and factions, in addition to the involvement of political forces. Senior academic leaders in the Mainland are not appointed through open search but instead are determined by the government.

Societies would be indeed miles away from the ideals of higher education if all our society and the media do is to circulate rumors to fan the flames, or if press reports concerning the manipulation of the selection of a university president or other academic leaders such as vice-presidents and deans are really true, or if we have lost the ability to conduct rational discussions on the basis of factual evidence. We would have nothing to be proud of, despite a remarkable rise in global rankings, outstanding research and teaching, excellent student performance, and self-assuring claims of democratic advancement.

Social customs and conventions do not come into being by themselves. It is the mission of social leaders and university teachers to promote education, research and service to the community in accordance with modern trends embedded in the ideals of the internationalization of higher education. Please do not interfere with the selection of university executives.

Be Courteous to and Respect Talents

When it comes to internationalization, one common view is that university students should have a global vision. Is that so? Why do we require university students to be internationalized in such a way, and not start with the teachers, the university and the government?

I am frequently asked the following questions. What salaries do you offer to attract professors? Why is there a shortage of international and overseas scholars in Taiwan and Mainland China? If your university is doing well in world university rankings, do renowned professors seek faculty positions elsewhere? How do you attract international students?

Most people would give answers that are closely related to salaries and resources. The English teaching environment and the reputation of a university come second as attractions for overseas talent. Such answers tend to forget that other fundamental issues should not be ignored in addition to sufficient funds and high rankings if we wish to promote internationalization in higher education.

University administration and democratic elections are entirely unrelated. Possibly under the influence of the election culture promoted by the superficial democracy in Taiwan and sometimes in Hong Kong, people in universities and society at large tend to regard talented applicants as mere contest-contenders or job-hunters, and some even believe that these applicants should be given tougher treatment in the recruitment process because of the high social status of university appointments. The outcome is, of course, a serious setback for internationalization.

It is understood that universities should recruit outstanding talent. Not only will outstanding scholars help to nurture excellent students, but they will also help to attract external funding. Outstanding scholars holding well-established positions will be put off by a haughty attitude and have no interest in taking up any position at arrogant universities. And those with no decent positions looking for better deals may be more willing to bend their knee but will probably not be the first-rate scholars we desire. Even young scholars starting their careers will choose to perch on a fine tree like a flock of birds. Scholars, young or senior, are willing to serve a university that is equally willing to respect and cherish them. Accomplishment is based on the readiness to learn, while understanding is based on the willingness to inquire, both of which require a humble mindset and a modest attitude as pre-requisites. Showing courtesy and respect to applicants is a basic attitude that society and universities should adopt.

In order to attract the right talent, we must make people happy to come to us from far and near. When hiring faculty and recruiting outstanding students, we need special arrangements to reach out proactively. My recruitment goal has always been to identify outstanding talents better than myself or those in the existing team, encouraging colleagues to get the best, even if it consumes energy and time. Faculty recruitment is not an easy task but particularly challenging when it comes to attracting accomplished scientists, often ensconced in established local and regional networks, often at world-leading universities, to Hong Kong. Usually, patience and persistence are key ingredients in the endeavor.

The questions most frequently asked of applicants across the Strait include: "Why are you interested in our university?" or "Why don't you apply for a position in other universities?" Or even: "Do you have other opportunities?" Could you imagine couples in love with each other who keep asking his/her partner: "Why are you interested in me?" or "Why are you not interested in others?" or "Don't you have others you are in love with?" How meaningless are these questions, and how lacking in self-confidence! For applicants, especially outstanding ones, it should be more appropriate to emphasize that "We are a distinguished university or department that enjoys high academic standing, and we hope you would give us thoughtful consideration. We welcome any proposals or suggestions you may have." With such an attitude, we will have an opportunity to find out where we can improve.

Those who gain talent, win the world. In this regard, beautiful Taiwan seems to be going the opposite way, treating people differently, as job-grabbers, and trying to exclude them. That may account for the lack of overseas professors and the brain drain in Taiwan. Take 2022 as an example: the number of Taiwanese full-time professors working at the eight UGC-funded universities in Hong Kong set a record high, reaching about 150. These professors are outstanding and considered academic pillars in any corner of the world.

Here is another example. Taiwan would view a senior academician at Academia Sinica who is interested in working in Hong Kong as talent outflow. However, Academia Sinica, supposedly being a first-class research institute, does not seem to mind the circulation of talent. If this is the case, Taiwan should try to open up and attract global talent to Taiwan, whether research scholars or students. It should drop the haughty attitude towards outsiders as if they were soliciting favors or alms. This kind of narrow mindedness reflects a failure to appreciate flair as the key to revitalizing society and bringing about rejuvenation. Instead of outsmarting others, we are actually on the losing side because of the loss of gifted personnel.

If we lose our self-confidence and competitiveness, global talent will not join us in cultivating an international perspective among the young generation and preparing them to live and work in a globalized world. If we are truly worried that Mainland or overseas students may take away student quotas from Hong Kong or Taiwan or even our jobs, we should try even harder to enhance the diversity of our talent pool and strengthen our competitiveness and our connectivity with the outside world. It is a pity that many local students, instead of enhancing themselves once they feel the pressure of strengths exhibited by others, start to whine, cry and blame others.

Without the backing of modern practices, recruiting international experts and scholars (not necessarily foreigners or those from other places) is unlikely to be successful. Without experts and scholars equipped with an international vision, it is difficult, if not impossible, to cultivate such a perspective among our students or expect them to be able to embrace cosmopolitanism. Being ready to recruit skilled individuals worldwide and embracing innovative ideas are the main driving force behind US prosperity.

Human resources are the main asset behind a society's competitive edge. If universities fail to put this idea into practice, the internationalization of higher education will be nothing but a fantasy. Universities and faculty should first achieve global standards before requiring students to strive for internationalization. As an ancient idiom says, never feel ashamed to ask and learn from your subordinates, and always be persistent in your sincerity to enlist the help of learned scholars. Keep knocking on the doors of sought-after talent until you finally succeed. The same thought process can be applied to the recruitment of faculty, staff and students. Some people have quit this traditional outreach practice, which Western societies acquired as they pursued internationalization. Are we simply adept at quoting ancient idioms?

Brain Drain

A quiet environment, reliable human resources and adequate funding are needed for scientific research. Professor Chen, a Taiwanese academic specializing in transmission electron microscopy (TEM), knows this well. Although Taiwan's electronics industry is highly developed, he never encountered anyone there interested in developing electron microscopes. Even though he had won many honors, and because he lacked funding for software and hardware research and was a misfit in a society that emphasizes interpersonal networking, Chen was getting nowhere. In fact, the mechanism for accessing teaching and research funds stopped him from developing high-end quantum electron microscopes and fulfilling his ambition to establish an industry for precision instruments. Luckily for him, he was offered a job in Hong Kong.

However, with only a few people controlling large-scale scientific research projects in Hong Kong, Chen did not know how to navigate the labyrinthine bureaucracy where only superficial procedures are followed and the results don't matter. This is why many technology firms have migrated north to Guangdong over the years. Fortunately, CityU offered Chen seed funding for a Time-Resolved Aberration Corrected Environmental (TRACE) transmission electron microscope while the Shenzhen Municipal Government followed the wisdom to set aside space in the Shenzhen-Hong Kong Cooperation Zone for Technology and Innovation and allocated 40 million yuan (US$5.5 million) in advanced funding.

The world's first TRACE-TEM prototype, which Chen designed, came out in early 2021, and in October 2022, the Shenzhen government gave Chen an additional US$110 million for leading basic research at the Institute of Physical Sciences plus a new 12,000-square-meter research building in ten years' time.

A false step in teaching and research can lead to an absence, or waste, of money. Brain drains occur because talent gets overlooked in some quarters but is appreciated elsewhere. Old-fashioned clichés prevent scientific research from taking root. Judging what or who is good is all in the mind, as the following poem explains:

> *In the Spring and Autumn period,*
> *People laughed at the brain drain from the State of Chu to the State of Jin.*
> *Today people across the Strait look at how talent from Taiwan is attracted to Hong Kong.*
> *History may not repeat itself, but stupid people often like to repeat history.*

Publish Peer-Reviewed Papers

There is bound to be output in whichever industry or business is chosen, and higher education is no exception. A university's output can be seen as published research papers, patents, teaching and research books, software and hardware design, and so forth. What we are referring to below is the publication of research papers.

Until half a century ago, many universities in the world were not expected to pursue research. They were regarded as the moral enterprises of society, and university teachers rarely produced any research and only taught in the classroom according to the curriculum. If there were some research outputs, they were not evaluated or reviewed. Even today, we can still see many claims and assertions regarding teaching and research that are neither evidence-based nor validated by proof. Therefore, it is necessary to emphasize the importance of universities publishing evidence-based and peer-reviewed academic papers or outputs.

Universities now put a premium on the publication of academic papers as a key indicator for measuring the research achievements of academic staff. With the exception of perhaps art and design, academic staff are required to publish academic papers based on research in their special fields of interest or disciplines, and these are peer-reviewed, validated, and sometimes even put into applications before being counted as output. Universities under pressure to produce research output place exceptional emphasis on the number of published papers. Lately, the number of citations for each paper is also emphasized or often overemphasized in order to demonstrate utility and impact.

In trying to publish papers, we should guard against the pitfalls of parroting or recycling other people's ideas with no real contribution to innovation or indulging in callous sentimentalism on the pretense of being an author of originality. Otherwise, the so-called publications will add no value to creativity and may even mislead the reader by causing confusion.

With the rapid growth of academic journals in recent years, we are witnessing a huge proliferation of papers submitted for review. I have come across a substantial number of submissions that were only slightly revised versions of other researchers' work but presented as the authors' own research achievements. Some of them didn't even bother to check the academic value of the original papers. Nor were they bothered by the superficial, insignificant and sometimes meaningless conclusions drawn by these papers. They were happy with their own output within their enclosed world, oblivious to what was really happening in the academic world.

Many conceived of the excuse that it would be difficult for research on local issues to be accepted by international journals for publication. But in fact, this is not true. There are articles based on local birds, fish and archaeology published in top international journals. Influenced by the current fast-food mentality, which emphasizes speedy output, pioneering research on important and complicated issues such as energy and healthcare is rarely conducted, although it is critical for societies across the Strait and can have a global impact. Many people are simply happy to repeat work on recycled topics because they are easy and handy.

The situation is similar to what some writers of martial arts stories did in the early days. They wrote only one word for each line as a way to get more royalties. Counting papers is easy, but assessing the quality of a paper requires vigorous peer review. An emphasis on counting quantity only, without the involvement of professional judgment, demonstrates a basic distrust of one another.

Focusing on fast production for speedy results is not limited to academia. Often the media across the Strait would rather publish superficial stories that are highly sensational, although full of exaggeration and distortion, than serious, thought-provoking articles. When being challenged, they would either waffle or brush them aside. It is also exceedingly popular these days to cite someone out of context to suit one's own needs or interests.

Subcontractors of Academic Papers

Subcontracting plays a vital role in the production of goods and services. Company management has increasingly resorted to subcontracting to other firms or persons to undertake aspects of a larger project to reduce production costs, enhance efficiency and increase productivity.

While the role subcontracting plays in manufacturing should not be dismissed, its presence in different domains could be a concern. In Taiwan and Mainland China, and to some extent Hong Kong, subcontracting is expanding rapidly into different areas, starting in manufacturing, penetrating politics, and quietly infiltrating the ears of people, affecting education and other sectors. If change is needed, where should we begin: folk customs, the style of our officials, or that of our scholars?

For example, when publishing is regarded as a key indicator of internationalization, faculty start finding ways to publish more. This gradually becomes what I refer to as the subcontracting of academic papers, and some academics behave more or less like subcontractors.

More and more academic papers are churned out by paper production teams, involving too many dispensable authors to increase output. The corresponding author mainly assumes a managerial role in the production chain. So under the drive for cost-saving, output maximization and the disguise of teamwork, quantity is emphasized over quality, and independent scholarship is sacrificed for mass production. This means that complex, time-consuming and vigorous research can lose ground to frivolous, sensational studies that require little effort or supporting evidence but are highly popular. Because of the diffusion of responsibility inherent in subcontracting, identifying liability is sometimes unclear. The drive for speedy publication may create perverse incentives for unprofessional or unethical practices such as cheating to achieve quick results. Many of the ethical problems that result from this kind of subcontracting are discussed in Chapter 14.

Since 1980, universities in Taiwan have swung from one extreme of not requiring publication to the other extreme of requiring academics to get their work into journals. To rectify the second extreme, universities in Taiwan, then universities in Hong Kong since the 1990s, and universities on the Mainland since the 2000s, almost without exception, classify academic papers into categories based on the academic journals in which they are published. They use categories A, B and C, the Science Citation Index (SCI), the Social Sciences Citation Index (SSCI) and even the impact factor to benchmark the citations of a published paper. In some cases, the h-factor, an author-level metric that attempts to measure the citation impact of the publications of an individual scholar considering that individual's most cited papers and the number of citations made by others, is used to determine his/her research achievements.

Obviously these measurements cannot apply to all disciplines; it is inevitable that the lower downs will generate countermeasures to subvert policies set by the higher ups. Hence, to put it mildly, these measures are stop-gap solutions only and are better than nothing. They seem to suggest that universities are not mature enough to judge the quality of their own faculty's academic publications. To put it bluntly, determining the quality of an academic paper by counting the number of words is a lazy way to cope with what needs to be done due to our inability to understand the papers.

Let me further illustrate the point with some easy-to-understand examples. Is the value of an article based on where it is published? Were Nobel Prizes awarded to Yan Mo and Charles Kao because of the publishing house or some particular SCI or SSCI journals where they published their work? Were Oscars awarded to Ang Lee's films because of their star-studded casts or the film studios that produced or released these films? Would anyone remember the record company that released the songs of Elvis Presley or Teresa Deng? Were major academic prizes awarded to papers purely on the basis of the journals where they were published rather than on their quality and value? Obviously, the answers to these questions are all negative.

Albert Einstein published fewer than 100 papers. The winner of the 2015 Nobel Prize in Medicine, Tu Youyou, described in the Epilogue of this book, had 108 counts of super low citation and seven counts of extra low h-index factor for the papers she wrote, including those written in Chinese, which sounds somewhat incredible to many people. And even the outstanding papers written by Genichi Taguchi, a quality guru, could hardly be found at one time in many university libraries. Academic papers with genuine foresight and insight will eventually stand the test of time and create ripple effects worldwide.

Research should be based on one's professional interests and curiosity. In assessing the quality and importance of research, universities emphasize impact and relevance for solving real-world problems as well as overall quality. The publication of a paper should be the natural outcome of the research rather than for the purpose of meeting a set quota. First-rate teachers in progressive universities can be classified as belonging to this category. Although the number of papers, the academic journals in which the papers are published, and the number of times the published articles are cited, etc., are not necessarily unimportant, they pay more attention to the substantial impact of the research and its relationship with practical problems. Professors at the forefront of academic research should be committed to such a practice instead of churning out papers that have no substantial impact, like subcontractors.

Universities conduct research innovation and knowledge creation for the purpose of enhancing problem-solving capabilities. Hence, university curriculums should emphasize more research driven by real-world problems rather than exclusively by abstract speculation. Although this is a simple fact, many people still fail to understand and argue against it, and even fewer people put it into practice. Viewing universities as factories for manufacturing academic papers is a total misconception.

Publishing should be making a substantial point. As the editor-in-chief for *IEEE Transactions on Reliability*, I strictly upheld this principle. We would revise and edit all submitted papers that were innovative, even if not written in good English; on the other hand, we would reject without hesitation papers with no substantial content, though written in perfect English.

If we refuse to publish our research results and oppose having them reviewed or validated by independent parties, internationalization is still flawed. If we are concerned merely with publishing papers and pay no attention to the actual impact, globalizing higher education will become problematic.

Ju Quan

Taekwondo, a highly popular form of martial arts in South Korea, is a combination of Korean, Japanese and Chinese martial arts that hone the practitioners' fighting will and defend themselves in combat. It was introduced to Taiwan in 1966 and renamed Ju Quan (Ju Boxing) to remind the Nationalists who moved to Taiwan from the Mainland after its defeat not to forget to reclaim their lost land. Ju Quan Teams were formed that were affiliated with the Marine Corps Academy, responsible for training cadets to be physically strong and to undertake unarmed combat.

Fifty years ago, I served as Second Lieutenant in the tank camp of the Marine Corps. Ju Quan was an essential daily exercise. Although the instructors with Sandan black belt skills could easily break bricks, tiles and wooden boards with well-aimed punches and kicks, the officers and soldiers usually did nothing but practice the basic stances. No one was taught any of the brick-, tile- or wood board-breaking courses because that was not the ultimate goal behind practicing Ju Quan.

After close to two years of training, I believe we can also "break" certain bricks, tiles and wood boards as long as we exercise our *qi* (energy) by "discarding distracting thoughts and concentration." Skills are built from practice, and output from research accumulates step-by-step and grows naturally. Hasty and inappropriate methods simply backfire.

6

Communicating Rigorously

The use of language is deeply entrenched in human culture, and there are different approaches and understandings. One way is to see language as a system of communication that enables humans to exchange verbal or symbolic utterances. In addition, language carries social and cultural purposes, such as signifying group identity, social stratification as well as social grooming and entertainment. Language has the function of enabling humans to request help, inform others, and share attitudes and feelings. Of course, language allows us to review history, state our current situation and forecast our vision for the future; a technologically advanced society needs to use language to convey and explain the results of scientific and technological research and development.

According to the Confucian educational philosophy in ancient China, mastering the Six Arts was the key requirement for scholars with higher education. The Six Arts, as spelled out in the *Book of Rites*, refer to a core set of philosophical ideals comprising six disciplines in aristocratic education before the Zhou dynasty: ritual, music, archery, charioteering, calligraphy and mathematics. Among the Six Arts, calligraphy refers to literature as well as writing, verbal and composition skills. Therefore, the Chinese education concept is identical to the notion of education in the West. The only difference lies in what language for communication should be used.

Human languages are highly open-ended. The structures change as they are employed by their speakers at separate times to suit their needs. In the early days, before Taiwanese students went overseas to study, they had to attend a seminar specifically hosted by the Ministry of Education that was nothing more than an introduction to the daily customs and commonly used expressions in the countries they were heading to. Teachers advised everyone from the very beginning that we should try not to use Chinglish expressions like "Long time no see" when we wanted to express "I haven't seen you for a long time"! Many years later, my overseas friends always greet me with "Long time no see" on such occasions. The customary greeting "How do you do?" in the early days has long since disappeared.

The world is changing rapidly and getting more complicated. Mastering language skills is not enough anymore. Instead, we emphasize that writing for the purpose of conveying truth should be the right way. Therefore, "poetry expressing will and writing carrying doctrine" on the function of literature are universal truths.

Languages can easily become extinct, and language loss occurs when it is displaced or de-emphasized because of a lack of users. Latin, a classical language belonging to the Italic branch of Indo-European languages, used to be an integral part of Western education. But Latin is rarely taught today. Certain languages come and go, but truth and knowledge stay. When one learns a language but fails to follow the truth or gain knowledge, language carries low utility for internationalization, and it will be impossible for the knowledge that can be passed on to future generations to exist.

However, communication does not necessarily depend on language, as in the case of political communication, where the ulterior motive is often to infuriate and impede others. In international politics, interests come first. The language you speak plays no part!

Mutuality in Communication

The family members of an MIT student who committed suicide in 2009 sued the institute for failing to take the necessary measures to prevent the death of their child who had had mental health issues. Similar cases often occur elsewhere around the world. For example, a graduate from Hong Kong sued a university because she had not found a "rewarding job with prospects", despite obtaining a first-class degree. We also have students suing professors for failure in examinations on the grounds of undue stress, or brazenly trying to dictate their curriculum content, or complaining about rising tuition fees. In addition, we have seen graduate students protesting over their low stipend or excessively long working hours. During the turmoil in Hong Kong in the second half of 2019, Mainland students protested that the university did not protect them and demanded high-profile punishment for demonstrators, while Hong Kong local students asked the university to drive away Mainland students. In 2022, with the continual worsening of COVID-19, some refused to be vaccinated, and some asked the universities to refund their fees, etc.

These actions reflect a mentality among students who hope to have an equal business partner relationship with the universities nowadays. Sometimes, there is a hostile and unreasonable tone on the student side. It is no longer a relationship based on principles of morality and justice.

Universities, therefore, must strictly abide by the teaching and research rules, continuing to fulfill their teaching and research tasks on the one hand and treat those whom they teach as peers on the other.

Gone are the kinds of pure and non-instrumental relationships based on mutuality and high morals between teachers and students for the pursuit of knowledge and truth.

How have times changed! Universities in today's higher education have probably evolved from their role in top-down didactic teaching to a kind of more egalitarian role in communication with students as their fellow peers. Let us consider some individual cases.

Communication Requires Cultural Understanding

There is an apparent lack of communication between students from divergent backgrounds in Hong Kong. Some local Hong Kong students brought up under a British-style education since childhood tend to look down on those from Mainland China, regarding the latter as country bumpkins. Yet, in recent years, they have discovered that not just a few Mainlanders have excellent academic performance and high proficiency in English, and some even have a heavy purse, too. Then the Hong Kongers' sense of superiority suffered a setback in feelings of inferiority and other complicated feelings. Cybercrime is rampant nowadays. In the fall of 2021, more than 30 students, all of them from the Mainland and some top students with a GPA of 4.0, in the dormitory, have been defrauded of nearly US$2 million.

On the other hand, while Mainland students recognize the strengths of their local counterparts, they find many of them ignorant about Chinese culture and hence utterly unjustified in their disdain for non-locals. Thus, the Mainlanders' earlier feelings of inadequacy became mixed with an increasing sense of self-pride, leading to a complicated and confusing mindset. The integration of the two groups is not easy, and there are often misunderstandings. We should note also that the so-called "mainlandization" trend has blurred the physical, social, cultural and psychological borders between mainland China and Hong Kong, which further complicates communication.

In recent years, Hong Kong society has experienced a tumultuous period of rising tensions. First, we had the Occupy Central movement in 2014, and then the Anti-Extradition Law Amendment Bill Movement in 2019. During this period, political movements, both on and off campus, formed a division between local Hong Kong students and students from the Mainland. The more impulsive and extreme members resorted to violent and seemingly endless confrontations with each other. In fact, both groups have overlooked the trend of "mainlandization" which will blur the physical, cultural, political, and psychological borders between Mainland China and Hong Kong.

Then, there is yet another group of non-local students from around the world. Though a small number, they form a highly visible group on campus. In their eyes, ethnic Chinese students are generally friendly but may behave strangely; for example, some are introverts who avoid eye contact, while others are so assertive that they will force their way through a door even though there is a female ahead of them, much to the dismay of the male foreigner holding the door open for her. Yet, from the opposite perspective, students from abroad are seen as mostly badly-behaved beer-drinkers and club-goers.

In Taiwan, Mainland students tend to be scrutinized under a magnifying glass. Unless living an extremely quiet life, they are more likely to be criticized for whatever they say and do. Mainland students have no one to turn to for help. I guess Hong Kong and Taiwanese students studying on the Mainland have to try hard to adapt to the Party-led campus environment. Someone asked me the difference between students across the Strait and those from the US. It is true that students from all over the world are different and have their own characteristics, but the biggest difference between American students and students from across the Strait, according to my personal contact and observation, is that American students are usually natural and consistent with each other.

The above communication barriers apparently have nothing directly to do with the different languages people speak. They are more likely to be the result of cultural background and values, as well as the lack of communication and respect for international norms and mutual understanding. As we all know, the only way to dispel misunderstandings is by opening up and enhancing communication. In both Hong Kong and Taiwan, since local students are the majority on campus, they should demonstrate grace and broad-mindedness in taking the initiative to welcome and communicate with non-local students. As for non-local students, they should take advantage of their studies in Hong Kong or Taiwan to make friends with local or non-local students and immerse themselves in the local culture in addition to pursuing their studies. If you cannot even take care of yourself, how can you help take care of the world? Following the same logic, college students should ask themselves how they can communicate with the outside world if they cannot even communicate among themselves. Indulging in the empty talk about internationalization without observing international norms and the rule of law is futile.

What I experienced at Iowa State University many years ago can be used as an example. One time a student from Mainland China was caught cheating during an examination. Everyone was talking about how the student should be punished. But one American professor stood up for him, saying the student should be dealt with leniently because cheating might be an integral part of Chinese culture. That is only misplaced leniency. Honesty is a universal value. If what was said about Chinese culture being different is indeed true, how are we to react to such a statement? You might think that the professor was deliberately trying to ridicule Chinese culture, but he was actually defending the student. You might wonder where his view of Chinese culture came from, but he was certainly not discriminating. Whose fault is it if he holds such a misguided opinion?

Many Chinese students studying abroad in the US initially feel discriminated against by locals. But after some first-hand experiences, they realize that these claims of discrimination might have more to do with a person's psychological makeup. On the other hand, students from across the Strait seem to have an admiration for Westerners even if they have not had any direct contact with them and do not necessarily know their culture.

All these contradictory phenomena seem to have little to do with any language barrier.

Communication Should Be Genuine and with Substance

Human communication lies in sincerity. Excellent communication enhances integration and boosts morale. Internationalization of education requires appreciation and respect for local mores and values to make headway and gain acceptance. Normally, making a start is difficult. Luckily breaking the ice between people is easier than a ship trying to cut through the ice in the Arctic. Just give full play to a creative mind to think of the content to fill the gap as well as find the right words to convey the ideas.

During my school years, we regularly listened to Chiang Kai-shek's Double Tenth (National Day) speech, characterized by a strong vernacular Ningbo accent, which was ridiculously hard to understand. Later, I learned from my Mainland Chinese friends that Mao Zedong's Hunan accent was no less difficult to follow. But what is interesting is that, while their accents were hard to comprehend and sometimes even amusing, we never had any problem understanding the messages that Chiang wanted to deliver to the people of Taiwan, while the Mainland Chinese on the other side of the Strait understood Mao's directives perfectly well and carried them out without fail.

It is easy to imagine Chiang and Mao not actually understanding each other in the language they used when negotiating. But when looking at history, we often find people who were not compatible either in appearance or speech but could agree completely as dislike-minded people.

Such a phenomenon clearly indicates that the tools of communication, whether language, pronunciation, or accent, are not essential for successful communication. Instead, the message and the content are more significant. In some cases, language itself is the least valuable tool.

Whether you agree with me or not, two giant leaders of the last generation across the Strait who managed to mobilize millions upon millions of people depended more on the power of the message they delivered than the language they employed.

Likewise, despite the language barrier, many couples in mixed marriages enjoy an intimate relationship and a genuine meeting of minds. Conversely, people who start with minor verbal quarrels and end up fist-fighting often speak the same language. This is partly because they can be hurt easily by the foul language they both understand well. That is, the value of communication depends more on the message than the medium. The appeal of ancient literary works rarely lies simply in an extensive display of flowery language. Communication does not necessarily rely on words, whether softly spoken or shouted out loudly in public.

One may see the moon using a finger as a pointer, but the finger itself is not the moon. Some people tend to be enthralled by the articulate rhetoric of a few charismatic speakers and regard them as a model for imitation. In the end, these people might acquire comparable levels of diction and eloquence, but they might experience obstacles to social advancement.

Wherein Lies the True Beauty of Tang Poetry?

The importance of a specific language in assessing quality is not as significant as imagined. I can use poetry to illustrate how the importance of subjective meaning in communication goes beyond mere spoken sounds or written representation.

During my middle school years in southern Taiwan, a classmate's father told me that reading Tang dynasty poems aloud in Mandarin could not give full credit to the charm of the rhymes. They had to be read aloud in the Hokkien dialect. When I went to college, a Hakka classmate said that Tang poems sounded most beautiful when recited in the Hakka dialect, which is an ancient language. I found him convincing after hearing him reciting a few stanzas. Then when I came to Hong Kong, many local Hong Kong people bragged about how Cantonese was the language to bring out the elegance of the rhymes and authentic beauty of Tang poems. Mandarin fails to achieve this, whereas according to them, Cantonese has retained more of the diction of the Central Kingdom of ancient China.

Hearing that, I began to harbor some doubts.

Several years ago, I went on a business trip to Chengdu in the middle of a scorching summer and happened to see under the canopy of a tree a crowd of people gathered around a woman in her seventies or eighties. Driven by curiosity, I walked up and listened to her reading out some Tang poems in the Sichuan dialect. The sound and intonation were so melodious that she seemed to be almost singing.

By then, I became interested in doing some research. Even though I do not understand Japanese, I asked a Japanese friend to read some Tang poems in Japanese. Then I read aloud myself a Tang poem I had found that had been translated into English. To be more thorough, I even asked an American friend to read it for me. Driven by curiosity, I asked the Dean of the Business College at CityU, who is South Korean, to try them in Korean.

I began to get some answers. But of course, I needed to try reading aloud the following Tang poem, "Viewing the Moon, Thinking of You":

As the bright moon shines over the sea,
From far away you share this moment with me.
For parted lovers lonely nights are the worst to be,
All night long I think of no one but thee.
To enjoy the moon I blow out the candle.
Please put on your nightgown for the dew is thick.
I try to offer you the moonlight so hard to pick,
Hoping a reunion in my dream will come quick.[1]

As suspected, it read beautifully as well!

But how is that so? The true beauty of a Tang poem lies in its inherent charm, and not just in the rhymes, in its aesthetic sensibility and not just in its composition. Otherwise, there would be no difference between a poetic verse like "The drifting soul of the purple moon exudes the fragrance of fallen flowers" and advertising slogans that are pleasant to the ear but easily forgotten afterward. A good poem has sublime content; it sounds beautiful regardless of how it is read, and not necessarily in which language, and it has the same unforgettable impact.

In the early summer of 2020, when the COVID-19 pandemic seemed at its worst in Hong Kong, a Japanese friend mailed some face masks from Tokyo to Hong Kong. On the package, I saw printed the last two lines of Wang Changling's Tang poem "Seeing off Imperial Censor Chai."

---

[1] Composed by Zhang Jiuling and translated by Ying Sun (https://language.chinadaily. com.cn/a/201909/13/WS5d7af820a310cf3e3556b5ae_4.html).

> *The Yuan River connecting other rivers takes you to Wugang;*
> *On parting with you my heart is weighed helplessly down.*
> *We'll share the same clouds and rain though separated by a mountain range;*
> *The bright moon belongs not to a single town!*[2]

The greetings from the Japanese friend transcended language barriers, country borders, clouds and rain, and thousands of years.

In addition, the popular heartfelt regard from Japan at that time also included an excellent line in the *Book of Songs* from more than 2,000 years ago: "Fear not the want of armor, for mine is also yours to wear." Confucius used the word "innocent" to evaluate this classic from Confucian culture. The Japanese now use this famous line to express their determination to combat the pandemic together. With wide circulation, the quote has become well memorized. Innocence is an element that is lacking today among college students across the Strait.

Languages carry doctrine. Regardless of which languages or dialects we use, Mandarin, English, Hokkien, Cantonese, Hakka, or Sichuanese, no matter how good they sound, and if we attend to trifles to the neglect of essentials, education will deviate from basic standards! Obviously, communication needs to have some substantial content and inherent charm, rather than depending on language only. Indeed, poetry expresses will.

Popular Courses at Harvard

That brings me to some of the courses at Harvard University that students, regardless of their disciplinary background, may want to take. Some of the courses, understandably, are more appealing than others. "Justice: What's the Right Thing to Do" taught by Michael Sandel, a well-known professor in political philosophy, is among the most popular.

This course was broadcast to several universities overseas and is one of the open courses at Harvard. Sandel's lectures are uploaded onto YouTube, creating a global classroom. Viewers see a lecture hall packed with more than 600 students, all enthusiastically engaged in the active exchange of teaching and learning, with questions flying in all directions.

"The Principle of Economics" is another popular course offered by Gregory Mankiw, who believes that "Learning the basics of economics is essential for being an informed citizen, and it is a good foundation for

---

[2] Adapted from an online translation.

many career paths." With a distinguished professor at the lectern, it is only natural that the enrollment numbers for this economics course remain high.

These popular courses are all taught in large classes. In my study of the relationship between teaching and research, I have pointed out that content is the most important aspect of a course.[3] The quality of the interaction between the teacher and students is determined by the substance and content of a course. If the content is rich and lively, the quality of interaction will not be affected by the number of students present in the classroom. This is true regardless of the discipline, be it science, social sciences or humanities. It is why all the above-mentioned courses offered at Harvard attract hundreds of students. If the content is poor, even one-to-one teaching can put a student to sleep.

Communication and Distorted View of English

Whenever people talk about internationalization, many emphasize the importance of English proficiency, as if proficiency with the English language is the only pathway.

There are people who advocate using English as the language of instruction, even in the absence of evidence to prove that it could improve learning efficiency. But what is the purpose of using English as the language of instruction? To acquire proficiency in English by studying academic subjects? Or to acquire professional knowledge through learning English? Or simply to follow a fad under the pretext of internationalization?

Is communication really as simple as fluency in languages? The exchanges between Taiwan and the rest of the world are inferior to those of Hong Kong. Apart from domestic political issues, Taiwan is not much concerned about what is happening in the world. Hong Kong, a cosmopolitan city where people from all over the world gather and interact, has a long history of embracing the world. One would assume that its universities are naturally highly internationalized. However, there are still differences and misunderstandings in society's views and communication on internationalization.

More often than not, they fail to see the forest for the trees in promoting internationalization. They tend to overemphasize the importance of

---

[3] See *Clarifying Some Myths of Teaching and Research* by Way Kuo and Mark E. Troy, National Tsing Hua University Press, 2009.

English proficiency, failing to recognize that international standards are by far the most important. We need not go extremely far back, only a few hundred years, to realize that English was not always the most popular language. Before that, French, German and the Latin languages were once popular. Right after World War II, English with a Japanese accent attracted attention. Recently, English with a Korean or Indian accent, the most affluent ethnic group in the US, or with a Chinese accent, is enjoying the spotlight.

When we talk about the technological achievements of the 20th century, we cannot ignore Genichi Taguchi, the Japanese quality expert who developed a revolutionary methodology based on his groundbreaking research on quality design for enhancing the quality of manufactured goods. This methodology, known as the Taguchi method, has been extended to engineering, technology, economics and the service industry as well. His contribution to quality enhancement in such a wide spectrum of areas is second to none in the contemporary world. I knew Taguchi well. His English was terrible, yet it did not affect the effectiveness of his theory and methods, nor did it stop people in different fields from adopting his methodology, which had a far-reaching impact on quality assurance.

Some people are proud of their command of English but talk with no substance; Genichi Taguchi's English may be poor, but people do not seem to mind because what he says makes good sense. I worked in US universities for many years and have known teachers with great command of elegant English, and yet their teaching quality leaves much to be desired. On a few occasions, I have met some officials who speak perfect Oxford English but with a lot of clichés. These cases serve to prove the point that effectiveness should be the focus of communication rather than the tool of language. Or, as the Confucians would say, language is merely a vehicle for culture. We should look first at effectiveness before we think about the language medium. As the old saying goes, "Things have their root and their completion. Affairs have their end and their beginning." Otherwise, it would be meaningless to put the cart before the horse, as was described by the Tang poet Li Bai (李白) in his poem about a bookish old man from Lu State who stuck to quoting famous lines from the *Five Classics* until his death, without ever putting principles into practice.

In addition to the story about Taguchi's poor English with a heavy Japanese accent, which did not stop him from having a sweeping influence over the world, allow me to tell you a more recent story about how culture transcends languages. It demonstrates that language is not necessarily a barrier to effective communication between people sharing the same goals.

James A. Schamus has collaborated with film director Ang Lee for many years. He was the producer of *Hulk*, the Oscar-winning movie *Brokeback Mountain*, and the Golden Bear award-winning movie *The Wedding Banquet*. He wrote the script for Lee's *The Ice Storm* and participated in the writing of *Crouching Tiger, Hidden Dragon*; *Lust, Caution*; and *Eat Drink Man Woman*. A leading independent film producer, Schamus teaches film history and theory at Columbia University's School of the Arts. He understands well the need to achieve a proper balance between artistic demands and commercial profits in the real world of filmmaking. He does not speak Chinese at all. His understanding of the Chinese philosophers Zhuang Zi (莊子), Lao Zi (老子) and the Confucian and Mencian doctrines came from translations read before he started collaborating with the two Chinese scriptwriters for *Crouching Tiger, Hidden Dragon*, which was written in Chinese only. However, these inconveniences did not stop him from contributing to the success of Lee's movies.

English, Chinese, and Korean

As I mentioned in Chapter 5, as editor-in-chief of a professional journal, I have never used language to judge whether a paper should be accepted or not. You might wonder why. Regarding the importance of English proficiency, let me tell you a story. When I worked at Texas A&M University as department head many years ago, I had a PhD student from South Korea who demonstrated a reasonable academic standard, but his English was extremely poor. I suggested that he should draft his doctoral dissertation in Korean and then have it translated into English. On hearing my proposal, another South Korean student told me it would not work because no one could comprehend what that student wrote in Korean. So, the English language is not the key point. It is not just South Korean students who have problems with English. Several of my American students failed to convey exactly what they meant to say in their academic reports even though they were writing in pure American English. So, no, English is not the key point.

Here is another entirely different story.

The baby-boom generation in Taiwan highly regarded Ke Qihua's *New English Grammar*, one of Taiwan's most popular English textbooks. However, Ke Qihua had never studied in the US or Europe or even stepped outside of Taiwan. But his grammar book was looked upon as the "Bible", a must-read for those who wanted to learn English. The book was popular because it had real substance. It benefited many Taiwanese who went overseas for higher education and later returned and became successful. Many people think that plain language will not travel everywhere, but in fact, having just literary elegance and no substance is worse. Somehow, we have quite a few people on both sides of the Strait who prefer form to content.

Here is another story about a well-known figure.

Kai Lai Chung is well known for his groundbreaking contributions to probability theory. He is second to none among Chinese scholars in the sphere of probability. But he speaks English with an accent so strong that neither Americans nor I can easily understand him. When he was a professor at Stanford, his students rushed to the president's office to complain. Do you know what the president told the students? "Professor Chung is our university's valued asset. If his lectures are incomprehensible, it should be your problem." Frankly speaking, I can list dozens of well-known expatriate professors in the US who speak broken English. There are also a number of non-native Chinese teachers in the US who enjoy a high reputation everywhere and are much respected in the academic community, but their spoken English is far from proficient.

I would like to say something based on my writing experience when I first came to Hong Kong.

About 12 years ago, I authored an article for a local Hong Kong newspaper, *Ming Pao*, in which I used the Chinese words *biaodi* (標的, meaning guideline, target, or standard of behavior or conduct). A local reporter published his comment in the paper questioning the use of words that he had never heard of and even ridiculed it as Taiwanese-style Chinese. When he saw the criticism, history professor Pei-kai Cheng exclaimed his surprise that someone would actually publicize his or her ignorance in the media. He even wrote an open rejoinder to the reporter, saying he should have looked up *biaodi* in a dictionary if he was unfamiliar with the words. The reporter was ignorant of the fact that Chinese culture had been better preserved in Taiwan. The main point of this story is not about knowing or not knowing *biaodi* but more about a person's cultural upbringing, or lack of it.

Young people in Hong Kong, in general, know little about Chinese culture and yet are unwilling to learn. How can they communicate with others even if they speak fluent English but have no knowledge of their own culture? What do they have to communicate?

Here is a scene I encountered while dining at McDonald's.

At the end of October 2021, I went to McDonald's in Festival Walk when I saw two male adults cursing each other in Cantonese, using such acrimonious and vicious terms that I was afraid they were coming close to blows. Just at that moment, a McDonald's waitress separated the two with a smile. One of them went away angrily while the other mumbled something, his anger not yet appeased. In any case, one smile finally resolved the dispute.

Let us take a look at the relationship between English and problem-solving.

My friend Lee is an alumnus of the University of Hong Kong. In the sweltering summer of July 2015, some problems related to personnel management issues happened on campus. This subsequently led to a long email trail of exchanges back and forth between the alumni and the university, looking more like submissions for a writing contest. In the end, Lee decided to extract the "gems of wisdom" from these email messages and turn them into English writing samples for use with his students. You can imagine how lively his teaching is, deeply enriched by his personal research and creativity, using examples from real-life communication to illustrate the beauty and elegance of different language usage. Nevertheless, they provide no real solution to the problems, don't you agree?

Let us take a look at the relationship between language and academic research.

People who speak English are considered superior in Hong Kong, which is why before 1997 and afterward, to a large extent, high schools that use English as the medium of instruction have been more popular among Hong Kong parents. The emphasis on English has been consistent, although science and engineering continue to be neglected. Shing-Tung Yau, winner of the Fields Medal in 1982, and Daniel Chee Tsui and Charles Kao, who were awarded the Nobel Prize in Physics in 1998 and 2009, respectively, are the only graduates of Hong Kong secondary schools to have been awarded a Nobel Prize, a rare phenomenon in the old days. Yau and Tsui graduated from Pui Ching Middle School, where classes are conducted mainly in Chinese. This is no coincidence. Several other great scientists who received their secondary school education in Hong Kong also graduated from Pui Ching and made their name in the United States.

While it cannot be said that Chinese is necessarily helpful for research, it does not hinder their scientific achievements. What we should ask instead is, why do many of the Hong Kong high school graduates who learn in English perform poorly in scientific research? Or even, why haven't these high schools produced masters of literature, history, finance, law, and economics?

I have another real story demonstrating that language is not necessarily the prerequisite for success.

Yeung Lam Wai-ying co-founded with her husband Yeung Kin-man a multi-billion-dollar high-tech company called Biel Crystal Manufactory. The couple, who originally came from Hong Kong, founded the company from scratch. She was based in Huizhou, Guangdong province for decades. A hard-working person, she doesn't talk much; nor does she speak much English, least of all Mandarin. Yet, just as "all the beauty of spring could be distilled into something plain and simple like turnip", she was assessed by *Forbes* magazine in 2020 to be one of the world's 100 Most Powerful Women. Like autumn leaves, beauty is inexplicable.

Finally, allow me to relay a wide-off-the-mark comment.

In 2021, Hong Kong appointed a senior government official. Those who opposed the appointment said the appointee did not have a college degree, while those who supported it said the appointee spoke good English. All irrelevant to the subject!

Long story short: we must communicate with our hearts!

Writing Contests

I have been in Hong Kong for more than a decade and have expressed my regret about the students' lack of proficiency in Chinese, not because their Chinese pronunciation is not good, or they use the wrong words or sentence order, but rather because their logic is unclear and their tone is insolent, which is worrying. As with some big shots who like to show off by using bombastic words and then mentioning some inexplicable stereotyped old tunes, which they themselves may not understand completely, it is even more unbearable.

When I first came to Hong Kong in 2008, a well-known public relations writer came to me and assured me that he could write the best Chinese and English speeches. He showed me some of the speeches that he had written for local celebrities. They were all immersed in nothing but flowery language and adorned with beautiful words. To be more accurate, they read like submissions to writing competitions or perhaps beauty contests.

Many of us have attended lectures where the speaker might appear highly eloquent and expressive, but his or her speech was hollow and empty of meaning. By the time the audience returned home, they could hardly remember what the speech was about or what the message was. On social occasions, I have seen speakers rattling on, non-stop and unperturbed, on just about any topic that had come to mind, but one that was completely devoid of meaning and substance. To be frank, many of those talks are sheer nonsense. Perhaps this hipster-like language is just the face mask worn by politicians to deceive listeners; still, many get deceived!

Currently, English enjoys the widest currency in the world. So we cannot afford to ignore it. However, it is not that important that one should be able to speak beautiful English or Chinese since such an ability is not an absolute prerequisite for effective communication nor a determining factor of a person's accomplishment or lack of it. A staff member in my university spoke good English but was often rejected by co-workers because of poor performance. Effective communication depends on attitude, sincerity, logical thinking and substance. Writing that is contrived, dominated by bias and meaningless rhetoric blocks communication, litters the mind and provokes anxiety.

Schools in Hong Kong promote biliteracy and trilingualism. The former refers to written Chinese and English languages, and the latter to spoken Cantonese, English and Mandarin. But effective communication goes beyond making mere linguistic sounds. Overemphasizing the importance of linguistic skills for effective communication in English or any language, and neglecting the systems of thought and logic in which they are embedded, is like being asked to eat the outer skin left after the meat has been disposed of, i.e., it's hard to swallow.

While the ossified form of writing, *baguwen* (or 8-legged essay, which stands for empty formalism, saying nothing at great length and with tiresome posturing) used in the Chinese imperial civil service exams is well past its use nowadays, societies across the Strait, unfortunately, are still focusing their time and effort on competing in various kinds of writing contests, adding a new chapter to the 60-chapter late-Qing dynasty novel, *Officialdom Unmasked*.

International Students on University Campuses across the Strait

People make new adaptations and pursue internationalization to assimilate the best of other cultures and the latest scientific and technological research. In Taiwan, where democracy prevails, many universities are experiencing great difficulty recruiting enough students. In Hong Kong, where English is a communication medium, the concern is how to attract overseas students.

According to statistics from the Ministry of Education in Taiwan, the total number of degree-seeking overseas students in Taiwan was 61,970 in 2018. The number of freshmen from the Mainland studying in Taiwan was 707. At the same time, suffering from low birth rates, the number of college students, which is already relatively small, will continue to decrease. The number of universities has increased disproportionately while student recruitment has become a severe problem for higher education at all levels, from undergraduate to master's and PhD programs. Despite the shortage of non-local students, outstanding Mainland students are prevented from studying in Taiwan for political reasons. Reduced funding sources because of the large number of universities, outdated management systems and cumbersome procedures, misplaced efforts on wasteful and non-essential activities, and the lack of vision and strategic planning obstruct the pursuit of internationalization.

How does Hong Kong fare, then? Hong Kong has a long relationship with Britain and uses English to its advantage. It used to be a gateway to Mainland China and prided itself as the intersection of Eastern and Western cultures. You would expect overseas students to be flocking here. But in reality, relatively few non-Chinese students come. Out of the 17,891 full-time first-year freshmen enrolled in UGC-funded undergraduate programs in 2017, about 2,500 came from Asia, including Mainland China, while only 79 came from the rest of the world. Multiply the above numbers by four, and you will have the approximate total number of non-local university students in Hong Kong. Up to now, few have come from Britain.

In North America and Europe, a single university may easily have at least the same number of international students enrolled on their campus as the total number we have studying in Hong Kong. Nowadays, even Shanghai or Beijing has more international students than Hong Kong and Taiwan combined. This begs the question, why? Why are so few non-Chinese students coming to Hong Kong? Or, for that matter, why so few from Taiwan? In fact, almost none came from Taiwan to Hong Kong before 2008, the year I started to work at CityU. Therefore, really, how internationalized is Asia's World City?

On several occasions, I came face to face with some highly polished female interpreters in Beijing. Their American English sounded extremely pleasant to the ear. I even discovered some of them had never left China, not to say visited North America. It is amazing how they could learn to speak beautiful and impeccable English only with the help of a recording instrument.

That is until one day when I heard an interpreter translating the Chinese phrase *ban jin ba liang* (six of one, and half a dozen of the other), which literally meant "half a *catty* and eight *taels*." In the traditional measurement system, one catty equals 16 taels. Hence "half a catty" should mean "eight *taels*." But the interpreter had no idea of the different measurement systems and mistakenly translated the phrase to "half a kilo and five ounces." This made me realize that even polished interpreters can be handicapped by their lack of contextual knowledge.

There are, of course, other amusing translations, for example, translating *xiao xin di hua* (slippery surface) into "slide carefully", *su zha da chang* (deep-fried large intestines) into "explodes the large intestines", and *tan lian ai* (dating) into "make love." And the way *The King's Speech*, winner of the Academy Award for Best Picture, was translated into 皇上無話兒 in Hong Kong, which could be interpreted as "The Emperor has no dick", was almost scandalous. Taiwan has a different and more appropriate translation 王者之聲 (*Voice of the King*) for the movie.

A national university in Taiwan posted a note at its dormitory saying only visitors of the same gender may visit, but the English translation turned that into "only homosexuals allowed." How misleading! Apparently, perfect pronunciation and intonation in Chinese or English are not the key to a proper interpretation.

Overseas students go to study in Mainland China not because the Chinese like to use English. They go to Taiwan not because the Taiwanese encourage people to speak English. Many Hong Kong people speak English without any problems. Why are there so few British and American students studying in Hong Kong?

Asian Higher Education Market

We should note that internationalization is not a new phenomenon. It has been around since humans first started interacting and finding common causes and ideals. Two and a half millennia ago, state-to-state exchanges during the Warring States period, which began in the 5th century B.C.E., were the norm before China was unified as an empire. Confucius took his students on visits from state to state, speaking different dialects and visiting kings and noblemen. Was that not internationalization? The world continued to learn from China until the 17th century.

After the Industrial Revolution in Europe starting in the 1760s, the world began modernizing, and the West grew in power. The rise of America in the last 100 years depended on the driving force of internationalization, bringing talents from around the world. Now that East Asia is rising, one can learn just as much from the East as the world has been doing from the West in the last 200 years, which is why one should develop confidence in one's areas of strength no matter which culture one belongs to.

Estimates suggest that Asia will constitute about 70% of the global demand for higher education in 15 years' time. In anticipation of this development, the West has already started to respond appropriately. Have universities in Hong Kong and Taiwan thought about what we can do to contribute to the rest of the world? You will understand my point if you compare Taiwan and South Korea.

I have been observing developments in South Korea for the last 30 years. Like Taiwan, the majority of professors in South Korea have received a modern education. Some of the experts and academics may have graduated from distinguished universities in Europe, America, and Japan. This country is constantly re-inventing itself, buoyed by the enormous success of multinational corporations like Samsung and Hyundai, its increasing cultural exports, including its cuisine, TV programs, traditional medicine and its growing service industry, all of which are enjoyed throughout Asia.

To understand why Taiwan is in decline and South Korea is on the rise, we only have to compare how public infrastructure (for example, Taoyuan International Airport in Taiwan and Incheon International Airport in Seoul, as well as the airport express train services), international relations, sports development, political reforms, anti-corruption campaigns, legislative rights, etc., are being pursued or promoted differently in these two societies.

What is interesting is that South Korea's success has not been due to the ability of its people to speak fluent English, just as the rise of Japan's economy in the 1980s and 1990s was not built on biliteracy or trilingualism. In fact, both South Koreans and Japanese are known for their poor English skills, but the heavy Japanese accent in speaking English was once quite a fad, just like the attractiveness of speaking English with a French accent in the mid-19th century.

Neither Japan nor South Korea is known for foreign language proficiency. But Japan stands tall by communicating with the rest of the world through high quality, and South Korea is to be commended for striving as a latecomer to build its world enterprise through diligence and challenging work. As for the US, it has been leading the world for a century by communicating with the world through its advanced science and technology and American-style democracy. I wonder how my fellow compatriots across the Strait, who generally have better English skills than South Koreans and Japanese, will communicate with the rest of the world other than through English.

Without skin, there will be no hair attached. Internationalization grows from various cultures. In promoting internationalization, people across the Strait should, first of all, make serious efforts to preserve, develop and transmit Chinese culture and language, especially when Chinese culture and language receive unprecedented attention in the world today. Unless overseas students from all over the world, far and near, flock to the universities across the Strait to seek the knowledge they consider worth pursuing, we cannot brag about making any progress in internationalization, no matter how fluently we speak English. To put it more positively, is it not time to pay attention to other cultures, such as Chinese culture, when the pivot of higher education is moving to Asia?

Under internationalization, whatever we do can be seen, heard, and felt by everyone else and will be judged accordingly. The South Korean, Japanese and French experience tells us the only thing that counts is capability. It is the culture behind a language that really touches people's hearts. The pragmatism of the South Koreans and Japanese and their leaders has enabled them to focus their strength on innovation for seeking continuous development rather than empty talk. A change in attitude is important. The three places across the Strait should make full use of their own cultural characteristics, enhance their influence on the Asian and Western international media, seek cross-border cooperation opportunities, develop innovative education courses and research institutions with an Asian perspective, create new cooperation models and structures, and nurture growth points for promoting global progress.

Taiwan is where traditional Chinese culture has been preserved the best. But are there strategies in place to maintain and study it to make Taiwan the center of Chinese culture?

Light Up Our Campus with Humor

Where there are people, there is trouble. There are all kinds of politics no matter where you work, and the education sector is among the most political of all in my personal experience. Why can't we make campus a less political, more pragmatic, livelier and more relaxed place?

Humor varies greatly from place to place, and culture to culture. While Chinese humor does differ from Western humor, Chinese humor in different places of China has its own uniqueness. The terms they use for "chatting" reflect the local cultures: *longmenzhen* (setting up the dragon gate) (Chengdu); *kandashan* (talking about mountains) (Beijing); *tanshanhaijing* (talking about *Shanhaijing*, a classic book) (Shanghai); and storytelling by an uncle (Nanyang Chinatown). Taiwan's local customs and operas, and stand-up comedies nourished by the funny Hong Kong Cantonese language provide great materials and tools for humor. Actually, the role of humor has long been played by education and is more pragmatic as an escape from difficult or embarrassing situations. Whenever the economy is bad, we see a surge in student enrollment. The public seems to know that, instead of fighting hard at work during an economic downturn, they might as well prepare for the return of a better economy by studying. During war time, applications for graduate studies surge as a way to dodge the draft.

It is common sense that being literate is a skill, and people who can sign their names won't pay by cash.

There is, however, little room for humor, and people pay little attention to it in societies on both sides of the Strait due to the obsession with money-making, especially when there is a boom in the stock or property markets, and because of the highly inflammatory political environment. This is a pity, given that humor has many positive functions, such as providing a temporary protective shield from the vicissitudes and worries of life.

Returning to the East after working in the US for many years, I discovered, much to my surprise, how people in Hong Kong, either in the education sector or politics, tend to be very solemn at conferences and seminars. It is as if they were in a court of law trying to reclaim a debt. Not only is typical Chinese humor missing, but no one would do as Americans do on these occasions: crack jokes. Inside the classrooms are serious faces, and the atmosphere outside is dominated by sarcasm. Both young and old are equally contentious, with little time for constructive contributions. Most speeches are either trite or clichéd, or completely off tangent. No wonder young people in Hong Kong and Taiwan are enthusiastic about participating in social movements, even if the reasons for doing so are sometimes weak. Lunch meetings, walking meetings, and even running meetings are all common ways to have meetings in the US today. I brought them to CityU, but they failed to attract attention.

Recently I heard a conversation between a teacher and a student while taking a taxi in Taipei. It was a good-humored joke that proved that sometimes a teacher may learn something from students.

Here is how the conversation went.

"What is the difference between a frog and a toad?" asked a teacher.

"A frog is conservative, while a toad is progressive," the student replied, thoughtfully. To prove his point, he cited two popular Chinese idioms, one about a frog at the bottom of a well and the other about a toad lusting after a swan's flesh.

"The frog can see nothing else but a small part of the sky; it has a narrow vision that the world is only as big as the top of the well, whereas the toad is not inhibited by his limitations and is bold and forward-looking in his vision, which deserves respect. Even though a frog is beautiful, and a toad is ugly, appearance is not important," he explained.

Indeed, what is important is having a goal and an ideal.

In my line of work, namely, education, there is probably no better way than humor to bridge the generational gap between students and teachers. However, as humor is not factored into GDP, it can be seen as somehow inappropriate in the workplace, which, again, is unfortunate. While its benefits may be difficult to quantify, humor can clearly boost morale, diffuse tension, and even reduce staff turnover. If applied well on campus, humor helps to enhance teaching and research and promote higher education.

In a Taipei taxi, I once saw a joke on the screen attached to the back of the front seat. It was about a conversation between a teacher and his student regarding the Mayan myth about the end of the world.

A teacher asks one of his students: "What is the one thing you'd like to do most if the world does come to an end as foretold by the Mayan myth?"

"I'd like to be attending your class," the student replies with resignation.

"Is my class that appealing to you?" the teacher mutters to himself, puzzled.

"No but sitting in your class makes a day feel like a year," the student says matter-of-factly.

Are there really such teachers and students around us? The joke reminds me of my younger days in Taiwan when we used to have a compulsory course on the *Three Principles of the People*. Many students skipped the class. Even if they did not, they never really paid attention to what was being taught. And yet everyone passed at the end of the semester.

In recent times, the stories I heard were about university students eating, sleeping, or busy doing things with their mobile phones in class while the teacher was lecturing. Very few listened attentively.

On one occasion, a teacher woke up a student who had fallen asleep during the lecture and asked:

"Why were your eyes closed?"

"I was thinking over what you had said," the student replied.

"Then why were you nodding your head?" the teacher asked.

"I was in agreement with your point," replied the student.

"Why were you drooling?" the teacher persisted.

"Savoring the content of your lecture," the student answered.

Such students were severely criticized as a result, either for lacking self-respect or for wasting national resources. But did anyone ever stop and ask whether the fundamental problem was with the students, the teacher or the course itself if students could always get a pass at examinations through self-study and never paying attention in class? Should we not further ask whether such a course ought to be offered in the first place?

It is not funny at all to have courses that make students feel that an hour is as long as a year. But aren't there many courses like that around?

For me, though, I can never forget the inspiring classes I attended in high school, the teachers and the valuable contents of their lessons.

From Jokes about Teaching to Importance of Content

As the *Analects of Confucius* said, "If a person's natural qualities are more conspicuous than his accomplishments, he is likely to appear not so cultivated; if a person's accomplished trappings are more obvious than his natural qualities, he is apt to appear ostentatious. Only when a person's natural qualities and accomplished art perfectly match will we have a perfect gentleman." College education should aim at cultivating gentlemen with good manners. On the contrary, many times, vanity and superficiality prevail. Higher education in the three regions across the Strait gives emphasis to English over culture and tends to be ostentatious and shallow. It may not help with communication, but it proves the saying that a man with invariably fair terms and an inviting countenance rarely has a gracious heart.

"The Way is the essence of writing; writing is the leaf of the Way." (Zhu Xi, 朱熹) Languages carry doctrine. Content is far more important than language skills. A university should attach immense importance to language. However, I would not like to see students become masters of English or Chinese purely for uttering frivolities or wasting time speaking about trivia. There is already enough of that kind of talk in communities across the Strait. What is important is to appreciate that languages, to the utmost, carry doctrine.

Part II
INTEGRATION OF TEACHING AND RESEARCH

Teaching is empty without the devotion of the heart,
Research after all remains the utmost art.
Barely equipped with hardware and software,
Still it lacks, devoid of proper soulware.

Universities should have the vision to lead, but they also need to emphasize functionality by aligning with society's social and economic developments to find their niche. They have to capitalize on opportunities to build their strengths and distinctiveness and establish their edge as a hub for discovery, innovation and nurturing talent. Hence those in higher education must engage in both teaching and problem-oriented research to fulfill, on the one hand, the role of transmitting, imparting, transferring, and explicating knowledge, and on the other hand, the role of investigating, creating and innovating knowledge.

Teaching Enriches Research and Vice Versa

Universities in Taiwan, Hong Kong and the Mainland like to separate teaching from research. Research-oriented universities focus on research, while teaching-oriented universities do not. However, has anyone ever wondered why people who want to study give priority to universities that do not emphasize teaching while teaching universities that do not emphasize research keep awarding doctoral degrees? What kind of research-oriented universities that do not teach and what kind of teaching-oriented universities without research dare to recruit doctoral students? Why do those teachers who have never done research classify universities that only focus on teaching as teaching universities, while those who do research are regarded as research-oriented university professors?

Everyone seems to assume that people who do research don't know how to teach or don't even need to teach, while teachers who teach don't do research, and so, of course, they will not know how to investigate and seek the truth. Think about it again: do those who don't conduct research know how to teach? And do those who conduct research not know how to teach?

Teaching and research enrich and complement each other. Ideally, research should be embedded in learning, and the learning experience and process should feed into and orient the research. Teaching and research should serve to explore real-life issues, enabling us to gain mastery over the world rather than vice versa. The essence of what the ancient sages said about education is subtle and complicated. Their multitudinous notes and annotations often confound right and wrong, which is detrimental to higher education and goes against the true meaning of internationalization. Otherwise, innovation will always be like viewing the flowers through the fog: a fantasy that is out of reach!

7
The Essence of University

In addition to the invention of paper by Ts'ai Lun during the Eastern Han dynasty in the year 105, the Chinese invented printing, gunpowder, the compass and a number of original mathematical discoveries. As descendants of this ancient legacy of the Yan Emperor and Huang Emperor, many Chinese like to talk about these great discoveries.

When major breakthroughs in research were reported in other parts of the world, some Chinese immediately cited evidence from the ancient classics to claim that these discoveries were not new because such ideas existed in China long ago. Such claims may have some validity, but the question remains as to why ideas and concepts germinating early in China failed to thrive. In the West, the spirit of systematic investigation and the practical application of ideas is a time-honored tradition, a spirit that advocates inquiry into all phenomena through independent thinking and objective analysis.

It could be that many original ideas were indeed discovered by the ancient Chinese, but there was no systematic follow-up research to investigate, develop and bring them to fruition. The Chinese have not invented much else since the Song dynasty more than 1,000 years ago. Modern China has produced fewer inventions, if any, than the West's achievements. Learning has been a matter of faithfully receiving from the master his or her lifetime knowledge and wisdom that he or she had learned from predecessors, with great importance attached to annotating classical texts. It does not encourage people to discover, invent and innovate to surpass the knowledge of their predecessors. In scholarly interactions, the preservation of harmony and avoidance of arguments are emphasized, and as a result, right and wrong cannot be determined based on open discussions, and knowledge cannot be advanced.

Perfecting Skills Coupled with Research

Moving into the 21st century, China is committed to exploring how it can instigate long-lasting contributions to science and technology, the social sciences and the liberal arts and thereby support the sustainable development of the world as a responsible member of the international community. The importance of perfecting skills was discussed in *The Analects of Confucius* as "As you cut and then file, as you carve and then polish" and in *The Book of Changes* as "Aiming high." Yet, these conceptual statements need to be put into implementation through systematic practice and research.

The much-honored Chinese spirit often stalls. Here are some examples that illustrate how originality depends on sustained and practical research to maintain momentum.

Firstly, far back in Chinese history, democratic ideas such as "selecting individuals based on integrity and ability", "regarding people as the foundation of the state" and "the world for all" had already appeared in the ancient classics. But it was John Locke who first proposed the tripartite system of the separation of powers, an idea that the French political philosopher Baron de Montesquieu developed into the establishment of the executive, legislative and judiciary branches of government, resulting in the creation of political systems that led to the realization of democracy in European and American societies.

It took several thousand years before we witnessed how Westerners transformed ideas about democracy once propounded by the ancient Chinese into reality. Some may argue that the democratic representation system practiced today has met many obstacles over the years. Even if that is true, who has devised anything better?

Secondly, traditional Chinese painting is stunning, using the technique of the bird-eye view. Its exquisite artistic sensibility, color and brushstroke are carried forward by successive generations. However, the use of perspective as a technique to depict spatial relations was not a Chinese invention. It was imported from the West. Nor did Chinese artists ever devise any improvements or refinements, yet another example of the lack of innovation due to an overemphasis on the traditional education philosophy of simply receiving knowledge one-way without creativity.

Thirdly, the black powder used in Chinese alchemy in ancient times was later used to make fireworks, firecrackers, cannon balls and rockets. It was the only chemical explosive before the 18th century. Later improvements by the Europeans resulted in the invention of gunpowder and firearms that far exceeded early Chinese technology and were introduced back to China by Jesuit missionaries during the Ming dynasty. And the explosive power of the black powder was very much inferior to the dynamite invented in the West during the 19th century.

Fourthly, since the early days of the Republic of China, there have been many arguments explaining why China is technologically backward. One of the popular arguments blames it on the way Chinese is written, saying that Chinese is difficult to remember, difficult to write, difficult to type, difficult to input, difficult to confirm, and difficult to process scientifically. Unexpectedly, since the invention and improvement of computers from the West and the promotion and use of AI, pattern recognition, speech recognition and other software and hardware, the above claims about the Chinese being unscientific have all disappeared, while the beauty of the Chinese language, the only thing left behind, is far beyond the reach of other languages.

There are other stories. The crux of the problem is not that the Chinese do not learn but rarely do they question what they learn. The lack of an inquisitive mind to investigate the why explains their shortage in looking for better ways to improve things.

Joseph Needham, known for his research on the history of Chinese science and technology, pointed out that China led the world for 1,000 years with its empirical science and individual technologies, which had progressed incrementally and had contributed enormously to human civilization. What was the reason for such achievements?

The rich and colorful accomplishments of selecting civil servants, the government inspection system, private school education, and the "Hundred Schools of Thought" in China were more advanced than similar achievements in the Western world at that time. Another point to note is that civil servants in France are appointed according to their test scores; it requires to seal (彌封) individual names on the test papers when they are being marked. According to Gérard Marcou at Université Paris I - Panthéon-Sorbonne, this turns out to be an influence from the imperial examination system (科舉制度) in ancient China. Throughout Chinese history, there were occasional entanglements between religion and the state, but far less so than in medieval Europe. A distinct characteristic of Chinese culture was that religion and the state were kept separated.

Most of the sporadic inventions in Chinese history were the results of coincidence. Although some individual innovations were remarkable, they were usually unfinished due to either a lack of drive for perfection, wrong questions asked in civil servant selection examinations, or the selection of the wrong professionals. As a result, innovation lacked momentum and successors. What should we do then?

Ever since the Renaissance, especially after the 17th century, the Industrial Revolution in Europe transformed almost every aspect of human life by accelerating comprehensive advances in science, technology, medicine, philosophy, politics, economy, literature and art. This process is rather like the way research-based universities emerged in the West during the same period. Chinese society at that time, however, lacked sufficient critical mass for research and development. Instead, China dilly-dallied, muttering about vague glories from the past when it innovated in systematic, experimental, logical, proof-based scientific and technological research. That explains why natural science, industry, philosophy, social science, and invention in China have significantly lagged behind the Western world and Japan over the past two to three hundred years. Misled by politicians and skewered by populism, people on both sides of the Strait are obsessed with the old dogma that they don't quite understand, leaving them at a loss.

Investigation for New Knowledge

If we look around today, it is not difficult to find young students across the Strait equipped with all kinds of skills. They can recite their textbooks, know how to sing and play musical instruments, and are eloquent and skillful at games and sports. They have the ability to get high scores or even full marks in any examination so long as there is a well-defined scope and set of criteria.

From kindergarten to high school, the education system across the Strait has managed to churn out a substantial number of examination gurus. Even students who win science competitions in high schools and universities owe their success to heavy drilling and special coaching. They are the elite minority, but genuine interest may not motivate many. They will lag behind a dozen years when they start developing independent thinking and critical reasoning at graduate schools.

The essence of learning lies in questioning. As early as the Song dynasty some 1,000 years ago, scholars proposed investigation as the way to understand all phenomena and seek new knowledge, leaving no stone unturned to search for answers. This Chinese learning tradition might be the closest to modern scientific methods. That is why scientific research, which is a foreign term, was first translated into Chinese as *ge zhi* (short for *ge wu zhi zhi*, meaning "investigating phenomena to acquire new knowledge"). Only that which is acquired by investigating and understanding phenomena thoroughly can be called scientific knowledge.

But unfortunately, in the didactic education system of traditional China, independent investigating and questioning through *ge zhi* are not mainstream practices, as reported in today's news media. Such practices are likely to meet strong resistance and require great courage to overcome. Even someone as influential as Mencius, with a reputation for arguing, had to defend himself by saying, "I can't help it."

The emphasis on research is a subversion of the authority of traditional knowledge, opening the possibility of drawing different conclusions for the same problem studied under a distinct set of parameters derived from a separate set of definitions under a different time frame and perspective. That is to say, research does not lead to a single authoritative conclusion; there is always room for interpretation, discussion, and improvement. We should promote such a scientific spirit by incorporating learning and investigating into the primary and high school curricula.

Disputes over Teaching versus Research Universities

People in the higher education field like to divide universities into two separate categories: teaching and research universities.

For years, teaching and research have been treated as two parallel but separate enterprises in many universities, which is still the case across the Strait. It isn't only the average citizen but also those in the higher education sector who think research is the responsibility of research institutions and researchers, not that of university teachers. Some people even believe that research is perhaps not part of Chinese culture, and therefore university teachers do not have to be involved.

It is not surprising for people to have such an idea. The 19th-century British theologian John Henry Newman believed that cultivating the intellect through teaching universal knowledge was the sole purpose of a university.[1] There could be no place for research. According to Newman, scholars engaged in teaching were too busy to conduct research, while those engaged in research were too preoccupied to perform teaching duties. Universities across the Strait at one time used the priority of teaching as a ridiculous excuse to resist research as if they were going back to 19th-century Britain.

People who advocate the demarcation of universities into teaching and research universities like to prove their point by citing examples of research universities from Europe and North America as benchmarks. Such a view is not only outdated but also incomplete. Prior to the 20th century, there were hardly any universities that emphasized research, and hence there was no distinction between teaching and research universities.

---

[1] *The Idea of A University* (Regnery Publishing, 1999, original version 1852).

The Humboldt University of Berlin, established in 1810, was the first university in history to incorporate research into higher education. This German research tradition in higher education was picked up later by other European countries. The US had a later start, encouraged by a number of concessionary policies issued by the federal government in support of the establishment of private universities at the end of the 19th century. A group of institutions such as Johns Hopkins University and the University of Chicago began to incorporate research and innovation into their vision and offer advanced degree courses beyond bachelor's programs.

Although North America's higher education system was developed on the basis of the European model, it has outshone its origins. Despite being latecomers to the scene, North American universities that emphasize research have since the 1920s become the mainstream for higher education institutions.

Simply put, before the 20th century, universities prided themselves on teaching. Research was not on the agenda. But since the early 20th century, research has been recognized as integral to university education, incorporating the spirit of investigation to generate new knowledge and emphasizing teamwork over individual achievement. In the mid-1950s, although some public universities continued to be engaged in undergraduate teaching only, the majority of them invariably incorporated research into their programs, the most notable being UC Berkeley.

Research and Teaching, Not A Zero-Sum Game

The Hong Kong government often labels certain local universities as engaged in "applied research" and even uses outdated blue sky rhetoric to describe "non-applied research".

In the last 20 years, several Nobel Prizes in physics and chemistry have been awarded to researchers engaged in engineering research, including Jack Kilby, the 2000 winner in physics; Koichi Tanaka, the 2002 winner in chemistry; Charles Kao, the 2009 winner in physics; Andre Geim and Konstantin Novoselov, the 2010 winner in physics; and Isamu Akasaki, Hiroshi Amano and Shuji Nakamura, the 2014 winners in physics. Among them, Kilby who invented the integrated circuit, Kao who invented fiber-optic communications, and Geim and Novoselov who invented graphene, a two-dimensional space material, are inventors who have benefited humanity, and didn't discover abstract concepts. It is more so for the Nobel Prizes in physiology or medicine that emphasize applicability. Research is not like a romance between teenagers. There is little room for blue-sky fantasies. Research is research. There is no difference between ancient and modern applications, inventions or discoveries.

The National Science Foundation in the US requires applicants to list the functionality of any submitted research proposals, i.e., the physical meaning of the research proposals. In this day and age, how many disciplines are not problem-driven or application-oriented? Stay away from empty concepts. If there is such a concept as applied research, it should not be the distinctive feature of any university. In fact, universities aim at promoting mutual enrichment between teaching and research in various academic areas, not just in science and technology but also in business administration, humanities, law, social sciences, media, design, etc.

In the US higher education sector, universities that offer PhD programs are not divided into teaching or research categories. Take, for example, the 23 California state universities, which most people would think of as falling into the category of teaching universities since they offer only master's degrees in addition to bachelor's degrees. But professors from these universities conduct fundamental research as well. The only difference is that research at such state universities constitutes a lower ratio of their total workload. When applying for promotion, they have to substantiate their applications with research achievements.

For universities that are conventionally considered representative of the teaching category, including all the California state universities, hardly any of them offer PhD programs except in some extremely rare disciplines. For that reason, they might be more appropriately grouped under non-PhD awarding universities. It is usually difficult for these universities, where there are no doctoral assistants, to apply for research funds or engage in research activities.

For research institutes that conduct no research or universities that do not conduct much research, the latter should be called "low-research universities", instead of categorizing them as "teaching universities" to avoid the misconception that these universities maintain a low research profile because focusing on excellence in teaching is their primary goal.

Impractically and incorrectly dividing universities into teaching and research entities is like dividing ways for keeping one's health into two separate and mutually exclusive options: one dedicated entirely to diet and the other to sport. It is also like categorizing a happy marriage into materialistic and romantic, neither ideal nor romantic. Such a dualistic way of conceiving the relationship between teaching and research reflects an outdated notion. This is often further justified by the fallacy that such a separation would enable some universities to concentrate on achieving excellence in teaching. But in reality, one finds that these universities can neither carry out research nor teach well.

For a university without any research achievements, its teaching lacks a solid foundation. This explains why it will not be able to produce insightful textbooks and will have no way to enhance its academic prowess. Therefore, if the higher education sectors across the Strait want to catch up with world standards, they have to eliminate misconceptions or outdated thinking. They need to appreciate that the relationship between teaching and research is not a zero-sum game and make a sincere effort to integrate them. After all, even teaching requires pedagogical research on how best to teach. Research acts like the "conductor" for teaching, like an ingredient in Chinese herbal medicine that enhances effectiveness.

Whoever Questions, Learns

Students go to college to build a foundation for their careers. They should not concentrate on studying what is related only to their major. They should read widely and consider developments in other scientific and research fields. To work in a university, one must have a mission or sense of responsibility for promoting the advancement of knowledge. Unfortunately, few people appreciate such a basic concept, nor do the majority of people realize the importance of creating academic space in money-driven cross-Strait societies.

To foster change, I started the President's Lecture Series: Excellence in Academia as a platform for CityU scholars to share their academic investigations with students and faculty across the campus community. The lectures have covered a range of subject areas, from global warming to the contemporary significance of Confucianism, the relationship between material technology and society, cloud computing, biostatistics, virtual art, ethnic minorities, biomedical engineering, One Health, and subjective probability, among others.

In addition, CityU hosts a series of Distinguished Lectures[2] throughout the year. The speakers include winners of the Nobel Prize, Fields Medal and Turing Award, and renowned poets, writers and scholars on topics as diverse as emerging infectious diseases, nanotechnology, rule by virtue (*wang dao*) in the 21st century, big data, the creation of poetry and novels, prospects of energy, issues on environmental protection, academic freedom, the global supply chain, and international relations in Southeast Asia, for instance.

---

[2] It was approved by CityU Council in April 2023 to be Way Kuo Distinguished Lecture Series.

These two lecture series, plus several dozen other academic forums, help disseminate the latest advancements in research and knowledge development, attracting at least 200 to 300, and sometimes as many as 600 to 700, attendees to each session. The interaction between the speaker and the audience is often lively. In some lectures, the audience simply doesn't let the speaker go! But very few local Hong Kong students have ever attended. It seems that the situation is similar at other universities in Hong Kong unless their presence is a requirement. Such academic lectures do not arouse the interest of local students, media reporters or the usually vocal faculty and staff.

In addition, academic culture is affected by disdainful remarks and criticism often uttered by non-professional outsiders who sometimes wish to meddle in academic affairs. North American universities are much more robust and willing to spend time and effort exploring academic issues. Americans are far less likely to speculate about university work or interfere with a university's academic operations.

Enlightenment comes from great questioning, while small awakenings stem from minor questioning. If you do not ask questions, you cannot learn. Teachers and students in universities across the Strait who are not engaged in research are not proactively creating an academic environment to support research, nor can they innovate or ask questions.

Lately, I have learned that some young people are puzzled by society's apparent lack of understanding of the e-generation. But shouldn't we be equally puzzled by people's lack of understanding that knowledge advancement is the core mission of a university?

Teaching without Research is like Driving after Drinking

There is a joke about a motorist arrested for driving under the influence of alcohol. He argued in his defense that he had to drive home because he had drunk too much and could not walk steadily. If we compare walking to research and driving to teaching, it is obvious that clear-headed thinking is essential for both. Without the capacity to think clearly, one can neither drive safely nor do well in teaching and research; otherwise, we will waste the time of the young people entrusted into our care.

Disciplines that are not supported by research have no depth and should be kept out of universities. Universities are differentiated as good or bad in teaching and research; there is no differentiation based on teaching or research activities! Otherwise, they are simply wasting their free academic environment like a drunkard who can neither walk steadily nor drive safely.

8
University Positioning

In Chinese history, we often hear how thwarted scholars, unable to realize their aspirations, chose to live a hermit's life, indulging in self-appreciation and staying "far from the madding crowd." With the world shrinking, living a hermit's life is possible in appearance only. Today, spiritual cultivation is undertaken in the mundane world rather than by living in seclusion or evading reality. We must transcend the world by facing up to real challenges.

If one feels one's aspirations are not fulfilled even though one has read many books, could it be that one has read the wrong books or set the wrong goals? If the former is true, we should not blame others for our failure and instead make some self-adjustment. If the latter is true, then the wise step is to re-examine our goals. Most people in the past set fame and wealth as their goals. No wonder so many felt thwarted. For scholars today, their goals are more diverse. But it is unavoidable that there could be serious gaps between social reality and the ideals in the books one studies. This calls for a review to examine ways to minimize or eliminate the gaps.

The higher education sector entered a chaotic state similar to that during the Warring States period (770 B.C.E. to 221 B.C.E.) in Chinese history. As pointed out in Chapter 7, grouping institutions into teaching and research universities out of convenience deviates from reality when we look at today's advanced universities. Such action doesn't align with the latest trends in higher education.

Four Types of Universities

Starting from the 1980s, universities in Taiwan took the lead in Asia in emphasizing the role of research in higher education. Universities in Hong Kong and Mainland China made similar adjustments in the 1990s and 2000s to reflect the role of universities of the time. They are nearly half a century behind Europe, the United States and Japan. In spite of the shift, classifying universities lagging in research as teaching universities in this part of the world is an insult to learning. It suggests that a university weak in research can teach well. In fact, many universities not so strong in research are not necessarily successful at teaching, either. They could lag far behind in practicing the integration of teaching and research.

Unlike community colleges and short-term vocational schools, universities today can be classified into four categories, but each one contains teaching and research components.

1. Universities with an emphasis on liberal arts education: Typical examples include Princeton and Dartmouth in the US. They promote a solid education in the liberal arts, and their teaching and research are conceptually oriented with the broad objective of developing the intellect and advancing humanities. Liberal arts education is the ideal advocated by institutions on par with Ivy League universities. Such universities are usually small; tuition fees are high (six to sixty times the tuition of public universities across the Strait); they are more like elite universities and usually possess excellent research institutes focused on the humanities and science. In recent years, Princeton has adjusted its abstract ideal of a liberal arts education under the growing influence of information technology.
2. Professional universities (or schools) with an emphasis on professional education programs: These universities focus on high-level professional training that is closely related to societal needs and applications, with MIT being the crème de la crème. Due to a heavy professional curriculum, plus internships and project work, as well as accreditation requirements in many cases, worries persist that there isn't enough time to cover all the courses required for the various professional programs. Therefore, the curriculum is centered around individual subjects. Their teaching and research are problem-based, with an emphasis on innovation. Their graduates are specialists and practitioners, and their contribution to society is tangible.
3. Comprehensive universities: UC Berkeley is a typical example of such universities. In December 1980, the US federal government enacted the Bayh-Dole Act (Patent Rights in Inventions Made with Federal Assistance), encouraging universities to collaborate with industry to convert research achievements

into new products and production methods and promote the commercialization of academic inventions. The original mission of land-grant universities established after 1860 was to teach agriculture, engineering and business in order to equip students with practical knowledge and career-oriented skills. By the 1980s, many of these universities had expanded into comprehensive universities, covering a spectrum of disciplines. Lately, the focus has shifted to cross-disciplinary integration. The University of Wisconsin-Madison, which became a land-grant university in 1866, and Texas A&M, which was established in 1876, are typical examples.
4. Specialized universities: These universities usually concentrate on a single subject. Juilliard School in New York City, known for cutting-edge dance, performing arts and music education, is an example. Others include the medically-focused Mayo Clinic College of Medicine in Minnesota and the Karolinska Institutet in Sweden. Their curricula differ from a four-year liberal arts university: the former emphasizes depth while the latter focuses on breadth. Universities with a single subject have played a vital role in the old education system in the former Soviet Union, Mainland China and the university systems in France and other European countries. But nowadays, many European universities have migrated to the North American system. The trend is toward consolidating specialized universities into professional universities or comprehensive universities. Despite that, universities with a single subject remain ideal for gifted individuals.

Adequate financing is key to the success of higher education. The above four categories, which are based mostly on faculty interests, are not the same as other tiers of government-sponsored tertiary education. The latter are based mostly on student aptitude, interests and sometimes financial needs, such as research-only institutions like the Chinese Academy of Sciences and the Weizmann Institute of Science in Israel; state-sponsored technical colleges; two-year community colleges; and short-term vocational schools.

Universities in North America have emphasized team research and have taken the lead in introducing research into the undergraduate curriculum. In October 2018, MIT announced a US$1 billion initiative to establish a new college of computing that would train the next generation of machine-learning mavens who can benefit those in the fields of social, biological and physical sciences. This is not the same as the learning style in universities across the Strait and many other places, where universities are less forward-looking, and students are preoccupied with quantity and taking as many credit-bearing courses as possible without fully comprehending what they are studying. Constantly raising the level of higher education through sustained and cutting-edge research diverges from traditional thinking and is worth paying close attention to.

To put what is best into practice, we should avoid wasting time on a mechanical teaching mode, eliminate the passive classroom learning mode and encourage the integration of teaching and research. Universities that offer education based on vacuous concepts emphasizing merely the granting of degrees, a large number of majors and English as the medium of instruction, at best, play the role of "compradors" in higher education. They are unlikely to be able to make any profound and substantive contributions to teaching, research and innovation.

Some people may learn the doctrine earlier than others; some may be masters in their individual fields. Recognizing that students come from various backgrounds with individual characteristics and their own forte, Confucius promoted "teaching students in accordance with their aptitude", which coincides with the principle behind the four types of universities I have categorized here. Each type of university offers opportunities for the diverse needs of students. Mencius treated it as one of the three pleasures in life to be able to teach all the talented people in the world. The essence of education lies in recognizing talented people in the world first and then teaching them in accordance with their aptitude.

What else for a University besides Teaching?

The best among the four types of universities mentioned above nurtures talented students through a dual emphasis on teaching and research. Science and technology are advancing each day. If teachers do not conduct research, their knowledge and skills merely repeat the scientific and technological achievements of others before them. How can they make a mark with their teaching without contributing to the continuous advancement of knowledge? How can they justify their place in society as a university teacher if they do not engage in research and constantly update their knowledge and skills? Likewise, university teachers would have no way to assess or verify their research findings if they do not teach and are only engaged in research activities. Even medical doctors and engineers need to update their knowledge regularly. Shouldn't university teachers do the same?

Unfortunately, such a simple and clear logic for the integration of teaching and research is neither fully understood nor completely embraced by society. Worse still, when professors are required to do research, some people will argue that teaching is marginalized, under the misconception that whoever is engaged in research will be impeded from teaching well.

Excellent universities provide outstanding education, leading in introducing progressive ideas in teaching and learning to high schools. For example, they are responsible for the many revisions to the teaching materials for high schools and primary schools over the last 50 years, the introduction of set theory in high school mathematics, the use of computers and the internet in high schools, adaptations in high school history textbooks, and the online Advanced Placement courses open to high school students, and so forth. These initiatives come from universities that are outstanding in teaching and research, which can never be described purely as research- or teaching-based. In addition, the explanations of world-respected teaching theories, the commonly used teaching tools (whether software and hardware) or the cutting-edge university textbooks on literature, history, medicine and other subjects deemed classics rarely come from universities with poor research.

Most universally acclaimed education theories in teaching and learning have been developed by traditionally well-regarded research universities. I can't think of any significant achievements in teaching and learning that originated in so-called teaching universities.

What most people think of as research universities are, in fact, heavily involved in both research and teaching responsibilities. As the name suggests, universities that offer master's or PhD degrees must conduct research and apply for research funds. The more competitive they are the more government subsidies and private donations they can secure. Robert M. Rosenzweig, former president of the Association of American Universities, observed in 1982 that the best North American universities were "an amalgamation of basic research, research training, and undergraduate education conducted by the same group of people doing all three things at the same time." There was no differentiation between teaching and research.

At one time, universities in North America were classified into Research I and Research II universities, depending on differences in funding. Hence, universities that received a smaller amount came to be regarded by some people as non-research universities. That kind of differentiation is the outcome rather than the cause of classification, and the differentiation is relative rather than absolute. Rising stars like Georgia Tech and UC San

Diego, whose academic reputations rose in the 1970s, and the Polytechnic University in Brooklyn, New York, which has been in decline after passing its prime due to lack of funds like many other less competitive universities, exemplify the idea of the survival of the fittest in the evolutionary process.

Universities that place dual emphasis on teaching and research stand at the forefront of society and are always ranked top in league tables. They are the top choices for high school graduates applying for tertiary education as well as for companies hiring graduates. It is extremely rare today for a university to assume a key role in education by just teaching without conducting any research.

Students Are the Reason for Universities to Exist

Since the 1980s, four major American initiatives for reinvigorating universities have been deployed. These included Ernest A. Boyer's model of scholarship in 1991; the 1997 Kellogg Commission on the Future of State and Land-Grant Universities; the 2014 Kevin Carey report "Building a New AAU: The Case for Redefining Higher Education Excellence"; and the 2016 Reinvention Collaborative at Colorado State University.

A common theme running through these studies and reports is the emphasis on the student-centered concept as the fundamental approach to improving higher education and redefining excellence based on a university's creative research and success with student learning as well as the success of its graduates. The ideal is that a first-rate university integrating teaching and research is also a first-rate student university.

Breathtaking developments in data science and machine learning in the recent decade are rapidly transforming our industries and workplace. It is projected that by 2030, half of today's jobs will become obsolete by automation. In light of these unprecedented changes in society, universities themselves must change and do so rapidly. Their operations must become effective, efficient, and flexible enough to prepare students to meet the challenges and take advantage of the new economic opportunities that technology will eventually create.

In the midst of these changes, the humanities and social sciences will remain crucially important to industry. At the same time, liberal arts and humanities students need to accept new tasks, such as understanding data, facilitating collaboration with technology disciplines, providing historical perspective, and therefore "[humanizing] technology in a data-driven world." Humanity majors need to help students strengthen their quantitative skills and enable them to be analytical to avoid dogmatic statements.

In addition to building fundamental skills, college degrees will need to prepare students early for lifelong learning by augmenting the teaching of reading, writing and arithmetic with critical thinking, communication, creativity and cultural fluency in their curriculum. Ultimately, it is the quality of university education that determines its success in responsibly and effectively harnessing both hardware and software, thereby engaging in planning and implementing the changes necessary for preparing students to embrace the challenges and opportunities presented by technology in a world of increasing automation.

Without students, universities won't exist and won't be able to contribute to society. The laxity of teachers leads to a lack of discipline. "Student-oriented university" should not mean condoning students, debauchery, awarding degrees, or quid pro quo between teachers and students. The principle is easy to understand, just as coaches urge their players to score on the court and be happy off it, instead of condoning the players to be happy on the court and cry off the court.

Remove Restrictions and Establish Clear Positioning

In this fast-changing world, how do we abandon outdated practices and wholeheartedly embrace the integration of teaching and research if we want to catch up with the more advanced?

First of all, we should remove the many restrictions on higher education and allow universities the autonomy to make decisions on such operational matters as the use of funds and the recruitment of international students in order to enrich the learning environment. The government is responsible for monitoring the overall outputs and formulating basic principles for pursuing social developments. It should set the general direction for the development of research and education and create the relevant reward mechanisms for incentivizing performance.

There should be regular coordination among the relevant offices and units, such as education, technology, national defense, environment, healthcare, and so forth, for the formulation of a set of strategic development themes, serving as the blueprint for funding commitment and systematic implementation. For example, in addition to being interfered with by troublesome non-academic matters, universities in Taiwan and the Mainland face many other problems: too many universities, too many irrelevant courses, too many research institutions, too many regulations, and too much government micro-management. At the same time, they are handicapped by not having enough time to explore and design their future, while their research funds are diluted, insufficient and incomprehensive, and there is a lack of long-term, sustainable education plans based on systematic simulation. Moreover, they face a degree of chaos: research and teaching are messy, industry development themes are unclear, and laypeople poke their nose into professional business and try to lead the experts.

Secondly, every university should have its own specific mission. Given limited resources, they should position themselves clearly by taking reference to the four types of universities listed in the previous section ("Four Types of Universities") and formulate a strategic plan to guide development. Regrettably, universities across the Strait lean towards empty talk, bragging about their whole-person education, their capacity for training university students to become erudite in the liberal arts, skilled in communication, knowledgeable about the past and the present, and highly proficient in English. By offering many courses, they claim that their students are equipped with both local knowledge and an international perspective, are responsive to societal needs, innovate and enjoy leisure, and are able to define their historical positioning.

After all these claims, many of the graduates they churn out are just mediocre, with no strong suit or forte for meeting the demand for high-level human resources or solving more general problems. As a result, some of them don't even know the basic principles behind conducting themselves. They babble about their aspirations before graduation and, unfit for a higher post but unwilling to take on a lower one, they often end up accepting low-pay jobs with poor career prospects, much to their frustration and puzzlement. How can one expect a college education to train a crop of students to become experts in all trades? How sad to see young students misguided by their education, leaving their talents and potential unrealized?

Public toilets in Taiwan were dirty and smelly, but few people cared. Instead, some politicians, attending trifles and neglecting the essentials, talked about promoting the use of the bidet (immunity toilet), confirmation of what is written in the first chapter of *On Bureaucracy* (*Huan Hai*): "Instead of investigating their (the officials') performance, much of the blame is focused on the inadequacy of the public." Similar phenomena are observed in higher education. Instead of paying attention to the actual content, attention is focused on packaging. Students deserve to be educated according to their individual talents. This is also the university's obligation.

Once the university is well-positioned, it should focus on doing practical things instead of constantly originating innovative ideas and talking about illusory concepts. It is impossible and not necessary for a university to offer everything.

Bai Juyi's Idea about the Hermit in Between

Bai Juyi (白居易), a Chinese Tang dynasty poet, once said in his *Preface to New Lyric Poetry*, "whether it is about the nobles and courtiers, or about the ordinary folks and simple things, each poem comes from real life, rather than from the set patterns of literary form." To promote the representation of real-life people and situations, it is necessary to portray pain and suffering in society. It means having substance in what one says and writes about. He further illustrated this point in his poem "The Hermit in Between":

> *The greater hermits stay in court and market,*
> *the lesser hermits enter the cage of the hills.*
> *The cage of the hills is too cold and dreary,*
> *court and market are too noisy.*
> *It's better to be a hermit in between,*
> *hermit in an auxiliary post.*
> *It resembles service as well as retirement,*
> *not too busy, nor idle either.*
>
> ...
>
> *Only such a hermit in between,*
> *can bring himself peace and good luck.*[1]

He thinks that "If poor, you suffer from cold and want; when rich, you have many troubles and cares." To be a lesser hermit means being poor and having to face hunger and cold; to be a great hermit means being rich and having to face many troubles and cares, which may not be something ordinary folks can tolerate. Therefore, he chooses to be a hermit in between, which "can bring him peace and luck." It means living your life in silence, without suffering from hunger and cold or taking your mind and energy. The life of a hermit in between is designed for the ordinary folks engaged in practical things. It is worth considering.

Some people can very well be greater hermits; others can only be lesser hermits. However, most of us are suitable to be hermits in between. Once we understand this, we will be able to avoid the snares of whole-person education and make our choice out of the four types of universities. Only thus can we avoid the pitfalls of doing what we shouldn't while neglecting what we should.

---

[1] From *Critical Readings on Tang China: Volume 3*, edited by Paul W. Kroll, Brill, 2018.

9
Pitfalls of Misaligning Whole-Person Education

We often hear people talking about how education should be people-oriented and how we should pursue the unity of humans and nature. Some people like to talk about "whole person education", regarding it as the goal of higher education. Why is that the case?

Hu Shih, a well-known Chinese scholar and a graduate from Columbia and Cornell in the 20th century, never cared about Chinese hypocrites and their rules and openly violated them. Today, people in Taiwan, Hong Kong and the Mainland still talk about how education should be human-centered or promote human unity with nature. But what does whole-person education mean? Is it more empty talk? Hu Shih pointed out that people should talk less of -isms and do more to face real problems. Adults mess around, and so do young people.

Bernard Shaw's Stephen

In *Major Barbara*, a play written by Bernard Shaw, an arms industrialist in Europe is trying to figure out how to help his son, Stephen, into a career. He wonders if Stephen has a turn for literature and art, philosophy, the stage, the Bar or medicine. Stephen, who has studied at Harrow, a full-boarding public school, and Cambridge, claims that he has no intention of becoming a man of business in any sense as he has no capacity nor taste for it. Irritated, his father asks if there is anything he knows about or cares about.

Stephen declares that he knows "the difference between right and wrong." His father is hugely tickled that someone who has "no capacity for business, no knowledge of law, no sympathy with art, no pretension to philosophy" but only "a simple knowledge of the secret that has puzzled all the philosophers, baffled all the lawyers, muddled all the men of business, and ruined most of the artists: the secret of right and wrong." He jokes that his son must be a genius, a master of masters, a god who "knows nothing; and he thinks he knows everything. That points clearly to a political career."

Has the university degree education produced many administrative leaders like Stephen in *Major Barbara*, who know nothing and yet think they know everything?

Whole-Person Education: A Historical Perspective

In ancient China, a whole person might refer to someone who had mastered the Six Arts. How about today? It would probably be inappropriate to claim that a whole person today should possess these Six Arts like the ancient Chinese did. But for the growth of each student, the philosophy contained in the Six Arts is important.

When Ron Miller first proposed the whole-person education concept, he aimed to develop a person's emotional and cognitive abilities so that a young student could be transformed from a self-centered person into a responsible adult. In addition to cultivating the abilities of writing, reading, and arithmetic in the curriculum, he proposed that an education system should foster character traits such as caring for the self and others, responsibility and reverence. Interestingly, there is an overlap between these six attributes of whole-person development with three of the Six Arts in ancient China: ritual, calligraphy and mathematics.

First of all, physical health is the foundation of success in learning. A first-class university attaches great importance to sports. In the early years, students at Tsinghua University on both sides of the Strait had the ethos of morning jogging. Every time there was a school celebration, everyone had to run a few kilometers, and a prerequisite for graduation was to complete a swim test of 100 meters. Some people laugh at how many US universities emphasize sports, forgetting the fact that the best universities at sports are Stanford University on the West Coast, Duke University on the East Coast and the University of Tennessee. Stanford, which is top in teaching and research, spends about US$100 million every year on its 35 sports teams.

Sports competitions reflect the positive competition that exists among universities. The spirit of sports leads us in the right direction. Two of the six arts students in ancient times were expected to master—archery and chariotry—correspond to the integrity promoted in sports today. Confucius once said, "A gentleman usually does not consider competing with his peers. If he should be engaged in any competition, it shall be the competition in archery. Before the competition, he shows his respect by making a bow with his hands folded in the front as he ascends the hall, and after the competition, he drinks a toast to his competitor's well-being. Even in his competition, he remains mild and temperate as a gentleman." What Confucius emphasized here exemplifies the spirit of excellence in sports. Excellence in academics and sports reinforce each other. Does anyone teach young people to strive for academic and sports excellence?

The major difference lies in the emphasis in modern education on fostering global perspectives and social responsibility and spotlighting skills for problem-solving, innovative research, and interpersonal communication. Modern society emphasizes team spirit, caring for the environment and multicultural awareness. In other words, students are expected to learn how to effectively communicate, interact and respect others. Such views seem to be impeccable, but to what extent can a concept like whole-person education take root and bear fruit in the local soil? And when should we introduce such concepts to the next generation?

In addition to treating "being able to teach all the talented people in the world" as one of the three delights in life, Mencius considers another delight for a Confucian gentleman if he has "no occasion for shame before Heaven when looking up and has no occasion to blush before men when looking below", a universal vision and one of the three pleasures hardly mentioned today. Feeling no shame when looking up or below sets the testing standard for a just gentleman or gentlewoman. It is a joy to lead a righteous and upright life without guile. After all, a gentleperson's words should have substance, and his or her actions should persist. But I am afraid that few people can achieve this today or, worse, few want to. The late US President John F. Kennedy once said, "Ask not what your country can do for you; ask what you can do for your country." Not so many people today can do this or want to, either. Even adults haven't thought about doing it. How can we expect young people to do it?

A blind spot in whole-person education is neglecting to nurture a sense of responsibility. We can scale new heights only by maintaining ecological balance, protecting the earth, making up for shortcomings, and ensuring sustainable survival. Polluting the environment is a disaster for any country or society. No one should feel happy about this situation, but how many people do anything about it?

Pseudo-ethics

Chinese society likes to boast of its commitment to ethics, considering it a sublime standard. The promotion of whole-person education may have something to do with it. But it becomes a cliché when people behave in ways opposite to what they repeatedly claim. Politicians like to advertise that they are willing to be "tested by the highest criterion." In fact, people who make such a claim can't even meet the lowest criterion!

Many people may have little regard in their hearts for social norms or basic decorum, and when it comes to laws and regulations, they adopt selective compliance based on personal interest and preference. Many have little respect for people from different ethnic or social backgrounds and might even blatantly discriminate against them. Comparatively speaking, Westerners or China's neighbors, the Japanese, are more rule-abiding; they would not do things they are not supposed to do and manage even trivial things attentively. For example, they yield to strangers while walking past them and are more inclined to regard everyone equally, discounting class or rank.

There exist in universities in Hong Kong and Taiwan far more complex and detailed rules and procedures for promotion and appointments, but they also have far more disputes and controversies over such matters. Even more incredible is that student organizations have learned to establish systems for checks and balances. A similar situation is seen on university campuses in Taiwan. In this regard, student organizations at US universities are more collegial and collaborative.

For example, student organizations in universities in Hong Kong follow the model of separation of powers as in a political regime. The students' union maintains the executive function, the council monitors the students' union, and an editorial board publishes reviews on the students' union. They provide checks and balances and monitor and occasionally impose sanctions against one another. Some even act like political opposition parties, listing as their top priority monitoring and checking on university operations. But universities should be a venue for learning about cooperation and working together as a team to serve fellow students. It is not healthy for young people to be so preoccupied with checking on one another as political organizations do. They should not regard themselves as political organizations. They are neither for profit nor power, and so why is this emphasis on checks and balances instead of emphasizing consensus and cooperation?

These student governing societies, usually supported by only a few participants, have large financial accounts that are not supervised. Some even use public funds to buy private insurance. They provide a breeding ground for political fanatics. Often due to special motives, Hong Kong universities cannot produce a president for their students' union through elections. Many university student unions in Hong Kong were registered as external societies according to ordinances and regulations in the early years, and from 2021 individual universities have ceased recognizing these student bodies at different levels.

What the superior loves, the inferior adores exceedingly. What is the cause of pseudo-ethics among the young generation?

A Professor's Lament

In my decades-long academic career, I have seen several professors demoted for foul play. Not too long ago, a senior professor at a university in Hong Kong was found to be teaching in name only. While he was listed as the primary instructor, he never appeared in class. A special committee investigated the case and found that many of the courses this professor had set up were taught by graduate teaching assistants over the years. He earned the salary, his work was done by graduate students, and the undergraduate students taking the courses were fooled. Therefore, the committee ruled to reduce this person's salary. It was discovered later that the professor was even an editor for an international professional ethics journal. The person who strongly recommended his promotion declared that he was an outstanding philosophy expert specializing in whole-person education.

This more recent story reminds me of the lament my professor, Ching-yu Hu, made in the old days. Many years ago, I attended his course on international law at National Tsing Hua University in Hsinchu. Hu used to serve as ambassador to Argentina and was both knowledgeable and witty. At one time, he was in charge of a training institute for judges in Taiwan. Once, a young trainee accused the older generation of government officials of corruption. That, according to the trainee, was why the Nationalists were driven to Taiwan from Mainland China. As a learned scholar, Hu felt ashamed because the criticism was valid. Later, however, he read in a newspaper that the young judge who did well on the course and had criticized his predecessors for being corrupt was jailed for corruption himself. Hu lamented that the next generation was not necessarily better than its predecessor.

Fifty some years have passed since Hu voiced his concerns. Today corruption on both sides of the Strait is just as rampant. And the higher the degree, the greedier people may become. Those who know, study and enforce the law may break the law; those who claim to be whole persons may be especially imperfect. Although I believe that the next generation should fare better, I can't really be sure that they will not be corrupt, particularly when I heard that a university students' union had been formally sued for fraudulent accounting.

These examples are found everywhere. What kind of world is this? What kind of education is whole-person education? Many of the literati are immoral, while literary-minded youths learn to bluff. Why is it that our whole-person education has bred so many good-for-nothings?

On my trips to Beijing, I often make time to chat with my long-time hairdresser about everything under the sun. Once, I had the opportunity to consult her views on graft and corruption. She said there are many irresistible temptations, and officials are just like mosquitoes that can't stop sucking blood. So long as the small mosquitoes are fed, people may still have some peace. But if the officials are changed all the time, we will never have any peace since the new mosquitoes will replace the old ones. So, if what my hairdresser said is true, there is really no end to dishonesty.

As the proverb goes, better the devil you know than the devil you don't. Looking at corruption on both sides of the Strait, we see how new officials are as corrupt as the old and how junior officials copy their seniors' deceitful ways. Those who have been corrupt will continue to be, those who have never been will learn to be, the bold ones will be big, and the timid ones little. Even the hairdressers have to get used to the situation and can only pray that they will be less corrupt. The best is not to change officials frequently as they take turns to corrupt others, sucking blood from batch to batch.

It is easy to dodge the spear in the open but hard to avoid a stab in the dark. Do you believe that? Many regard general education as an important element in whole-person education. Does this so-called general education ever help to prevent such devilish behavior?

Blind Spot for Youths

The whole-person education proposed by universities in Hong Kong and Taiwan seems to lack substance, failing to provide even basic training in social manners and civil duties. Mainland China believes that the introduction of whole-person education in Hong Kong and Taiwan emphasizes liberal education. However, such a move might turn out to be futile, like, as mentioned before, looking for fish in the trees.

Instead of proposing whole-person education, an idea that may sound quite lofty, it might be more practical for young students to start with the smaller things in life before entering university, like being courteous when taking escalators, opening doors for others when walking in and out of classrooms or toilets, and refraining from rushing, scrambling, pushing or elbowing others when walking in the streets or getting on or off buses or subway trains, or going in and out shops.

If healthy and if the distance is manageable, we should all exercise more, walk more, take fewer elevators and cars, walk on pedestrian paths, stop at red lights and move fast at green lights. Try not to talk in the local language if there are overseas visitors present in the classroom or at a meeting; try not to sail straight between people talking face to face; avoid talking loudly over mobile phones on subway trains; and refrain from ignoring others by looking at your mobile phones at formal meetings. These are basic social manners.

People in the modern world should care about nature. To treasure valuable resources, they should not distribute unnecessary T-shirts or useless souvenirs, hold unnecessary meetings, chant empty slogans, send anonymous messages, record conversations with others without permission, and not try to be online influencers by disseminating fake/virtual text or pictures. While dining at self-service restaurants, line up rather than jump the queue; do not take up seats before you get your food; take only what you need to avoid leftovers; return the utensils to the collection counter and push back your chair after the meal; and clean up any mess you drop on the floor. These small gestures are as easy as lifting one's little finger and will benefit others as well as yourself. So, why not adopt these practices first?

Are university students on both sides of the Strait at least able to observe such basic decorum in social intercourse whether we talk about whole-person education or not?

Lately, I have heard several cases in Hong Kong about graduating students who were late or simply did not show up for job interviews. This is puzzling. But there is an even more incredible story. A graduate I heard about signed a contract with a major company but failed to show up on the first day of work. When the company called, he simply said he did not want to work there. Apparently, this is not an isolated case. There have been several cases of graduates failing to show up after signing a contract. Such behavior indicates a lack of respect for others and contracts in the workplace.

Universities are civilized communities; criticisms and challenges can have persuasive power only if they are based on deeply critical self-questioning, courageous soul-searching and logical argument. Truth is not to be decided by majority votes nor attained by mere shouting. Young people like to stand against authority, but shouldn't they challenge themselves before confronting others? Opposing those in charge might provide an outlet for venting frustration, but only by seriously questioning oneself can one really demonstrate one's strengths. René Descartes once said, conquer yourself rather than the world!

On February 7, 2020, in response to the coronavirus pandemic, CityU launched CityU-Learning, a real-time, institution-wide, comprehensive online teaching platform that ran according to the original CityU timetable. Over 1,000 Mainland Chinese students objected to this measure, arguing that "tuition fees were paid for classroom study", "the degree would not be recognized on the Mainland if we studied without seeing the professors in person", and "it didn't count as university education if the equipment of the university library was not used", etc. They thought it reasonable to ask for a tuition fee refund.

More than a year later, in June 2021, when the pandemic in Hong Kong had eased after many people had been vaccinated, CityU planned to return to in-person classroom teaching in September. Again, nearly 1,000 students from the Mainland protested in a very public manner. This time their reasons were "accustomed to online learning", "unwilling to travel back and forth between the Mainland and Hong Kong", "classroom learning may cause COVID-19 infections", "home-learning is more convenient", "difficulty getting a Hong Kong travel permit", and so on. Matters boiled down once more to demanding a refund.

From January 2022, with the Omicron variant of COVID-19 severely disrupting daily life in Hong Kong, CityU continued to adopt an online and classroom dual-track teaching mode, requiring that students returning to campus should be vaccinated unless they were exempt for any special reasons. Again, our plans were met with complaints ranging from "we will be infected if we go back to school", "there is no guarantee with the jab", "dual-track teaching mode is unfair", etc. The bottom line was once again to gain money.

Blind Spot for Adults

Hong Kong is known as an international metropolis. So why is it that prosperous Indian and Pakistani residents whose families have lived in Hong Kong for a century and who have contributed to the prosperity of the region are largely ignored by Hong Kong society? Why can't foreign domestic helpers become permanent residents in Hong Kong no matter how long they have lived here, while others can as long as they have lived in Hong Kong for seven years?

Do those fighting for democracy in a free society show the same respect and demand for equality with different ethnic groups? More precisely, do they respect the rights of foreign domestic helpers at the same time as they clamor for their own human rights? Have they ever been concerned about the freedoms of others? Are they ready to recognize the same liberties for visitors from other parts of the world in demanding civil liberties? When it comes to pursuing justice, to what extent are they able to follow the principles of fairness and respect the rule of law? Has it ever dawned on people who reject immigrants and advocate localism that Hong Kong and Taiwan were both originally places for immigrants? Despite talking about living with dignity, can they really not bend to power, position, money or wealth, or not look down on the poor? Is the ulterior motive for removing autocratic regimes and bureaucracies to establish a new bureaucracy and autocracy under one's own control?

There is greater environmental awareness in the 21st century. Shouldn't we try to acquire a better understanding of technology and nurture a more sustained interest in learning about culture? Since the colonial era, Hong Kong has lacked a democratic, technological and cultural vision, and its education policy has been unclear. In a society preoccupied with finance and money-making and not interested in investing for the future, few students pick science and technology as their first choice for university or a career. At the same time, there is a distinct sense of neglecting science and technology and an indifference to history and culture. Students write extremely poorly in Chinese and lack civic awareness, all of which are part of the overall problem.

Advanced information technology in modern society has greatly facilitated interpersonal communication and the free flow of information, but if we can't observe basic decorum in everyday interactions, we won't make much progress even if we possess a high intellect and sophisticated tools, not to mention that those hiding in the virtual cloud can disseminate false information or bully and defame others. This is simply atrocious!

Why are students required to receive whole-person education while adults are not required to do so first? Whichever way you look, there is no way universities or society can take pride in having any sense of achievement in promoting whole-person education. Merely chanting slogans is not the way to promote whole-person development. Where will this lead us? Shouldn't we be more rational and moderate instead of just uttering pretty words?

Many people misapply the US understanding of general education to universities across the Strait. They have obviously forgotten that etiquette has been necessary for young people in Chinese culture since ancient times. So why can't university students obey the same everyday etiquette found overseas? Why are they asked to acquire whole-person development at such a late stage? Isn't it equivalent to what Confucius used to say: "The Rites of the Six Arts are lost, so go find them in the countryside"?

Has any Hong Kong youth ever expressed the slightest interest in such issues? Isn't the blind spot for youths also the blind spot for adults?

Parenting

Behavior reflects culture, and culture shapes behavior. Culture is not only the foundation of a society; it is a way of life reflected in the way one treats others and oneself. How should we treat the natural environment in concrete ways through our behavior rather than with just empty talk? Personal habits, behavior and value orientations are integral to a person's cognitive and affective development. This makes me think of a popular book called *The Young American: A Civic Reader*, a must-read for primary and high school students.

This publication cultivates in readers a sense of patriotism and civic wisdom. It says that a decent citizen should possess a democratic character, which can be summarized as "Do not do unto others what you would not have them do unto you", which sounds like classical thought. It also says that a person's dignity has the highest value, and one must learn to control oneself. A good citizen must understand himself/herself and should not be egotistical. The goal of education is to nurture the overall quality of a person and foster the development of a democratic character for responsible citizenship and for learning how to respect oneself as well as others. More than 2,000 years ago, Confucius proposed overcoming oneself and observing the ritual as a way to achieve harmonization between the development of our cognitive and emotional capacities. Have we tried to learn from the past to gain new insights for the future in our promotion of whole-person education in Hong Kong and Taiwan?

Does anyone teach young people to promote virtue and an upright character? The emphasis in Chinese culture on a proper upbringing is universally essential and practicable. A worthy person commits to the fundamentals, for all courses of action will proceed once the fundamentals are established. Cultivating one's character and putting one's family matters in order come under the basic sense *Bildung* needed to conduct oneself in life. I am surprised that no one in Taiwan, Hong Kong or the Mainland talks about it!

Character development begins at an early age. Why hasn't anyone talked about proper parenting or childrearing? Teaching children how to behave properly? Do adults know how to behave properly? Have they had proper parenting?

The formative education designed for young people by societies across the Strait encourages starting early with basic tool-handling skills. We should not wait until young people are in college when their character is more or less formed and expect universities to start nurturing their whole-person development. This would be like emphasizing the importance of brushing one's teeth but not until the teeth have already decayed. Universities should concentrate their resources on generating cutting-edge knowledge and professional skills to prepare for a forward-looking career and the world of work.

In his *Book of Rites*, Confucius once quoted an expression from *The Book of Changes*, saying, "The gentleman should be careful with the beginning; a miss is as good as a mile." The cultivation of a Confucian gentleman is valuable in the beginning as well. It will be too late to talk about whole-person education at the university. It will be a misuse of university resources if we wait until college to promulgate whole-person thinking while home and early education fail to address character development in the formative years. Otherwise, how about people who never go to college? Does it mean they have no chance to become a whole person? Based on my experience, many ordinary folks who have not gone to college appear to be whole and wholesome.

While you may find that people upholding justice are mostly those in despised jobs, deceivers are often among the highly educated, which is a well-known quote from Cao Xueqin (1710–1765). It still applies today to societies across the Strait, even if it might be a bit exaggerated. One can elaborate more, but there is really no need to labor the point.

Professionalism

Societies across the Strait do better in prevention than innovation. They talk less about teamwork and ignore professionalism. They always try to strike a balance by implementing intricate regulations under the cumbersome and indecipherable organizational structure. As a result, "bad outcomes happen with correct methods." Anyone paying attention to Jeremy Shu-How Lin's performance in the NBA will notice that his assists are as highly regarded as his points. They help his teammates find the hoop, and baskets don't have to be scored by "me", which is the essence of team spirit.

Students from the Institut Polytechnique de Paris in France, as well as university students in Singapore and Israel, must undertake military training. These universities specialize in science and engineering. The presidents of such universities believe their students become more mature, reliable, and self-disciplined after they have completed their military duty. These graduates truly understand team spirit, meet the requirements for excellence in academics as well as sports, and many eventually become responsible political leaders.

When we discuss issues such as democracy, freedom, human rights, feminism, the rule of law, race, systems and regulations, etc., emphasizing teamwork, listening to others, being fair and respecting others are absolute principles that teachers and students need to abide by, not checks and balances. Among the three places across the Strait, Hong Kong society may abide by statutory rules, but its awareness of team spirit leaves much to be desired. As for Taiwan and the Mainland, their recognition of professionalism and team cooperation trails far behind.

On September 9, 2009, Obama was addressing a joint session of Congress when Joe Wilson, the South Carolina congressman, pointed at Obama and twice shouted, "You lie!" The Republican whip thought Wilson's behavior was a breach of decorum and civility, damaging the collective reputation of the Republican Party. The House voted to admonish Wilson over his "You lie" outbursts. Almost at the same time, people working in a support group in Wilson's district resigned because they felt ashamed of his conduct. It is the same during presidential elections. The rivalry is fierce, and so are the debates when the race is on. But once the election is over, past contentions are put behind. Fair play, or fair competition, as it is well demonstrated, is a display of team spirit and professionalism.

In a similar case, Elizabeth Lauten, a staffer for Republican representative Stephen L. Fincher, was compelled to resign on December 1, 2009, after a backlash following her critical remarks on Facebook about how Obama's daughters dressed. In the Trump and post-Trump era, US society is becoming more divided. As a result, the long-standing tradition of "arguments between gentlemen" has vanished.

These examples show that basic rules must be observed when conducting scientific research or responding to social issues, and relevant practices have to be appreciated. This spirit of professionalism and commitment to excellence in academics doesn't seem to be promoted as much in societies across the Strait as in Japan, South Korea, Europe and America.

The culture of cooperative, democratic communities helps young people to transform themselves from individualistic entities into socially responsible citizens. Even in a young country like the US, every university or high school student must take history lessons about the state where the school is located, in addition to national history.

In Hong Kong, however, high school students don't have to take history lessons. This omission creates a chasm between the emphasis on science and technology on the one hand and the lack of a sense of history and identity on the other. To bridge this gap, students should study Hong Kong's history to understand its unique developments and special social, cultural and political circumstances in order to develop a sense of purpose and mission and to become committed citizens. Both Taiwan and the Mainland have revised their history from a political point of view to align it with their own political parties' stances. Someone who does not even know his/her own history has no roots and can easily be blown adrift like dust in the wind. One wonders what kind of education has landed them in such a situation.

Those who do not follow good practices, and do not appreciate professionalism and team spirit, are not qualified to be modern citizens. In that case, people across the Strait will continue to be spiritual vagabonds, poor with nothing left but money. They are not qualified or have the necessary prerequisites to talk about innovation or entrepreneurship. Relatively speaking, communities across the Strait seldom promote social development nor pursue professionalism in their education curriculum. Sun Yat-sen started his republican revolution in Hong Kong more than 100 years ago. It seems the concerns he had regarding Chinese disunity still apply today.

A Wonder Woman: a Contemporary Story

Sister Xi grew up poor in southwest China. When she was three years old, she became seriously ill and eventually had to drop out of school at the age of six. Life was tough, so in the 1980s, when Sister Xi was still young, she decided to try her luck and traverse the mountains and rivers all the way to Hong Kong, having heard about the city's booming economy.

When she first arrived in Hong Kong, she was a stranger in a strange place, not knowing a soul. She found a job cleaning toilets. Taiwan, Hong Kong and the Mainland use the same language, share the same culture, and have the same unhealthy habits. The public toilets in Hong Kong are just as dirty and stinky, notoriously grimy and unsightly. The average cleaners would just do a superficial job by swiping and sweeping the easily accessible areas, unwilling to stay for long. But Sister Xi took her job seriously, cleaning everything until the facilities were spotless, from the ceiling to the damp corners. Sister Xi's diligence won appreciation from the cleaning company and she was soon promoted to a junior supervisor position.

Hong Kong, where the East meets the West, has inherited the southern Chinese culture, on the one hand, with a distinct class differentiation and severe discrimination against Mainlanders. Due to the language barrier, Sister Xi was often teased as a "Mainland girl." To better integrate herself, she made tremendous efforts to learn Cantonese. On the other hand, Hong Kong has embraced Western culture and values. Sister Xi's employers liked her very much because of her sincerity and dedication. She later switched her job to work as a dishwasher in a restaurant and was promoted to restaurant manager. With her focus and dedication, she shone in everything she did.

Thanks to her enthusiasm and energy, Sister Xi got into the textile industry through a friend's connection, starting with sewing and knitting. Stitch by stitch, she built up a new business in the field. At the same time, she doubled as a buyer. One day, her boss wanted to ship a load of ready-to-wear garments to Yokohama, Japan. In a rush, she was entrusted with the responsibility of escorting the shipment, even though she had no previous experience dealing with Japan. When the cargo entered the port, both the cargo and Sister Xi were detained due to a problem with the declaration procedures. The customs officer asked for the owner of the shipment to come forward. Sister Xi took full responsibility without revealing anything else. The Japanese did not believe her, no matter what she said, but they couldn't find any further information despite repeatedly questioning and threatening Sister Xi. Finally, impressed by her loyalty, the Japanese customs treated her to a meal and bought her a ticket back to Hong Kong. After arriving home, her boss, grateful to her for not reporting him, gave her a venture fund to start her own business.

With her accumulated experience, she used the funds to establish her own garment factory. She was personally involved in foreign trade, expanding the ready-made garments business from Hong Kong and Taiwan to Southeast Asia. Even though she did not speak any foreign languages, she was bold and cautious and traveled across the oceans to Europe and the US. Finally, Sister Xi succeeded in accumulating a certain amount of wealth.

Because she had not received any formal education, others often took advantage of her. She decided to donate her wealth to provide others with learning opportunities and make them knowledgeable and literate. Despite her success in her career, Sister Xi still lives a frugal life and speaks Cantonese with a strong accent as well as simple English. She also maintains a modest lifestyle and takes care of everything by herself: no house cleaner and no dependence on others. When going out, she takes the bus or subway, never feeling lonely or the passing of time.

Life itself is education. We should never judge a book by its cover. Sister Xi only knows how to contribute and never seeks to make herself known. I think nobody would dare say Sister Xi is not a whole person. We know from her story that she didn't have schooling, not to mention a "whole-person" education. University education has its value, but it is not the appropriate time to start nor the only platform for whole-person education.

10
Strategies for Nurturing Generalists and Specialists

A doctoral candidate I supervised 30 years ago came from a prestigious university on the Mainland. When I mentioned to him how the Japanese regarded ancient China's Zhu Xi as a God, he asked, "Zhu Xi? I've never heard of him." When I said Zhu Xi had made great contributions to 理學 (a rationalistic Confucian philosophical school, also known as Neo-Confucianism), he asked, "Do you mean 物理學 (physics)? What contributions had Zhu Xi made to China's physics?" I was dumbfounded by his question.

Twenty years ago, I relayed this anecdote to another candidate pursuing doctoral studies under my supervision. He was also from a leading university on the Mainland. However, I was surprised when he said, "Professor, I'm sorry, but I, too, have not heard of Zhu Xi. Can you tell me why he is such an important figure?" When I relayed the same story a couple of times later to some Hong Kong graduate students, I got similar answers: "Sorry, but we don't know who Zhu Xi is, either. Is he a celebrity in Taiwan?"

Doctoral candidates with little general knowledge are no longer a joke. Like students in Mainland China, those in Hong Kong don't know much about their native Chinese culture and, in fact, aren't required to take any history courses before they enter university. If doctoral students are like that, isn't it even more worrying for graduate and undergraduate students?

The Meaning of A Doctoral Degree

The Chinese term *Boshi* (博士) is the translation for a doctoral degree. The term dates back to ancient times. During the Qin and early Han dynasties some 2,000 years ago, *Boshi* was an official position held by learned scholars who were well-read and commanded a wealth of knowledge spanning the past and the present. He oversaw the imperial library and served as a royal adviser. Emperors of the Qin and Han dynasties, whether on official tours or presiding at court, were often accompanied by a *Boshi* seated to their left and right. One of the early Han dynasty emperors, Wudi, set up the official position of 五經博士 (Five Classics Boshi), whose duty was to educate students in the five classics. Since then, *Boshi* has been charged with the specific responsibility of transmitting knowledge about the Confucian classics in China. What about the *Boshi* across the Strait nowadays?

The imperial examination system in China was abolished during the late Qing dynasty about 120 years ago, and some Chinese students went abroad to study. After attaining a doctoral degree, they were called *Yang Jinshi* (洋進士, which literally means "someone who has passed the imperial examination in the West") because they were regarded as equivalent to having passed the imperial examination in feudal China.

Later, the term *Boshi* was used to refer to "someone who has a doctoral degree." The word *Bo,* which has the meaning of being broad, is retained because it sounds too good to be left out. In fact, many Chinese expressions carry the word, *Bo*; for example, *bo lan qun shu* (well-read), *bo xue duo cai* (learned and versatile), *bo da jing shen* (broad and profound knowledge), and *bo gu tong jin* (erudite and informed). In addition, we have such terms as *bo wu guan* (museums) and *bo lan hui* (exhibition conventions). All these terms starting with *bo* carry implications of extensive knowledge and profound scholarship or inclusiveness and all-embracing.

In ancient China, scholars liked to regard themselves as learned and all-embracing. Yet, despite their claim to know everything about the past and the present, have they ever been able to create an independent school of thought based on their knowledge? People today have the same problem and are unwilling to admit that they do not really know everything. Society also generally believes that if a top student can attain a doctoral degree after years of study and is called *Boshi*, the person will definitely be extremely broad in his/her knowledge and is well-informed about everything (*Bo*). Whether they know everything about the past and the present, or can create an independent school of thought is not an issue!

But in reality, this does not seem to be the case. With the rapid advancement of science and technology, various academic disciplines have been increasingly divided into smaller branches of studies. The scope of study pursued by a doctoral student becomes much more narrowly defined, focusing on only a small area of the discipline. In many cases, they are not familiar with other areas of the same discipline. Someone once made a typo and wrote *Boshi* (博士), doctor, as *Botu* (博土, "土" for ignorance). The error is inspiring. If one is too focused and knows nothing else, they are truly *Botu*!

People in the West are aware of the situation, which is why they define doctoral degree holders as "people who supposedly know a lot about a little something." In fact, there is nothing in the English term "doctoral degree" that suggests being erudite or all-round. Therefore, the thought that comes to mind is that the translation of a doctoral degree should perhaps be changed from *Boshi* (博士) to *Zhuanshi* (專士), meaning specialist in a little something, which seems more appropriate. A doctorate is only an academic degree title symbolizing that the holder has mastered a specific area of study or profession.

I have met many world-class scholars who do not hold a PhD degree, such as the 1987 Nobel Prize chemistry award winner Charles Pedersen and the 1988 medicine award winner Gertrude Elion (excluding Nobel laureates in highly subjective fields in literature, peace and economics). Since the beginning of this century, several Nobel laureates, including Jack S. Kilby, winner of the Nobel Prize in Physics in 2000; Koichi Tanaka, winner of the Nobel Prize in Chemistry in 2002; and Tu Youyou, winner of the Nobel Prize in Physiology or Medicine in 2015 and the only Chinese Nobel winner in medicine to date, do not have PhDs. Though most Nobel laureates have PhDs, this qualification did not prevent those mentioned from being recognized for their scientific and technological achievements.

At the same time, many people who do have PhD degrees behave in ways that are inappropriate for their highly educated backgrounds. In our society, a disproportionate number of people are willing to do considerable research and fact-checking to find the underlying cause of problems, compared to the number of people with degrees.

Many teachers who do have a doctoral degree may not be qualified to do the things they are trained to do. They may have a certain degree of learning but are not erudite; they may specialize in a certain field but lack profound knowledge or, worse, their knowledge is neither broad nor profound. Which type contributes more to society, I wonder, the real scholars who do not have a PhD degree or fake scholars who do have a PhD degree but are just drifting along accomplishing nothing?

Usually, one should have some knowledge about ordinary things. But some people behave, as a Chinese proverb states, as if they have neither tasted pork nor seen a pig run. If our academic climate is governed by politics and shallow, vulgar opinions, we will fall far behind advanced standards. Therefore, it can be said that the lower-class idles away doing nothing; the middle-class acts according to rules; the upper-class acts creatively. Many people crave the title of a PhD degree without looking into the meaning that such a degree carries. And that is the reason why many

PhD degree holders across the Strait are pursuing unrealistic illusions about the title they now possess.

Society is confused. We have moved from the ideological attitude of being broad to the current situation in which the PhD students, as I mentioned previously, know little or even nothing about history. Aren't we encouraging the cultivation of professionals and demanding that they should be erudite as well?

Multicultural and Cross-disciplinary Knowledge

Ever since John Nash dismantled the framework of the zero-sum game, a win-win relationship that is both competitive and cooperative has become the foundational principle for collaborative interaction. Higher education and scientific research industries rely on multi-dimensional cooperation for success. Many scientific and technological topics today involve a multiplicity of disciplines. Take energy, for example. Energy is related not only to technology but also to environmental protection, the economy, politics and social psychology. In formulating energy policies, we need to follow rigorous procedures, carefully weigh the benefits and costs, and objectively evaluate advantages and disadvantages.

While corn may be used to produce clean biofuels, it may aggravate the world's food shortage problem. Solar power is renewable, but the production of solar panels consumes energy and creates a blot on the landscape. Wind power is clean and renewable, but it is not stable and endangers birds. Hydropower is clean, but the supply is unstable because of unpredictable weather conditions, while dams can impact neighboring communities downstream. However, around 70% of the world's electricity comes from coal, the mining of which alone is responsible for taking hundreds of thousands of lives in China a year, to say nothing of the effect on global warming and the radioactivity of the coal cinder. Nuclear energy is clean and inexpensive, but there are constant worries and disputes over its safety.

Here's another example. The WHO reported on February 25, 2015, that in 2012 around 6.5 million people had died, that is, one in eight of total global deaths, as a result of air pollution, confirming that bad air is the world's biggest environmental health risk. However, the general populace doesn't seem to understand the destructive power of burning fossil fuels (especially coal and natural gas) for generating electricity and heating. Nor do they care about the dire consequences of global warming, oblivious to the need for vigorous research and analyses in order to address the issue of sustainable development. Moreover, about 30 % of the world's population lives without or with only a limited supply of electricity. We, as fellow global citizens, are in the same boat. If only a minority of the world's population gets to benefit from the outcomes of cutting-edge technology while the well-being of those living in underdeveloped areas is ignored, we can foresee the spread of disasters.

Whether we are talking about biofuels or solar power, wind power, nuclear power or new energies, or new technologies like graphene, all require research and development. In 2013, Bill Gates called for timely investment in developing clean energy and energy efficiency plans, but different energies incur different costs and risks. Should we not put a priority on investment in researching low-cost and low-polluting energies, then charge according to cost ratio, and use part of the proceeds for reinvestment in new energies?

The Nobel Prize in Physics was awarded to Syukuro Manabe, Klaus Hasselmann and Giorgio Parisi in 2021 for a study they conducted fifty years ago that predicted the effect of global warming with precision. The conferment of the Prize broke with tradition, evidence that the Earth's environment should command our attention, and underscored the importance of collaboration across fields.

In general, education should focus on delivering subject matter that has critical importance for everybody. In assessing different options, we need to take into account environmental pollution, reliability and public risk involved in the entire energy life cycle. As we find ourselves in the era of the digital economy, the wealth gap between countries is worsening. Facing the realities of a range of issues outlined above, policymakers and universities have a compelling obligation to deal with these problems. They should leverage the collective wisdom of different disciplines to ensure a supply of energy that is reliable and sustainable, and protective of the environment.

The primary purpose of education in societies across the Strait has been to ensure admission to a premier institution of higher learning. To this end, the streaming of students takes place early on in high school or even elementary school, with students focusing on one particular field of study in the liberal arts or sciences or business. This process severely limits the scope of learning. As students improve their grades, the scope of their subjects is further narrowed to achieve superior results for admission to prestigious universities. Unsurprisingly, even when they eventually graduate with a PhD, their knowledge is still extremely limited and narrowly based.

Professionals need an exceptional EQ (Emotional Quotient) to adapt to the increasing demand for knowledge integration, a global trend today. Young people may have to change jobs five or six times during their careers.

They need to be able to adapt, possess multiple talents and continually learn new skills to cope with these changes.

In fact, many views have been expressed by the Chinese in the past over the issue of specialist versus generalist or depth versus breadth in education. Ch'ien Mu, one of the greatest scholars of 20th century China, once commented that people paid too much attention to specialization, forgetting that transdisciplinary knowledge and understanding are, in fact, the most important. Our scholars had neither ambitions nor significant achievements. Every few years, a new crop of scholars replaced the old, but the country was always lagging in scholarship. What Ch'ien Mu said eighty years ago still applies today. Much of this lack of advancement is a deficiency of research. Without sustained research, the knowledge our PhD holders have learned in science and technology as well as in the humanities will become obsolete.

Many of today's challenges have to be addressed by cross-disciplinary collaborations and multi-sectoral contributions. Even if a team is formed involving *Zhuanshi* from different disciplines, the collaboration won't work without some basic understanding of one another's specialization. The same person working in the same field may have to take up a variety of roles during their career. No matter what field one works in, one needs to upgrade one's knowledge and skills. It is also important to develop transdisciplinary knowledge and understanding to expand one's intellectual base.

What is the relationship between cross-disciplinary knowledge and understanding and the much-talked-about general education, then?

General or Confused Knowledge

General education is becoming increasingly popular across the Strait and is considered an important part of whole-person education. Some people claim it's been copied from the United States. But this is misleading.

The former president of Yale University, Richard C. Levin, once said the core of university education is general knowledge, aimed at cultivating critical thinking rather than merely passing on practical knowledge and skills to prepare students for their future careers. His comments seem reasonable. But when under closer scrutiny, a couple of points can be debated.

First of all, universities that mainly focus on general education and the liberal arts are but one type of university out of the four listed in Chapter 8. Levin's view about university education and those who emphasize liberal arts education might be admirable, but it may not be suitable for the majority of average students. It definitely does not cover the education mission of all universities. The above point is illustrated by Levin's joining Coursera after leaving Yale to serve as CEO of the MOOCs platform for the development of online education, a position that entails a quite different education mission.

Secondly, general education has gained increasing importance in universities across the Strait in the last few years because of a misguided effort to introduce American-style education. As a result, general education became associated with something superficial and shallow, not intellectually challenging enough to meet the demands of the professional disciplines. Under the name of general education many universities offered fun and appealing but non-academic courses, such as qigong, music and dance, movie appreciation, pollution prevention, love matching, animation world, social movements, etc. These are more extracurricular courses that will dilute the value of a degree and waste seemingly precious time and energy when incorporated into the curriculum.

Many general education courses are relaxed, extensive, superficial and messy and are well-liked, with few people opposing them, which seems to be one of the sequelae caused by low tuition fees. But can this be considered general education at all? It was chaotic knowledge then, and it is still chaotic knowledge now.

Humanities-focused four-year colleges are unique in the US, with programs that provide a broad education base and develop students' ability to adapt to different career pathways. General education, as the foundation of a liberal arts education, is perhaps considered essential for Ivy League schools because the students they recruit are usually among the top, with a solid academic foundation and well-balanced development. They are usually quick on the uptake as well. Besides, there is no need to prepare graduates for certain accreditation with humanities majors. In Taiwan, Hong Kong and the Mainland, there are few, if any, universities similar to such Ivy League universities. Therefore it may not be a good example for every individual or every university.

Most state-funded universities in the US do not run general education courses, only some general requirements for subjects such as English, state history, etc. For professional programs such as those in business schools and engineering departments, the curricula certainly have built-in broadening academic components, but they are not called general education. Instead, they are generally circumscribed by specific majors, such as economics and engineering economics, the study of which is intended to support or facilitate. In order to be mature enough to practice professionally, students entering the schools of law, medicine or veterinary medicine are required to complete a 4-year preparatory college education first. As with European universities, which are steeped in the humanities and arts, the design of the curriculum is fairly flexible. There is no such a thing as general education, either.

Starting from 2012, all universities in Hong Kong adopted a four-year undergraduate curriculum, just like universities in Taiwan and Mainland China, and general education was introduced to fill up the additional year. This education reform could be a good beginning. Why do I say, "could be"? Because general education *could be* a plus factor if it is well designed and properly implemented. Otherwise, it might put professional education at risk, creating undesirable consequences instead of fulfilling the original purpose.

If general education courses can be completed through self-study, the wrong outcome might transpire. Why do I say "might be" again? Here is a handy example. In the spring of 2021, the Hong Kong government announced that the liberal studies (general education) curriculum would be reduced and the compulsory assessment criteria would be changed to a simple pass/fail. The importance of reducing general education was self-evident, but a correct decision was based on incorrect reasons because the Hong Kong government believed that general education was the cause of the social unrest in 2019 and therefore mistakenly believed that general education was not as important as national education. Though named general knowledge, what was initially taught in primary and high schools was not knowledge but social movements. Liberal studies came and went quickly. If we had known it would come to this, why did we bother in the first place?

To remain important and relevant, general education courses should deal with highly topical issues that have far-reaching significance. Depending on the type of universities to which they are admitted, students can select a few basic courses from various disciplines during their first and second years, and they begin to specialize in their chosen majors only when they reach the third and fourth years. It is important that these basic courses have depth and vigor and must stand the test of academic merit rather than being shallow.

If we value these basic courses, it is important to have experts offering forward-looking, contemporary courses that would be difficult to learn through self-study, such as courses in philosophy, economics, data science, etc. Aim high or you may fall below even the mediocre. In order to incorporate contemporary scholarship into the curriculum, it is a promising idea to invite top academics to deliver lectures to freshmen and sophomores, which in turn can broaden the students' interests. That is why academics at advanced universities in the US in the same league as Nobel laureates offer lectures to freshmen, which can lead to fantastic results. In addition to making English a compulsory subject, universities in the US are proposing to make biology compulsory, too. Has anyone across the Strait considered such an innovative proposal? Does any university have the courage and foresight to consider adopting such a measure?

If general education refers to basic literature, history and philosophy courses, most university students across the Strait are already assigned to different streams of study before entering under a system of educational triage based on an early separation of science and humanities in high school. Such general education courses may not be universally applicable. Other than that, the priority for certain universities is to prepare students for the accreditation requirements in certain professional careers and to become experts in their specific fields. This explains why in general students tend to be more narrowly focused on their pre-college life, making it difficult for them to take general education courses at universities. They should have taken the fundamental liberal arts education and learned to be decent human beings in their pre-college life instead.

The primary goal for many students at college is not to seek general knowledge in a large number of areas at the expense of gaining in-depth professional knowledge and expertise in their chosen field, not even to mention that often the broadly defined general education courses are too elementary to be meaningful. Although in-depth general education courses may be useful for outstanding students, I doubt they apply to the average college students.

In fact, many accomplished scholars or entrepreneurs did not acquire their ideas or change their way of thinking through university education; some might not have taken their university studies seriously or not have been to college at all. Isn't it intriguing that these scholars or entrepreneurs who have not received any general education can control our daily life or be cited as general education models?

While universities across the Strait emphasize the importance of English, have they thought about making Chinese studies compulsory? Do they realize that, as we admire the moon, living souls on the moon, if there should be any, might be admiring our planet? Or did they require that students majoring in the humanities take logic and mathematical philosophy? "Autumn moon over Mount Emei, so like a half wheel / Its reflection in the Pingqiang River with its current flows." (Li Bai) Can we claim to be well-cultured simply because we have read a few books on the arts and literature?

Is there concrete knowledge in general education?

Several dozen specialist professors are concurrently affiliated with the Collège de France in Paris, which dates back nearly 500 years. In recent years, the majority have been academicians and scholars of the caliber of Nobel Prize winners and Fields Medalists. The professors at the Collège de France offer non-degree courses covering a variety of disciplines, including the humanities, social sciences, mathematics, physics and chemistry, biomedicine, energy, and environmental protection, and so forth. The content varies from year to year according to the professors' research. A professor is invited to give lectures only when he/she has undertaken highly significant research, in keeping with the notion that great masters must teach profound knowledge if one is to keep abreast of advances around the world and encourage people to understand the essence of an issue thoroughly. The practice of the Collège de France is consistent with the practice at leading universities in the US, where senior professors teach basic freshmen courses in physics, chemistry, biology and English that, despite being basic courses, contain commendable principles that only experts can explain well.

The key to education is to ignite curiosity and encourage students to use rational thinking to analyze and explore. Why travel long distances and spend money on college if the general education courses offered are no better than materials readily available from TV programs, films or what can easily be learned by oneself? Worse still, some of these courses are simply fragments of populist propaganda.

It is important that the education we provide can develop the students' talents and interests. General education does not aim to nurture any specialized skills or knowledge and may not really benefit our students, especially most average students. The traditional practice of encouraging students to take more credits, learning things without fully understanding them or simply swallowing a set of dogmas without thoroughly digesting them can produce at best a group of immature pedants who are excessively critical about society but extremely weak in introspection and self-discipline.

According to the ancient Chinese philosopher Zhuang Zi, life is finite while knowledge is infinite. Pursuing the infinite with the finite is bound to fail. Therefore, it is impossible and futile to try to know everything. But without a solid foundation built across different disciplines, it is impossible to develop innovative ways to address problems. Even general education courses, whether easy or difficult, must be developed by specialists in their respective disciplines in order to prevent them from being shallow or superficial.

Ch'ien Mu's comments in his *On Studying Chinese History* are worth quoting as an illustration. He once said people studying history should start by concentrating on a particular era and then follow up by reading general history to give it context and a new perspective. One should repeat the same reading pattern, choose another era, one era at a time, and make a significant effort to study it, after which one should then turn to reading general history again. Only by studying history in such a way can one gain a thorough and integrated understanding of Chinese history. His views on studying Chinese history can be applied to the study of other subjects or disciplines. We should specialize in one or two related disciplines at each stage, then integrate the knowledge before moving on to engage in further studies on that foundation. In fact, no matter what the specialty is, history should be a must-have subject for everyone, and it should be learned as early as possible.

Cooking

Buddhist masters advise people that, for personal development, one must "focus on one thing at a time and spend long hours cultivating it".

The same principle applies to preparing food. A head chef may specialize in certain cuisines, but he or she must first understand the principles of the science and art of cooking. A cook cannot concentrate on any particular cuisine without having developed an overall understanding of cooking in general. Master chefs need more than general knowledge if they want to become more specialized. It is the constant interplay between reviewing general culinary principles and experimenting with specific recipes that brings about excellence.

Lao Zi once said that we should "govern a great country as we would cook a small fish". Outstanding teachers with profound professional expertise are the same as expert chefs. They are both committed to vigorous research, experimentation, and application. Inferior teachers can churn out nothing but inferior students.

11
The Successful Evergreen Tree

The development of a society is inseparable from education. An ideal education has an uplifting function for the individual, freeing the mind from quandaries and confusion. Education involves a learning process. Even the great Chinese philosopher and teacher Confucius was not born with innate knowledge. Due to his love of knowledge, he studied hard to acquire it. Therefore, a university will not be a university unless it enhances knowledge and doesn't use that learning as an ornament or to gain favor; otherwise, it doesn't deserve its status in society.

And yet education is not necessarily associated with the university.

Math and the Tuhao (Newly Rich Hillbillies)

Before I start a description of the usefulness of academic degrees, I would like to share a story related to solving a common arithmetic problem. A newly emerging group of people called Tuhao (newly rich hillbillies) on the Mainland usually give people the impression of being rather arrogant, showing off their wealth in bags of cash, a sign of despotic vulgarity. Many people look down on them, trying to outdo each other by ridiculing them. But I heard a unique perspective about a Tuhao recently. Although this person has never been to college, he runs a prosperous business, a sure sign there is something on offer.

The son of this Tuhao was puzzled by the following arithmetic problem: "There are 34 chickens and rabbits, with 92 legs in total, placed in a cage. How many chickens are there in the cage, and how many rabbits?"

Unbelievably, this chicken and rabbit math problem has baffled many people. I believe it may take a lot of people a lot of time to brainstorm the solution.

An engineering student might start by assuming that there are X chickens and Y rabbits, so two variables....We are already at a total loss before all the definitions are given.

The Tuhao, instead, gave the solution to his son right away. He said: Assume both the chickens and rabbits are well trained. With one whistle, both the chickens and rabbits will raise one leg, and we will get 92-34 = 58; with a second whistle, another leg is raised, and we will get 58-34 = 24. By then, all the chickens will be sitting on the ground while the rabbits will still be standing on two legs. Therefore, we will get 24/2 = 12 rabbits and 34-12 = 22 chickens.

People specializing in liberal arts and humanities might find the above problem baffling, not knowing where to start since it is probably not so easy for them to understand. Those studying politics and law may relate the question to some kind of conspiracy theory, having a bee in the bonnet and taking the wrong actions. Those specializing in finance and business might see this as a social networking problem and therefore look in the wrong direction and knock on the wrong doors, whereas students and teachers specializing in science, engineering, medicine and technology are likely to turn a simple problem into a complicated issue, hoping to tackle it by solving a set of equations with two variables. Ordinary folk specializing in certain professions might devise a solution of sorts through trial and error. But once the combination of numbers is changed, they will be at a loss again.

The Tuhaos might come across as unrefined hillbillies, but the money they make doesn't drop from the sky. The above-mentioned Tuhao has no academic degrees, but his mathematics, crude as it may sound, has the essence of concrete knowledge, and it's not to be sneered at. Although trivial, there is something worth noting here. It is true that we can learn something in the company of other people.

As pointed out in the previous chapter, inferior PhD and bachelor's degree holders are found everywhere in a society flooded with degrees. According to a recent report, Mainland China now produces more doctoral degree holders than the US. Can this fact alone place China at the forefront of the world in terms of research and development in science and technology or in the humanities and social sciences? If not, the rapid growth in the number of PhDs at China's universities only serves to illustrate how eagerly Chinese people hanker after titles.

Shanghai is known to be a city where it is exceedingly difficult to apply for residency due to its rapid development. However, in order to spearhead its science, technology and innovation advancement, a policy was announced on July 1, 2015, that permitted foreign talent in such fields to apply for work visas directly and to live in Shanghai. More recently, I learned that non-locals, including people from other parts of China, need high-tech knowledge and advanced degrees to be granted such visas or residence permits. This might be counted as one advantage of having a degree. But on this basis, Mao Zedong and Chiang Kai-shek would not have been granted permission to reside in Shanghai if they were still alive today. Of course, even medical scientists like Tu Youyou, the only Chinese Nobel laureate in Medicine so far, would have been kept outside Shanghai as well. Stories like Tuhaos are readily available. Is it not worth paying attention to?

Degrees Are Not Equal to Knowledge and Expertise

Due to the traditional attention paid to education, Chinese people all over the world value degrees, with very few exceptions. Some even deeply believe that the more degrees, the better. In fact, the length of one's life cannot determine the richness of one's life. Some successful people did study at well-known high schools and universities. The training and nurturing they received might have played a role in their career advancement. However, it is entirely possible that they would have succeeded even if they had not attended those well-known universities. A diploma or degree from a prestigious school is no guarantee of success in one's career. An emphasis on education is commendable, but an emphasis on degrees may lead us astray. If one's attention is focused entirely on degrees, one won't succeed in one's career but rather will be wasting one's precious time. Why?

Based on my observations over the last few decades, students with excellent academic scores in middle school do not always continue to rank top once they get into college; outstanding university students may not have successful careers or be the most competitive in the job market; PhD holders from respected universities are not necessarily the best researchers or excellent teachers, either. The best professors or most accomplished researchers do not always come from famous universities. It is a lamentable but common phenomenon that having a degree does not equal knowledge and expertise.

I once read the self-introduction on the webpage of a middle-aged Hong Kong government official who bragged about his outstanding results in high school and university as well as the reputation of those places where he studied. But he never mentioned what other accomplishments he had achieved since then. It gave me the impression that he had not done well in his career. And indeed, it turns out that his life was really not going anywhere, and he had to live in the past and indulge in reminiscing about the academic qualifications he had collected over time.

We may compare an academic degree to the jersey a football player wears. It may show to which team a player belongs, but it does not necessarily indicate how well he can perform on the football pitch, and wearing more jerseys, even of prestigious teams, will not help one play the game and certainly not guarantee to win. In addition to degrees, one must have knowledge and expertise, which can be compared to the ability to score in a football match. If a person cannot score or perform well, what good is it to wear the jersey of a famous football team? Some people feel proud of owning a number of degrees, some even from prestigious schools, but just like owning a number of jerseys, they are useless if that is the only thing they can brag about.

In the 2022 Taiwan elections, some candidates were suspected of plagiarism in their master's thesis. The news attracted a lot of public attention and led to significant criticism. Influenced by populist sentiment, some people in Taiwan tend to be oblivious to reason and sentimental as a rule. They never care about "professionalism" and "knowledge." During the election, however, "academic theses" and "degrees" all of a sudden become highly significant. Some people even started to question the value of certain degrees, which happens if society ignores actual scholarship and equates a degree with knowledge.

This controversy regarding the type of degree is not an isolated case. Our society values degrees more than real scholarship. Since there is an unhealthy trend to inflate one's degrees in the political sector, there will be people in the academic world who "cooperate", helping to "dress up" and "gild" the degrees. While peerage titles and official positions are purchased and sold in officialdom, diploma workshops exist in the academic circle. When there is a demand for academic credentials in government, many politicians launder their qualifications for the purpose of acquiring specific positions. At that point, the nature of degrees has been corrupted completely. The credentials originally represented by these degrees are completely gone.

Given the demand in society, universities are delighted to offer incredible degrees and programs in response. As a general rule, the curriculum in universities across the Strait can be burdensome, but few are willing to conduct a critical self-review to cut down on courses with low merit and utility. On the other hand, as long as a degree is granted, people tend not to question whether the curriculum content is useful or not, resulting in a situation where there is a saturation of degrees, but without soul. Many blindly follow because they want degrees. Moreover, graduate school is sometimes regarded by some as a temporary shelter during tough economic times.

After all, a degree is nothing but a certificate of qualification. It will not guarantee a satisfactory job, achieving a high salary and living a happy life. Even degrees earned through really demanding work only serve as stepping stones to kick-start careers and are not for advancement for the rest of one's life.

In an ideal situation, degrees should indicate the holders' knowledge and ability. But the higher education offered under the current system cannot guarantee that there is a correlation between degrees and the level of knowledge. At the same time, many phenomenally successful people from different occupations don't have degrees and don't need them as a prop, either. It is the university's responsibility to review these phenomena and to narrow the gap between knowledge and degrees.

Since an ideal university doesn't exist, there is a great deal of room for improvement. The general public across the Strait values degrees because they provide a convenient way, for lack of a better way, to assess people's knowledge and expertise that would otherwise be difficult to gauge. In that sense, degrees still have limited use.

Someone once said: I was born intelligent—education ruined me. I won't claim that degrees are useless, but I am quite certain that the content of quite a few programs offered at universities in our part of the world can either be learned by self-study or contain little learning value if any at all, mainly because teaching and research are not integrated into much of these programs. Instead of wasting time on these programs, the students could have fared much better by engaging themselves with the real world to gain concrete knowledge and skills. From this perspective, some university or graduate courses that undermine the students' intelligence don't deserve our time and effort. Sure enough, there are people ruined by their degrees without knowing it!

Knowledge and Expertise Do Not Equal Practical Experience

A substantial number of people in societies across the Strait have bachelor's, master's or doctoral degrees. Some even boast of having several doctorates. What else do we need, other than academic degrees, knowledge and expertise to live a successful and fulfilling life? Many successful entrepreneurs and visionary leaders are in more occupations than we can count at the end of the last century or the beginning of this one. They share some common qualities: self-discipline, passion, ideals, vitality, determination and perseverance. They have finally created a fruitful career through persistence.

Of course, many highly productive people have benefited from a congenial environment. The eight Chinese scientists who have been awarded the Nobel Prize in Physics and Chemistry are good examples. The open and free higher education and research environment in Western societies is a key condition for their success. I also happen to know that quite a few Nobel laureates, Chinese included, were not at the top academically during their student years.

Often at social events, many prominent Hong Kong industrialists tell people modestly how little formal education they received. What they say is most interesting. They are prominent not only because of their success in their respective fields but also because of their immense contributions. While they might not have attended university, they are far from being people with little education. In reality, they have not only managed to acquire education in their own way but have also excelled in applying what they have learned in real life. What they have achieved in terms of knowledge, skills and professional expertise is much more advanced.

Likewise, their counterparts such as Yonghao Liu in Mainland China, Shanshan Zhong (the wealthiest person in Mainland), Ng Teng Fong in Singapore, Terry Kuo and Bruce Cheng in Taiwan, and Bill Gates of Microsoft and Michael Dell of Dell in the US do not necessarily hold higher degrees while some are without even a first degree. Yet each one is a pioneer, whether in hi-tech or business, and their achievements are publicly acknowledged.

Those even younger, like Larry Page and Sergey Brin, founders of Google, Jerry Yang and David Filo, founders of Yahoo, and Elon Musk, founder of Tesla, did not complete their doctoral programs. Mark Zuckerberg, founder of the social networking portal, Facebook, Travis Kalanick, founder of Uber, and Gautam Adani, the ex-richest man in Asia, did not even finish their undergraduate studies.

The life experience of successful people in all fields shows that many make their interests their profession and their profession their interests. It was reported that Daniel Tsui, Nobel laureate in Physics 1998, thought of physics experiments as games even before he won his prize. In his view, so-called research is nothing more than doing something fun, interesting and challenging, but you get paid. This is the best example of the seamless integration of personal interest and work.

A *Time* magazine profile details how Apple's CEO Tim Cook spends his day. He wakes up at 3:45 every morning, does e-mail for an hour, goes to the gym, Starbucks for more e-mail, and then works. This is his daily routine, with no exceptions and no shortcuts. Successful people love what they do and take pleasure in it. They never slack off. It is like what Confucius said, "Understanding something is good but not as good as being interested in it, which in turn is not as good as being able to enjoy doing it."

Knowledge and expertise represent abstract concepts that must be verified and implemented. Therefore, as one comes to the end of one stage of academic life and begins thinking about future directions or determining goals for further studies, it is advisable to base one's college or career choice on considerations of what is really the most suitable for oneself. Only if we select what we love and love what we select can we be sure that in the next several decades, we will be wholeheartedly devoted to our learning and career, not only for our own benefit but also for society.

Academic qualifications or even practical knowledge are still not necessarily a special pass to success. This statement applies to all places and eras, whether it is the "sixth graders" in Taiwan, the "post-90s" in Hong Kong, the "77th and 78th class students" on the Mainland who went to college after the Cultural Revolution, or people from any other regions or eras. Only those who have clear goals and take rigorously scrutinized courses can really see the value of a degree.

Education effectiveness can be determined by whether we have solved any problems or created any problems instead. When I was a child living in Nantou, Taiwan, we used to see blue skies and white clouds. In front of our house was a small river where we used to catch (or dig up, to be exact) clams. Behind the house was a slope leading all the way to the hills. During the day, we saw a lot of dragonflies; at night, fireflies could be seen flying in the green field. But when I visited Taichung and Nantou in early 2018, I realized what air pollution really meant. It was also reported that lung cancer had sky-rocketed in the region (see Table 17.1). Taichung and Nantou used to rank at the top in terms of air quality. How come the environment has deteriorated to such a state even though people with academic degrees and many deeply knowledgeable about environmental preservation flock our streets? How come we can no longer find clams and dragonflies?

The situation can be explained by comparing academic degrees with playing basketball. The degrees people have may be compared to the natural body height of basketball players. It only serves as one parameter. One must also have learning, which can be compared to the scoring rate. However, the scoring rate doesn't guarantee winning the game; the same way as knowledge doesn't mean effectiveness. It is labor to no purpose if a person with learning cannot put his/her learning to practice. It is like a person who writes flamboyantly without making a point. We need to apply what we have learned at the right place, at the right time, using the right method and to the right people.

The competition is intense. Everyone should get rewarded on the basis of his/her capabilities and contribution. One can hardly expect to reap the rewards just by resting on one's laurels. People who have been living too long under the illusion of the omnipotence of degrees and taking privileges for granted will find themselves in great distress when this realization finally dawns on them.

Experience May Not Stand the Test of Time

To search for talent, professional recruiters ask as much as possible about an applicant's potential in a range of areas. A degree from a prominent school will not make one shine in the job market or in a profession. Knowledge will not necessarily work, either. Instead, over-reliance on one's academic qualifications or even knowledge can limit oneself from giving full play to one's talents and creativity, eventually ruining one's future. At times like this, the experience becomes essential. But experience may not stand the test of time.

In my work in higher education, I often hear interviewees emphasize that they have a lot of experience. Some say they have direct familiarity with teaching; some explain they have industry exposure; others say they have a rich research background; others claim they know about fundraising. But how valuable are such experiences? Are they able to stand the test of time, or will they disappear like fleeting clouds, to be forgotten easily?

For example, many people have dated, but how many really understand love? You might be able to cook, but can you rustle up delicious dishes worthy of a successful chef? Driving is a skill many acquire, but how many people have never been in a traffic accident? Who's not fond of talking? But is building a coherent argument your forte? Joggers run regularly, but how many know the key to running? Many people have studied, but how many can identify what studying is all about? Many people have taught, but do their students remember them? Making connections is fine, but is it possible to raise funds through these networks? Are the rich necessarily happy and the poor unhappy?

A person's experience cannot always stand the test to prove its value. Only testable experience is worthwhile. Therefore, we should not be surprised that less experienced doctors might sometimes cure a serious disease, whereas an experienced doctor might worsen a patient's condition. Why do we often hear that cars don't break down because of driving but because of repairs? That's because the mechanic's experience does not always stand the test.

A perfect example, which may also be an exceptional one, is the famous Dujiangyan irrigation system in Chengdu, southwest China. The project was completed in 256 B.C.E. Its theoretical foundation is still considered sound, even by modern standards. For more than 2,000 years, thousands of miles of rolling plains in Sichuan province have been made fertile by irrigation facilitated by this system, benefiting hundreds of millions of people. Completed in ancient times, the project still commands the admiration of engineers and specialists today. Its designers-cum-engineers, Li Bing and his son, did not take courses in modern physics. Yet they must have studied some relevant subjects and, more importantly, applied what they had learned to this timeless irrigation project, which has stood the test of time.

Ordinary people can hardly expect to emulate Li Bing and his son. But even in our everyday jobs, we can, and should, exert ourselves to assist—not resist—improving society, however small those improvements might be. For that reason, we should bear in mind the principle of studying for application's sake and keep on learning and working in that spirit. By application, I mean we should ensure that the effect of our work benefits the community and improves people's lives. The things we depend on to make the application happen, be it language, tools or degrees, are only secondary.

Take Nothing for Granted

Every fall, the announcement of the year's Nobel Prize winners creates a buzz. But do people know that Jean-Paul Sartre, the French philosopher known for his existentialist philosophy, declined the Nobel Prize in Literature in 1964? After learning the news, Sartre's response was that "a writer's standing in the realms of politics, society, and literature can only be actualized in what he writes, in the creative work he produces, from which he gets his complete fulfillment. It cannot be replaced by any kind of prize or award."

I have heard of several similar cases and know people who have declined similar or lesser prizes. In 2006, Grigori Perelman, a forty-year-old Russian mathematician from Saint Petersburg, was offered the Fields Medal, which is awarded every four years with a monetary sum, for his proof of the Poincaré conjecture. He declined the medal and chose to live in modesty like a real hermit with his mother.

About 30 years ago, a friend of mine, Jack, was teaching at Iowa State University (ISU). He usually liked to criticize his employer. One day, the college dean told him during his performance appraisal that he would need to adjust his attitude toward ISU. My friend did not accept the comment and said he would rather quit if the academic environment were not congenial. And even if he were offered tenure, he would not necessarily accept it.

About ten years ago, another friend of mine, Wu, who was working at the University of Washington in Seattle, came to Hong Kong as a visiting faculty at one of the local universities. At the end of the three-month stint, he did not receive the exact amount for the honorarium that had been agreed upon. Instead of reasoning about the shortfall, which might have caused bad feelings, he returned the cheque, saying, "Please accept that as my free service." What a neat way to handle a difference! This kind of lofty spirit and upright behavior is indeed exemplary.

A Chinese scholar, Wang Anshi of the Song dynasty, penned a well-documented story called *Lament over the Oblivion of Zhongyong* about a child prodigy named Fang Zhongyong. The Fang family had been farmers for generations. Zhongyong knew how to compose poems and create inscriptions by the time he was only five years old, even before he knew about writing tools. Crowds of people went to his house to ask for his works. His father tried to profit from his son's special talent by charging money and keeping him away from school to further develop his potential. Years passed, and Zhongyong, having reached the limits of his talent, eventually became ordinary. Accomplished people work hard day in and day out. That applies to geniuses as well. Even a child prodigy will eventually degenerate into a mediocre person unless he or she works hard.

Wang Anshi wrote about lamenting how talent can waste away through a lack of cultivation. If someone as gifted as Fang Zhongyong could fall into mediocrity because he did not receive a proper education, how about those who are just average and have no special talent?

Learning is boundless. Therefore, while degrees are not necessarily essential, education and learning are.

A Few Thoughts

When I was deciding where to go for my graduate studies, the benchmark I used for selection was the quality of the teachers in the target discipline rather than the reputation of the university. I made the right decision. I have benefited a great deal from some of the greatest educators. Besides conducting professional research, I learned from them how to judge the quality of a scientific paper and how to select my research projects. Such experiences have not only been beneficial for my professional research but also a great asset for my work later as editor-in-chief of an academic journal.

Working as an academic journal editor taught me that excellent scientific papers should be clearly articulated, precise, concise and free from pedantry. The function of language is to describe a fact clearly and explain a point plainly. The purpose of authoring an academic paper is to make a point, emphasizing logic and rationality rather than flowery language to create indecipherable text. It is far better to state and explain the fact in plain language.

Whatever our profession, we should strive to be evidence-based, focused and concise in our communications, i.e., making our points succinctly without exaggeration.

When I first started teaching, I met a department head known for his deficient performance. However, we can learn something from everyone. For years, he was the kind of teacher I did not want to be because of his inadequacies and mistakes. But I learned a lot by witnessing how he made his errors. This experience was immensely helpful when I moved into a higher-education leadership role. There is no way that academic degrees or scores can record the invaluable experiences of extraordinarily successful or unsuccessful people. A degree is far from being enough, or even necessary, for achieving success. What is important is embracing the spirit of learning and doing one's best in what one loves.

We can only earn public recognition by making a real contribution rather than idling through life. I often tell students that there is no such thing as a free lunch; instead of asking what society owes us, we should ask how best to apply our efforts to win society's recognition.

A Farmer's Advice

A few years ago, at a dinner gathering in Xi'an, China, one of the guests talked about a friend of his, a farmer in the countryside whose son, a recent graduate, was about to leave for the US for further studies. The bright future for this village boy drew a lot of praise and admiration from the other villagers. However, it was the father's wise advice that moved me the most.

He told his son that what really counts when studying abroad is not how much he would learn or what degrees he would obtain. After all, that can be done in China. What's important, once he's abroad, is to learn how other people manage their affairs and to take note of the systems and institutions that have created the strength of their society. No degree can substitute for these insights.

What a perceptive advice! Such wisdom far surpasses that of many of our PhD holders, and that applies to both those who deserve it and those who do not deserve their degrees.

We will only be paying lip service to internationalization if the education system remains self-enclosed and bureaucracy continues to rule while mistakes are simply glossed over. With evil intentions, learning by receiving degrees is likely to be a pretext for gaining undeserved recognition or benefits. Under such circumstances, the overemphasis on degrees today is like a reincarnation of the old practice of selecting people for official posts through imperial exams. Instead, it would be more meaningful if we emphasized the utilization of education for the well-being of society.

On the university side, it has been a grand challenge for educators to maximize the benefits of education beyond granting college degrees collectively. The more difficult mission is to accomplish how to make college education a necessity rather than a decorative ornament. See the Epilogue of this book for a detailed summary of this philosophical question.

An academic degree should be more reflective of the actual level of knowledge and expertise a college graduate receives than just a piece of paper with no substance. If learning is of value and we studiously apply the learning in practice, anything can be achieved. From this, the scene of crying when chanting the two sentences that took him three years to compose as written by Jia Dao, a Tang dynasty poet, can be understood. Also allow me to use the poem "On Hollyhock" composed by Chen Biao, a Chinese poet of the Tang dynasty, as a footnote for the farmer's advice:

> *Alas, my heart goes to the hollyhock flowers in front of me,*
> *Hundreds of them in various colors, purple or ruby-red.*
> *Even though their beauty matches that of peonies,*
> *They are not valued because of their multitude.*

12
Students and I

Quality education can enlighten students' minds and cultivate their potential. University provides a relaxed and pleasant learning environment where students meet by chance for pre-employment training to find the right job after graduation. I have been a student and a teacher. The only difference between master's or doctoral degree students whom I have supervised and myself is that I may have learned the "doctrines", or the Way of things, earlier. Therefore, I treat them on an equal footing, no matter their ethnic, gender, racial or geographic background. Students are the main body of the university, and I have had many truly gratifying experiences with these regular students.

I ushered in and put into practice the One Health concept when I took over the presidency at CityU in 2008. Over the years, I led thousands of CityU faculty and staff, students and alumni in the Standard Chartered Hong Kong Marathon every year in spite of cold wind and rain, except in 2020 and 2022 when the race was canceled due to the COVID-19 pandemic. Occasionally, we teamed up for international competitions outside Hong Kong. Most CityU athletes and I compete in the 10k race while the rest run the full or half marathon. We have also invited students from special schools to run side by side with us on many occasions, hoping to promote social inclusion. I have experience in long-distance and cross-country running and know that, through participation in long-distance running, we meet like-minded friends, promote sport for all, and work together to enhance community cohesion and morale. I have stayed connected with quite a few long-distance running friends, too.

If we want to cultivate team spirit, it is better to walk the walk than simply talk the talk. To achieve this goal, I often visited the homes of students from different backgrounds, academic disciplines and levels of achievement, especially students from less affluent families. During my visits, I learned about their home environment, their views on CityU and their study needs. I took these opportunities to chat about the standards of modern universities, encouraging students to learn to stand on their own feet, strive for improvement, develop independent thinking, and learn to respect the views of others.

According to "Family Sayings of Confucius" (*Kongzi Jiayu*),

> *As a flower of noble character, the orchids that grow in the deep valleys release their fragrance even if no one is around to appreciate it and shrivel because of the cold. The scent as sweet as the orchids will never change, the heart as tenacious as the orchids will never move.*

Here are some memorable student stories. These students were like the orchids that released their fragrances without seeking fame.

Tim-yan and Kay

Tim-yan, who has some physical disabilities, studied applied sociology. She is outgoing, optimistic, willing to help others, and performed well academically, aspiring to study for a Master of Social Work. Volunteering is part of her daily life, having worked as a DJ at Radio Television Hong Kong, the public broadcasting service in Hong Kong, while still in high school and one summer as an intern at the Legislative Council (LegCo) of the HKSAR government. She used an old-style wheelchair to move around the Mass Transit Railway (MTR), a major public transport network in Hong Kong. She got in and out of elevators, crossed the street without any complaints in all kinds of weather, was never late and never left class or gatherings earlier than others. Tim-yan said she didn't want an office job and that salary was not a priority. Instead, she wants to serve society and help people in need.

Kay, who studied physics, experienced attention deficit hyperactivity disorder as a child, but since then, he has achieved excellent academic scores and aspires to commence further academic studies. He excels in physics and mathematics, unfazed by any challenge, no matter how difficult. His major interest was reading science journals, and he picked one from a stack of publications and put it in my hand as we spoke one time. He is a rare young person for Hong Kong, an oddball, so to speak, someone interested in the more abstract theories of science.

Both Tim-yan and Kay performed well in their studies, and neither came from an affluent family. They wore a smile when they chatted with me individually, never bringing up any request for financial support. They thanked CityU and society as a whole. When pressed with the question,

"How can the University provide more support?", they both smiled and asked, "Do we have the opportunity to go on an exchange tour?"

CityU has no problems providing them with an exchange opportunity, given their academic scores and motivation.

Neither Tim-yan nor Kay are like certain big shots who grab by extortion and fight over trifles. It was a pleasure visiting their families. I have no doubt that Tim-yan will become a well-respected social worker one day and Kay will shine in the physics sector.

Po-yan and Kiki

During a visit in March 10 years ago, I got to know Po-yan Sze, who, though suffering from a terminal illness, insisted on continuing her studies at CityU. In what was in other ways a regular visit, I was deeply touched by her extraordinary tenacity in holding fast to her goal. Accompanied by her teacher, Maria Cheng, I visited her and her parents several times. The last time I saw her was in the hospital. Very weak, she read me Du Fu's poem "Going up the Gate Tower of the City of Yanzhou" 《登兖州城樓》:

> *Visiting my father in the City of Yanzhou,*
> *I ascend the South Gate Tower for a first look out.*
> *Hanging clouds connected Mount Tai and the sea,*
> *To cities of Qingzhou and Xuzhou, level land stretched.*
> *Nothing remains round the wreck of the Qin stele that stands*
> *Or the crumbled rubble of King Lu's Palace.*
> *Forever seized by melancholy for things of the past,*
> *My heart trembled with hesitation.*

Knowing that her days were numbered, I was moved to tears. The poem "Seeing Spring Off on the Last Day of the Third Moon" by the Tang dynasty poet Jia Dao (賈島) came to mind. Spring was ending in the midst of the setting sun, but I was still hoping for a miracle.

> *It is precisely the thirtieth day of the third moon,*
> *When good time parts from me who dolefully croon.*
> *Through the evening you and I shall stay up today*
> *For it is still spring ere bell tolls in the morn ray*[1]

---

[1] http://www.smallstation.net/forum.php?mod=viewthread&tid=2535

Spring ended that year, as in other years. Po-yan passed away after receiving her CityU diploma from my hands at her hospital bedside at a specially arranged graduation ceremony.

Po-yan was not a student with excellent academic scores or a successful career. Anyone bedridden with a severe illness for more than two years could only achieve mediocre scores. Her early death deprived her of an opportunity to realize her potential fully. Po-yan might not have been profoundly wise, but she was dedicated to pursuing knowledge. The University did not provide her with whole-person education, either. She did not have the full opportunity or strength to receive an education designed for the average student. I saw, though, that she had a good family education. I saw from her eyes that she accepted her circumstances with good grace even when she was experiencing excruciating pain. While she must have felt frustrated at times, she never complained, sustained by her deep sense of gratitude until she finally realized her dream.

Po-yan loved studying. She was able to achieve her goal through tireless striving. She was finally able to leave the world peacefully. She was what I would call a whole person, even though her youth tragically came to an abrupt end, just as it was lamented in one of Tao Yuanming's (陶淵明) poems, "Old Styled Verse (VII)":

> *There is no cloud in the evening sky;*
> *The vernal wind has warmed the eye.*
> *A songstress loves the tranquil night;*
> *She drinks and sings till first daylight.*
> *As night is soon replaced by morrow.*
> *How can the fair not sigh with sorrow?*
> *The moon looks brighter amid cloud;*
> *The flower among leaves seems proud.*
> *Every beauty has her day,*
> *But how soon will it pass away!*[2]

Yan Mo, the Nobel Prize Winner in Literature, once said when the majority is crying, we should allow some people not to cry. When crying becomes a performance, we should allow others not to cry. More often than not, students are our teachers. Po-yan is just one such example.

Life may not be perfect, but the will is infinite.

---

[2] https://www.istudy-china.com/old-styled-verse-vii/

On September 30, 2016, I visited Hung Mei-ki (Kiki), a Department of Translation and Linguistics freshman, and her mother at their family home. Kiki suffered from a rare muscle disease called myofibrillar myopathy.

After that first meeting, we often ran into each other on campus. Whether in the chilly winter, sweltering summer or breezy days, she was always accompanied by her mother and full of smiles. Even though she required a wheelchair and ventilatory support throughout the day, she was an active and optimistic participant in university life with many friends. She promoted an inclusive campus culture for students with special educational needs (SEN) as CityU's inclusion ambassador and found out about SEN services and SEN students at local universities in Macau on behalf of CityU.

She pursued her studies with great enthusiasm, maintaining particularly good academic standards and earning a number of scholarships each year.

The sky is clear without clouds at sunset,
The spring breeze feels warm on the face.

The 2018 scholarship established under Po-yan's name was awarded to Kiki for her academic performance.

On May 16, 2020, Kiki was admitted to the intensive care unit at Kwong Wah Hospital. Her body weakened. Unable to endure the pain anymore, she fell into a coma. I visited Kiki in the evening with a heavy heart. She had submitted her graduation thesis before being admitted to the hospital as if she knew what would happen. I again presented a Diploma of Bachelor of Arts (First-class Honours) and the Honour Cord for distinguished graduates at a hospital bedside to Kiki's mother.

A few years before, I had presented Po-yan with a graduation certificate in the late spring. Although she was bed-bound and in great pain, she read me a poem, "Going up the Gate Tower of the City of Yanzhou" (登兗州城樓) by Du Fu (杜甫). It was difficult for Po-yan to endure the hardship and keep going. But she did.

And now I saw another young role model for a whole person. The sun was setting and even if Kiki could not respond when I presented the award, her sudden rapid breathing told me she sensed me standing beside her.

Let me quote Zheng Banqiao's poem "Bamboo Stone (石竹)" to express my praise for Kiki.

Between broken rocks striking my root deep,
I bite the mountain green and will not let go,
From whichever direction the winds leap,
I remain strong, though dealt many a blow.

Moved by this story, which was published in the media, the Ng Teng Fong Charitable Foundation called me and donated for setting up a special Kiki Hung Scholarship in appreciation of her great perseverance in the face of difficulties. The scholarship would help with funding students with physical or mental challenges.

Persistent, unyielding, forward-looking and striving for excellence. I will always be proud of Po-yan and Kiki. I hope our young friends will be just as committed to learning.

Follow Basic Norms

In May 2010, a number of presidents of well-known world universities attended the Fourth Chinese Foreign University Presidents Forum in Nanjing. When they were asked about the gap between Chinese higher education and world-class universities, several replied that China was at least 20 to 30 years behind the US. The former president of Peking University, Zihong Xu, expressed that China did not have any first-class universities at that time. These comments echoed my experience with the universities across the Strait.

Based on my observations and personal experience, one of the reasons Chinese universities lag behind is the prevailing culture in Taiwan, Hong Kong and the Mainland, i.e., people like to talk about high-sounding doctrines but ignore basic norms, rules and standards that should be observed in everyday social life.

According to *Datong* (Great Harmony, or Great Community) in the chapter on *Li Yun* (Conveyance of the Rites) in *The Book of Rites* (禮記), the promotion of the Great Way relies on a commonwealth concept. Inscriptions that can be seen everywhere in Taiwan include the four virtues of loyalty, filial piety, benevolence and love; and concepts often mentioned in Hong Kong, such as whole-person education, great virtue as water, and moral education. They are all about Chinese culture.

But we see a different picture in real life. Take Mainland China, for example. We can see striking slogans everywhere, and they never fail to impress. Some are startlingly aggressive and oppressive, yet we still witness pedestrians and vehicles embroiled in all kinds of frays and collisions on the roads in Mainland China and southern Taiwan as well; and in Hong Kong, we see people push and shove while getting on and off trains, despite the ease and convenience of the transport system.

Regarding university education, while we may have the hardware and software comparable to advanced world standards, a crucial element is still missing or leaves much to be desired: soulware. By soulware, as discussed elsewhere in this book, I am referring to the kind of mindset and professionalism that I have been promoting in higher education, which is what we admire as the basic integrity of intellectuals. There are clues to be found where soulware is missing.

The Great Harmony clearly states at the beginning: "When the Great Way prevails, the world belongs to all the people; people of virtue and competence are chosen to govern the country; honesty is valued, and people live in harmony." In trying to advocate democracy, some people often overlook the need to adhere to basic human values and social ethics, forgoing our humanity and civility even before any democratic progress can be achieved. If the democracy currently implemented in Taiwan is based on individual and party affiliation, how can people who are talented, trustworthy and peacemaking be selected? Instead, those in power are dishonest and harm the public for private interests. Higher education and the mentality and behavior of young people are misled.

A university campus is a microcosm of society. Cumbersome rules and procedures and detailed policies that regulate university operations do not protect us from unruly protests, anonymous letters and angry complaints. More unwieldy and complicated rules and regulations are then drafted to deal with the discontent, resulting in an ever-expanding system that's too complex to be effective. In this respect, we seem to tilt more towards an excessive reliance on rules for determining and justifying decisions in comparison to Western society. More generally in the West, decision-making depends more on the rational judgment of authorized individuals and is therefore less mechanical and more efficient. But this could only result from having appropriate soulware.

In my student years, I often thought Americans and Europeans advocated egoistic individualism while the Chinese emphasized nationalism and communitarianism. After living and working overseas for many years, I began to realize that people across the Strait are the most individualistic of all, while Westerners do better in teamwork and cooperation. Universities in the US do not talk about whole-person education all the time. Rather, it's demonstrated more indirectly in people's daily behavior. There is no rampant patriotic indoctrination in American society, and yet Americans are full of patriotic sentiments.

Therefore, if we want to improve universities, we should stay away from meaningless doctrines and start by learning to observe basic norms and simple rules in our everyday interactions instead. In trying to advocate democracy, some people often overlook the need to adhere to basic human values and social ethics, forgoing our humanity and civility even before any democratic progress can be achieved. Tim-yan, Kay, Po-yan and Kiki are vivid examples of whole-person education.

A Warm Story of the Old Days

I encountered a situation more than 30 years ago when I was teaching at Iowa State University. After the students had taken a test, I would distribute the marked papers back to the students, explain how the questions could be solved, and write down the correct answers on the blackboard.

When class was over, a young man came to me to request some points, saying that his answer was correct, but I had deducted 10 points by mistake. I looked at his answer sheet, and it seemed that there were traces of revisions. I recalled having seen that one of the papers had been written in pencil and wondered if this could be the one. I remembered being particularly careful while grading that paper because the use of a pencil was so unusual. And there was no possibility of making a mistake. But I couldn't be 100% sure whether the young man in front of me had altered his answer sheet after seeing the answers on the blackboard.

An idea came to me. I decided not to respond to his request right away. But I did not want to embarrass him, either. So I said: "Why don't you go back and see if your current answer is correct? Come and see me tomorrow if you are sure about it." I thought if he returned to me the next day, I would give him back the ten points. But he never showed up.

Everyone has greed. It is the greatest good if one can correct one's mistakes. That young man still has a conscience.

Part III
SEPARATION OF POLITICS AND EDUCATION

When the heart has gone astray, the sickness of politics will set in.
The superior man is here to expound on the Realm of Reason:
While the East and the West diverge on learning,
Neither would claim to depart from soulware.

Since assuming the Presidency of CityU in 2008, I have established teaching and research as explicit themes for development and, in so doing, may have set the trend. A university must focus on its tasks and adhere closely to the principle of the separation of politics and education. It does not serve politics, just as politics does not dominate the university.

A university is the majestic hall of learning in search of truth. The separation of politics and education is the root of campus autonomy and academic freedom, and also a drive to promote scientific research and innovation. Government officials, politicians, the police, the news media, political and social organizations and all other external forces with associated distinguished personages from the political and commercial realms should not meddle with the workings of the university. The faculty, staff, students, parents and alumni should not use the university platform to discuss issues unrelated to learning and research or bring to campus unrelated street politics and populist movements. Academic governance is not to be confused with street politics.

In concrete terms:

1. A university does not provide outsiders with a platform for the dissemination of personal political views in the service of political and commercial interests and other goals.
2. To consolidate its status as a research and education center, a university must maintain a teaching and learning environment that upholds neutrality and academic freedom. External forces should not interfere with or influence the academic governance of a university under any excuse.

3. With mutual respect, people can express different opinions and discuss them rationally within the bounds of the law. No individual or organization should be allowed to use the name of the university to propagandize, promote and conduct political gatherings or run for public office on and off campus or on the internet. Of course, this does not mean that a university teacher or staff member cannot have his or her political stance, nor does it mean that he or she cannot participate in political movements as an individual outside the university.

The Origin

The separation of church and state refers to the decoupling of the arrogance of religious organizations and the authority of holders of state power. Separating religious authority from state governance dominates political science in Europe and the Americas. In Chinese, the term is often mistranslated to mean the "Separation of Politics and Education "(政教分離) implying the "Separation of Politics and Religion". Though this translation has generally been accepted as correct due to repeated usage for hundreds of years, it is by no means appropriate. In the original, the point is to prevent the church from interfering with the authority of the governing class and to prevent the governing class from consolidating its position by relying on the power of the church.

The entanglement between religion and the state originated from the harmful interdependence of religion, the church and the rulers during the Middle Ages in Europe. The period was marked by a great many religious wars, especially between 1096 and 1291. With the blessings of successive Popes, European crusaders conducted a series of military campaigns in the Holy Land in the Mediterranean region.

At that time, the church had the monarchy under its wings because of its overwhelming power and influence. After all, those who seek profit often band together for nefarious purposes. Gradually, the monarchy became more autocratic, with the church's blessing.

The church and the rulers were united, each using the other for their own purposes, resulting in something that can be called the "Union of Church and State" or the "Inseparation of Church and State". Subsequently, there was a lack of genuine distinction between the two, and they often became interdependent and mutually beneficial. The integration of the church and the state was common elsewhere in addition to Europe, for example, in the history of the Middle East, South America and China. Despite their differences, such integration of religion and the state stirred up huge storms.

Perhaps the university didn't exhibit any obvious social influence in the early days. Neither the church nor the monarchy interfered with university governance; therefore, whether there should be academic freedom or not was not a concern, nor was there any apprehension regarding campus autonomy. Only when a university had matured and taken shape did people begin to discover the power of knowledge. Driven by interests and power, the church and monarchy worked hand in glove to take over the governance of universities, which they saw as parasitic tools to control, in addition to controlling the spirituality of the common populace and riding roughshod over secular power.

This craving for power is the same past or present, at home or abroad. The schemes may come in different shapes, but their purpose is the same, almost always similar in appearance. So, after the vice of the integration of church and the state, religion exerted tight control over the universities, which was, in essence, the root of the "integration of religion and education". Universities fell under the spell of churches. The history of the University of Vienna in Austria is a typical example.

As time went by, political power and university governance became inextricably linked. Political hands began to get involved with and depend on the university, which led to the integration of politics and education. Despite their differences, governments, society, the young and old, and men and women see this integration as profitable. And this process is far from over until this day: Taiwan, Hong Kong and the Mainland, like brothers and sisters, not a halfpenny the worse, are now following this same path.

After the French Revolution in 1789, with the "Declaration of the Rights of Man and of the Citizen" (*Déclaration des Droits de l'Homme et du Citoyen*), the "Separation of Church and State" was pronounced as a principle of governance. Although Catholicism was once again restored as the national religion under Napoleon I, France passed a law (*loi du 9 décembre 1905 concernant la séparation des Églises et de l'État*) in 1905 affirming the concept of a secular state. The law was based on the three principles of secularism: the neutrality of the state, the freedom of religious beliefs and public authority in connection with the church.

To this day, France bans conspicuous religious symbols, including religious clothing, slogans, and promotional documents, in primary and high schools.

The US was the first country to stipulate the separation of religion and state at the constitution level. In 1791, the First Amendment of its

Constitution stated that "Congress shall make no law respecting an establishment of religion or prohibiting the free exercise thereof." In addition, the resources of the state should not be used to assist, abet or suppress religious organizations. However, religious organizations continue to influence the ruling parties in the world today, the US included. Taiwan and Hong Kong are no exceptions in this regard. For years, religion has consciously or unconsciously directed the transition of political power. On the other hand, political authority in Mainland China strictly controls religious activities. On principle, at least, it would appear that those across the Strait have not fallen into the kind of embroilment that the church and the state experienced in the Middle Ages in Europe.

While a university seeks truth and reason, politics thrives on fallacies and treachery. Truth and reason are not compatible with deceit and rhetoric. In the US where religious power and ruling power are kept apart, political, educational and research activities are clearly separated. The population of a university ranges from several thousand to several tens of thousands, including staff, faculty, students and parents. Given the size, the resources of a university are considerable. That is why to avoid politics interfering with the university's operation, political parties or individuals that pursue their own interests, including candidates running for office, are not allowed to appear on university campuses under false pretences. Staff members are not permitted to use their office computers, telephones and other facilities to engage in electioneering or other political activities. Students are not supposed to pursue political benefits as students. Those in office should not use the university as a political platform, nor should they seek to affect the university's working through political parties or students. Otherwise, they will violate the principle of the separation of politics and education.

This principle can be traced to the establishment of Humboldt University of Berlin in 1810. In 1967, the University of Chicago issued the Kalven Report, stating that universities must be politically neutral in order to uphold campus autonomy. In other words, in order to encourage and defend campus diversity, universities must rise above current political fashions, passions and pressures. The Kalven Report was by no means a legal document, but it was nevertheless upheld as the standard for higher education. In 2009, the president of the University of Chicago, Robert Zimmer, reiterated that only when universities had autonomy could academic freedom be assured.

The separation of politics and education is the bedrock for progressive universities in the US. Higher education may not be perfect, but the US is able to keep politics and education apart. The principle is applicable universally. The constitutions of many European countries have stipulated academic freedom at different levels. Other countries and regions, such as Georgia and Japan, strictly observe the same principle by including a clause on academic freedom in their constitutions.

However, Taiwan, Hong Kong and Mainland China refuse to write academic freedom into law, which seems to have violated the principle of the separation of politics and education over the years. Universities are seen as a political tool, and degrees are more to raise the status of politicians. Political figures have become idols for blind worship in Taiwan. One only needs to observe the manner and frequency with which these political figures appear on university campuses to see that the interference of politics in education and the use of education to assist politics have reached a critical degree there. The phenomenon is so well-known that there is no need to labor the point.

While politics and religion are kept apart, many people including those in the media, governments and political parties join in the common pursuit of politics as a religion. Political parties reject one another in ways that surpass religious wars in terms of intensity. The preservation of academic freedom and campus autonomy is the core value of universities and the key to success in higher education.

The mingling of politics and education poses harm to innovation and, as such, is the Achilles' heel of the internationalization of higher education.

People, Culture, University

Two historical figures associated with the University of Bologna set a precedent for universities by questioning authority and paying attention to the humanities. One of them, the Italian poet Dante Alighieri, triggered greater humanistic thinking in universities and thought circles when his epic poem *Divine Comedy* contributed to ending the darkness of feudalism and ushering in the Renaissance. The other person, Polish astronomer Nicolaus Copernicus, began a revolution in human epistemology when he challenged the geocentric view of the universe, one that the church had upheld for centuries, by establishing a mathematically based heliocentric alternative.

Western democracies hope those in power will show the way to social progress. Many are enamored with the US political system, but in copying Western democracies, they do not approach it with a proper mindset for defending the welfare of the people. Their efforts, therefore, often fail. In any case, American democracy is not entirely free of problems.

A reasonable education system has to be built with due consideration to human and cultural factors. In democratic movements in many places, as soon as people are put in power, they immediately become the driving force behind the politicization of education. Again and again, social movements have implicated and exploited universities in their grappling for interests and power. Government officials eye up the affairs of universities, hoping to gain power and benefits by getting involved. What people at the top love, the general populace will follow suit. Therefore, students, the media and even faculty and staff think of universities as a haven where they can seek personal gain. Don't blame the general populace for being unwise when people at the top lack benevolence.

Universities are not government subsidiaries and the university president's senior staff are not at the authorities' beck and call. Yet the administrations across the Strait cannot, or won't, understand these basic principles, while members of the public accept them in accordance with their general understanding of what constitutes right and wrong. Years pass and the worries and concerns persist, with teachers and students failing to question the situation and remaining confused for life. Academic freedom and university autonomy are nothing but hot air.

The key to the overall success of society hinges on a state of mind, and it is the same with the progress of a university. The flourishing of a university is like turning an arid desert into a blossoming garden. It depends on the separation of politics and education, a principle that we must learn to observe. In order to preserve a safe and free academic environment and cherish the multiplicity of ideas, we need to maintain political neutrality. No external powers or players should be allowed to encroach upon the university campus.

Unfortunately, that politics mingle with campus is becoming the norm across the Strait. For example, university campuses are often used as free platforms by political parties to promote their political views or for elections[1]. Politicians utilize populism cunningly while populism intoxicates politicians. However, the general populace is usually blind and populists are led by ignorance. As a result, the nature of higher education has shifted.

Without the separation of politics and education, it will be difficult to realize campus autonomy and academic freedom.

---

[1] *United Daily*, May 28 and June 19, 2023.

13
External Forces that Interfere with Soulware

The university originated in Europe and spread around the world to thrive in places like North America and other countries and regions where different causes and effects, to varying degrees of effectiveness, influenced the development of higher education. Culture has a direct impact on a university, and if the essence of that culture remains unchanged, the university does not change, either. And if a university does not adhere to a code of ethics, academic freedom is wasted, and the foundation of the university's operations will be shaken.

Various interest groups like to influence the operation of a university. The media, different organizations and corporations, political parties, alumni and even student organizations are always waiting for an opportunity to get involved. Of course, it is the government in power that has the greatest opportunity and desire to get its hands on universities. Even in the US today, political interference can be seen on many university campuses. Often they come from the state governments, causing confusion to faculty and academic leaders.

As reported by *The Australian* on November 19, 2021, Ian Jacobs, Vice-Chancellor (VC) of the University of New South Wales, and Michael Spence, VC of the University of Sydney, resigned because of political intervention. What is more worrying is the threat to academic freedom, which is the biggest challenge to Mainland Chinese researchers, according to Tim Pringle, editor of *The China Quarterly*, in a September 2022 interview. In this regard, with political interference commonplace in Taiwan, Hong Kong and the Mainland, the freedom these researchers enjoy is probably more than 30 or 50 years behind that of their counterparts elsewhere.

Oude Universiteit Leuven in Belgium

In 1425, Pope Martin V built the Old University of Leuven (Oude Universiteit Leuven, OUL). During the Renaissance, Belgium was ruled by Spain, Austria, France and the Netherlands. OUL was ravaged by war. During the French Revolution, the First French Republic occupied OUL. Belgium was placed under the Kingdom of the Netherlands in 1815 after the defeat of Napoléon Bonaparte, and King William I established the State University of Leuven (Rijksuniversiteit Leuven) on the old school site. In 1830, Belgium became independent. Five years later, nine Catholic cardinals restored the Université Catholique de Louvain.

Entering the 20th century, the university, which has experienced many vicissitudes of life, was severely damaged by two world wars. In 1968, the Catholic University of Leuven split into two schools, each with about 30,000 students. The Dutch-speaking campus stayed in Leuven to become KU Leuven (Katholieke Universiteit Leuven), and the French-speaking campus moved to New Leuven to become UC Louvain (Université Catholique de Louvain). I had the pleasure of talking to the presidents of both universities separately.

Obviously, over nearly 600 years of its history, KU Leuven has been exposed to the dual influence of the church and the state. "A thousand sails pass by the wrecked boat / And ten thousand saplings shoot up beyond the withered tree." (Liu Yuxi, 劉禹錫) Today, the two universities have been reborn and are full of vitality. They are among those world-class universities that uphold the principles of the "integration of teaching and research" and the "separation of politics and education", and KU Leuven is recognized as the most innovative universities in Europe. It is worth exploring their research innovations and educational innovations.

University of Vienna, Austria

The University of Vienna is one of the oldest universities in Europe and a prestigious hall of learning. Sigmund Freud, one of the world's most influential thinkers and the father of psychoanalysis, is an alumnus. According to its official history, the University of Vienna was exposed to the dual influences of the church and political leaders when the Jesuits entered the city in 1550, which represented not only the integration of the church and the state, where religion came to interfere with the politics of the ruling class, but also the integration of religion and education, where religious forces infiltrated the university campus.

The inextricable relationship between the church, the government and the university continued in Vienna until 1778 when the University eventually succeeded in removing the requirement of religion from its admission criteria. In 1848 and 1849, petitions from students brought about a revolution in Vienna. When the revolution was suppressed, the Thun-Hohenstein education reform became a point of transition in the Austrian education landscape. Henceforth, the freedom to teach and learn, which reformers had fought hard to obtain, came under protection.

Vienna was famous in Europe in the late 19th and early 20th centuries for its Jewish culture. But in the small hours of November 9 and 10 in 1938, known as the "Night of Broken Glass", Nazis and the SS attacked Jews living in Germany. The persecution quickly spread to Austria. In fact, as early as 1930, under the demagoguery of anti-Semitism, the University of Vienna had already set stricter requirements to limit the number of Jewish students admitted and shown a tendency to persecute Jewish students. In 1938, the national socialists assumed power in government, and Jews died in staggering numbers in large-scale massacres. Many Jewish students were eliminated.

The disturbances continued until 1945 when Jewish culture and society gradually returned to a state of stability in Vienna. In 1975, the University Organization Acts established strategic guidelines for democratization. Universities were finally delivered from the morass of mixing politics and education. The University of Vienna refers to its history of 650 years as Colorful History, an apt name that captures its ups and downs.

Of course, what happened to the University of Vienna could have happened to other ancient universities in Europe. For all we know, it might happen again. The history of the Humboldt University of Berlin brings to light yet another picture.

Humboldt University of Berlin

Known as the mother of Modern Universities, Humboldt University of Berlin, which I visited on June 25, 2019, is well known for its close integration of teaching and research and the 55 Nobel laureates closely associated with it. Its name, which has changed several times, was altered once more in 1949 in memory of its founders, the Humboldt Brothers. Famous for its research-oriented, Humboldt-style higher education, it is a model for the University of Tokyo in Japan and Johns Hopkins University in the US.

The university that Qian Zhongshu describes in the novel *Fortress Besieged* is based on Humboldt University, which turned out to be the birthplace of

Marxism. The following are closely connected with Humboldt University: Friedrich Engels, Arthur Schopenhauer, Georg W. F. Hegel, Albert Einstein, Max Planck, Niels Bohr, Christian Heine, Otto von Bismarck, as well as Chinese philosophers, calligraphers and painters such as Yu Dawei and Pu Xinyu.

The Humboldt Brothers upheld the belief that a university is the sum total of knowledge (*universitas litterarum*) and that teaching and research should go hand in hand. This echoes the idea of the integration of teaching and research that I proposed earlier. To the brothers, a university should explore the world of science, philosophy, and the cultivation of morality. The latter makes up the essence of a person as a member of society and, as such, concerns the overall development of character. It has nothing to do with any specialized ability or technique. A university has to withstand solitude, defend freedom and remain untouched by political, economic and social interests. That is the separation of politics and education.

In 1949, the Democratic Republic of Germany, better known as East Germany, was occupied by the Soviet Union, and East Berlin, where Humboldt University is located, was the designated capital. Having experienced the devastation of the Nazi regime and intervention under communist rule, Humboldt University started to decline. After such twists and turns, the glory of the former years is no more. Since then, it has not produced a single Nobel laureate or any scholar of note. The Berlin Wall was dismantled in 1990, and on October 3 of that year, the two Germanys became one again, with Berlin as the new capital. Humboldt University slowly returned to its original path on the east side of the former Berlin Wall. A great deal of distress was experienced over the years, but to dwell on those memories is too painful. Humboldt University must pick up its journey and tread the long road ahead.

In October 2021, Professor Sabine Kunst of Humboldt University resigned as rector shortly after my interview with her in protest at the German parliament's amendment to the Berlin Higher Education Act, with the government mandating that all university professors be granted tenure. Her resignation demonstrats the need for the separation of politics and education.

George Washington University and Washington University in St. Louis

There are some people in current Taiwan's ruling party, the Democratic Progressive Party, who seemed to think of themselves as members of the 15th-century espionage agency under the leadership of the eunuch during the Ming dynasty in China, wielding power as if the monarchy system had been restored. Take the Master's Thesis-gate Scandal in 2022 as an example. Many in power, starting from the president, consistently defended the paper in question, interfered with university governance, and confused the state with education. Although fraudulent degrees are reported from time to time, whether the accusations are confirmed or not, such a reaction from a state administration would not have happened in advanced countries. Take G. Santos, who won the U.S. House of Representatives election in 2022, as an example. *The New York Times* reported his fictional CV on December 19, 2022, including a degree from City University of New York. Republicans, including some House Members, questioned his integrity and asked him to resign from the House of Representatives.

In the video series "Beyond Boundaries: Dialogue with Presidents of World's Leading Educational Institutions", I had a dialogue with Mark S. Wrighton, President of George Washington University (GWU). Before he took over at GWU in 2019, he had been Chancellor and Chief Executive Officer at Washington University in St. Louis for 24 years. Both universities have achieved remarkable success under the leadership of Wrighton, who can be considered a living dictionary for American higher education.

Both universities are named after George Washington. Washington University, located in the Midwest town of St. Louis, is one of the top 20 universities in the US and is one of the "Hidden Ivies". Twenty-five of its alumni and faculty have been awarded a Nobel Prize. Its main founder and president, William G. Eliot, graduated from Columbia College, the predecessor to GWU.

GWU is located in the heart of Washington, D.C., the capital of the United States, adjacent to the US Department of State and the Ministry of Finance and only a few blocks from the White House and Capitol Hill. It has cultivated many top professionals in politics, diplomacy and law for the US and the world. Notable alumni include former US Secretaries of State John F. Dulles and Colin Powell, 28 governors, 128 members of the Senate and House of Representatives, as well as political leaders in many countries.

GWU attracts teaching and research elites and cooperates with many US government departments and international institutions in studying international affairs and policies. These political figures may exert a huge influence but never interfere with the university's governance. Otherwise, it would be a scandal. Bob Woodward, one of the two journalists from *The Washington Post* who broke the Watergate scandal in the 1970s (and the newspaper that popularized the slogan "Democracy Dies in Darkness"), studied Shakespeare and international relations at GWU.

The institution can be considered a living dictionary for the separation of politics and education. It is worth it for Taiwan to reference and model itself on it to avoid evolving into a dark democracy.

First-rate Higher Education

What is first-rate higher education? What is a first-rate university?

There are many merits in the governance and operation of US universities, which are the best in the world. As mentioned in Chapter 1, American higher education—with an academic atmosphere free from political interference, equal emphasis on teaching and research, integration of academia and enterprises, diversity, meritocracy, accountability at all levels, peer evaluation, professors in charge of academic affairs (not administrative affairs), among others—has been a role model for academically advanced universities around the world that have indirectly driven economic growth and social prosperity, and significantly contributed to science and technology in the 21st century.

Altogether 636 people won the Nobel Prize in Physics, Chemistry, and Physiology (or Medicine) from 1901, when Nobel prizes were first awarded, to 2022. Of that number, 310 awardees, or 49%, worked at US institutions of higher learning. If we narrow the focus to the last 24 years, the number of American scholars winning the Nobel Prize is 104, or 55% of the 190 awardees. The US performance stands out from the rest of the world. Perhaps you are not aware that those 310 awardees were scattered at more than 60 universities all over the US, not just a few elite universities that people across the Strait aspire to enter. Such a phenomenon indicates the excellence of America's higher education system. Any of top 100 public and private universities in the US (not in the world) could win a Nobel Prize. The breadth and depth of excellence of American higher education far surpass other countries and areas.

The recognition of a Nobel Prize in disciplines such as physics, chemistry, biology or medicine represents an objective scientific and technological accomplishment, behind which must lie some indicators of a first-rate university. In other words, a top university must have first-rate academic disciplines, teaching staff and facilities, and abundant financial resources. In addition to the necessary hardware and software, a first-rate university must be equipped with an appropriate educational ideal, an excellent management mechanism, and an open and free campus culture and academic environment. In short, first-rate soulware and the integration of teaching and research are required.

A university must possess a variety of resources and use them well before it can be ranked among the most advanced institutions. In general, universities across the Strait are well-equipped in terms of campus buildings and research facilities. They are trying hard to catch up with the world's most forward-thinking institutions regarding faculty, materials and curriculum design. But in terms of the right mindset or soulware, there is plenty of room for improvement.

Soulware is an ideal that places a high premium on the profession of teaching and research, academic quality and social benefits. It refers to the fundamental principle that all who are associated with education—faculty, administrators, students, committee members who affect the decisions of a university or even members of the society—have to submit to. It is explicitly stated or implied in the mission of the university, its teaching philosophy and the direction of its research.

Compared with their first-rate counterparts, universities on both sides of the Strait lag behind in soulware, which is partly the responsibility of society. The Chinese community attaches great importance to education, which is a merit, but the public must shoulder the difference due to low tuition fees and exorbitant higher education investment. If the return brought by education is not commensurate with society's investment, the effectiveness of universities will be compromised. This is a result of the lack of emphasis on accountability, quality, productivity and merit, all of which are the essential features of soulware.

Where does the soulware of our universities lag behind first-rate universities? The history of Oude Universiteit Leuven in Belgium, the University of Vienna in Austria and Humboldt University in Germany provides many clues. How can we shorten the distance between them and us? President Michael M. Crow of Arizona State University lists three vital factors that American universities require if they wish to be outstanding. As they may serve as a footnote to the soulware that I advocate, I will introduce them here:

1. Campus Autonomy
   Since American state universities receive part of their funding from state governments, it would seem they would have to bow to the political authorities because they are on the supplicant's end of the deal. In reality, however, for the most part, America's higher education system takes pains to keep university governance separate from political pressure. Once funding is decided, the state government respects campus autonomy, leaving the universities to decide on academic

matters and governance issues. These include decisions on staffing structure, hiring, remuneration, promotion and retention, as well as overall academic development. The university that enjoys autonomy will not report to any organization or individual other than its independent board. Politicians, government officials, legislators and the media are kept outside the gate and are prevented from interfering with operations. Students are also not allowed to participate in school administrative affairs without authorization.

However, the governments across the Strait are ensnared in a web of intricacy, and their support for university teaching and research is not necessarily generous. Government officials lord over universities and non-specialist bystanders, with their uninformed criticisms, have a tendency to interfere. Their dabbling in university governance through phone calls, emails and campus visits is commonly seen.

2. Free Competition

    Campus autonomy gives rise to another kind of education ecosystem: competition. Evidence shows that competition allows American universities to excel, although the competition has to be courteous. It is good that US universities can compete strongly to recruit professors and students and attract research funding and private donations without government meddling. In the last 50 years, the performance of US universities and their departments has been tightly connected to investment, university leadership and faculty recruitment, among others. By comparison, universities across the Strait are so obsessed with issues such as what areas to research that they lose sight of the bigger picture and their overall plans begin to drift. On their part, governments know only to follow precedent while the general public has already decided that funding ought to be allocated in accordance with old established rules. Thus, free competition fails to attract the attention it deserves, and governments generally regard it as a thorn in the flesh.

3. Market Mechanism

    To enhance competitiveness, progressive universities use the market mechanism to recruit the best talent globally in order to raise academic standards and build their brand. However, the structures of universities across the Strait are still largely discipline-based, and there is a definite inclination to overemphasize numbers. Funding from the government is also subjectively determined by quantity, which severely restricts innovation. While universities in North America recruit scholars and students from all over the world, governments across the Strait decide on the number of admitted students for each discipline based on estimates of labor demands. When the student numbers are not determined by market forces, the result for education is not necessarily accurate. No wonder such a gap exists between projection and reality.

The higher education sectors across the Strait possess their own strengths and weaknesses. Compared with that in the US, there is an entanglement of interests and deficiency in soulware. "Controlling the university" is increasingly common in approaches to higher education.

Teachers' Union

The three governance factors for American universities identified by Mike Crow of Arizona State University very often hit a brick wall in Taiwan, Hong Kong and the Mainland.

As an example, trade unions have their own values. At one point, the law protected trade unions in Hong Kong, and their actions were unrestricted, giving them greater freedom and influence than their counterparts in the West. In fact, Hong Kong universities offer faculty members considerable free rein; they enjoy much greater academic freedom than trade unions traditionally enjoy on behalf of the humble workers. In addition to academic freedom, university personnel in Hong Kong are further protected by teachers' unions, which are supported by law. These unions are often managed by staff members and teachers who are not academically promotable. Many teachers' unions consider themselves to be the opposition party to the administration. Taking advantage of the free academic environment in the universities, they build connections and play street politics on campus, directing protests and even running for elections. They have their fingers in every pie, spoiling academic freedom but failing to gain the welfare that staff members are due.

In August 2021, the 48-year-old Hong Kong Professional Teachers' Union was dissolved because of political reasons. Paradoxically, the union grew out of a failure in Hong Kong to separate politics from education, and yet it was terminated by a failure to separate politics from education.

Though universities across the Strait have individual working conditions different from those in the US, the phenomenon of a teachers' union veering from its proper role has never occurred in American universities. Even though teachers' unions exist in a few American universities, they work for improved pay and benefits for members, keep politics at arm's length, and sidestep academic affairs. Union leaders in US universities don't use their groups for their own political ends. In fact, teachers' unions seem at odds with the academic atmosphere of a university campus.

There is a Taiwan Higher Education Union, but the extraordinary phenomenon seen in teachers' unions in Hong Kong has never appeared in Taiwan universities. Some unions for graduate students at Taiwan's universities sometimes find themselves at loggerheads with universities on salary and work hours, occasionally led by political parties for political gains.

Social Factors for Disparities in Higher Education

While it is relatively easy to assess a university's academic accomplishments as well as how innovative its teaching and research staff may be, it is more difficult to educate students to become independent, forward-thinking pillars of society. When nurturing students, a university should not set its sights only on the first job their graduates successfully apply for; they have to prepare their students for the second and third jobs. A progressive university should consider how to transform today's students into the mainstay of society twenty or thirty years later. For that reason, a university should train students in interpersonal communication skills, especially for working with people from different backgrounds.

It is the same with the recruitment of teaching staff. When appointing a teacher, a university should consider not only the applicants' current performance but also assess their future potential for promotion to associate professor and then full professor within a designated period of time and whether by the time those candidates reach 40 or 50 years old, they will have established a name for themselves in their area of expertise. This way of thinking corresponds to the Confucian observation that if people have not made their name by the age of 40 or 50, they are never going to be noteworthy, an evaluation that's not only helpful to the development of a university but also to the individuals involved in urging a job applicant to self-reflect lest that person falls into the wrong line of work from the outset and be plagued with regret later in life.

Many highly accomplished Chinese scholars concentrate on their teaching and research, realize their talents and make striking contributions in the West without any distractions. Obviously, universities across the Strait still need to strive hard to provide that same kind of environment to nurture excellent talent, pioneer new fields of knowledge, and be proud of groundbreaking results.

Compared with the situation in North America, many traditional cultural practices and entrenched malpractices across the Strait are responsible for the failure of local talent to live up to their full potential. The obstruction originates mainly from the following social issues, which have existed in communities across the Strait for a long time and which are what I call the absence of soulware:

1. Entanglement of industry, government and university
   Professors teaching in universities across the Strait take up concurrently key positions in government and industry, and officials enjoy working in education and industry as well. In addition to their employment in academia, they acquire a sense of superiority for their triphibian involvement. They fail to recognize that industry, government and university are three distinct spheres. As each has its own professional expertise, it requires a person full of commitment to become accomplished in any of them. At the same time, it creates conflicts of interest that are often difficult to resolve. Rather, in the boundless ocean of learning, professors should focus their hearts and minds on teaching and research, and with the exception of innovation and community service, they should leave all other matters to others.

   Universities emphasize collaboration in industry, academia, and research, but under clearly stated procedures, professors should stay away from entangling themselves with concurrent appointments even when they work to bring together these three areas. For those who are involved in all three domains, being discreet and diplomatic might serve them well in politics and industry, but the same attributes may not be congenial to academic work. It is understandable if only a few people have simultaneous appointments in all three domains by force of circumstances, but this should not be the aspiration for those not interested in teaching. Otherwise, all they have is a fanciful dream in which nothing can get accomplished.

2. Failure to understand the contemporary mission for a university
   Many people don't understand what higher education is, and they don't know that they don't know this, which is a serious problem.

   A position at a university is often mistakenly viewed as a lucrative sinecure with a bunch of attractive benefits. Traditionally, someone who was good at academic study would see a career of officialism as their next step. Such thinking has its own historical reason, but it continues to haunt us like a ghost that refuses to be exorcised. I'm often taken aback whenever I hear university students expressing a wish to follow in the footstep of ancient intellectuals, planning to use their academic degrees as a steppingstone to officialdom. Apparently, besides the widespread phenomenon of fawning over people with a glib tongue, retrogressive bureaucratic thinking is still deeply entrenched in the soul of these people.

   When people tell me that they want to work at a university, I ask why. They answer that the salary is high and the benefits are generous. They think of the university as a place where they can enjoy an easy-going life. We would have to review the situation if individual staff members give society the impression that they are lazy, especially when universities are a platform for conscientious people to innovate and create new knowledge, where they face demands for an even higher level of professionalism than in the past. University faculty should update their knowledge through research due to the free flow of information and the popularization of a university education these days. Students are no longer members of the elites. Increasing globalization means that universities face intense competition. If they don't strive for excellence, they are likely to fall.

   Societies across the Strait don't quite understand that universities carry a weighty responsibility but are fond of expressing their opinions on academic matters. Society should respect the professionalism of universities and their mission today. As Confucius puts it, "To claim you know something when you know it and to admit to your ignorance when you do not – this is knowledge."
3. Misplaced mindset by the government
   Government officials keep tight control over universities, fearing insubordination. The general public places high hope on the academic degree; so sometimes the government

believes that controlling the university will indirectly mean controlling the granting of degrees and, in turn, the students. In this way, controlling the universities becomes the way and the direction of exercising their power. This is drastically different from what goes on in the US, and the clean and refreshing ambiance conducive to academic research one finds there. In Taiwan, Hong Kong and the Mainland, falling in line with the government is more important than being innovative. This is why, no matter what, rules have to be set down for universities to follow.

Hong Kong follows the UK system of assessing the performance of universities. Every six years, the UGC conducts the Research Assessment Exercise (RAE), inviting external reviewers to assess the standard of research publications. When these research publications have already been reviewed by specialists in the field before publication, why do the same publications have to be assessed later by external reviewers who may not even work in the same fields, especially when government funding is determined by the outcome? It is simply a waste of human and material resources. What marginal utility does it have? Similar instances can easily be found in the Mainland and Taiwan, termed "Third-world inferiority syndrome".

Judged by fair and unsolicited competition results, ranking research output from different universities in Hong Kong is sometimes hard. Quite often, universities with relatively low government support perform better. That is why the consistently lop-sided funding strategy of the government goes against the pursuit of excellence, thereby weakening the overall academic performance that might have come from free competition. This situation is indirectly reflected in how students decide on their specialty. In picking what they will study, they look for guidance to the ranking, a subjective criterion at best. The result is that the educational resources are not put in areas where they can live up to their effectiveness.

Respect Creativity

What to do with creativity, then? In American universities where there is mutual respect between people for professionalism, innovative ideas are openly discussed, but across the Strait, people may not appreciate creativity. Many are happy to be No. 2, letting others be the first to take the risk while waiting to see if there's any room for opportunistic manipulations before taking action. Yet, while many communities across the Strait lack creativity, they copy other people's ideas well. For example, if there's a successful beef noodle restaurant or mobile phone shop, dozens of other noodle restaurants and mobile phone shops will quickly sprout across the street.

Talk about ideas? Why bother? Is the time ever right to talk about ideas? Is it due to a deep-rooted flaw in the traditional Chinese mindset that people don't respect other people's ideas, seemingly only interested in undercutting others? They are only interested in stealing the fruit of labor from other people or waiting for the moment to use every possible means to gain privileged information about other people's innovative projects, which they then manipulate to create copycat products. To them, creativity, initially a practice of educational theory, is like a special meat recipe to be duplicated for profiteering in their own chain of BBQ meat stores.

A case in point is the obstructions encountered by CityU's innovative proposal to establish an internationally accredited school of veterinary medicine in collaboration with Cornell University. When the plan was announced in 2008, CityU faced many hurdles and excuses to stop the approval process. Some even used information from unknown sources to duplicate CityU's idea and were bold enough to use privileged information to set up a copycat program at a different university and lobbied Cornell to change the working partner. Some of them were legislators as well as government officials, and even from special media groups. Come to think of it, this could not have been the first incident of its kind. Given such a lack of respect for other people's creative ideas, it is clearly hard for innovation to take root.

It is not enough for an advanced university just to recruit outstanding faculty and bring cutting-edge teaching and research onto campus. Universities won't be able to realize their full potential and benefit society if unhealthy habits and traditional mindsets remain strong and the speed for change is too slow. Each profession has its own rules and conventions. Higher education is a broad but professional subject facing many issues. In addition to freedom from government interference and media disruption, and support of society, all parties concerned need to uphold the code of conduct, strive hard to fulfill their professional duties and do the utmost to maintain academic integrity while at the same time staying away from social and governmental factors that impede creativity.

Where Dao is, so is the Teacher

Academic freedom, campus autonomy and the separation of politics and education are the three components of an ideal higher education. However, in practice, these ideals do not turn out as expected.

In the famous essay "On Teaching (師說)", Han Yue of the Tang dynasty wrote, "Where Dao (the Way) is, so is the teacher." If one abandons the Way, one may be high up in the official world, but his empty rhetoric will only confound the public. It takes us farther and farther away from the wisdom of the ancients, and the internationalization of education will become an unreachable goal. It is not advisable to be obsessed with the minutiae of operations but overlook the bigger principle. In internationalizing education, people seem to be overly concerned with trivial details. Conversely, they want to settle with quick solutions and their own biases, disregarding the harm that the entanglement of politics and education will bring to academic freedom and campus autonomy. These long-standing malpractices have their historical causes and are not peculiar to any social sector or individual.

In an open society, people may easily get into a disagreement over political and economic issues and hold on stubbornly to their views, brooking no compromises. Universities can easily become the bone of contention or be used as a platform where people with different political and economic views can strike out at one another. The separation of politics and education should be respected on both sides.

Outsiders should not meddle with universities' activities; in turn, universities should stay away from street politics. The staff and students of a university should not make use of public resources for their own ends, hijacking the campus and using it as a free site for the propagation of their own political views. Universities are never known for their political and public relations acumen. At times of unrest, it is inadvisable for them to be involved in street politics or public relations games. Yet, these are precisely the traps that ensnare higher education across the Strait. That the universities have frequently fallen into them indicates that higher education has a lot to learn.

Keeping politics and education within their own domains is an issue that has to be confronted. Anyone can contribute to society and be recognized when becoming a specialist. We should allow specialists to take care of academic affairs; outsiders do not need to encroach upon their territory. People who know nothing about academic affairs often confuse them with power and mistake the courteousness that people show them for the respect that is their due. Marching under the banner of the righteousness of their own making, they bring pressure to bear on the universities through the media. The best thing for them is to find another line of work and leave higher education alone.

The cornerstone of creativity and innovation is an unbiased mind that can see things as they are. The clear-eyed readers will see that compared with the advanced higher education in the US, various entities in the education system on both shores of the Strait stand in awkward opposition to one another, like bickering children. They remind us of the proverbial turtle who makes fun of the horseshoe crab for lacking a tail; they present quite a ludicrous spectacle.

A university has an obligation to set an example. In the face of difficulties, it should not go adrift with the trend but maintain a positive mindset and adjust its pace. Society has to respect the professionalism of higher education and refrain from bandying empty words. The government should do the same. Teachers should take the lead to show their students not to engage in vacuous rhetoric. In order to foster a free, safe and creative academic environment, we have to cherish a diversity of cultures, advocate individual freedom and refrain from interfering with the academic freedom of others. Only then can the fermentation of irritable and dissatisfied emotions be halted, and the social differentiation caused by chaos be avoided. Otherwise, other disagreements and conflicts will arise.

It takes wisdom and perseverance to preserve the political neutrality of university campuses. If the Kalven Report can be taken as a benchmark of soulware, then the three societies across the Strait have fallen behind the US by half a century.

Ingesting without Digesting

People across the Strait have always had high regard for learned and talented individuals, who, for their part, are proud of the breadth of their knowledge. They are avaricious in knowing more but do not bother to seek deep understanding. Neither do they know the importance of verifying the things they hear about. To them, the whole purpose of studying is to advance in the official world. Conversations with *My Guests in The Western Chamber* (西軒客談), a book written in the Ming dynasty about reading and writing, uses food as a metaphor for knowledge. Gourmands might binge, ingesting huge amounts of food and drink, but in the end, what is consumed has to be digested before the nutrients can be absorbed to nurture the body and sustain strength. Otherwise, everything is in vain. Food becomes tasteless and, in the end, harmful.

As for ordinary people, their academic credentials may not mean anything, even if they have read extensively. Like a culinary expert who ingests food without digesting it, they may not know much about the many volumes of books that they have crammed into their brains. Other people may not understand them for all their learning, and they become a burden far from getting any benefit. In fact, the more books they read, the greater the likelihood that their careers may be harmed and flounder.

Hong Kong is a gourmet paradise. Nutritious food benefits the body and tastes as delicious as the presentation. To wolf down a meal like a ravenous beast is a travesty. Even snacks sold on the street, *wonton* or *char siu*, have to be prepared with special care before they get any recognition. Otherwise, there will be no market for them. If we care at all about the substance and value of a university degree, we should realize that more is not necessarily better. Knowledge, like food, is not to be gulped down. Why, then, do we reproduce other people's ideas in higher education without really understanding them?

Hong Kong universities have changed to a four-year curriculum. It is time that we thought independently, shaking off the outdated mindset and re-orient our higher education towards effectiveness. We should consider why we want to stick to the very rules and regulations that even the British abandoned. For Taiwan and the Mainland, isn't it time to relax our political grip over universities, keep in mind the goal of benefiting society and return higher education to the hands of specialists and let them decide the direction of research and university affairs?

If we can allow people the freedom to choose which restaurant to eat at, why is there a need for politics to guide the direction of universities? Why do we allow street politics to influence universities, and why are public officials permitted to dictate over university presidents? The advanced higher education in the US deserves to be reflected upon by Taiwan, Hong Kong and the Mainland. We should minimize our interference in people's natural needs. The same is applicable to higher education.

Academic and higher education must be independent of external forces. Think no evil. This sums it up all:

> *Dipping simultaneously into industry, politics and academia,*
> *A scholar gets fat while the country gets thin.*
> *A thin scholar can be fattened still*
> *But there is no cure for an emaciated country.*

14
Stains in Academic Freedom and Campus Autonomy

As the seedbed for the quest of truth, knowledge creation and innovation, academic freedom provides the opportunity for professors and students to engage in academic exploration and ensure that external forces will not interfere with their studies, teaching and research. It encourages them to express their academic views and publish their research. In the words of Albert Einstein, academic freedom is the right to publish and transmit knowledge and truth. The concept is clear and is recognized universally. Academic freedom is the first element of the separation of politics and education.

Knowledge transmission, creativity and innovation are critical to human well-being and the progress of a civilized society. We can only extend our knowledge through freedom and flourishing schools of thought. As Thomas Paine wrote, "It is error only, and not the truth, that shrinks from inquiry," words that recall the idea of *gezhi* promoted by Zhu Xi. Restricting academic freedom not only suppresses the dissemination of knowledge but also stifles reasonable judgment and action.

The modern concept of academic freedom comprises three layers. First, academic freedom refers to freedom from political interference in the curriculum and academic affairs under the leadership of an academic institution. For example, a university decides its academic topic, hires its teaching staff, formulates admission criteria and graduation requirements for undergraduates and postgraduates, and determines its academic mission and operational priorities. Second, it refers to academics' freedom from retaliation related to their choice of research and teaching but excludes blanket protection against views they express under every possible viewpoint. The third refers to the freedom of academic inquiry. Inquiries unrelated to academic matters are not subject to the guarantee of freedom. In recent years, academic discussions have been required to adhere to codes of ethics. In other words, academic freedom does not mean unlimited freedom.

The Definition of Academic Freedom

The American Association of University Professors' view on academic freedom is that academics "should be careful not to introduce into their teaching controversial matter which has no relation to their subject." The prerequisite of the pursuit of academic freedom is that the matter under discussion is academic and that the discussion itself is academic in nature and procedure. In the absence of academic elements, or should the matter at hand be unrelated to academic inquiry, invoking the name of academic freedom is inappropriate. Regardless of one's political stance, one should refrain from meddling with university teaching, research and governance. To pursue extra-academic interests under the guise of academic inquiry is to stray from academic freedom. Any misuse of academic freedom is inadvisable and should not be encouraged.

The responsibility to defend academic freedom transcends national boundaries, especially in an era when international collaboration is growing steadily. Academic circles have shown their determination to defend this freedom and have taken measures to prevent infringements. According to a report on October 30, 2018 in the UK's *Financial Times*, out of concern for the integrity of academic freedom, Cornell University's School of Industrial and Labor Relations terminated two of its academic exchange programs with Renmin University of China. This may be the first but by no means the only case of suspending international collaborations between universities in recent years. According to a November 5, 2018 report in the *South China Morning Post*, out of concern for the infringement of intellectual property, the medical school at Johns Hopkins University temporarily decided not to admit overseas scholars. It is widely reported that many leading universities in the West have suspended the Confucius' Institute for reasons of alleged interference in academic freedom.

Very often, academic freedom is used as an excuse for the most abusive behavior, such as shouting at colleagues, publicly berating students or staff members, maligning supervisors or other university administrators, and shirking professional duties. I know of colleagues and students who believe that academic freedom allows them to say anything to anyone in any situation. One colleague told me that even if she indulged in slander and character assassination, as long as she believed she was telling the truth, she would be fully protected by academic freedom. Needless to say, such behavior is inappropriate in any work setting. A flawed personal view should not be taken as an excuse for breaking a rule.

In February 2018, the National Association of Scholars, a non-profit politically conservative advocacy association in the US, published a reference document on the history of academic freedom. According to the

Association, "Freedom-loving Americans, liberals and conservatives alike have begun to work to formulate new doctrines of academic freedom, so as to fend off these new threats" as imposed by "rioting students and illiberal ideologues" on American campuses.

Those very words from the National Association of Scholars can be written equally about the rebellious slogans during the 2019 unrest in Hong Kong and the unruly behavior of the rioters who disrupted order in the name of academic freedom. The mentality that the world comprises only friends and foes poisons academic freedom. Unfortunately, mistakes can happen at any time. On the other hand, academic freedom restricts the authority of those in power and discourages them from imposing a particular position or viewpoint on universities and prevents governments or external interest groups from using educational institutions for propaganda purposes.

Boats may float on water, but they can also capsize. On the one hand, academic freedom is restricted; on the other, it is abused. People can exploit any incident as an excuse to make disgraceful demands.

Academic Ethics

Academic ethics refers to the norms and moral codes that must be observed when conducting research and engaging in academic activities. Issues pertaining to academic ethics have received the attention of higher education. Every now and then, it transpires that, under the banner of academic freedom, professors fabricate their research data, PhD students claim authorship of papers that they purchase, and under-the-table tansactions in the selection of university presidents are secretly exchanged.

The voting rules for selecting the president of Academia Sinica in Taiwan in 2016 were abruptly changed following an alleged setup. Many members were disappointed, while suspicions of a "black box" operation circulated in the media courtesy of certain political operatives. Often, when this kind of suspected misconduct is challenged, efforts are directed toward whitewashing any potential scandal rather than ensuring that any possible fraudulent behavior never happens again. A similar scandal broke out in 2018 when members of the ruling Democratic Progressive Party were again allegedly involved in jeopardizing the selection of the president of National Taiwan University.[1]

---

[1] See *The Backbone of the University: A Story of Defending University Autonomy*, in Chinese by Tu Yang and Chung-Ming Kuan, China Times Publishing, Taipei, 2023.

Immanuel Kant believed that humans regulate their behaviors according to goodwill and apply the categorical imperative of moral law to fulfill their duties, by which humans are treated as an end, not as a means. Any action that is based on utilitarian or hedonistic considerations lacks moral meaning.

One case I remember to this day involves David Baltimore, a molecular biologist, Nobel laureate, and President of Rockefeller University. In 1991, just 18 months after he became president, he resigned from his position for defending a female colleague who co-authored an article with him. She was later cleared of the charge of research fraud while Baltimore did not once come under any suspicion of research misconduct.

Another high-profile case occurred in Japan in 2014 when Haruko Obokata, a Japanese postdoctoral researcher at Japan Laboratory for Cellular Reprogramming at the RIKEN Center for Developmental Biology, was accused of fraud. She claimed to have developed a radical and remarkably easy way to create a stimulus-triggered acquisition of pluripotency cells that could be grown into tissue for use anywhere in the body. Obokata and her coauthors were charged with research misconduct. Yoshiki Sasai, one of her mentors and coauthors, was Japan's foremost developmental biologist. He took his life, and she disappeared from public view for more than a year.

Western morality is committed to seeking truth and conclusions, while Chinese morality is largely grounded in the moral theory of shame and the innate goodness of the heart. As observed, this is why in the West and even in Japan and South Korea, if someone is discovered to be involved in academic misconduct, he or she apologizes or steps down right away, which at least shows that they are courageous enough to admit to their shameful wrongdoing. This is what I refer to as soulware, as explicated by Mencius more than 2,300 years ago. In the Jin Xin chapter of the *Book of Mencius*, it is stated that "The superior man has three things in which he delights, and to be ruler over the kingdom is not one of them. That his father and mother are both alive, and that the condition of his brothers affords no cause for anxiety; —this is one delight. That, when looking up, he has no occasion for shame before Heaven, and, below, he has no occasion to blush before men; —this is a second delight. That he can get from his kingdom the most talented individuals and teach and nourish them; —that is the third delight."[2]

Who among us in Taiwan, Hong Kong and the Mainland can claim that "when looking up, he has no occasion for shame before Heaven, and,

---

[2] James Legge, *The Works of Mencius* (1960) pdf version, pp. 458–459 https://starling.rinet.ru/Texts/Students/Legge,%20James/The%20Works%20of%20Mencius%20(1960).pdf

below, he has no occasion to blush before men"? If, as teachers, we lack self-reflection, how can we demand that our students abide by what is right?

Even though societies across the Strait have adopted many aspects of Western culture into their way of life, many so-called scholars still lack the spirit of truth to guide them in their ethical conduct. They cannot and dare not ask, "why must we use the word 'profit' since the counsel likewise given could be counsel to benevolence and righteousness" because they often fail to meet the basic Chinese standard of putting righteousness before profit. They like to resort to procedural justice, as if it is the totality of morality, while it is, in fact, considered to be the lowest common denominator in contemporary ethics, although they also have difficulty in living up to this minimum ethical requirement (by Kong-Kuo Huang).

Laundering master's degrees in the political circle in Taiwan is a growing trend. Professors fail in their gatekeeping duties, and students plagiarize and cheat. Most people admit their wrongdoing and step down if their falsified qualifications are revealed, but politicians cling to their posts by igniting populism. These actions violate academic ethics and the basic principles of honesty, a far cry from the moral standards generally observed in Western and Japanese societies. A court case in Taiwan in 2022 caused an uproar. A large number of plagiarism suspects and whistleblowers came forward. With great fanfare, some even held public hearings on "dissertation protocols". In the case of university autonomy, there is hardly any need for the government to step forward or for political parties to act, smearing each other online and then bleaching the situation offline. In ancient China's chaotic Spring and Autumn period, people fought against lies, fallacies and dirty wars. In the current situation, cheating happens in political circles, and a similar trend is observed in academia. The hot entanglement of politics and education adds bad debt to the chaos of academic degrees.

The mindset of upholding academic morality does not come easy. Those in power in society are always ready to abandon reason. Yet they set themselves up as behavior models for the younger generation. As a result, their crooked ways only lead to more transgressions down the line. In everything they do, they are guided by political considerations and self-interest. Democracy gets twisted to become populism. There is no god or shame in the mind of the people, and nobody in academia bothers to talk about academic ethics. The result is that many people in academia despise morality and ethics. It is, therefore, not at all difficult to understand why no one ever bothers to point out improper behavior when they see it.

A Chinese idiom says, "when an orange (*ju*) tree grown south of the Huai River is transplanted north, it grows into something else (*zhi*)". Unfortunately, the same can be said of an apparently ideal plan introduced to places across the Taiwan Strait. The plan changes shape like a Transformer, i.e., a human-like robot. As a result, fake degrees with no soul or content are rife, a situation that is hard to bear. What is particularly exasperating is when politicians sign up for on-the-job master's programs that serve only to whitewash their academic attainment. I raised this issue a few years ago, but no one noticed or cared. In recent years, news about fake academic attainment and plagiarized theses is often on the front pages alongside major Taiwan news stories, to the bewilderment of readers. But we should not be surprised at all: This situation is created by traditional Chinese culture and the blindness of the soul.

What's strange is that politicians seem almost compelled to lie to unprecedented levels, a phenomenon that is now trending to become the norm. To ensure the populace has faith in its rulers, all politicians running for public office, from the president down to parliamentarians, should take a polygraph test, with no pre-test tutoring. Only those who pass possess the basic qualification. This is the only way we can maintain healthy soulware and ban opportunists who lie repeatedly.

Other Examples of Violations of Academic Ethics

Madame Roland famously said, "Oh Liberty! Liberty! What crimes are committed in your name!" There are also common examples of abusing academic freedom and seeking quick success.

In 1998, Andrew Wakefield and 11 other scholars published an article in *The Lancet* claiming a link between the MMR (measles, mumps and rubella) vaccines and autism. Even though this matter was eventually deemed a carefully crafted piece of fraud, after multi-party reviews for over a decade, the damage was done. Rumors spread, and the MMR vaccination rate dropped, followed by a rise in the number of reported cases of measles in the US.

Infamous scandals include stem cell research at Seoul National University, the fabrication and falsification of research data by a professor at MIT, the fabrication of research results by professors at the University of Tokyo, the fraudulent computer chips of digital signal processing produced by a professor at Shanghai Jiao Tong University, the mixing of data in the development of a new drug at the Institute of Biological Chemistry at Taiwan's Academia Sinica, and the plagiarism of multiple papers supervised by a single professor at NTU and others. Similar ethics violations have occurred at Harvard and Rockefeller University over the years.

There is, moreover, a kind of publication mania in the academic world today. Submitting the same article to different journals and colluding among peers to engage in mutual citations are common phenomena. Some have even tried to fake publications using computer simulations or rigging the list of coauthors without seeking the proper consent. Such unhealthy behavior resulting from the blind pursuit of numbers in academic publications, though not uncommon worldwide, is particularly prevalent in India, Taiwan and Mainland China. Every now and then, we hear about cases where in the name of academic freedom, many scholars forge data, plagiarize and infringe upon the works of others. International academic journals or national research grant-giving agencies blacklist some.

Different from the cases of fraudulence mentioned above, recent violations have touched on areas such as genome editing and gene modification using the CRISPR/Cas9 system, a highly controversial area that has caused great concern among bioscientists in recent years. In 2015, the technique attracted the attention of many biologists. Some believe that ethical considerations should not stand in the way of scientific inquiry. Such a cavalier dismissal of academic ethics may exist in the eyes of scientists whose work involves experiments with the human body. Their skewed value system has given rise to many controversies.

Campus Autonomy

Campus autonomy is the second essential element of the principle of the separation of politics and education. Like medicine, finance, architecture and other professions, university governance has its own culture and unique organizational structure: Professors take care of academic matters and administrative issues are left to academic executives such as college deans and departmental heads.

As universities have to be concerned with issues such as funding, engagement with stakeholders in society, the recruitment of students and so forth, it is unrealistic to expect complete campus autonomy. In fact, no university with complete campus autonomy exists in reality. For example, during economic downturns, universities must seek ways to compensate for the lack of sufficient funding, allowing government, legislative bodies and private foundations to influence their operations and academic direction. In terms of organizational structure, a university may be governed by an independent board or council (Hong Kong), or the Ministry of Education (Taiwan), or a political party (Mainland China). They are responsible for planning the overall development direction of government-funded universities. No more, no less. Universities in some countries are entirely autonomous, with some having no supervisory government bodies. Such an ideal system is unimaginable in societies across the Strait, nor can it be achieved under the current circumstances.

There is yet another obstacle in the way of campus autonomy. Government officials and the general public often like telling universities what they perceive to be the focus of teaching and research. Like the taxi drivers mentioned in Chapter 3, they freely offer their opinions, prefacing and concluding their remarks with the disingenuous proclamation that they respect institutional autonomy or are completely open-minded regarding university matters. When repeated over and over again, they make their listeners feel uneasy, wondering about the subtext.

Half a century ago, when people on both sides of this Strait met, it was customary to greet one another with the phrase, "Have you eaten?" In primary schools, the first thing teachers did each day would be to check if the students had brushed their teeth. In those years, regular meals and brushing one's teeth every morning and evening were not necessarily the norm, which is why they became a common topic of conversation. Similarly, when people across the Strait today dwell excessively on campus autonomy, it is definitely a sign that it remains a matter of continuing concern in need of regular checking. Try asking your colleagues tomorrow if they have eaten or brushed their teeth. They will probably consider you a complete nut!

However, because universities in Taiwan, Hong Kong and the Mainland lack independence, this question needs to be asked again: Do universities enjoy autonomy? According to Chung-Ming Kuan and Johannes Hsiao Chih Sun, the university law in Taiwan puts inappropriate restrictions on university autonomy to a great extent (*The Storm Media*, December 25, 2022). Not much about such laws is discussed in Hong Kong and on the Mainland. Regarding university autonomy, Hong Kong fares better than Taiwan, while Taiwan fares better than Mainland China. However, the road ahead is long and far. We may have to seek high and low relentlessly for any improvement.

Campus autonomy is one of the essential elements of the success of American universities. As it is the norm for American universities to exercise autonomy over academic affairs, there is no need to go out of one's way to highlight it. The more external interference there is, the less campus autonomy there is, and the lower the chance of creativity's success (See Chapter 26). Creativity at universities across the Strait is experiencing tremendous difficulties. It is not surprising that the principle of campus autonomy is reiterated hypocritically.

As far as Taiwan is concerned, street politics have stormed across university campuses like unbridled horses since democratization. As is well known, external parties became involved in the selection of the president of NTU in 2018, which seriously undermined the university's autonomy. In 2022, student activists at NTU once again blatantly practiced "political scrutiny…by professional students and the 'new party-state system' manipulating from behind…. Was it the Cultural Revolution of the 1960s? … Torturing to check personal 'loyalty level'?" The above translated quotes are from Yang Du, a Taiwanese journalist who calls such phenomena "demons of the mind".[3]

Demons of the mind come from the absence of soulware.

Blind Spots of the Mind

No matter how well-educated, we all have our blind spots, weaknesses, gaps or hidden biases. These are areas for improvement and growth. I call them the blind spots of the mind.

On several occasions, I have asked audiences comprising world-class scholars, professors and students at prestigious schools, business leaders and other people known in their particular fields to solve a puzzle. I have a piece of paper with nothing printed on one side and a map printed on the other. I then tear it into small irregular pieces, letting the audience see only the blank side but not the side showing the printed map. I ask all of them to put the torn pieces together.

With vacant expressions, they do not know how to begin, but there is nothing difficult at all if they know the secret behind the paper. On one occasion, a child turned over the paper, discovered the map, and quickly reassembled the pieces. For this, I have composed a poem, "Blind Spots of the Mind":

> *Politics may blind us with its rhetoric.*
> *Scientific and technological advances strengthen education.*
> *Difficult as it may be to assemble the torn pieces of paper,*
> *Flipping it over frees us from the blindness of the mind.*

Embedded in this poem is a call for separating politics and education, which is necessary to create an academic atmosphere fostering innovation and creativity.

There is a traditional belief that as long as people keep to themselves, they will be left alone. Teachers and students in Taiwan and Hong Kong believe they can enjoy or abuse academic freedom. The writing and circulation

---
[3] *China Times*, October 10, 2022.

of anonymous letters is but one of the examples of the outlandish misuse of academic freedom. Taiwan and Hong Kong universities have tolerated many instances of vicious speech and disorderly conduct in the name of academic freedom, which is absent in the Mainland. Anyone engaging in similar behavior on an American university campus would be sent packing.

Water can remain clean up in the hills, but it gets murky once it flows down the mountains. Since "once an official, always an official", bureaucrats always look to interfere with campus autonomy. They do not shy from expressing their opinions under the flimsiest of pretexts and enjoy issuing administrative orders to redefine the academic order within their narrow political points of view. On their part, the media either report on the most trivial matters or bend to the wishes of politicians, ready to abet them in the shameful game of flattery or denunciation. Such underhand wheeling and dealing will not find an audience in the US government or media.

Treating academic freedom as a smoke bomb that breaks the rules is no better than having no academic freedom or even worse. Higher education is a profession, and it is best left to specialists, not to outsiders with insufficient know-how, lest it becomes a mere device for political scheming. The blindness of the mind is precisely the blind spot where political power overrides universities and power corrupts the education system.

The Philosophy of Cai Yuanpei (蔡元培)

Cai Yuanpei, a well-respected Chinese educator, put forward these basic principles for Chinese universities more than 100 years ago. First, they should be independent and autonomous. Second, they should enjoy freedom of thought and academic pursuit. And third, academic freedom and freedom of thought depend on a correspondingly free social and political environment. While the first two principles are often quoted without appropriate actions, the third one is rarely mentioned.

If campus autonomy cannot be upheld and there is no true academic freedom, internationalization is simply empty talk, and it is impossible to run a high-quality university.

So what are the criteria for a healthy social system? In short, it is the separation of politics and education.

Without soulware, Cai Yuanpei's ideal of academic freedom is still reeling after more than one hundred years of devastation from political forces. In the final analysis, the development of higher education is now at the adaptation stage of infant mortality in Taiwan, Hong Kong and the Mainland. The free social and political environment is not found in any of the three places that will serve as a foundation for freedom of thought and academic freedom in higher education. Not only do the governments across the Strait enact elaborate rules, but they fear their control is insufficient. They meddle with a university's work, creating a visible (or invisible) wall that separates us from what we aspire to: innovation.

I could continue, restating that universities should not serve politics. But a short poem should suffice for now:

> *Flowers will not blossom across the Strait*
> *Until a spring breeze reaches the very end of the earth;*
> *The tree of innovation will not sprout*
> *Until academic freedom is endowed.*

15

Mechanism of the Separation of Politics and Education

After World War II, the light of the free and liberal US dazzled, leading the world in economic development. Riding the waves of political and global economic development, the three Chinese communities across the Strait sensed the international trend and joined the US-led global system, which facilitated US leadership in global higher education. In the humanities, the arts, technological innovations and other fields, US universities have attracted and nurtured numerous talented young men and women while the widespread use of English has become a concrete but subtle consequence resulting from America's world leadership.

Undoubtedly, the steady progress of a society or a country depends on the solid support of the economic system. In the same way, a progressive higher education system is backed up by a stable political and economic environment. Investment in education should be seen as a special investment for society and not merely an item of daily expenditure. That American higher education has become the mainstream for the whole world is a manifestation of the progress of American politics and economics, something Americans can take pride in.

Although American universities enjoy high academic freedom, they do not operate in a vacuum. They cannot avoid external interference entirely, nor are they immune to changes in the political environment.

Academic Freedom in the US

For more than one hundred years, American scientists have worked with colleagues from all over the world. At the same time, international students and colleagues are recruited into the academic community in the laboratories, classrooms and research networks. Some of these collaborators come from countries and territories where academic freedom has not yet improved. For this reason, defending freedom and the right to pursue knowledge becomes challenging.

While US universities generally enjoy high academic freedom, these fundamental values are sometimes threatened. In the 1950s, the world was polarized into the democratic and communist camps, which looked upon each other with hostility. With its strong anti-communist stance, American society sought to marginalize the Soviet Union and Communist China. The white terror staged by the ultra-rightist Senator Joseph R. McCarthy exaggerated the scale of communist infiltration, inciting public figures in the political, artistic, literary and higher education arenas to report on one another, resulting in what was known as the "Red Scare". Many scientists and performing artists were implicated, such as the actor Charlie Chaplin.

In the McCarthy era, a court judged that the philosopher Bertrand Russell was unfit for teaching at City University of New York. Yet many stepped up to resist the assault on academic freedom from inside and outside the university. The most famous case of all involves the president of the University of Chicago, Robert M. Hutchins. Because of his testimony, an unjust bill that would have infringed on academic freedom failed to pass.

In 1960, John F. Kennedy became the President of the United States, changing the ambiance of the country and stressing the importance of civil liberty. The university campus became more peaceful, which led to more international students enrolling at US universities, injecting new blood into scientific and technological development.

After the 911 terrorist attack in 2001, outside forces once again sought to influence US universities by stipulating what courses to offer or what students to recruit. University management came under external pressure, leading to the termination of employment of some teachers and thus depriving them of a platform for the expression of their views. George W. Bush, the US president at the time, signed into law the Uniting and Strengthening America by Providing Appropriate Tools Required to Intercept and Obstruct Terrorism Act of 2001, also known as the USA Patriot Act. The Act expanded the right of the government to collect information on potential terrorist activities, clearly stating that the government has the right to collect information on the electronic communications of the public, including telephone numbers, emails and websites, directly or indirectly infringing on the privacy of individuals, and violating the human rights of immigrants, refugees and minorities.

In an article in the October 2004 issue of *Harvard Business Review* titled "America's Looming Creativity Crisis," Richard Florida, an expert on economic competitiveness, elaborated on the connections between American success and immigrants. He pointed out, "America's growth miracle turns on one key factor: its openness to new ideas, which has allowed it to mobilize and harness the creative energies of its people ... But the United States doesn't have some intrinsic advantage in the cultivation of creative people, innovative ideas, or new companies. Rather, its real advantage lies in its ability to attract these economic drivers from around the world. Of critical importance to American success in this last century has been a tremendous influx of talented immigrants ... This talent has helped make the US university system and innovative infrastructure second to none."

In the post-911 presidency of George W. Bush, universities relied on contracts and grants from the federal government. At the same time, they experienced all kinds of influences from commercial circles, rich donors and the government, making it difficult to maintain independence. In 2007, the Ad-hoc Committee to Defend the University spelled out some of the effects of the influences from organizations outside the university, including maligning scholars, exerting pressure on the management, and circumventing or disrupting established academic governance procedures. In retrospect, one sees similar phenomena in Taiwan, Hong Kong and the Mainland to this very day, but no one questioned that.

During Obama's presidency, the House of Representatives passed the USA Freedom Act in 2015, reducing the government's power to monitor and collect information on the people's communication records, setting the American spirit back on course.

The waves had by no means calmed down when the US again suffered another bewildering onslaught of politics. In 2017, during the first few weeks of Trump's term as president of the US, the ultra-right gathered at the Unite the Right rally in Virginia, followed by more demonstrations in Berkeley, California and other cities. After the disturbances and riots at Berkeley, Trump used Twitter to threaten reduced financial support for UC Berkeley on February 2, 2017, an abuse of power that confirmed the pressure universities suffer when they are beholden to the federal government for financial support.

Federal financial support for universities endows those in power with authority to give and take, a process that threatens academic freedom, which is why the government is generally lambasted for abusing power. In addition, after his ascendency to the presidency, Trump signed a number of new ordinances, including banning immigration from countries with a population of mostly Muslims, which ran contrary to the open policy that has contributed to the prosperity of the US for many years. The presidents of 48 universities strongly criticized Trump, urging him to take corrective measures.

The Impact of Strained Sino-American Relations on Higher Education

In July 2018, to reduce the trade imbalance between China and the US and bring manufacturing jobs back home, Trump began a trade war with China, imposing tariffs on Chinese products valued at over US$500 billion, ranging from 10% to 25%. This is the largest trade war in economic history so far. The US and China have imposed punitive tariffs on each other's imported products.

The political scuffles have directly affected both countries' economies. Although American investment in China remained relatively stable till 2021 at a level of approximately US$13 billion a year, according to a survey by the American Enterprise Institute, China's investment in the US slid from US$54 billion in 2016 to US$16.7 billion in 2021. This large-scale reduction primarily reflects Chinese investors' concerns caused by the trade war, with the US's increasingly rigorous scrutiny of investment by Chinese companies and China's restrictions on capital outflow.

Universities in the US enjoy legally given autonomy in governance, mission and development, but under different historical circumstances, long-standing universal values such as academic freedom and campus autonomy have been challenged. For example, teaching and research collaboration between universities and industry can increase competitiveness and bring about scientific and technological breakthroughs, which is regarded as mutually beneficial. However, due to a federal investigation into sanctions and violations, MIT decided in 2019 not to receive research funding from Zhongxing Telecommunication and Huawei.

From 2018, out of concern for espionage and the theft of intellectual property, the State Department began shortening the duration of visas for Chinese students in cutting-edge manufacturing fields such as aviation, robotics and AI and required them to reapply for visas every summer when they returned home, thus increasing the possibility of visa denial. In November 2018, the Department of Justice set up a China Initiative to affirm the priority of cases prosecuting Chinese for stealing commercial secrets and guaranteeing that enough resources be channeled to these cases from government departments to ensure speedy and effective conclusions. Subsequently, many Chinese scholars have had their visa applications rejected. In 2019, the US again tightened the review of Mainland Chinese students' visa applications, resulting in students who had returned to China on vacation failing to return to university campuses. On November 19, a hearing held by the House of Representatives indicated that the FBI was focusing its efforts on disrupting academic exchanges as well as the exchange of research personnel between China and the US.

Since 2019, the willingness of some US universities to cooperate with their government to confront China has created a toxic atmosphere. Cases of ethnic Chinese professors being harassed are seen everywhere. The Thousand Talents Program, a plan launched in 2008 in China to recruit leading international experts in scientific research, innovation and entrepreneurship, is considered by the US government as "theft under the disguise of academic freedom". Anyone involved with the program, or a similar program called Changjiang Scholars Program, would invariably be questioned and investigated. For those who had scientific research exchanges with China, the lucky ones (in mild cases) were persuaded to take early retirement, while the unlucky ones (in more severe cases) were investigated for espionage and were prosecuted, imprisoned or are awaiting trial.

The new Cold War between the US and China shows signs of reviving the Red Scare of McCarthyism. Visiting scholars, technological exchange personnel and American Chinese scientists have come under suspicion and are subjected to acts of exclusion and even prosecution. On the surface, the target is scholars from Mainland China, but a prevalent sense of insecurity ensues. For this reason, many higher education and non-profit advocacy organizations, including the American Association of University Professors and the Association of American Universities, issued a joint statement to express their concern over the situation of the Chinese scientific research community in the US and their belief that some government departments were making groundless accusations that restricted academic freedom and affected the development of American education and industries. They called for fair treatment of Chinese scholars and researchers.

The interchange of talent involves pushing and pulling. Due to the upward adjustment of salary packages for professors in the Mainland and the unfriendly atmosphere for Chinese scientists in the US, many top-notch scientists have chosen to return to the Mainland or come to Hong Kong. There are indications that the brain drain from China to the US is ending while the number of returning students from the US to China continues to increase. According to a 2020 report on Chinese returnees from overseas, approximately 30.6% of overseas Chinese talent aged 30 to 40 chose to return to China; while the rate for the age group 20 to 29 is as high as 52.2%. At the time of writing, Biden was said to have relaxed restrictions on scholars from the Mainland to encourage them to stay. Between the pushing and pulling, there are signs that the number of returning Chinese scholars and experts is slowing down in 2022.

The Accelerated Impact of Pandemic on Higher Education

At the end of 2019, COVID-19 broke out in Wuhan and quickly spread to the rest of the world. At present, the occupation that is most severely affected by the pandemic may not be construction, retail, transportation or the catering industry, but education.

Politics can override education in many ways. At one point, the Trump administration attempted to stop international students from entering the US by issuing an executive order. The Taiwanese government took a similar step. At the beginning of the pandemic in 2020, the Taiwan government issued a ban on students from the Mainland, subjecting them to discriminatory treatment. Some were stopped at the airport, and some could not return to Taiwan after they had left. In August, the government opened its door to international students, but out of political considerations, only Mainland students were not allowed in. Many universities in Taiwan expressed concern.

The health crisis triggered by COVID-19 upset the way of life and economic activity all over the world. Travel was restricted, commerce was affected, and academic exchange was disrupted. The US government held the Chinese government responsible for the pandemic.

After China adopted the open-reform policy, the number of students studying overseas increased rapidly. In 2000, only 60,000 Mainland students were studying in the US, but by 2019/2020, the number exceeded 370,000. Those studying at the university accounted for 1/3 of all foreign undergraduate and graduate students, paying aggregate tuition of US$15 billion. One-third of the tuition income of American universities came from international students from China. Sino-American relations have continued to be tense. During the three-year pandemic, the increase rate of Chinese students going to the US for overseas studies was only 0.8% in 2019/2020. In the golden period ten years ago, the rate of increase once reached 23.5% (see Table 0.1). After it reached the high point of 372,532 in 2019/20 year, the number of Chinese students in the US dropped by 14.8%, yielding a figure of 317,299.

Due to the raging COVID-19 pandemic and political and economic tensions, it was difficult for students from Mainland China to study in the US. Instead, they turned to Hong Kong. In the fall of 2022, we saw significant growth in the number of Mainland students applying for undergraduate and postgraduate studies. Taking CityU as an example, the number of applications for master's programs was close to 80,000, more than double the previous year, even though CityU can enroll just over 4,000 such students.

In English-speaking countries such as the US, UK, and Australia that recruit international students, the biggest economic achievement of the education industry is the high tuition fees from international students, which are frequently several times higher than fees for home students. For example, in the UK, home students pay approximately £9,000 per year, but an international student may have to pay close to £26,000 a year. COVID-19 has brought about an unexpected financial impact. If the trend persists, the number of international students will continue to drop, and universities that depend on this income will be significantly affected.

Moreover, while online teaching put forward to address the need to maintain social distancing may have alleviated the pressing teaching problem, it did not provide the best learning environment for some students, particularly those from low-income families without a stable internet connection or a learning environment free from disturbances at home. All of these led to a drop in enrolled students and the interruption of international exchange.

The Self-Regulating American Democratic System

In their common goal of preventing China from surpassing the US, the Republican and Democratic Parties have arrived at a rare consensus in their attitudes towards the question of China. In the presidential election at the end of 2020, candidates from both parties adopted an aggressive strategy towards China and depicted the other party as being controlled by Beijing, with the hope of boosting their own status while crushing the opponent.

In view of this, over 90 famous scholars from the US and other places joined with former government officials to issue an open letter on April 3, 2020, calling for Sino-American cooperation to deal with the global crisis brought on by COVID-19. Among those who signed are Madeleine Albright, former Secretary of State; Chuck Hagel, former Secretary of Defense; Winston Lord, former Ambassador to China; Kevin Rudd, former Prime Minister of Australia; Joseph Nye, a well-known American scholar; and Lawrence Summers, former President of Harvard University and former Secretary of the Treasury.

One day prior to that, 100 Chinese scholars, writing as civilians, issued "An Open Letter to the People of the United States From 100 Chinese Scholars" in the international journal *The Diplomat*, indicating that the new coronavirus represented the most serious crisis to global public health and asking that everyone fight the pandemic together rather than "complaining, finger pointing and blaming one another".

Events took an unexpected turn. Under the catalytic changes brought on by the new coronavirus, higher education in the US has veered off course and yielded strengths that used to draw talent from around the world, its morale suffering a severe blow. The trade imbalance with China and Trump's insistence on putting America first only worsened matters. The Department of Homeland Security and US Immigration and Customs Enforcement declared new regulations targeting foreign students on July 6, 2020. Scholars and students from many countries were denied entry because they were viewed as external enemies to US technological development. Higher education was affected; old wounds from the 1950s reopened.

The original plan was as follows: If universities implemented online teaching in the Fall semester, foreign students holding F1 or M1 non-immigration visas would not be allowed to remain in the US and would be deported. The Department of State would not issue visas to the 1.1 million international students at these universities. Likewise, Immigration and Customs Enforcement would not allow them to enter unless they chose face-to-face teaching or a hybrid mode. The Trump government used the pandemic as an excuse to turn away more immigrants.

As soon as the new regulation was announced, Harvard University and MIT jointly filed a lawsuit in the District Court in Boston, preventing the enforcement of the new guidance and declaring it unlawful. Denouncing it as "cruel and reckless," they requested that the court block the government from executing the policy. Two hundred or more universities expressed their support for Harvard and MIT.

The new policy was meant to pressure universities into opening up campuses to physical classes in complete disregard of possible health and safety risks, yet another example of politics interfering with education. Feeling the heat, the US government rescinded the new policy just over a week later.

Due to changes in policy during the latter part of Trump's presidential term, what used to be a normal academic exchange activity between China and the US could be construed as a crime. Scholars from the Mainland were ostracized and could be blamed on the flimsiest of excuses. On January 14, 2021, MIT mechanical engineering professor Gang Chen was charged with concealing contacts with China in an attempt to secure US$19 million in federal research funding, an action that was part of the China Initiative put in place by the Department of Justice which already charged around 10 American scholars and six visiting scientists.

Not long afterward, Professor Yoel Fink, a materials scientist at MIT, drafted an open letter to MIT's President L. Rafael Reif. The letter, co-signed by 100 professors, pointed out that Chen's allegedly concealed connections constituted routine academic activity while President Reif publicly clarified the nature of the collaborative project between MIT and the Southern University of Science and Technology, calling for an open and inclusive academic environment and fair treatment for Chinese scholars. At the same time, MIT offered to cover Chen's legal fees. A year later, a federal judge dismissed all charges.

The US population comprises immigrants, and America is known as a melting pot of races. Although segregation was abolished in 1964, systemic racial discrimination still exists in American society, with whites discriminating against people of color, including African Americans, and older immigrants discriminating against the new. The problem won't simply go away. Police brutality in May 2020 that caused the death of George Floyd, an African American, represents only the tip of the iceberg. The outbreak of the new coronavirus prompted Trump to refer to the pandemic repeatedly as "Chinese pneumonia" and "kung flu," once again highlighting discrimination against Asians and fanning the flames of hate crime. In 2020, assaults on Asians, especially elderly Asians, were on the rise.

In view of this, in a rare move, the House of Senate overwhelmingly passed the COVID-19 Hate Crimes Act, intended to reduce the increase in violent incidents against Asian Americans triggered by the new coronavirus. The Act was put to a vote in the House of Representatives and was finally signed into law by Biden. On April 26, 2021, the website of the Department of State announced the lifting of the ban on Chinese students entering the US. Beginning on August 1, students holding F1/M1 visas could enter the US thirty days before the start of the semester. However, students from China, Iran, Brazil and South Africa must satisfy specific academic requirements before they are allowed in. Without academic exchanges, any educational system that isolates itself will become a hindrance to progress.

Acts of hatred against Asians are motivated by different factors, including the execution and operation of higher education. Hatred will probably not be eliminated at any time in the near future. Yet the self-regulating mechanism of the American democratic system still deserves respect.

When Will Politics and Education Be Separated in Taiwan, Hong Kong and the Mainland?

In the last thirty years, the three Chinese communities across the Strait have caught up with the trend to improve their higher education. Taiwan was the trailblazer, followed by Hong Kong and then the Mainland (See Chapter 3). In terms of outcomes, the Mainland shows the largest improvement, with Hong Kong second and Taiwan bringing up the rear. Theoretically, a rigid framework cannot deal with a fast-changing world. The Chinese government is highly centralized with poor transparency, but on matters that need to be corrected or adjusted, it acts decisively, bringing about obvious results. The improvement in higher education is a case in point. Taiwan, which takes pride in its democracy, often sees people in official positions putting the party before the state. The tendency to focus on the local prevents people from seeing beyond their personal bliss. The university system there is a complete mess (see Chapter 5), and the hard days are by no means over.

There are strengths and weaknesses to any system. Democratic countries and authoritarian states have their own limitations. A rigid system might be resistant to changes, and one with flexibility might change, but perhaps for the worse. In addition to the system itself, the leaders' abilities, knowledge and experiences are important. There are a right and a wrong way; the two are not mixed.

Over the years, I have been a frequent traveler, exchanging views with leaders at nearly one hundred universities. Having met with the presidents of several dozen top-notch universities, I realize that people in power intervene in university affairs in various ways. The involvement of the US and Canadian governments in education is the lowest, and there is almost no interference in France and Israel. In Europe and Australia, university presidents have resigned because of the encroachment of politics on university campuses. In Taiwan and the Mainland, academic leaders have gotten into a mutually beneficial relationship with those in power out of a sense of political correctness. More often, feeling powerless, they acquiesce to the meddling of politics. The Hong Kong government, feigning action in one place while making moves in another, visited universities privately through its representative, the UGC, making a verbal request for the introduction of the National Security Law curriculum, the execution of government decrees regarding university classification and others so that it could complete these tasks without losing face. Why couldn't they simply learn from the US and set laws or issue regulations openly for easy execution?

The difficulties inherent in keeping politics and education apart call to mind the separation of the church and the state in the Middle Ages. It might be an exaggeration, but higher education across the Strait could probably be described like this. There are many bad guys and good guys on the Mainland because people reveal their feelings more readily, and bad guys and good guys can be identified instantly due to a weakened cultural foundation; but there are no bad guys nor good guys in Hong Kong because people (the young or old, who are both supple and weak under the influence of the old colonial rule and the new, more authoritarian rule) excel at sitting on the fence. So it is hard to differentiate the good from the bad even though, occasionally, there are some horrible people around. In Taiwan, though, there are many bad guys and even more onlookers. The social media can turn you into an overnight internet celebrity and then attack you brutally at will. The daring are arrogant; the timid are humane. The bad guys are ferocious, like piranhas in the Amazon River that attack humans. Not wanting to stir up trouble, the good guys slip away at the first sound of thunder.

The separation of politics and education is an ideal state that no countries or societies have completely reached. What sets the American system apart from that of the three Chinese communities across the Strait is that the former has a self-regulating mechanism capable of adjusting within a short time. American society is proud of its democratic system. Those in leadership positions enjoy tremendous power in office, doing practically anything they want, but there are always some in the Congress, and the general public, or among successors, who prioritize the state, make timely adjustments and safeguard the status quo. American society provides a platform that allows people with different opinions to express their views, allowing truth to emerge through debate and argumentation.

According to the recognized contemporary Western standard, be it Taiwanese society that practices fake democracy, Hong Kong society that does not know what democracy is, or Mainland society that does not recognize Western democracy, the self-regulatory mechanism lacks transparency and lies beyond the reach of common people. Those in power, or, for that matter, other social groups, are not inclined to self-reflect, and the silent majority feels the need to play safe. Weighty scholars tend to withhold their views on Taiwan, Hong Kong and the Mainland, unlike those in the US who take to the public sphere to address issues of concern. Universities rarely make their positions known because, up to now, in the three communities across the Strait, to quote Cai Yuanpei, "a correspondingly free and social and political environment" is still unavailable (See Chapter 14).

In retrospect, internationalization is not unique today. The Spring and Autumn period, which began in the 8th century B.C.E, the Warring States period, which dates back to the 5th century B.C.E., and the Renaissance in 15th and the 16th century Europe are concrete examples of greater global connections. In the evolutionary process, internationalization and localization alternately rise and fall. It is understandable that the process may double back and that the good might sometimes come with the bad. But in the long-term, it is an unalterable trend that the world will move towards global integration.

In a world where political hacks outnumber bona fide politicians, the separation of politics and education seems a distant, unreachable goal.

A Dialogue with the Chief Executive of Hong Kong

Carrie Lam, the former Chief Executive of the HKSAR Government, visited CityU on August 4, 2021. We said that the overall quality of Hong Kong universities is not too bad, even though they do not measure up to universities in Japan and Singapore, nor do they compare with those in the Mainland, such as Tsinghua University and Peking University. There are also signs that Hong Kong universities are falling behind South Korean universities and members of the C9 League in the Mainland. When higher education in the Mainland is rapidly moving forward, it seems to falter in Hong Kong. This, in a way, sounds like a warning that not advancing means falling behind.

Then Carrie Lam referred to an outdated distinction between "applied research" and "basic research" as a way to differentiate the roles played by various universities (See Chapter 7). We asked her what she meant by "applied research." For years, people have considered themselves superior to universities and directed the Chief Executive without understanding that all research should be relevant to societal needs. There are books to read and research to do. Applied research and basic research—there are right and wrong ways, but there is no mixing of the two.

To be sure, universities are by no means dispensable ornaments. An ideal university can elevate a society's humanistic consciousness and economic development. In present-day Hong Kong, where the labor resources have reached saturation point, social progress has to rely on teaching to increase the marginal advantage of cultural and economic growth. Yet top- and mid-level educational bureaucrats advocate the acquisition of special talents and techniques that Hong Kong needs at a high cost rather than nurturing local talent. That senior government officials in Hong Kong almost without exception send their children to study overseas is clear proof of their comprador mentality.

Moreover, student housing is an extremely important part of university education, but the Hong Kong government initially ignored the shortage at almost all universities. Campuses are small and crammed, and sports facilities are inadequate. Finally, in July 2018, under the proposal from Carrie Lam, part of the request for building dormitories was submitted to the legislative body. Already late in coming, the discussion moved at a ponderous pace. There is not much one can do but hold one's breath and wait.

At the end of February 2022, the number of confirmed cases of COVID-19 in Hong Kong reached a new high, and all quarantine and hospital facilities were full. In response, the government intended to requisition student dormitories as isolation facilities. Not to mention whether this awful idea was justified, with the serious shortage of student housing, where are the required beds?

When students or graduates accomplish something on their own, independent of the provision of policies, the government gets puffed up with self-importance. For example, in the summer of 2021, as soon as news broke that the Hong Kong team had given its best-ever performance at the 2020 Tokyo Olympics, winning 1 gold, 2 silver and 3 bronze medals, the government could not wait to claim the credit.[1] But really, what have they ever done over the past decades for university sports? Some universities have indeed paid attention to their sports programs and scored great success in the last dozen years, but no one has given these achievements any thought. The smart, polite, eloquent Carrie Lam was speechless at this juncture.

Why do higher education circles in Taiwan, Hong Kong and the Mainland rarely scratch the surface of what matters to the authorities? When will enough progress be made for them, like the US, to be able to regulate themselves? When can people in power be fair and just in treating the universities, rather than act like a slippery loach?

Refreshing breeze and bright moon for me,
Deep water and scorching fire for you.
I will come forward with happy events,
Leaving disasters to you.

---

[1] See the TVB Evening News on Chief Executive visiting Hong Kong athletes in Xian, September 26, 2021.

16

University: The Seedbed of Social Movements?

During the colonial period, Hong Kong was less a man's land (See Chapter 3). At the beginning of the post-1997 period, the UGC was set up to oversee universities, but it did not involve itself in personnel matters. In recent years, the government, students and even the media seem to be eager to stick their fingers into the university affairs. Should they find themselves in the mood, they butt in and offer their opinions as if they owned the place. In Taiwan, under the guise of democracy, the ruling party may interfere with personnel affairs of universities. In the Mainland, the party is the government in name and in reality. The two work together to realize the highest principle of combining politics and education.

Universities should march ahead of the times, but every now and then, those in Hong Kong and Taiwan are swamped in the wake of populism. Or worse, like beachcombers, they pick up what society discards. The intermix of politics and education is deeply rooted in Taiwan and the Mainland to varying degrees, and set deep in the bones of the political parties in both places is the desire to direct the universities. Why and for what purposes?

Social Malady

There is a belief in government circles that as long as universities are brought under control, political power will be stable and the job of governance will be easier. It is unclear which is the chicken and which is the egg, or perhaps it is a characteristic of Chinese culture that makes people reason in that manner. Some people in society use university students as a leverage against the government when they are not in control, hoping that, at a very low cost, they might gain a fraction of the marginal advantage needed to get among the ruling circles.

Some people at a university are pure of heart, and others less so. The former are shy, timid and unwilling to express their views even when they do not like what they see. The impure, however, are brash, looking for opportunities to strike out for personal gain. Whether it is the government that seeks to control the university or students who look upon the university as a base for their resistance against the government, in their eyes, the university is merely a hotbed for social movements.

Universities in Hong Kong respect suggestions from the community. For example, in the last ten years, it has come to our attention at CityU that there have been requests to rename the university to reflect our development better. Proposals of all sorts have been made, no less than several dozen in number. We have held an open attitude with regard to these proposals, listening carefully to suggestions and maintaining lines of communication with staff and alumni. There is no predetermined position on this matter nor a conclusion yet.

However, because some professors have made public their suggestions, there circulate now in public a few future names—Nanyang University and Huanan University being two of them. None of these names are found in CityU's plans, and nor have they been recognized by the University in any way. Yet some individuals and the media seized upon these names and for reasons that are not entirely selfless, blew them out of proportion and gave them a political spin. The rumor mill then began to turn, making a mountain out of a molehill. Indeed, what is the fuss? What business is it of those who are not related to the university—government officials and the media—whether CityU is going to change its name and what new name it has chosen? The back-seat driver has taken over the steering wheel.

Events like this are by no means rare in Hong Kong, but I have yet to see the American public or media spread rumors against universities in this way. And to be sure, I have not heard of students and professors in American universities protesting and rioting against the university because of social issues. American universities are not the place to cultivate political movements, nor are they allowed to be. American students are not and will not be used as chips in a political deal. That is just a tacit agreement accepted by all, having been established over a long period of practice.

Some may ask, isn't it true that American students have taken part in many demonstrations?

Yes, protests and demonstrations on American campuses often occur spontaneously, especially in the last century. Many large-scale demonstrations and conflicts occurred over the conscription for military service during the Vietnam War.

Student Movements in the US

Student movements in the US began in the 1920s over issues ranging from segregation and racial discrimination in the early years to civil rights in the 1960s, from the anti-Vietnam War to the anti-Iraq War, from the sale of firearms to the human rights issues as well as questions of peace and democracy, police accountability, multiculturalism, the rise in education costs, the cancellation of student loans and others.

Regardless of the issue at hand, there is a common point in these movements; that is, they all reflect the students' concern about injustice in society and their willingness to be involved. Apart from cases that are directly and concretely related to campus, such as the racial discrimination on the campus of the University of Missouri, Columbia in September 2015 that sparked off a series of protest activities including occupation, hunger strike and boycotting football matches and campus stores, all other student movements are initiated from society. They target society and not the university over social issues. These movements are by no means partisan, including the following:

1. In the 1960s, student movements sought solutions to social problems such as racial discrimination and racial injustice. The start of the US civil rights protests can be traced to February 1, 1960. A group of young African American students from North Carolina Agricultural and Technical College sat at a Woolworth's whites-only lunch counter in protest against the segregation system. By the end of March, the movement had spread to 55 other cities in 13 states, drawing young white people into its ranks. They staged peaceful protests in libraries, beaches, inns and hotels, shops and other places that practiced segregation. The protests continued unabated, reaching a boiling point in 1968 and ending with the occupation of five buildings on the campus at Columbia University by over 1,000 students who were violently removed by the police. Known as the Morningside Park Protest, the protest also targeted the Vietnam War, conscription and racist policies.
2. In 1964, in defense of the rights of freedom of speech, academic freedom and political freedom, students at UC Berkeley started the Berkeley Free Speech Movement. This movement was closely tied to the Civil Rights Movement

and Anti-Vietnam War Movement, with the three echoing one another. These movements are subsequently seen as the biggest and the most effective student protest movements in the history of the US.
3. The 1965–1975 US Vietnam War protests, from Students for a Democratic Society (SDS) Teach-ins to the Kent State University shootings, represent some major landmarks in the student movements in the US. Teach-ins extended the anti-war protests to the classroom and were first organized by the SDS at the University of Michigan, Ann Arbor, in 1965 to protest against the war strategy of the US government. On May 4, 1970, National Guards opened fire at protesting students at Kent State University, killing four and injuring nine. The incident is called the May 4 Massacre and led to a boycott of classes by 4 million students and the closing of more than 100 universities. The incident changed the American public's view on the US's role in the Vietnam War.
4. Occupy Wall Street started on September 17, 2011. Nearly 1,000 demonstrators marched on Wall Street at the center of the financial district in New York City. Thereafter, demonstrations spread to university campuses. At the University of California, Davis, demonstrators staged a peaceful sit-in at the campus square. When students refused to leave at the request of campus security, pepper spray was used. The police anti-demonstration action was captured on video and quickly spread over the internet. Two years later, the court ruled that the university would have to pay $30,000 to each student sprayed.
5. In 2017, Trump was elected President of the US. Protests broke out in universities and cities across the east and west coasts of the US. The University of Texas, Austin, was one of the first universities to stage a rally and boycott classes. Students raised banners emblazoned with the words "Love Trumps Hate Protests" and "Students Against Trump". Other universities where similar protests were held include Temple University, Ohio State University, Florida State University and the University of North Carolina, Chapel Hill. On February 1, 2017, students marched on the Stony Brook University, New York campus to protest Trump's order to ban refugees, immigrants or individuals from seven Muslim countries from entering the US.

Student Movement – A Lofty Ideal

Women's rights activist Malala Yousafzai is dedicated to the education rights of Pakistani women. At 17, she was awarded the Nobel Peace Prize in 2014. In 2017, when she was nine, Ridhima Pandey, an Indian girl, sued the Indian government for taking no action to address climate change, thus making it inevitable that the next generation would suffer. In raising the consciousness of global warming and climate change, Greta Thunberg, a young female environmental activist from Sweden, organized the "School Strike for Climate" outside the Swedish Parliament and spoke at COP24 in 2018. On March 15, 2019, 1.4 million students all over the world responded to her call for action. In 2021, at COP26 held in Glasgow, Scotland, she once again spoke out, bluntly charging that the conference was a sham and a "greenwashing" public relations stunt and had nothing to do with addressing climate change.

Another noteworthy incident in the environmental protection movement is a 2017 court case brought by 21 young Americans, ranging in age from nine to 20, against the American government and energy companies for not taking proper action to address the problem of global warming, thus encroaching upon the rights to life, freedom, and property as guaranteed by the US Constitution.

Thunberg comes from an affluent country and Pandey from an underdeveloped one. The data at their command may not be entirely accurate, but both carry with them an aura of virtue that elicits respect. When the air is woefully polluted in the three societies across the Strait and when thousands and thousands of people are holding protests across the world to demand speedy actions on the use of fossil fuel and air pollution, where are the young people in Hong Kong and Taiwan? (As demonstrations are not allowed on the Mainland, I do not mention the young people there.) Why aren't there noisy young people in Hong Kong and Taiwan, like Thunberg, Licypriya Kangujam of India, the young Americans, or Pandey, the young girl from India fighting climate change?

Let us not forget students' crucial role in achieving political change on the Korean peninsula. During the Japanese occupation of Korea, the main goal of the student movements was to fight for national independence from Japan at events such as the March 1 Movement in 1919 and the Gwangju Students Movement in 1929. After World War II, the major demands of the student movements, especially the April 19 Movement in 1960 and the May 18 Gwangju Democratization Struggle, were anti-authoritarianism, anti-corruption, democracy and uniting North and South Korea.

South Korean students deserve our praise and tears for their valiant adherence to principles.

France is famous for its long history of resistance, insurgency and revolution. French students are known as *jeunesse revolutionnaire* (revolutionary youth). This is why even though student movements are not as widespread as in other places when they happen, they are often related to issues of people's livelihoods. The "May 68" was a large-scale anti-establishment, anti-capitalism and anti-war ideological struggle waged by students in 1968 that attracted many foreign students to France in a show of support. The student movement prompted trade unions to mobilize 9 million members to take industrial action, which proved to be the longest since World War II, eventually leading to Charles de Gaulle's ousting in a referendum. After that, other noteworthy student movements include the 2003 protest against the Iraq War, in which France did not participate, and the protest against the CPE-First Employment Contract in 2006.

All the protests and demonstrations mentioned above were not driven by self-interest. No one has been known to become rich or famous because of their involvement.

It should be clear why, after returning to the East to pick up my first official job in Hong Kong, I found it hard to adapt myself to the entanglement of politics and education in this part of the world. In particular, I could not understand that some treated the university as an instrument for venting their anger over politically driven social disturbances. Why didn't they go to the source of the problems if they felt they were in the right?

The racial segregation system, or apartheid, in South Africa started during the Dutch colonial era. Cecil Rhodes, a 19th-century British politician, businessman and founder of the Rhodes Scholarship, was considered the "architect" of South Africa's notorious apartheid laws. South African university students were involved in uprisings and protests from the 1950s to 1994 when apartheid ended after a national election. But nightmares are not easily dispelled. A student protest broke out on March 9, 2015, against a statue of Cecil Rhodes at the University of Cape Town. The campaign was like spring thunder: It awoke people from their dreams and quickly developed into the "Rhodes Must Fall" campaign, which in January 2016 reached Oriel College at the University of Oxford where students protested against a statue of Rhodes located on college grounds.

The movement to remove such statues swept the globe after colonial suzerainty retreated in the 20th century. This particular student movement was the beginning of global anti-colonialism of another kind. Only Taiwan and Hong Kong have been unmoved.

The May Fourth Movement

Many student agitators in Hong Kong and Taiwan like to shine a positive light on their actions by comparing themselves with the participants of the May Fourth Movement. That is mixing apples with oranges. Nothing can be more far-fetched.

In a narrow sense, the May Fourth Movement refers to a patriotic movement driven by young students in modern Chinese history. On May 4, 1919, more than 3,000 students from 13 universities in Beijing gathered in Tiananmen Square. Filled with righteous anger, they held high their heads against the Paris Convention's decision to transfer Germany's vested interests in Shandong to Japan and sparked a series of nationwide demonstrations, parades, petitions, strikes and violent resistance to the government. In the end, the Chinese representative refused to sign the Treaty of Versailles.

In a broad sense, the May Fourth Movement was a matter of conscience initiated by students and intellectuals. It was part of the New Culture Movement from 1915 to 1926 that promoted the use of the vernacular and pushed for the progress of civilization and academic prosperity. During that period, intellectuals underwent a deep reflection on Chinese culture and advocated a way of life guided by science and democracy in search of a strong China.

Whether one takes the narrow or broad sense of the term, the May Fourth Movement is regarded as a watershed in the history of China. Its call for enlightenment, including science, democracy, human rights and truth and its advocacy for the use of modern language, continue to have a strong appeal even today. The leaders of the movement were all elites at universities, many of whom became figures known for their profound learning, such as Fu Sinian, Wen Yiduo, Qu Qiubai, Cai Yuanpei, Hu Shi, Chen Duxiu, Liang Qichao and Lu Xun. Some of them became pioneers in advocating academic freedom.

The student movements in Hong Kong and Taiwan today cannot be compared with the May Fourth Movement in terms of spirit, background and goal or the capability and knowledge of the participants. The two cannot be put together for comparison.

Nevertheless, from the angle of the separation of politics and education, the May Fourth Movement has its drawbacks; so deep-seated are some of the backward habits of China. Led by literary figures, the Movement could boast of success in popularizing the use of the vernacular, but apart from that, the overall result is lackluster. Even today, one hundred years later, the old ways have stuck with us. The advocates of the May Fourth Movement raised the banner of democracy and produced no results, mired in empty rhetoric as we still are.

And in science, we have not produced anything worthy of note, either.

Social Movements and Official Career

In the past, when a person was good at book learning, the next natural step was to become a state official. The purpose of studying was to carve out an official career—such was the rule set down by the courts. Looking with a positive light, one can see this behavior as a way of recruiting the learned and the capable to the government; in a negative light, however, this was the government's way of winning over intellectuals to the service of the court. The two existed in a state of co-dependence. Whether one chooses to do good or bad in one's official position or work for one's own interest or the interest of the people depends on one's conscience. This relationship between the court and intellectuals goes back a long time, and its invisible guiding hand is still shaping the government, society and universities across the Strait. This is another difference between the education system and society in China and the West.

Ancient and modern times differ, too. In the three societies across the Strait, what one sees more often is people who have done poorly in their studies but aspire for a career in government.

The agitators of today's mass movements often start from the university. Though without much accomplishment, many strive for a seat in the legislative branch without putting forward political opinions or become a party official, as these positions cost them nothing. The more boisterous a person gets, the higher the office they may aspire to, and the more abundant the returns. In the name of democracy, populistic support is indispensable for a candidate to get elected. That is why the ambitious among some students and low-grade teachers use the university as a platform to participate in mass movements as a warm-up exercise to fight for a future official career.

As for genuine learning, many of them do not really care as they know well that they can graduate once admitted (See Introduction). Many populist students choose the easy "soft" subjects to earn their degrees. Who knows what they have really learned! Some teachers know too well that promotion is not for them, and since they already have an iron bowl in hand and nobody is going to fire them, they might as well do what they want. Elections do not rule a country; the Taiwanese-style election culture ruins people's hearts and breaks that of higher education.

Young people who engage in social movements should harbor some ideals. Have they spoken up for the economically less privileged? Do they have the courage to rebuke the corrupt and the do-nothing government officials? Apart from issues that concern their interests, are they ready to stand up against policies that harm higher education? Or speak on behalf of the environment? Do they pay attention to the exceptionally high rate of work-related incidents in Taiwan? Are they concerned with the effect of climate change in Taiwan, Hong Kong or the Mainland, or the connection between air pollution in these three places and global climate change? Can they resist the temptation of getting all worked up over political issues tied to their self-interests? Can they stay away from impure and corrupt political pursuits whose motives are far from clear? Can they take the lead in conflicts without craving a better official position for themselves?

Are they afraid of the distance of the journey because they lack aspiration?

Let's lower our threshold a little more. Can young people wait until they have accomplished something concrete in society before seeking personal gain, official positions or legislative seats? During the social movements, some young people in Taiwan and Hong Kong aligned themselves with their cronies or were sentenced for other crimes. Take a look at the social movements in Europe, America, India and South Korea. Why are they so different?

Zhuge Liang (諸葛亮), a well-known Chinese statesman and military strategist from the Three Kingdoms period (220–280), once said, "People whose aspirations are not firm and whose ideological thinking is not broad tend to indulge themselves in affairs and emotion, accomplishing nothing and getting mixed in with a mediocre crowd, and inevitably falling into low-class society." Isn't this scenario wholly believable?

Raising the Red Flag Only to Sabotage It

The Chinese Communist Party (CCP) rose to power through mass movements and student protests. In Mainland China, it goes without saying that the CCP works hard to strengthen students' loyalty. Why do people at odds with the CCP in Taiwan and Hong Kong want to employ the same methodology to voice their opposition to the red flag while wearing masks?

Mass movements and student protests should speak up against injustice in society. However, they have become ways for young people to get rich and acquire power. If this is not unique to Hong Kong and Taiwan, it is at least more developed here than in other places. How come people who oppose Chinese authoritarianism are the most Chinese and most authoritarian? Once in power, why do they raise the flag of democracy to counter democracy?

In discussions, teachers and students must respect academic ethics and adhere to the principle of peace and rationality. Political mafias like the agitators for mass movements must not be allowed to come into university campuses to stir up trouble. The energy of our young people should be the power that pushes society forward. Only by working and living together can we find a way to uphold social justice.

A Little Story of a Little Kindness

Recently, I heard a little story that is quite shocking.

One day in May 2021, a man in Florida took his young Labrador retriever for a walk. An alligator suddenly jumped out from a pond, grabbed the dog between its teeth and dragged it into the water. Without thinking, the man pressed hard the alligator's eyes with his thumbs, blinded the alligator and pulled it out of the water until it let go of his dog.

This alarming incident was witnessed by a teacher who happened to pass by. Later, the man talked to the press, saying that for him, there is no turning back from saving his dog. He must charge forward to let the alligator know that he would not make things easy for it. The alligator indeed retreated, and he and the dog suffered only minor injuries.

Our world is a compassionate place. Incidents like the story above show that real compassion can be found anywhere. From what I can see, however, chances are that it is not found as frequently in Taiwan, Hong Kong and the Mainland as in the US. In times of danger, people in these three places might not want to step up to lend a helping hand. If they do, it's only after considering how their involvement will affect them. The Americans, with their warmth, naivety and unaffectedness, do whatever comes to mind. They do not bother with all these unnecessary distracting thoughts.

When I was in the Marine Corps in Taiwan, we stood by a basic principle: when I charge forward, you will watch my back. Is it a principle too hard for ordinary people to understand?

The difference in character can be seen clearly in personal education and cultural attainment. A telling sign is that in Taiwan, Hong Kong and Mainland China, the government and people like to refer to rules and dogmas, which they use to harangue and intimidate. Who knows what those rules mean. The crooked among them learn to rehearse them well until they know them like a song, but when they act, they are timid, each and every one of them. The most daring among them might get to the point where they will urge other people to charge forward while they stay behind to watch their back—nothing more.

Putting aside what is right or wrong, we can consider the recent demonstrators in Hong Kong and Taiwan. They pick on the weak and stay away from the strong. Universities, which have nothing to do with what they are fighting for, became an easy target for their violent behavior.

Is it a revolution? Interestingly, in protesting and rioting, they covered their faces but held sharp weapons in their hands. Prancing around in their arrogance, they charged ahead violently as if to brook no resistance. Yet when the pressure came, they were the first to run. They whimpered as if they had lost their loved ones when they were arrested, creating such mixed and contrasting feelings. These unpromising people are worlds apart from the protestors in South Korea and Japan.

Here are more examples. White students at the University of Cape Town in South Africa in the 1960s fiercely opposed apartheid. They held several large-scale protests and even fought the military and police. Without hiding their real names, they defied beatings and arrest. On January 6, 2021, more than 2,000 demonstrators stormed the Capitol Building in Washington, D.C., disrupting the ongoing electoral count. They faced off against the Capitol Police in broad daylight, charging into the building through the door with their heads held high. None acted like those sneaky rogues in Hong Kong in 2019 who covered their faces or wrapped themselves in black. Then, on the second anniversary of the attack, Biden said political violence would not be tolerated in the US, and indeed there is nothing to be glorified about these rioters.

Justice? Is it just a word on paper to show that they have not completely forgotten it?

17
Populism: The Stumbling Block of Academic Progress

The world has become diversified. The communist society of today is different from its former self at the beginning of the 20th century, just as the capitalist society of today has changed considerably from that of the past. Communism and capitalism take components of each other and are no longer two mutually exclusive camps. Yet populism and power-mongering remain the same in our communities.

For their own benefit, some go out of their way to pander to the masses, giving public events a skewed interpretation in the public arena. The media put on their sheepskin coats and sway with the wind. Rather than adhering to the professional spirit of neutrality, objectivity, fairness, justice and public interest, they cater to public demand in the process of gaining political and economic rewards for themselves. The former is the result of working under the specter of populism, and the latter is the vulgarization of the media and the internet.

The section on *Art and Literature in Han Shu* (漢書藝文志) says, "But the confused have lost sight of profound and mysterious truths, while those whose job it is to dispel heresies have chosen to follow the times and depart from the right path. They would rather curry favor with the people through startling pronouncements and following in their footsteps." Such actions are reminiscent of those who ride on the waves of populism and are used in battle as axes by political mobsters.

Populism, Taiwan Style

Most of the time, Taiwan manages to keep religion and politics apart, but participants in mass movements treat politics as a religion and practice it fervently on campus. At times, the government echoes the populist sentiments when carrying out its policies, respecting the wishes of the people on the surface but working for ulterior motives in reality. At other times, it takes the lead in guiding populism, putting aside its proper work of governing.

Communications scholar Joe He views populism as a trend of thought that emphasizes the values of ordinary people to the extreme. It takes popularization as the ultimate source of legitimacy for all political movements and political institutions, using irrational responses among common folk to radically reform society. However, such actions often backfire and cause long-term harm. Populists oppose elites and expert authority and are highly exclusive. They have no tolerance for opposition or "bystanders". The populist movement in Taiwan may stem superficially from the anti-authority demands of ordinary people, but in fact it is exploited by those who collude with populists to gain control.

The insightful words of Wang Bohui, the plant manager of the Fourth Nuclear Power Plant in Taiwan, reported in *The Storm Media* on April 18, 2021, will serve as a footnote to the argument in this chapter. In the report, Wang mentioned a sociology student at NTU who, after taking part in social movements, now understood how populism affects Taiwan. He offered a definition: a populist policy is one that conforms to the wishes of many people but violates the objective interests of the public. For example, if a candidate promises free transportation for all, he will certainly please voters, but such a move will violate the objective public interest. This is populism. In the past 30 years, universities have mushroomed in Taiwan, engulfing almost all villages and townships. Such a move must have helped the advocates and supporters of the building of universities to hop into the political arena, which fits with this definition of a populist policy. (See Chapter 3.)

The student gave another example: The Fourth Nuclear Power Plant is an important public project critical to Taiwan's energy resources development. However, discussions about it were not undertaken from a professional perspective but were instead driven by the hunger strike of Lin Yixiong. Taking advantage of Lin's situation, the government peremptorily declared the project closed, showing how one individual can be used to hijack public policy. Turning to yet another example, the student pointed out that years ago, the former mayor of Taipei City, Huang Dazhou, put forward a strong case for the demolition of the Chunghua Market Bazaar and the illegal structures in the Da'an Park area and for straightening the course of the Keelung River. Huang was torn to pieces by public opinion, but future events showed that his plan not only solved the problem of flooding but also laid down the foundation for the orderly development of the Neihu district. All these constructions are the pride of Taipei today.

Any public construction project is bound to arouse two opposing views. The way to deal with such a dilemma is to consider the best interests of all, giving due respect to professionalism. To appeal to populist sentiments is to create public fear, which is by no means a normal or correct way. Lingering problems will definitely surface sooner or later.

Following an official order, the two generators of the First Nuclear Power Plant and the two generators of the Second Nuclear Power Plant were shut down without any thought regarding the storage of the used fuel. After the suspension of the use of nuclear power, only Linkou, Datan and the highly polluting Hsieh-ho power plants remain in operation. Would this result in a power shortage? After the referendum in December 2021, the whole government was mobilized to manage the proposed solution, i.e., to make way for a highly polluting natural gas pipeline by destroying a 1,000-year-old algae reef that would pave the way for new power plants. This solution is more like digging another hole to fix the original hole. This is government-led Taiwanese populism.

Power Shortage, Power Outage

Due to human error, the ultra-high-voltage substation in the Lujhu District of Kaohsiung tripped four generators at the Hsinta Power Plant owned by the Taiwan Power Company on May 13, 2021, leading to a power outage in the northern, middle and southern parts of Taiwan. The power supply to 4 million households was interrupted. Four days later, the No. 1 unit of the Hsinta Power Plant malfunctioned and was shut down, resulting in the May 17 power outage, affecting approximately 660,000 households. On March 3, 2022, another major power outage caused by the same power plant (Hsinta Power Plant) affected 5 million households and disrupted the water supply. Whether it was human or technical errors that caused the outage, when places all over Taiwan had to take turns going without power due to an incident at a power plant, affecting several millions of people, the weakness of the power supply gets fully exposed.

Power supply is tied in with industrial and commercial development as well as the security of the state. The power outage in Taiwan became a hot topic of discussion. All at once, people wondered whether Taiwan had a power shortage and what measures should be taken to remedy the problem. Objectively speaking, this is a professional question, but once politics got into the mix, a cacophony of voices broke out. One cannot but be reminded of the blackout on August 15, 2017, and the ensuing controversies over Taiwan's power shortage.

When I was interviewed by the Taiwan media that year, I gave a comprehensive answer in laypeople's terms to a question on energy resources and environmental protection. The basic issues behind the power outage of May 2021 are the same as those of August 2017, and the answers I gave then still apply. Power supply safety involves several basic factors: energy policy, energy structure, spare standby power, the reliability of the energy network and a fair electricity fee structure. I will address these issues briefly below.

Energy is a necessity in modern daily life. It comes from different possible sources, including hydropower, thermal power (coal, oil, natural gas), power generated from nuclear, wind, solar, biological, and other sources (e.g., geothermal energy, the tides, marsh gas, etc.), making up what is called "rainbow energies." In terms of efficacy, safety reliability, sustainability, environmental protection, resources reserve, economic affordability and value, these sources have strengths and weaknesses. When formulating an energy policy, one must consider balancing environmental protection, economic well-being, reliability and sustainability. Countries and regions have different resources they can dip into, which must be considered when deciding what combination of "rainbow energies" to adopt.

Taiwan lacks natural resources. Ninety-eight percent of its energy is imported. Forty-eight percent of it is consumed by electricity, 39% by petroleum-based transportation and the remaining 13% on other uses. Petroleum, natural gas and coal comprise 85% of the energy resource consumption. Such a high rate of fossil oil consumption is rare, placing Taiwan top of the highest per capita emissions for both carbon dioxide and sulfur dioxide, two to three times higher than the average emissions for the whole world.

Nuclear is a clean energy. It has served Taiwan for more than 40 years, and so far, there is no scientific report of direct or indirect casualties. However, under the slogan of "a nuclear-free homeland", the development generated of nuclear energy has encountered many obstacles, replaced by electricity generated by highly polluting thermal power, departing further and further away from the emissions reduction target of the United Nations.

Like having a spare tire in the car, the base-load power reserve is one of the keys to ensure the safety of the power supply. Electricity consumption changes all the time. A high base-load reserve will have a lower chance of power outage; conversely, one with a low base-load reserve will encounter a higher chance, which increases exponentially. If there is a risk, accidents occur. That is why, to satisfy users, advanced countries usually carry an electricity reserve of far more than 15%. However, Taiwan's spare standby power is often much lower than 10%, at an "alert stage" of 6%. Naturally, the chance of a power outage is relatively high.

Human error is always one of the factors that cause a power outage and should be considered in the reliability calculation. The authorities maintained that the reason for the series of power outages in 2021 was not "a shortage of power" but human error, the outdated power grid, the surge of electricity use due to the heat wave and severe drought, and the generation of electricity by renewable resources at a level lower than anticipated. The ultimate reason, however, is that there is an insufficient electricity reserve. Power supply is intimately connected with people's livelihoods and the economy. How can we afford to base our plan on the best-case scenario and not equip ourselves with sufficient reserve? Besides, electricity depends on a stable energy source, such as thermal or nuclear power. Wind, water, solar energy and other renewable resources are affected by climate conditions and are not suitable for producing electricity reserves.

Taiwan is surrounded by the sea, with a natural environment like Japan. We cannot turn to an external power grid for support, and the supply of electricity naturally must withstand a higher risk. That is why even after the Fukushima Incident, Japan resolutely returned to the use of nuclear power. Japan's Prime Minister stated in August 2022 that seven more idled nuclear reactors will be restarted in the summer of 2023 to stabilize the country's power supply by 2050 and make up for the shortfall in carbon reduction. The government further plans to develop new nuclear power plants and may consider extending the operating period of existing plants.

It is extremely important to maintain the reliability of the power grid. The outage of 2017 and 2021 in Taiwan is precisely caused by the weak power grid. The base load is unreliable, and the reserve capacity is low. Any errors will definitely cause a power outage.

There is no free energy in this world. The price of electricity should reflect the cost of generating it. In determining the price, besides the cost of generation, transportation, and transformation, one should consider safety, reliability, the cost of the well-being of sustainability as well as the sense of social, psychological and national security. Different energy sources come with different degrees of risk and pollution. The ideal formula for calculating the price of electricity is for consumers to choose the electricity source that they are willing to accept, according to which a price can be calculated by taking into consideration the distribution of sources, the quantity consumed, the cost of production, the risk during the life cycle and the pollution cost. Also, the price of electricity is extremely low in Taiwan. The government should consider setting a policy to encourage electricity saving and the rational use of electricity.

Using nuclear power to generate electricity will help to replace the use of highly polluting fossil fuels such as coal and natural gas. At least, it will speed up the transition to clean, renewable energy in the future. Nuclear power is recognized as the best energy source to solve the problem of global warming. Why can't Taiwan undertake the all-round simulation introduced in Chapter 4 for the environment? In the absence of a long-term plan, the government is fighting a losing battle in areas such as energy policies, environmental protection and higher education. When professional voices are silenced, nobody dares speak out. Only the energy sycophants are left to flatter the government's populist ideology.

A dozen years ago, I talked about how energy was a social security and a national security issue, emphasizing how it needed to be independent of political passions and populist considerations. Few got the point. However, after the outbreak of the Russian and Ukrainian war in 2022 and the subsequent impact on the energy supply to Europe, the point is now well made. Taiwanese democracy is driven too much by politics rather than concern for people's livelihood. Education is for decoration.

Using populism to drive its policies, the Taiwan government operates in much the same way it runs an election: good at handling news; weak at solving problems. Stepping into the 21st century, when the world views nuclear-generated electricity as key to providing low-carbon energy, the authorities are unwilling to take a holistic view and instead opt for an anti-nuclear stance. In May 2021, Taiwan ran short of water, electricity and vaccines. The pandemic escalated again in the late spring of 2022, with new cases reaching a new high. There was a shortage of COVID-19 rapid test kits, and society was thrown into chaos. The problems of air pollution, power shortage and the mishandling of COVID-19 are all consequences of populism.

Random Thoughts about Hong Kong

Taiwan is my hometown. I was born and brought up there. It is where I completed my mandatory military service and where my most pristine memories reside. Although Hong Kong was a foreign place before I arrived here to work, it shares the same Chinese culture and written language. I learned, grew, worked and lived in these two places. I observed and thought, and would like to speak what is on my mind freely.

Hong Kong is where the East meets the West, and the new and the old come together—a matter of pride for the people living there. But people rarely notice that Hong Kong has retained the dregs of both Chinese and Western cultures along with the good. For example, if a university attaches great importance to results, it should focus on academic research to promote welfare. But young people in Hong Kong generally know little about history; nor are they willing to learn about it. They fail to acquire what is decent about the culture while ostentatious indulgence in empty rhetoric about traditional China lives on across university campuses and among the vulgar and the bureaucrats. At most, they can parrot a few outdated doctrines eloquently. Bo Yang, a historian and novelist, speaks of how Chinese people get lost in the soy sauce vat culture, a phenomenon still highly visible in Hong Kong and Taiwan in the 21st century.

Besides, Hong Kong people who defy superiors and maintain distance from subordinates sometimes reveal their anxieties and fears. The COVID-19 pandemic has been rampant for three years. "In the east, the sun is out; in the west, there is rain; it seems to be clear, but somewhat not yet clear, you may as well say." (Liu Yuxi) Hong Kong was torn between two extreme arguments, represented by the East and the West. The East demanded zero COVID-19 cases, lockdowns, compulsory universal testing and complete elimination of the virus; the West advised against universal testing or achieving zero cases, no more lockdowns and co-existing with the virus, with occasional opposition to vaccinations. As a result, the preferred outcome was not achieved because people didn't know how to choose the right path. The way ahead is difficult and divergent: which way to go? Whether oriental or occidental, while approaches may differ, the purpose remains the same. We have suffered rather than benefitted from existing in the meeting point of the Eastern and Western worlds.

The more one speaks, the more one departs from the right way. The stronger one's desires, the more harm caused. As far as the administration is concerned, the outdated bureaucracy and proliferation of rules and regulations under Chinese-style governance co-exist in Hong Kong, which jars with the culture of innovation. The complexity and length of the administration process, a combination of both Chinese and British bureaucracies, harm the breadth and depth of research in higher education.

Inheriting traditional British government attitudes, the government and the people in Hong Kong have adopted the unhealthy practice of ranking universities with similar backgrounds to justify funding allocation, which superficially categorizes students from different universities. Some officials take pride in their splendid early administrative track records and Oxbridge-accented English, which they believe places them a rung above the universities. Little do they know that their resplendent exterior has engendered discontent, foreshadowing disturbances to come.

Hong Kong is an open society. It is a strength that the government system is complete and rigorous and that the finances are clean and conservative. A rigorous system, however, can become too inflexible, fostering blind faith in rules. The academic atmosphere is lacking on university campuses. A minority of teachers adept at neither teaching nor research take advantage of their special positions to engage in activities unrelated to their duties, while teachers' unions bring political disputes onto campus. To complicate matters, some in society who stress academic credentials rather than academic expertise step out of their own fields and directly commandeer university affairs. On the surface, Hong Kong seems to stress campus autonomy, but in fact, overt and covert forces on and off campus are spoiling for a political fight. Young people imitate what they see in the adult world, and it is only natural that student associations turn messy.

Yet isn't it surprising that among these disgruntled university students, many of whom yearn for a brighter future, many aspire to become government officials? Thus the cross-breeding continues. Is this not the traditional Chinese culture we are all too familiar with?

Perhaps we are carrying too heavy a burden. I have offered suggestions on various issues to government departments, either orally or in written communications, in the hope that those in power would abandon outdated modes of thinking and allow experts to spearhead education, research and other higher education matters rather than continue to control universities. For example, for fifteen years, many have proposed sending delegations to the US, the world's leader in higher education. The UGC showed no response, seemingly so as not to expose their inadequacies and continue to deploy more familiar UK and Australian models. The British system of RAE is upheld, superfluously subjecting published papers to another round of subjective review to determine the allocation of funding (see Chapter 13). By creating work for idle bureaucrats, the government has established the rationale for its existence.

To Carrie Lam's credit, her government stressed innovation and invested abundant resources accordingly. Unfortunately, the government fell short of its intentions in resource allocation, management, personnel organization and keeping taps on social inequalities. A progressive university should be oriented toward results, and professors and students should be encouraged to put innovativeness into practice. Hong Kong people are known for their extraordinary IQ, but they know little about separating politics and education because the right atmosphere and relevant experience are missing. Minor officials think only of protecting their positions, while those higher in the echelons of power know all the tricks. Besides, there are others who plan to move into the official world under the banner of democracy. All have axes to grind.

The government should consider re-engineering its governance structure and personnel recruitment. Government officials should not consider themselves superior to the people, let alone the universities. With their high salaries, they should do more than just look at the rule book or busy themselves only with allocating money and producing reports while ignoring the basic but multi-faceted way of fully utilizing human potential.

What's more, they should not self-award British-type medals and awards in turns year by year.

The Mainland

For several decades, I have come into contact with many universities and research institutions on the Mainland and have worked with their old, middle-aged and young scholars. We range far and wide in our conversations. On the whole, Mainland professors are seasoned international travelers. They admire higher education around the world, but they are also confident in themselves. Just as they learn from universities in the West, they have opinions on internal governance, but do not follow them blindly, unlike Hong Kong or Taiwan, which seem to be bogged down by outmoded, conservative attitudes.

I have no experience of staying in one place on the Mainland for any length of time, but I can well imagine that living under the rigid governance model must be stifling. Higher education in the Mainland has made noticeable progress in its most politically relaxed period, benefiting from active academic exchanges with the international community, particularly the US, and the vast resources generated from its economic take-off following its WTO entry. However, as the once diminished Orwellian governance resurrected in recent years, universities are working under tremendous pressure to be "politically correct." Although the type of populist street movements in Taiwan and Hong Kong has little influence on university operations in the Mainland, the omnipresence of the "Big Brother" is exerting a chilling effect, especially on those working in areas related to liberal arts and social sciences.

In fields such as engineering and the natural sciences, higher education in the Mainland can boast some proud results, although they fall short of the ideal in some areas, especially in the direction of strategy and professional ethics. Subjectively, even as they recruit research and teaching staff from advanced countries, they keep the work of setting research policies in their hands. Objectively, mixing politics and education and enforcing opaque and infiltrated regulations erect a wall between them and the outside world. To international specialists, the attractiveness of working in Mainland China is limited. The direct intervention of Mainland authoritarian politics in universities is another version of the interweaving of politics and education, which is different from what occurs in Taiwan and Hong Kong. Yet the situation is not dissimilar to water flowing into the same sea.

On the other hand, as with Hong Kong and Taiwan, there are too many rules on the Mainland. The complexity of paperwork goes against the US goal-oriented spirit of higher education. There are many conferences on the Mainland, but they tend to be long. Due to the practice of linear ordering, the ruling elites enjoy tremendous power. The agenda is often announced only at the very last minute. Worse, meeting times can be changed at the final hour, creating all kinds of residual problems. Officials in the Mainland get rotated like a Chinese revolving lantern. Newcomers frequently might have to decide to alter their predecessors' teaching and research promises. While they revel in their new policies, the old guard is left in the lurch. In turn, the "newcomers" see their policies revoked by their successors. This is not a system designed to win trust.

Interestingly, the heads of departments, deans and presidents of US universities have great arbitration power, but in the three places across the Strait, more often than not, the committee decides. The only difference is that in the Mainland, the committee is directed by the Party, while in Hong Kong and Taiwan, it is directed by rigid rules. On the surface, the responsibility is shared by all concerned, which means it lies with nobody.

Pathology of Following Blindly the Wish of the Officials

In 1968, President Ma Ying-jeou and I graduated from Taipei Municipal Jianguo High School. Before I accepted an invitation to speak at the Office of the President in 2013, we were not acquainted. Apart from the information available in the media, we had only a superficial knowledge of each other as there was no overlap in our specialization and experiences. Ma Ying-jeou cared about people's livelihoods and believed in evidence-based scientific research. However, because he thought highly of my energy report, a few media, with their own intention, nicknamed me "Yo Ma" (Friend of Ma). There you have an unhealthy example of political parties' skillful use of populism and control over the media. Why is the President always placed sky high and not "Yo Kuo" (Friend of Kuo), or at least both could be on equal footing?

On the same note, nearly half a year after I arrived at CityU, the Hong Kong government appointed Leung Chun-ying as Council Chairman at CityU. He was, in other words, my direct supervisor. Since I was new to Hong Kong, I had no idea who he was. After some meetings, he agreed with the importance of the University's proposed collaboration with Cornell University and actively assisted in establishing the first 6-year Bachelor of Veterinary Medicine degree in Asia. In 2012, he became the Chief Executive of Hong Kong. By convention, he was also Chancellor of the eight UGC-funded universities, including CityU. In a sense, he was the head president of all universities, a legacy from the British Hong Kong government. It was a major surprise that some media insisted that CityU be labeled a "Fan of Leung". If truth be known, since CityU led by me produced the idea of a college of veterinary medicine, and Carrie Lam finally approved it, shouldn't they be called "Fans of CityU" or "Fans of Kuo" instead? Now that the vet college has implemented its vision for One Health, all sectors of Hong Kong thank the two former Chief Executives for supporting veterinary medicine, despite the odds.

The above examples show that a culture of subservience pervades Hong Kong and Taiwan. An official is considered superior to a university president, a habit that stems from the ancient belief that the court and intellectuals exist in a dominant/subservient relationship. The Mainland is no better. One by one, those in power crawl to the top until they are perched above university presidents. They have given us more than enough material to write a sequel to the 19th-century satirical novel *Exposure of the Official World*.

I was invited to speak about the importance of the "separation of politics and education" at over 100 high schools, institutions of higher education, professional bodies, government organizations and international conferences. During my lectures and other exchanges, people often ask what it takes to build a first-class university. They are looking for quick answers like a hungry person looking for a bowl of instant noodles. They don't give it much thought as long as their stomachs are filled. However, one must bear in mind that in order to build a first-rate university, there has to be a first-rate educational system, and that system has to be built on a correct social mentality, one that rids us of the pathology of blindly following the wishes of officials. If this sickness persists in Taiwan, Hong Kong and the Mainland, improvements cannot be expected.

Unstable Society, University in Trouble

The correct mentality is still lacking in the three societies across the Strait, and this illness forms a big part of populism.

CityU upholds the value of campus autonomy. Politics is politics, and education is education. The two do not mix. People on and off campus should not use the university as a platform to engage in street politics and destroy academic freedom. In 2008, I proposed and implemented the advanced discourse on higher education, "integrating teaching and research" and "separating politics and education". In 2022, the Senate at CityU officially incorporated "separating politics and education" as a "Basic Principle of Academic Governance". (See Appendix.)

That politics and education should be kept separate is a consistent article of belief for me, one fully examined in my 2019 book *Soulware: The American Way in China's Higher Education*. My views may have hit the nail on people's heads. Or perhaps, one can't discuss the ocean with a frog in a well and ice with a summer insect. The idea of "Separation of Politics and Education" aroused no interest in Hong Kong and Taiwan. Rather, it seemed to have touched a sore point in some quarters. Perhaps we inhabit different worlds. Their experience is so far removed from mine that we cannot communicate. The governments and students across the Strait made no comments at all on the basic principle of the "separation of politics and education," and the media did not have the courage to report it, either. Be that as it may, the book drew the attention of the Japanese. A Japanese translation of the book is now in print. In the book, I warn that if this principle were ignored, innovation would suffer, leaving behind a host of problems. Quicker than words can tell, sure enough, by the spring and summer of 2019, what the book forewarned had struck Hong Kong.

On June 9, 2019, in a protest against an amendment to the extradition law, people from all walks of life, as well as high school and university students, came out on the street. The police and citizens clashed. The situation was not created by the universities, and yet none of the campuses eluded rampant vandalism and disturbances. The damage to teaching and research was particularly woeful. Donors came to complain about students' role in the protests and clamored for the return of their donations. The whole system seemed to have almost collapsed; it was chaos inside and outside.

Beginning in June 2019, out of a concern for the safety and well-being of teachers and students, I telephoned the Hong Kong government, entreating it to consider the welfare of society. I cut down (and canceled) my overseas trips and remained on campus to prepare for any emergencies. I took the initiative to instruct two vice-presidents in charge of student affairs and administration to form the Emergency Response Unit and to maintain close communications with students and staff. I undertook a huge amount of coordination and replied to over 1,000 queries, and at critical moments removed blockades, installed protective railings, maintained order, arranged transportation and lodgings, and evacuated teachers, students and staff. We declared through announcements and public messages that CityU respected peace and rational behavior, calling on students to pay attention to safety. I made it clear that CityU would not tolerate any kind of violent behavior or bullying language. The campus suffered considerable damage during the disturbances, but clashes between different communities were relatively few. This had something to do with our timely decisions and the appropriate leadership.

CityU came under the assault of external forces on an unprecedented scale. Mobs from outside joined forces with populist students and politicians. With weapons in hand, they demanded to meet with the University President. They rioted on and off campus. In broad daylight, rioters in black masks went on the rampage, wantonly destroying campus facilities, burning Lau building, acting in a manner reminiscent of the Ku Klux Klan. On a moonlit night in November, they attempted to break into the President's Office and the Communications and Public Relations Office. The line from *Macbeth* came to mind: "Foul is fair, and fair is foul", and it seemed evil forces hovered "through the fog and filthy air," waiting for a chance to envelop the city. The Hong Kong government seemed out of touch and slow to respond while people vented their frustration on campus.

Throughout the development of these events in 2019, CityU kept to its fair and upright ways and demonstrated a full commitment to its mission. Council Chair, Mr. Lester Garson Huang, and the Executive Committee were united in their views that the President of the University should not meet with rioting demonstrators from off-campus, while the Cabinet issued a statement condemning the powers behind the destruction and called for the preservation of social order in support of the principle of one country, two systems. Amid the chaos, as the mainstay of academic research, CityU upheld the core value that street politics should stay away from campus and that the University focuses on its teaching and research tasks.

With the social unrest continuing into 2020, when COVID-19 was still largely unknown, people from different social sectors proposed on May 5 to form the Hong Kong Coalition by the Government. They invited presidents of all the universities in Hong Kong to participate. All the way through, CityU regards nurturing future pillars of society as a major aspect of its mission and is dedicated to contributing to Hong Kong through research and proactively raising funds to boost career guidance for students. Actions were taken on April 17, 2020, to invest over HK$10 million to help students prepare for the world of work. Although our decisions align with the Hong Kong Coalition's goals, we were a step ahead.

However, following the principle that politics and education should be kept separate, and as endorsed by Cabinet, I declined to join the Coalition, making me the only university president not to join.

A university should stick to its course and pay no heed to how the wind blows. It should not dance to the tune of street politics, and populist politics should not take precedence over universities. I persisted in my commitment to the separation of politics and education and did not once stray from it throughout the protests in 2019 and 2020. Another case in point was my response to a joint statement to support National Security Law, suggested by the Heads of Universities Committee (HUCOM). As law-abiding citizens, we comply with laws. Giving a joint political statement to indicate the support for a newly approved law is unnecessary. I declined to sign the statement released on June 1, 2020.

Throughout the various incidents in 2019 and 2020, political mobsters took advantage of the chaos to pursue their own ends. Among their number were those from Taiwan looking for an opportunity to wedge their foot in the doorway, propagating biased views while politics grievously perverted learning and order. Blameless students became their pawns, and Hong Kong, one of the new places, was turned upside down. As for those students arrested, CityU appointed lawyers to give them free legal service, posting bail for and defending them in court. However, the forces hiding behind the scenes, including politicians looking for opportunities to intervene in education with their own brand of dirty politics and self-serving personal attacks, disappeared and were heard of no more.

Let's make a long story short: movements go into reverse after they reach an extreme. In 2019, the social movement wreaked destruction on the universities under the slimmest of excuses. In 2021, the government issued its counter-attack by promulgating the National Security Act, enabling the hand of politics to inch further into university affairs. On the surface, peace has returned, although undercurrents continue to swell. The underlings were arrested and thrown in jail. In 2022, universities began picking up the pieces and arranged for convicted students to continue their studies after serving their sentences.

In chaotic times, the wise withdraw for self-preservation. They work day and night to stay true to themselves. While keeping politics and education apart is difficult, it is even more challenging for universities to cope with the aftermath. Haste makes waste. The dust may have settled down, but society is wrecked.

During the disturbances in 2019, letters from donors flooded into our offices asking for the return of their donations and the strictest penalties to be imposed on rioting students. In 2021, when events had begun to settle, another wave of emails and letters washed in. These were from the initially silent (but actually quite slippery people) who criticized CityU for caving in to students' demands and offering them refuge in 2019. They demanded to know which of the protesting students were supported by their donations. What a fickle bunch!

Warm-hearted Folk vs Hypocritical Whole Persons in Officialdom

During the unrest in Hong Kong in 2019, CityU received support from thousands of people, mainly from the general public. The counter staff at a nearby McDonald's were the first to reassure me. They said, "President, we will protect you if anyone makes trouble!" These workers exemplify warm-hearted folk expressing true feelings. Having experienced the world, one can't help but miss ordinary people when hearing the desolate sounds of autumn unrest.

Following colonial bureaucratic practice, government officials were arrogant and domineering during peaceful times, but they exhibited terrible habits common to traditional Chinese officialdom during times of turmoil and were often cowardly, secretive and evasive. Hong Kong claims to be where East meets West, and yet it is often neither the East nor the West, and only able to mouth high-sounding words, with no intention to accept the consequences while evading any responsibility to clean up the mess. I suppose British officials during the colonial days might not have been as disordered. No wonder people are dissatisfied and can't stop being critical.

The UGC, which oversees the essential and nonessential affairs of universities in Hong Kong and regards itself as superior, lay low during the 2019 social unrest, quietly avoiding trouble and leaving individual universities to face the challenges caused by the government. Gold ore is buried deep in the rock, accessible only by sifting out the mud and sand. In recent years, CityU has performed exceptionally well, but with its blind adherence to conventions, the conservative Hong Kong government has never fully supported CityU. In fact, it treated us shabbily. Logically speaking, as the aggrieved party, we should complain, but we continue to communicate with the UGC rationally and professionally and refrain from recrimination. It has taken many years for a social phenomenon to surface, and it is a mistake to blame one or two individuals. Since the goal is to obtain fair treatment, there is no point in openly airing grievances.

Anyone in our society should treat others respectfully. It is a pity that the governments and societies across the Strait have no understanding of the diversity and openness of universities. Nor do they respect the independence of the universities and academic freedom. There is little team spirit or self-respect.

The Hypocrisy of Populism

Populism is like the human crushes we have witnessed over the years. The list makes for uncomfortable reading: the Halloween festivities in Itaewon, Seoul, in 2022; the pilgrimage to Mecca in 2015; the New Year's Eve celebrations in Shanghai's historic Bund district in 2014; the Love Parade electronic dance music festival in Duisburg, Germany in 2010; the fireworks display in Akashi, Japan in 2001; the Weierkang Restaurant fire in Taichung, Taiwan in 1995; the New Year's Eve celebrations in Lan Kwai Fong, Hong Kong in 1993; and the football match at Hillsborough Stadium, UK in 1989. In too many cases, the crowd at the back kept pushing forward, not knowing those at the front had fallen and lost consciousness. The more people push, not appreciating the severity of the situation, the more people get crushed.

COVID-19 cases continued to surge in 2022. When the public was successively perplexed and disturbed by issues such as the Thesis-gate Scandal, the Digital Intermediary Service Act, tensions in the Taiwan Strait and overheated local elections, climate change was sweeping the world, including Taiwan. As a member of the global community, Taiwan had blundered in its carbon reduction plans and misplaced its priorities when handling energy and environmental concerns. The previous disasters were unstoppable, and so are the disasters to come. While air pollution is still a concern, the new issue is the rise in sea levels: the coast of Taitung has been eroded and roads hollowed out; the Tainan canal flooded the roads with no respite for several weeks; and the aquaculture area in Yunlin collapsed because of intruding seawater, etc. Despite old regrets and new worries, the government dismisses people's opinions. The populists ignore the issues as if they are unrelated to them. Ecological destruction, which may seem like a natural disaster, is human-made.

Table 17.1 summarizes the following types of average annual fatalities in Taiwan, Hong Kong, Mainland China and the US: nuclear power accidents over the past 40 years; earthquakes over the past 10 years; auto accidents over the past 10 years; COVID-19 over the past three years; and lung cancer over the past 10 years. The data point out that the most serious damage to people's lives turns out to be lung cancer, the leading cause of cancer deaths in recent years, resulting from unscrupulous politicians and passionate populism ignoring air pollution. Relatively speaking, earthquakes

Table 17.1 Annual fatalities in Taiwan, Hong Kong, Mainland China and the US over the indicated years.[a]

Accidents	Average annual fatalities[b]			
	Taiwan	Hong Kong	Mainland	US
1983-2022 nuclear power plant	0 (0)	0 (0)	0 (0)	2 (~0)
2013-2022 earthquakes	14.7 (0.62)	0 (0)	376[d] (0.26)	1 (0)
2013-2022 auto accidents	2,943 (125)	115 (15)	61,177 (43)	35,433 (110)
2020-2023 COVID-19	19,005 (796)	13,756 (1,809)	121,444 (89)[f]	1,164,718 (3,479)
2011-2020 lung cancer[c]	9,239 (392)	3,891 (524)	667,566[e] (473)	149,228 (450)

[a] Figures listed in the table may be slightly inaccurate due to reporting, but they shouldn't hurt the overall comparative analysis.
[b] Figures in the brackets represent fatalities per million population.
[c] Crude mortality, including tracheal, bronchial and lung cancer deaths in Taiwan and US.
[d] Mainland China and global statistics for 2009–2018.
[e] 2015, 2016 and 2020 statistics.
[f] As of May 24, 2023. China's reporting on COVID-19 was not transparent.

are natural disasters and air pollution is human-made, with the former far less damaging than the latter!

According to the eminent monk Venerable Master Chin Kung (淨空), "Efforts for environmental protection provide only superficial solutions. The 'root cause' is polluted human nature." Superficially, environmental pollution is caused by burning fossil fuels, but it is caused by polluted human nature, polluted feelings, polluted politics and polluted ethics.

He fears the result, but I am scared of the cause. While the ecological environment is adversely affected, the spiritual environment is even more of a concern. The government does not work at improving citizens' lives and does not worry about chaos and poverty. People change according to their environment. Human greed and confusion derive from a blindness of the soul, and a person possessing such traits is sick. Populism results from a blindness of the soul; populism pollutes the earth and plunges us into the abyss.

The world stands in turmoil. Societies across the Strait maintain their respective blind spots. Environmental pollution is a self-inflicted wound.

We have nobody to blame. Universities are not political battlegrounds. *Fenqing*, literally translated as "angry youths," have nothing better to do with their time than hang around. They are uncultured, incompetent and greedy for immediate gains and convenience. They unsheathe their broken swords, with their faces covered, and holding their blades upside down, they look around, puzzled. Who will be troubled by their faults, and who will benefit?

The higher education sector across the Strait is unaware that it is stuck in a pot of foul water. Ethics education receives little attention, while civic education has been taken off the curriculum. Universities indulge in vacuous discussions about whole person education (Chapter 9) or general education (Chapter 10) that is not understood by many while failing to follow the path of self-rule and discipline.

Where do these heart diseases come from?

> *The reason for speaking English results only from the blindness of the soul,*
> *While rattling like empty bottles is due to the disintegration of teaching and research.*
> *Chaos is the result of the entanglement of politics with education,*
> *Whole person and general knowledge education is nothing but a populist fantasy.*

Chen Peizhe and Anthony Fauci

In response to President Tsai Ing-wen's call to the people in Taiwan to get vaccinated with the domestically manufactured vaccine by the end of July 2021, Chen, a member of Academia Sinica, expressing his reservation on whether the Food and Drug Administration would be able to withstand pressure from the President, resigned from the vaccine review committee. In June 2021, from his professional perspective, he raised questions about the manufacture and the effectiveness of the domestic vaccine and stated that it would definitely not meet international standards by July. A spokesperson from the President's Office indicated that Chen's resignation was "incomprehensible and regrettable". Subsequently, the internet army and the "national machinery" were mobilized to launch a comprehensive lateral attack on Chen, sinking as low as using the populist method of insinuating that Chen and the communists were fellow travelers.

Let us look at what happened in the US at the beginning of the pandemic in 2020. Anthony Fauci, the chief medical advisor to the President of the US, held views that were based on science but different from those of the President. For example, when Trump announced that hydroxychloroquine used to treat malaria could be deployed against the new coronavirus, Fauci maintained otherwise. When Trump indicated that the vaccine would be available very soon, Fauci said it might take as much as a year and a half. When the White House declared that there were enough testing kits, Fauci stated frankly that the US testing capability fell short. All this shows that whether they agreed with him or not, few Americans would engage in endless campaigns to bad-mouth him.

Chen and Fauci are alike in their integrity and professional background. Neither resorts to flattery nor ignores science. As a medical professor unencumbered by any official post, Chen should enjoy full freedom of expression. In a normal society, he should be able to express himself freely. Fauci, on the other hand, is medical advisor to the White House and must be careful with his words. In this case, both Chen and Fauci decided to be guided by their medical conscience and, in their respective ways, ended up contradicting their presidents. Both uttered the same inconvenient truths under the same circumstances, and yet the two were treated differently. Fauci was regarded as a hero, but across the Pacific, Chen as a private citizen was hunted like a bear. This is how the American democracy differs from the populist kind in Taiwan.

"The spring flowers in the woods have withered/ The cold rain and wind torment the day." The way that Taiwanese-style democracy has violated Chen's personal rights is not an isolated case. Government leaders in Taiwan disregard norms and are shameless in using state apparatus to seek private benefit. Interference in the selection of the President of National Taiwan University in 2018 was a notable case[1], while the selection of the President of Academia Sinica in 2016 was equally intolerable. There were accusations that the rules for voting were changed on the spot while the authorities resorted to populism and cyber warriors to cover up their dirty dealings when academics questioned this inappropriate behavior and the media suspected "black-box" operations. Certain parties or politicians shamelessly persecuted higher education and academia in general, barely pausing for breath, as if they were entering an unpeopled land. The silencing of universities was even worse than when academic rights were violated during the pandemic or when the vaccine was launched.

Recently, I heard a story that conveys just what I have in mind. Ji Xiaolan (紀曉嵐), a scholar from the Qing dynasty, challenged He Shen (和坤),

---

[1] See *The Backbone of the University: A Story of Defending University Autonomy*, in Chinese by Tu Yang and Chung-Ming Kuan, China Times Publishing, Taipei, 2023.

saying, "You claim that you love the Qing court. Yet you amass great wealth for yourself." He Shen countered, "The Qing court allows corrupt people like me to amass great wealth. How can I not love it?" Love is not a mantra nor the exclusive property of politicians. Yet in the political arena in Taiwan nowadays, declaring love for Taiwan gives a person some kind of immunity. Whether you feel it or not, it is best to proclaim it. However, this kind of love for Taiwan somehow has a similar ring to He Shen's love for the Qing court.

By proportion, there are more degree holders in Taiwan than in the US, but the social value of a diploma is far lower in Taiwan than in the US. It is futile to have 1,000 half-blossomed trees, when none can be cut. From the trivial, one can divine the big. Taiwan was the first to adopt the advanced American education system. Yet it has now fallen to the bottom of the Four Asian Tigers and is left behind by the Mainland. If the same were to happen to Japan, we could expect to witness many resignations and deep apologetic bows.

The problem of populism comes from ignoring the importance of a person's character to sabotage academic progress. The result is disastrous.

Part IV
QUALITY AND EVALUATION

Taking in the beauties pleasant to the eye,
Each endowed with distinct quality and charm.
Evaluation determines rankings high and low,
True defects and merits can hardly be concealed.

Higher education has to respond to quality assurance, ensure teaching and research effectiveness, nurture talent for improving social well-being and enhance economic growth. Hence all sectors of society scrutinize universities in the hope that humanistic concerns and cutting-edge science and technology have been successfully incorporated into higher education.

The government, society and the media across the Strait look at universities through a micro-management or a nano-management lens and sometimes simply take over someone else's job based on irrelevant subjective views. In the US, on the other hand, a university's performance is assessed by its effectiveness and not by scrutinizing the details.

Don't We Need Exams?

When we talk about exams, we tend to think of students. But there is a great deal more to be examined. We seek knowledge based on facts, not only in science and technology. Research is implemented in education to enrich teaching and the operation of enterprises and government to enhance efficiency.

Exams are equivalent to evaluations and therefore are required. It's like saying you aren't allowed to eat because your diet is unhealthy. In any case, exams are not necessarily ineffective. After all, life is full of tests: closed-book, open-book and take-home tests, not to mention the unpredictable formats, venues or timing.

Apart from evaluating individuals, the effectiveness of higher education must be assessed. Therefore, universities and all individual organic entities closely related to higher education, such as the government and society, should be examined or evaluated. Whether politics and education are separated or the degree of separation is an important focus in evaluating higher education. In this regard, universities, governments, societies and traditional cultures are responsible for ensuring the separation of politics and education, especially the government, because it has the most power.

In Part III, we elaborated in detail the necessity, principles and practice of the separation of politics and education. However, evaluation bodies for reviewing the separation of politics and education do not exist. Otherwise, universities across the Strait would not have scored high in this respect.

The following chapters focus on examining the quality and performance of universities.

360-Degree Evaluation

Are the curricula in higher education across the Strait proceeding in the right direction? Are they asking the wrong questions and assessing the wrong directions by focusing on trivial matters of transmitting human knowledge, imparting necessary skills, and clearing up whatever may confound the mind without evaluating the effectiveness of studying the phenomena of nature and extending knowledge? We evaluate our students in many ways, only to make superficial improvements without examining the effectiveness of the integration of teaching and research or making research the essential element of contemporary education.

Universities that attract support and respond to society's overall planning and future development must be flexible and far-sighted when adjusting their research and teaching. Teaching, which was the sole focus of university education until the middle of the 20th century, is only one of the core responsibilities of higher education institutions today. In addition, we have to incorporate research into student learning to ensure alignment with societal needs and design innovative programs that match long-term planning.

Accountability requires a 360-degree evaluation of institutions, covering staff, students, employability, teaching, research, resources, tuition, environment, equipment, management, tangible hardware and software, and intangible soulware. It ensures that decisions formulated by traditionally protected higher education institutions will help strengthen connections between universities, society and industry. But those holding the government and the news media accountable should follow established rules and be answerable for their actions. They should refrain from interfering with academic matters or disrupting campus operations.

Under evaluations, organizations regularly publish rankings on universities and individual subject areas, which are well recognized. The purpose is to hold universities accountable for the expectations of students, parents, alumni, industry and other stakeholders. They provide concrete performance indicators for realizing responsibility. While it is not advisable for universities to focus only on specific rankings, it is problematic to ignore them.

Unfortunately, while people across the Strait may care about the quality of higher education, hardly anyone focuses on exploring the deficiency of soulware. Many people simply ignore soulware, letting politics interfere with education and governing schools with populist sentiments. Others ignore soulware and yet look everywhere for advocating scientific and technological innovation and social reform. It makes one wonder what's going on.

Public Opinion

In addition to those tangible rankings, there are other intangible, psychological and societal opinions about universities and university degrees worth noting.

In the US, which in my opinion, has the world's most advanced higher education system, the excellent state-funded universities are frequently questioned by the public and legislators. According to the results of a poll released in July 2017 by the Pew Research Center, 58% of Republicans and Republican-leaning independents in the US believe universities negatively affect the country. Over the years, the tenure system has been attacked, and doubts about a college degree's "return on investment" are frequently raised. In 2023, the tenure system is seriously challenged by the state legislature of Texas[1] and that of Georgia, Florida, South Carolina, North Carolina and Iowa.

All these points from a specified group of citizens may not agree with traditional views held by people across the Strait. In Asian societies, older universities carry weight and may only be criticized for trivial matters. People choose soft persimmons to eat, and universities rarely accept external doubts on essential matters. Universities are part of the public's assessment of the quality of higher education, and educators should constantly reflect; otherwise, our education will lag forever.

After the financial crisis in 2008, many American universities attempted to explore alternative sources of income, and some adopted aggressive economic development strategies. Some even invested in impoverished urban areas in order to encourage entrepreneurial and technological innovation parks, which can contribute enormously to economic expansion and job

---

[1] *USA Today* (April 13, 2023); *Texas Tribune* (May 27, 2023).

growth and ultimately transform the stereotypical public image of universities as "ivory towers".

However, have well-established universities across the Strait conducted any self-reflection? Or do they just follow in the footsteps of others while flaunting their history?

18
Review is the Father of Success

Education is regarded as a noble and enigmatic profession across the Strait. There is even the myth that scholars have an aversion to money. Do you believe that? Whether education is noble or not, let us leave it alone. But since education is a business, should it have a purpose, some steps, and some feedback?

Education, especially higher education, must be effective. It is not an abstract concept that satisfies the personal ego. Failure is the mother of success, and review is the father. Education policies must stand the test of analysis and comparison to achieve the best results and ultimately help with governance and public service. That is why we should pay heed to evaluation. Teaching, research, student performance, the value the university offers society, the administrators' policies, the effectiveness of legislative bodies and media reports should all be evaluated.

At one time, universities across the Strait seemed privileged with extra-territorial jurisdiction. Some even think it would be better for universities to retain their enigmatic appearance and continue to hide behind a veil, doing as they wish without outside interference. At the same time, people outside campus like to comment and criticize higher education, freely and ostentatiously, in idle gossip and sometimes even confounding universities with politics.

I often hear people lamenting the loss of the free academic atmosphere that prevailed in the early part of the 20th century and the loss of past university presidents known for their lofty character and open-mindedness like Cai Yuanpei and Fu Ssu-nien. In their opinion, people today are not what they used to be, and universities are no longer magnificent.

This line of thinking is wide off the mark. People hold such misconceptions because of the lack of professional evaluation mechanisms for gauging performance systematically. Do people really want to find out how, back in the day, Cai Yuanpei and Fu Ssu-nien led Peking University and NTU, respectively? If today's universities are to be run as they were 60 or 100 years ago, would they survive? Should universities still be called universities if they only enjoy freedom without demonstrating professional accomplishments? Can we talk about ideals in a vacuum, not paying any heed to the changes occurring around us?

Things Are Not What They Used to Be

Universities today have to raise money to supplement insufficient funding. They have to emphasize both teaching and research, ensure quality, update curricula, implement academic exchanges, cope with rising student requests for face-to-face dialogues, provide scholarships and subsidies as well as employment assistance, promote innovation and entrepreneurship, and deal with populism, abuse, politicians, demonstrations, and so forth. These responsibilities far exceed the imagination of universities of the early 20th century. Of course, we can hardly imagine that university presidents in that era could use today's governance models to deal with problems that Peking and Tsinghua universities faced in the past.

Universities in those days could afford to stay distant and indulge in lofty ideals and self-admiration in a sheltered, privileged and self-contained world. Universities today are concrete entities connected to the real world with high transparency, accountability and professionalism, subjected to intensive external reviews and evaluations. The fact that Chinese wisdom was kept closely within the confines of the ivory towers of universities around 100 years ago and not put into application helps to explain China's lack of development during this period.

When Madame Curie won her first Nobel Prize in Physics in 1903, Peking University was already five years old. Chinese universities remained unmoved when she was awarded her second Nobel Prize in Chemistry in 1911.

My point might be better understood if we compare Chinese universities from this period with universities established in Japan after the Meiji Restoration. Zhang Zhidong, one of the four most famous officials of the late Qing dynasty, introduced to China the diligent spirit and pragmatic industrial revitalization plans of the Japanese. But Chinese universities were not interested in developing practical courses for their curricula. The institution that the well-known Chinese scholar Lu Xun attended in Japan, Tohoku University, was established later than Peking and Tsinghua universities. But it achieved excellence, claiming Nobel laureates among its graduates.

According to the China Modernization Report 2015, published by the Chinese Academy of Sciences on June 6, 2015, Mainland China's industrial and economic level in 2010 was 100 years, 80 years and 60 years behind Germany, the US and Japan, respectively, in terms of industrial labor productivity, industrial value-added rate and industrial labor force rate. To what extent should Chinese universities from those early years be responsible for these poor results? Also, why is Taiwan only complacent with original equipment manufacturers? Why is there no scientific research industry in Hong Kong? Why can't the Mainland manufacture high-end steel and advanced semiconductors?

Quality and Quality Management

The fundamental concept of quality originated from AT&T in the 1940s. AT&T achieved efficiency through applying statistical control, which developed into today's concept of total quality management. In Mainland China, quality (品質) is referred to as 質量 (quality (質) and quantity (量), or measurement of quality), which seems to be a better term as it involves both the quantitative and qualitative dimensions.

After World War II, the US military promoted quality management and developed quality control procedures. In the 1950s, W. Edwards Deming, a US physicist, created Deming's 14 points, which evolved into the basic principles that underpin the plan-do-check-act procedures in quality management. On the basis of quality assurance designed by the US military, Joseph Juran and Armand Feigenbaum developed the concept of total quality management with the view that the quality process should extend to all operations and departments.

Japanese businesses embraced the quality management theories proposed by Deming, Juran and Feigenbaum and subsequently enhanced the quality of Japan's automobiles, electronics and food products, which were marketed all over the world where they remain highly popular, with no signs of declining. In recent years, the meaning of the quality management concept has been enriched and extended from product quality to procedure quality, from manufacturing to the service industry, medical care, information, government, judicial and higher education sectors. Product or service quality reflects the professional standard and reputation of an enterprise and is a manifestation of scientific and technological innovation and even a demonstration of a nation's institutional and social modernization. Every 10 years, the National Research Council in the US evaluated the research achievements of different disciplines in US universities and produced a report that is considered to be a benchmark.

The generic concept of accountability is an extension of the quality circle and the beginning of total quality management, emphasizing that everyone is responsible for what one does in the process, both horizontally and vertically, as a unit and as an individual.

Subject Accreditation

Prior to the 1960s, few people paid attention to quality control and few people thought of quality as the keystone for the success of an enterprise or product. They never saw the need to do anything except extol their own products. For example, the automobile industry never offered warranties in the early days. When quality became a principal concern, warranties were offered, marking the beginning of modern quality practice. It started with a one-year warranty, which was eventually extended to three, five and seven years. Some manufacturers even offer life-long warranties for key auto parts.

Today, with the advent of electric vehicles, automobile manufacturing, powered by sensors, is moving toward internet-based manufacturing, which is more intricately linked to customers, while parts are provided by suppliers and cars are assembled by third-party contractors.

Quality has gradually become a global, borderless topic, and higher education institutions are no exception. Universities are not businesses, but they are members of society endowed with two roles. Firstly, they nurture talent for society through education, which is subject to professional evaluation. Secondly, universities are commissioned by society to create new knowledge and conduct scientific and technological research, the outputs of which, along with the performance of its graduates, are subject to regular assessment.

Is there any quality assurance for university education? Is there any warranty for university graduates, who are a kind of product in a broad sense?

To ensure the quality of professional disciplines, professional associations have set stringent and uniform accreditation standards for respective disciplines, including engineering, business, medicine and veterinary medicine. These basic standards provide some guarantee for the quality of service that the graduates of these disciplines offer future clients such as patients or building service users. Professional accreditation is part of the evaluation of university programs. There are accreditation standards everywhere nowadays. Universities conduct teaching, research and service in accordance with these standards to gain public trust.

Teaching and Research Evaluation

Evaluation of teaching performance in universities started in the US at the end of the 1960s. Teaching and research are the primary mission of the university. For more than sixty years, teaching evaluation and evaluation of research based on the publication of papers have constituted the key components of the overall assessment. This established practice in the US has become widely adopted by universities worldwide.

According to the big data analyses from my book *Clarifying Some Myths of Teaching and Research*, professors who consistently get low scores in teaching evaluations from students are unequivocally in need of improvement in certain areas, while those who consistently get high scores deserve special attention.

A Hispanic-American professor in the department I worked in many years ago adamantly opposed student evaluations because he used to receive poor scores. I told him that, for a non-mainstream professor from an ethnic minority background, student evaluations of teaching were the most objective way to convince the university about an individual's teaching performance.

Setting indicators for teaching evaluations is relatively more difficult than for other areas. Notwithstanding the difficulty, it would still be better than not having any teaching evaluations and letting the department head evaluate your teaching performance subjectively. Student evaluations provide some reference for improvements. It is probably more beneficial than sitting in an office imagining the teaching performance of every teacher. There is hope so long as one knows where to improve; without student evaluations, one cannot turn things around for oneself.

Teachers who receive poor evaluations should be given a chance to explain. Other teaching performance indicators should be considered in addition to student evaluations. For example, have the teachers been involved in developing teaching software or textbooks? Have they helped students participate in part-time or full-time employment, overseas exchanges or internship programs? Have they helped students to secure grants or scholarships? Have they published any papers on teaching methodology or teaching-related research? In fact, these criteria should be important benchmarks for evaluating teaching performance.

One of the yardsticks for evaluating research performance is the publication of papers. Publishing is the natural outcome of research. The number of papers can be counted easily, while the quality of the papers should be judged by external parties over time rather than being self-assumed. However, we often hear people commenting that the number of papers is not so important. Instead, publishing high-quality papers is the goal. It might make sense if this view comes from people who have published such papers. But for people who have never published any papers or those who do not have the ability to publish papers, making such statements may sound like sour grapes.

Another important benchmark for evaluating research is success in applying for research funds. Several steps are involved, such as peer assessment and assessment by industry. No matter what methods are used, individuals must specify their projects' practicality, relevance and impact. These checkpoints for research evaluation might turn out to be more difficult to manage than publishing papers.

Take Heed of Rankings

Those engaged in education must stay vigilant, considering rapid changes. Higher education is like a business enterprise in a highly competitive environment. It must set benchmarks for the measurement, evaluation and revision of its operations and programs to keep abreast of what is happening around the world.

The emphasis on evaluation in recent years has positively enhanced the quality of university operations. We need to continue to evaluate higher education's contribution to society in terms of functionality and applicability. We should explore the value of theoretical and experimental research for promoting social well-being and seek improvements to teaching through research and to research through teaching.

The higher education sector has developed swiftly across the Strait over the last 30 years. In addition to the mushrooming number of new universities, an enormous number of institutions in medicine, finance and technology were converted, expanded and amalgamated to form comprehensive universities overnight. In many people's eyes, size and name have become the standard for evaluating a university. As pointed out in Chapter 11, university degrees may have little use, and we should emphasize real learning over degrees. With or without degrees, persistent effort is the key. In theory, the degrees granted by a reputable university can better guarantee that its graduates have acquired the necessary knowledge. Whether a university, new or old, does well or not can be determined by appropriate evaluations.

Accreditation and evaluation set a threshold for the minimum standard. The methodologies and components for ranking evaluation are constantly reviewed and updated to reflect relevant quality requirements. In addition to accreditation and evaluation, there are rankings arrived at on the basis of evaluation standards. In short, although the criteria and standards used to evaluate the quality of university teaching and research may not be perfect, the concept of evaluation is not wrong, and the conclusions reached, i.e., the ranking results arrived at on the basis of international standards, have value. Even so, certification and evaluation cannot guarantee excellence.

University ranking is a way for evaluation agencies to assess the quality of a university's teaching, research, service and outreach. Perhaps not everyone agrees with the evaluation criteria, the ranking results or the relative performance of individual subjects or universities, but it is undeniable that, in spite of being subjective to a certain degree, the indicators used are objective, comparable and peer-reviewed. What would happen if there were no international evaluations and universities were allowed to assess themselves? Likewise, many people claim that academic scores are not a comprehensive benchmark for measuring success but add that without them, it would not be clear that progress had been made. What's more, are there people who think academic scores are not important and take pride in deliberately getting a low score?

Those who have been teachers may have had the experience of seeing students coming for extra points after the test papers had been returned or the test scores published. However, how many teachers have encountered students requesting to reduce their test scores? Or are there students who have high scores but want to protest because they are worried about not learning factual knowledge? In fact, I heard that there were no examinations and no scores on the Mainland during the Cultural Revolution. Once the Cultural Revolution was over, exams were reintroduced.

When hiring employees, companies in Taiwan, Hong Kong and the Mainland usually take into consideration the academic reputation and ranking of the universities their applicants graduated from. Referring to the quality of the applicants' universities during the hiring process will motivate universities to improve their education quality in order to nurture high-quality graduates.

Rankings and evaluations are an essential reality, though universities should not be held hostage by ranking.

What Does University Ranking Represent?

In addition to professional accreditations, there are rankings based on evaluation results. In the 1980s, *USA Today* proposed the evaluation of universities and the *US News & World Report* was the first to publish the ranking results of US universities on the basis of professional performance.

It received a great deal of attention. University rankings that appeared 40 years ago as a quality assurance standard have helped to promote the modernization of global higher education.

With proper measures, nothing is beyond evaluation. Currently, there are three internationally accepted university rankings: QS World University Rankings, THE World University Rankings and the Academic Ranking of World Universities (ARWU). Every system comprises teaching and research indicators that vary across different systems with different indicators and weighting factors. Hence, there could be variations in the results for the same university. Just as some universities brag about their results in one ranking, another set is not so satisfactory. Only truly outstanding universities, which are few in number, are ranked consistently top in all major rankings.

Universities ranked in the top 100 in QS, THE and ARWU can undoubtedly be considered excellent. In what country or region are they located then? Table 18.1 below lists the 2022/2023 and 2012/2013 results of some universities in the US, UK, and some major Asian countries and regions in individual and all three ranking systems simultaneously, as well as the top 100 universities in the QS Graduate Employability Ranking. Based on the criteria listed in Table 18.1 on ranking in all three rankings, and considering the ranking in graduate employability, Mainland China, Japan and Singapore are obviously the top 3 in Asian higher education evaluations.

As illustrated in Table 18.1, 10 years ago, there were only two Asian universities, both from Japan, ranked among the top 100 in all three rankings. By 2022/2023, the number from Asia in the same rankings rose to 12.

Table 18.1 provides insight into the performance of universities around the world. Among the 12 top ranked Asian universities, nine universities do not use English as the medium of instruction. This indicates again that, despite perceptions, English is not necessarily the key to recognition for excellence in higher education; therefore, it shouldn't be used as an excuse for lack of recognition of academic merit.

Ten years ago, none of the universities in Mainland China ranked in the top 100 in the above three rankings, but today there are six. If a fourth criterion, i.e., the 2022 QS Global University Graduate Employability Rankings, is introduced, five universities in Mainland China are in the top 100 in all four rankings, two in Japan and only one each in Singapore, South Korea and Hong Kong. It can be said that Mainland universities have made the most progress in the world in the past 10 years. Higher education in Hong Kong and South Korea has made some progress and is heading toward excellence. We would reach the same conclusion even if the standards were relaxed and not confined to the top 100.

Table 18.1 Number of universities ranked in top 100 in the US, the UK, Mainland China, Japan, Singapore, South Korea, Hong Kong, Taiwan, Israel and Others.

Country/region	Number of universities Ranked Top 100				QS, THE, ARWU simultaneously	QS, THE, ARWU, QS 2022 Graduate Employability simultaneously
	QS 2023	THE 2023	ARWU 2022			
US	27 (30)*	34 (47)	39 (53)		23 (29)	21
UK	17 (18)	10 (10)	8 (9)		8 (8)	8
Mainland China	6 (3)	7 (2)	8 (0)		6 (0)	5
Japan	5 (6)	2 (2)	2 (4)		2 (2)	2
Singapore	2 (2)	2 (2)	2 (0)		2 (0)	1
South Korea	6 (2)	3 (3)	1 (0)		1 (0)	1
Hong Kong	5 (3)	5 (2)	1 (0)		1 (0)	1
Taiwan	1 (1)	0 (0)	0 (0)		0 (0)	0
Israel	0 (0)	0 (0)	3 (3)		0 (0)	0
Others	31 (35)	37 (32)	36 (31)		18 (14)	9
Total	100 (100)	100 (100)	100 (100)		61 (53)	48

* Numbers in the brackets represent the ranking results ten years ago.

Numbers talk. Evaluation reveals weaknesses and strengths. Ten years ago, 53 universities were ranked among the top 100 in all three rankings, among which 29 were American. Today, a total of 61 universities are ranked among the top 100 in all three rankings, among which 23 are American. If we bring in the fourth criterion, the QS 2022 Graduate Employability Rankings, a total of 48 universities are ranked among the top 100 in all four rankings, of which 21 are American. These results demonstrate that the excellence of US higher education is no accident. Moreover, most recently, 9, 12 and 15 American universities were ranked among the top 20 in the world in the QS, THE, and ARWU rankings, respectively.

It is crucial that we recognize the independence of these results. The ranking criteria were not designed in the US. Yet the US outshines everyone else. University staffing and academic programs are properly funded by the federal government and industries. US universities which have attracted talented professors from all over the world are known for their solid academic strengths and outstanding creativity. In many universities, more than half of the doctoral students are international. Many stay in the US after finishing their degrees, contributing enormously to economic development, social well-being and high-tech innovation. Only with sound soulware can higher education progress.

The ranking of universities in the Four Asian Tigers mirrors their economic status, with Singapore's universities taking the lead while Taiwan's universities remain at the bottom. South Korea, after experiencing failure in education reform, has started to grow again. Taiwan, which also has suffered a failure, has little courage to propose any amendments and at the same time dismisses the achievements of its neighboring region or countries, a strange mentality that is incomprehensible. It may make Hong Kong proud that some of its universities are highly ranked, but we must not forget that few first-rate universities exist across the Strait. Unless Hong Kong's higher education pays attention to soulware and truly rewards strong-performing universities, I predict that, after falling behind Singapore, Hong Kong may soon be outranked by universities in South Korea.

Such a result has its own causes. It serves no purpose to be complacent or compare the duration of university operations.

Ranking of Scientists

When the annual rankings are announced, some NTU alumni begin to complain. NTU has the largest number of published faculty papers among universities in Asia, so why does the ranking lag? Does it mean NTU students are not as competent as students in Hong Kong? This is a common question raised by many across the Strait, too.

While NTU alumni seem to have cause for complaint, it should be noted that the ranking results are not only about student quality. Regarding the methodology adopted, a university's ranking depends on or reflects assessment scores based on the set indicators and weightings carried by those indicators. What's more, it remains to be determined whether it is accurate to say, "NTU has the largest number of published faculty papers". By analogy, we may say the results of a sports competition reflect the rules set by the game.

So what are the research results for university professors around the world? Let the numbers talk again!

A research team led by John P. A. Ioannidis from Stanford's School of Medicine analyzed university professors' research performance. The most cited professors in various academic fields were ranked according to a systematic evaluation in 2022. This is the first categorized ranking list to evaluate the research results of individual professors to such depth. The subjects analyzed cover almost all academic disciplines, including mathematics, engineering, biomedicine, liberal arts, humanities and applications. The data analyzed the citation index rankings of scholars and experts who have published at least five papers in all subject areas and sub-categories. The evaluation includes the number of citations, h-factor, hm index adjusted by co-authors, comprehensive indicators of citations by different authors, and so forth, which are used as the basis for screening global scholars and experts in 22 scientific fields and 176 sub-fields.

Ioannidis's analysis of highly cited papers by global scholars and experts demonstrates their influence on their respective academic fields. Ioannidis's report is based on unbiased, publicly available data. Since the ranking aims to identify the top 2% of scholars in each discipline using peer comparisons, apples to apples, the difference in the citation rate of papers published in different fields doesn't affect the results.

Using the results of Ioannidis's analysis, we can analyze the number of scholars among the top 2% in each university. Based on this, I have listed in Table 18.2 the number of universities in the US, the UK and major Asian countries or regions in the top 100 worldwide with the most highly cited scholars in the top 2%. Because the number of professors in each university varies greatly, I have compared the ratio between the number of scholars in the top 2% in each university and the total number of professors in that university. Israel is the best-performing country in Asia.

Table 18.2 once again shows the superiority of American universities. In simple terms, half of the world's outstanding professors are in the US.

Table 18.2 Number of universities in the world's top 100 with the top 2% of scholars in the US, the UK, Japan, Mainland China, Singapore, South Korea, Hong Kong, Taiwan, Israel and others; and number of universities in the world's top 100 with "the ratio of top 2% to total number of professors in the university".[a]

Country/region	No. of universities in the world's top 100 with the top 2% of scholars[c]	No. of universities in the world's top 100 with "the ratio of top 2% to total no. of professors in the university"[b, d]
US	54 (86)[e]	57 (85)[e]
UK	14 (22)	5 (31)
Japan	4 (8)	1 (6)
Mainland China	1 (3)	0 (0)
Singapore	1 (1)	0 (1)
South Korea	0 (1)	0 (1)
Hong Kong	1 (5)	2 (4)
Taiwan	0 (1)	0 (0)
Israel	3 (4)	4 (4)
Others	22 (69)	31 (68)

[a] The analysis is based on the 2022 system evaluation report of John P.A. Ioannidis, Biomedical Data Science at Stanford University School of Medicine.
[b] Overall number of scholars in each university is based on the QS record provided by each university.
[c] Number of top 2% scholars in individual universities. For example, Harvard University, the number one in the world, has 1,472 in the top 2% scholars.
[d] The university with the largest number of top 2% scholars as a percentage of overall professors in the world is the University of Washington in Seattle, with 2,796 full-time professors and 1,096 top 2% scholars, a ratio of 39%.
[e] Numbers in the brackets represent the top 200 in the world.

The table shows that universities in Taiwan, Hong Kong and the Mainland performed poorly. Among the three, Hong Kong professors are better than Mainland professors, although it seems Mainland universities are far superior to Hong Kong and Taiwan universities in QS, THE and ARWU. Apart from Israel, only three Asian universities (Tokyo Institute of Technology, CityU and HKUST) are ranked among the top 100 universities in the world, with "the ratio of top 2% to total number of professors in the university".

Here is another example. Clarivate message published in March 2023 pointed out that NTU with a large faculty size has only four Highly Cited Researchers for 2022. This is far less than the number of faculty on the Clarivate list in a single academic department at many other universities.

Here is a phenomenon worth noting that confirms a previous point about some of the older universities on both sides of the Strait receiving disproportionately larger government funding and social attention. Because of the government's promotions and blessings, their local social impression scores, which contribute to the rankings, are extremely high. That is why even though the percentage of distinguished professors at universities like NTU in Taiwan, University of Hong Kong and Chinese University of Hong Kong, Peking University, Tsinghua University, and Shanghai Jiao Tong University on the Mainland are not ranked among the top 100 in the world, their overall university rankings are higher than other universities in their regions. Judging from a quality management point of view, this is a unique symptom resulting from the influence of Chinese culture, which will not help with the overall development of higher education.

Universities in Taiwan and research paper output by professors in Taiwan universities, whether measured by the world's top 100 or top 200 standards, lie at the bottom among academic faculty across the Strait. The ranking performance of Taiwanese universities has fallen far behind other Asian universities for several reasons. Firstly, Taiwan has roughly 15 times as many tertiary institutions as Hong Kong, even though the population is only three times as large. These institutions suffer from poor planning and insufficient resources, which result in inadequate facilities and substandard campuses. (These weaknesses may seem irrelevant to ranking performance, but they reflect the weakness of insufficient resources and attract criticism.) The uniform but low faculty salaries, low quality postgraduates and lack of administrative staff negatively impact the teaching and research environment.

Secondly, although many professors have studied abroad, the localization drive in Taiwanese society in the past few years has resulted in self-marginalization. Higher education is among the hardest-hit sectors. For example, it was a clever idea for Taiwan's then National Science Council (upgraded to the Ministry of Science and Technology in 2014 and changed to the National Science and Technology Council in 2022) to introduce the Graduate Student Study Abroad Program a few years ago, but Hong Kong was not covered in the program. Such self-imposed limits hinder the pursuit of excellence in research and development.

Additionally, academic and student exchanges with partner institutions abroad are insufficient, and there are few overseas professors in Taiwanese universities. Apart from academicians from Academia Sinica who teach at Taiwan's universities, very few international academicians teach on local campuses. By contrast, academicians from Mainland China, the US, the UK, France, Russia, Sweden, Australia and other countries teach and research at universities in Hong Kong. The stark contrast between the two places is visible. The fact that Hong Kong can recruit outstanding professors is probably due to the salaries.

Perceptions about universities can be misleading. The green hills still stand as before, along with a perpetually rosy sunset, i.e., the hills and sunset won't change simply because of perception. Ultimately, do some people dismiss international rankings because the results fail to align with expectations and an outdated mindset? If a nihilist insists that ranking systems have no value, does such a person's dogmatic mind and empty talk possess any intrinsic worth?

Controversies Regarding Rankings

Since the end of the last century, the biggest reform in higher education has been the enhancement of teaching, research and learning through the evaluation of universities in the wake of greater recognition of the importance of quality.

But unfortunately, society at large does not understand this completely. Debates started from the day that university evaluations were introduced. Some people are uncomfortable with what is evaluated; others disagree with the methodology; still others simply object to evaluations. As a result, we often hear people commenting that ranking is unnecessary so long as a university is well administered, forgetting that "well administered" can only be a conclusion based on results derived from ranking evaluations. Before ranking was introduced, a few dozen universities indulged in the sweet dream of proclaiming themselves among the top 10 in the world. But a "top" university must be based on systematic quality evaluations.

The evaluation of universities makes some people feel uneasy. Without evaluation, everyone is just muddling along, bragging about one's performance. The University of Southern California voluntarily withdrew its education school from the 2023 *US News & World Report's* graduate school rankings because it had provided inaccurate data for several consecutive years. In the *US News & World Report's* 2022 National College Rankings, Columbia University was removed from various rankings. As early as 2014, the University of Malaya boycotted the THE international rankings because it disagreed with THE's decisions on ranking. The Renmin

University of China and Nanjing University announced in 2022 that they would not participate in overseas rankings. Such a decision is viewed as conforming with the direction of China's overall educational development, and withdrawal may become a trend. The reasons the University of Malaya, Renmin University of China and the University of Southern California removed themselves vary.

These cases remind me of a novel published in Taiwan in 1975 called *The Boy Who Refused to Take the Joint College Entrance Exam*. The story, which created a buzz much like *Alice in Wonderland*, made it extraordinary for people to vent their frustrations and sense of helplessness and indulge in fantasies, spicing up life with some temporary topics for conversations, which eventually amounted to very little.

Interestingly, people who belittle university evaluation either come from universities that have performed poorly in ranking exercises or have been muddling through in an academically lax environment for so long that any improvement is unattainable. There are still others who say that ranking is not important when in fact, they are already working in highly ranked universities. Ranking is a useful reference. If standards are reasonable and the evaluations professional, no progressive universities will fail to pay attention, whether explicitly or implicitly. Just log onto the websites of many world-renowned universities and look. You will see how they take pride in their rankings.

Some universities that are weak in research often claim they are more distinguished in teaching. Such a defense is like poor people who consider the rich to be necessarily unhappy or ugly people who regard the beautiful as inevitably untrustworthy. It's like those who never exercise and think the brains of athletes are underdeveloped, young girls who fantasize that romance novelists are devoted to love, and so forth. The truth may not necessarily be so.

Universities that ignore research tend to object to evaluations. They complain about not receiving proper recognition, making them feel aggrieved. Likewise, some teachers challenge the adequacy of ranking under the pretext that teaching quality is hard to assess. But remember, statistical proofs show that teaching and research quality positively correlate with ranking results.[1]

Evaluation is based on quality and provides pointers to guide everyday life. Comply if it makes sense; ponder if it goes against common sense. Make more excuses for success than excuses for failure. For example, food

---

[1] See *Clarifying Some Myths of Teaching and Research* by Way Kuo and Mark E. Troy, National Tsing Hua University Press, 2009.

safety had long been a latent problem in Taiwan and Mainland China, not reaching the standard of quality evaluation, but people did not seem to care. Society was obsessed with the illusion of being a gourmet paradise until the food oil scandal surfaced. The potential problems of Taiwan's higher education, like its food safety problem, have long existed, and it is necessary to investigate and improve them through quality evaluation. Doesn't the same situation exist in Hong Kong and the Mainland?

A good match between the university degree awarded and the knowledge imparted is the direction universities should strive for, and ranking evaluations can help achieve that. Rankings are like stock indexes: They are necessary, critical and relevant. Of course, whether it is university ranking, scientist ranking or any specific ranking indicator, it can be good reference points but not the complete standards of quality.

Rankings consider indicators that vary according to different systems, and often include an impression score. Subjective ratings favor older universities promoted by the governments across the Strait. Also, private tutoring is widespread in communities influenced by Chinese culture. There will always be coaching classes if there are exams to be sat (see Chapter 7). Many universities prioritize rankings, setting strategies and drawing up agendas to achieve the best results, at the expense of basic concepts such as academic integrity and how higher education leads society. As an evaluation index, the ranking of a university should reflect academic achievement rather than ranking for its own sake. In this regard, universities in Hong Kong, Mainland China and Singapore could be overvalued, while Israeli and Japanese universities are likely undervalued.

It is universal that when it comes to making choices in education and related matters, everyone has a yardstick in mind for assessing learning, school reputation, graduate employability, fundraising, and so forth, irrespective of whether any tangible or intangible rankings exist.

So far, university ranking evaluations do not involve evaluating an individual's academic performance, teaching, research, etc. No matter who the target is, the evaluation must be reasonable, professional and humane. The goal of evaluation is to enhance the quality of education; therefore, the benchmarks should be clearly defined, rewards and penalties well specified, and the confidentiality of the person or unit under evaluation strictly protected. Lack of professionalism and respect for the evaluated party and violation of confidentiality are some of the flaws in the culture across the Strait that must be overcome.

Should the government or the education sector be interested in enhancing the quality of higher education, they should boost resources and focus on investing them strategically to ensure appropriate returns.

Ranking is not the goal, but the phenomena reflected in rankings are worth our reflection.

Delusional Donations

A certain university has an outreach center that was established many years ago. It claims to have accumulated 1,200 non-paying members. In January 2022, the center sent a letter to the public to inform them of its membership base and invite them to make donations of at least HK$300 to demonstrate their recognition of the center. Considering the easing of the pandemic, the center planned to resume normal activities (in fact, the pandemic was getting more serious at the time) to organize academic lectures and art performances.

Such a fundraising activity is questionable. First of all, a university is not a social welfare organization, and its identity is not recognized by multiple small donations. Secondly, the said university has invested tens of millions of dollars to support the outreach center. It pays heed to the value of the center and its role within the university; therefore, it doesn't care about small donations. The critical point is to enhance the quality of the center and calibrate its positioning with the university. It should seek recognition and confirmation of its effectiveness.

Like it or not, the amount of donations a university receives is directly proportional to its prestige and performance and sometimes even its ranking. Any center that creates a fanfare and openly asks for small donations is self-defeating and will not be respected. If it really wants to get recognition, it should concoct a well-thought-through plan and seek funding from foundations or government agencies. It will be counterproductive, something to be warned against, if it depends on minor donations; because it fails to get recognized.

The Cooking Oil Story

I visited Shanghai Jiao Tong University in the summer of 1995. A professor from the University accompanied me on a walk. Drawn by the fragrant smell of fried buns from a roadside stand, I wanted to join the queue when my companion stopped me, saying: The price for a large fried bun was only a few dimes, with vegetable and meat fillings, and fried, utilizing oil and electricity. The price also covered the stand owner's profit. Good cooking oil alone would cost more than the price. Therefore, he was sure that the source of the meat filling was problematic and the oil had to be gutter oil or swill-cooked dirty oil.

Instead of tasting the actual buns, I had to feed on illusions from a distance.

One morning in October 2013, as I entered my office, my secretary, Jane, stared at me and demanded that I apologize. Why? Because I was from Taiwan and had always praised the place where I grew up. The reason for her shock was that in the news that day, some Taiwanese food companies had been found to be using illicit ways to produce and sell adulterated cooking oil, and the Taiwanese food exported to Hong Kong might have been made using this tainted oil, or black-heart oil. Jane, who loves Taiwanese food, was understandably upset.

I apologized without hesitation.

A year later, it was reported that a Hong Kong trading company had falsified export declarations and exported adulterated lard used as animal feed to Taiwan. The Taiwan government immediately canceled importing Hong Kong lard and demanded that all oil products exported from Hong Kong, Mainland China and Macau to Taiwan first obtain official certificates.

This time, I jokingly demanded that Jane apologize on behalf of Hong Kong for exporting adulterated oil products to Taiwan!

The market is filled with bad oil products. Should we allow some people to violate the law without telling them about their wrongdoings? People on both sides of the Strait have lost confidence in such edible oils as lard and salad oil and are wary of each other. Who should apologize to the public in the end?

19
Rankings in the Humanities and Liberal Arts

Which is more important: a liberal arts education or an education in science and technology? Such a debate has been longstanding. In the early days, university education was for elites, and a liberal arts education was the core, with an emphasis on religion and philosophical explorations. This was true, be it in Bologna, Oxford and Cambridge, Heidelberg, or Harvard and Yale. Even in China, the academies from the old days and many of the modern universities established at the end of the 19th and early 20th centuries focused on a liberal arts education.

Goodnow's Advice

The preference for liberal arts over science and technology disciplines was gradually dropped in the Western world after the industrial revolution and during the Meiji Restoration in Japan when the clichéd talk of old traditions and values gave way to more practical learning. While China was still oblivious to the changing trend 100 years ago, Frank Goodnow, an American educator and the third president of Johns Hopkins University (1893–1914), called for a transformation at the beginning of the 20th century, demanding that due attention be given to scientific and technological education.

At the time, Goodnow was a legal adviser to the government of the Republic of China. In his book *China: An Analysis*, he pointed out that there was a long tradition in China of privileging arts education over technology. As a result, China's many liberal arts graduates had limited career pathways and had to compete fiercely for employment in government jobs. Goodnow advised that old-fashioned ideas and practices that gave preference to the liberal arts over technological skills should be discarded. He thought science should be promoted and China could thrive and prosper only by focusing on science. With a close look at the places across the Strait, this theory still represents the scientific spirit. As a matter of fact, at least in the first half of the 20th century, China failed to achieve scientific and technological achievements and lacked academic performance in humanities and social sciences, not to mention other academic performances.

Goodnow's remarks and foresight have been slowly adopted across the Strait after half a century. However, whenever knowledgeable people in universities and society at large discuss liberal arts education, they express three major anxieties. Firstly, they are concerned that liberal arts disciplines are in decline, with a decrease in student enrollment and humanities courses being compressed; secondly, research funds for liberal arts are decreasing; and thirdly, with the reduction in the number of liberal arts courses, students' overall cultural and artistic understanding, especially among science and technology majors, is diminishing.

Whether such anxieties are reasonable is not the point we wish to explore at this moment. Society may have different social concerns, and learning may have a different emphasis at separate times. But what is true is that teaching and research in the liberal arts and humanities are no less important even in the 21st century of scientific and technological innovation. Poetic works give expression to human sensibilities, and literary works communicate human aspirations. As subjects in the humanities domain, their teaching and research quality should be evaluated just like science and engineering disciplines and should not be left to the individual's subjective self-acclamation.

Cookie-cutter Selection of Universities or Majors

The universities I have served at in the US are all land-grant institutions. Take Texas A&M University as an example. It is not an Ivy League university, nor among the top 20 to 30 famous universities that the Chinese are familiar with. Yet, after the SAT results were announced every year, many high school graduates with full SAT scores would choose Texas A&M instead of other famous universities. In fact, citizens from every state choose to study at state universities instead of famous universities, even if they have full SAT scores.

In addition, American high school graduates are not divided into arts and science groups. Although some applicants prefer pre-med or such popular subjects as computer science and engineering, students' selection of subjects is diversified. High SAT scorers often choose subjects that young people across the Strait dismiss. The selection of various language majors is a common example.

Let us look at high school graduates across the Strait. Do we see students who have recorded full or high scores on their college entrance exams skip the few prestigious universities in the three places across the Strait that are equivalent to the Ivy League universities in the US and opt for ordinary universities? Are they even willing to choose a more down-to-earth university? Are they willing to drop popular majors and choose majors less recognized by common folks? How many students have chosen universities and majors according to their own inclinations instead of being influenced by family, other people or societal considerations? We know that answers to these questions are usually negative. When it comes to choosing a university or a major, those young people who babble about independence as a rule suddenly all bow down and go with the flow, which has become their common aspiration.

There is a normal distribution, with diversity, when high school graduates in the US choose universities or majors. In other words, students with high SAT or ACT scores or even full scores may have hundreds of universities and dozens of different majors to choose from, but there is a large deviation from normal distribution when high school graduates from both sides of the Strait choose universities or majors, in an unimaginative and cookie-cutter way, all trying to squeeze into a few universities or majors.

Subjects Take Priority

When it comes to humanities rankings, I have to say a few words about subject evaluations. A university's unique academic strengths are not necessarily reflected in its overall ranking. In this regard, individual subject rankings can provide a more useful reference point. Individual universities can reference their rise and fall in subject rankings and make the necessary improvements. This is another function. In fact, it is unwise for high school graduates to choose universities without taking into consideration the qualities of individual subjects. There can be huge variations between the ranking of individual subjects and a university's overall ranking, whether high or low.

It is rare for students from Europe and the US to choose universities without considering the performance of individual departments. But it is the opposite across the Strait, which may not help young students to make the best choices for themselves. High schools are obligated to provide guidance, helping students select appropriate subjects based on their interests so that they do not choose a low-ranked program at a high-ranking university. Take engineering, mathematics, and other related subjects as examples. In a pragmatic society such as Hong Kong, high school graduates interested in taking such courses almost always prioritize some of the older universities, even if they are not strong in such disciplines before they consider other universities whose engineering is ranked stronger in ARWU & the *US News & World Report*. Such behavior can land students in the wrong learning environment because their choices were not made based on the objective academic strengths of the individual subjects they want to study.

An ideal situation would be for students to choose their professions according to personal interests and aspirations and then apply for studies at universities that excel in such areas. It would be illogical and a waste, if one enrolls at a sports institute to study English or at a university noted for medical science to study business administration, or studies science and technology at a university excelling in literature or mathematics in a university known for excellence in the arts. Students in such enrollments will not get the best learning environment, wasting personal effort and social resources.

Likewise, graduate students or those pursuing PhD studies should choose as their potential supervisors outstanding scholars who specialize in the same professional fields as their interests instead of giving too much attention to the rankings of the university or even the department. One should look for the best supervisor, department, or university only on the basis of one's professional interests.

American Strengths in Arts & Humanities and Social Sciences

American universities outshine the rest of the world in science, engineering, and biomedicine, but do they hold the advantage in the humanities, arts and social sciences?

According to the QS World University Rankings 2023, American universities constitute one-third (16) of the top 50 universities in the Arts & Humanities or Social Sciences & Management categories. Among the top 50 in the Times Higher Education (THE) World University Rankings of Arts & Humanities 2023, there were 17 American universities. Among the Social Sciences, there were 23.

The 2022 ARWU ranking is the latest information available at the time of writing and is considered more academic-oriented than THE and QS. In the Sociology ranking of the 2022 ARWU, published by Shanghai Ranking Consultancy and once led by Shanghai Jiao Tong University, the first and the third universities were American. Among the top 20, there were 16 American universities; among the top 30, there were 24; among the top 50, there were 34. In previous rankings by QS, THE and ARWU, the ratios of top programs offered by American universities in the humanities, arts and social sciences remained the same to a considerable extent.

Take MIT as an example. Although it specializes in science and technology, it is renowned for its world-leading humanities and social science programs. The 24 professors in its history department offer about 70 professional courses in areas covering Ancient, North American, and European history. These faculty members are known for their high-quality teaching and research, which is ranked top in the world.

In addition to science and technology, American strengths in liberal arts, social sciences and humanities are unsurpassed.

Substance Matters in Academic Innovation

In addition to hardware and software, developing cutting-edge disciplines depends on ideas as the timely and pertinent driving force. Comparatively speaking, liberal arts and social sciences are less dependent on hardware and software and therefore enjoy an advantage in terms of resource requirements over science and engineering disciplines, which depend heavily on hardware and software.

According to statistics, although funding in all areas of research in Hong Kong is seriously low, the ratio of government investment in the liberal arts and social science disciplines is higher in Hong Kong than in North America. A similar conclusion can be drawn from the situation in Taiwan and Mainland China. The National Science Foundation of the US provides basic scientific research funding for universities. Though the humanities and social sciences are not within its ambit, American strengths in the arts and humanities and the social sciences are not affected at all!

The US has been leading the world in the liberal arts and social sciences for over a century. Investment in China studies and Japan studies is a clear example. Johns Hopkins' China studies program is world leading. Other American universities, like Harvard, Columbia, UC Berkeley and the University of Washington in Seattle also have first-rate East Asian or China studies programs. Conversely, how many authoritative organizations or academics who are experts in American studies can we find across the Strait? It all boils down to the fact that a healthy soulware is the reason American universities are the forerunners in higher education in the world.

Some argue that it is hard for universities across the Strait to compete in social science research publications because of Western society's predominance of English as the language of communication. But to what extent is this so? Will they make breakthroughs by authoring research in the humanities and social sciences in Chinese?

Language plays only a supporting role in innovation. The predominance of English in the 20th and 21st centuries is largely because countries leading in innovation are English speaking. America is an innovative country not because of the use of English. In other words, it is not because of English that a certain country or culture should replace America in the future. If a country is able to generate groundbreaking innovations, its language will gain global currency and become universal. Therefore, a lack of English language proficiency is not an excuse for a lack of innovation. Besides, even though English is widely used, it is not the most popular language in human history in terms of the number of speakers. Chinese could very well become the world's lingua franca if the Chinese develop innovative ideas that impact progress and benefit well-being.

Substance rather than language (see Chapter 6) matters in higher education. Increasingly, topics pertaining to traditional Asian culture and arts, social transformation, philosophical inquiry, economic analysis, scientific and technological development, as well as political ecology, cross-Strait relations, social welfare and reforms, and so forth are becoming important in the 21st century. Along with China's economic and political rise, many issues related to Asia's humanities and social sciences are hot topics for academic research. They need to be studied with a scientific method to evolve into distinctive fields of specialized knowledge.

Evaluation Applies to All Professions

In summary, the progress of universities and academic disciplines depends on the right kind of soulware, not just software and hardware. "Quality first" should be the common denominator for all professional disciplines. The first-class soulware mechanism is suitable for the development of all disciplines, including natural and mathematical sciences, humanities, social sciences and the arts. No disciplines are exempt, nor can any disciplines claim sole ownership.

It is known that faculty in the humanities, social sciences and liberal arts in the US are paid far less than those in engineering, business, and medicine, while faculty from all disciplines at universities across the Strait are paid about the same. However, as pointed out in the previous section, American strengths in the liberal arts, social sciences and humanities are unsurpassed, but the contributions made by university faculty across the Strait in the same disciplines generally attract less attention. This makes us wonder why.

Higher education reflects local culture, and reforms will inevitably impact that culture and face challenges and resistance. The existing local culture across the Strait embedded in the campus environment, social ecology and the organizations that control higher education policies and resource distribution may not be amenable to the values of academic autonomy, free competition and the market mechanism, which are necessary for the cultivation of a healthy academic environment. And yet, it is only by embracing such a notion of developing excellence that universities can hope to become advanced.

A healthy mindset is a prerequisite for all disciplines, including the natural sciences, mathematics, the humanities, social sciences and liberal arts. There is no exception or exclusive privilege for any discipline.

Stories about my Colleagues

Some people hold the view that while awards such as Nobel Prizes for scientific and technological research can be a measure of success, they doubt they can be an adequate measure for other professions. Some even question whether any correlation between the quantitative evaluation adopted by these prizes and the quality of excellence in the liberal arts and humanities can be established.

A writer friend of mine insists that others could not appraise the quality of her work because they would not know how to assess the aesthetic quality of literary output. I replied that if she refused to be evaluated, she would have no chance of getting the prestigious literary prizes she pined for.

Here is another story. Concerning an evaluation exercise in 2021, a liberal arts professor was not happy with their evaluation, saying, "Every one of the four papers I submitted is an A grade paper. Several dozen outstanding professors from our department also submitted papers for evaluation. How come there seem to be only three A-grade papers from the evaluation for the entire department?"

This is an interesting question. I cannot comment on whether the RAE evaluation is fair or not. But the outcome was based on conclusions reached among liberal arts academic peers in the exercise, and that academic assessment should not degenerate into mere self-assumption.

While the details of the assessment system may be open for further discussion, we cannot ignore the contribution of evaluation within higher education. Moreover, plausible claims about governments and universities in Hong Kong and Taiwan investing too much in science and technology and too little in the liberal arts and humanities must be subjected to objective verification.

Today, we heed Goodnow's wise words from a hundred years ago, not because we want to replace "preference for liberal arts over technical skills" or "preference for technical skills over liberal arts". Rather, his advice is to heed science. I can go a step further and say that we should heed scientific evaluation, with no exception for any discipline. While students shouldn't choose their majors in a one-size-fits-all, cookie-cutter way, they shouldn't use the same approach for choosing programs and universities.

20
Tuition, Salary Comparisons of Professors and Graduates

While working at Texas A&M as department head, I tried to recruit professors at competitive salaries and look for opportunities to promote existing professors within the department. For outstanding faculty, I gave out awards that they deserved. But I never asked the university to adjust my own salary. One day, when comparing the salaries of faculty members, the dean discovered that the department head's salary was low, and so he took the initiative to increase my remuneration. It will be a win-win if we try to encourage and reward performers by increasing their salaries!

Though higher education is not a for-profit operation, appropriate financial planning, such as proper income and expenditure budgeting and financial resources distribution, is still essential. Profitable or not, without a complete business plan, there will be no success; without investment, there will be no return. When we think about others, others think about us. If the country prospers, the people will be at peace. Although tuition and remuneration packages do not necessarily determine happiness, they are related. Therefore, this area is worth analyzing and comparing.

Income and Degrees

Recruiting people who do not have sufficient understanding of the importance of integrating teaching and research for cost-saving purposes will only reduce the quality and value of higher education. The phenomenon to be discussed below is both an alternative economic miracle unique to Taiwan and an alternative facet of the failure of its higher education policy.

Because of the frequent education reforms in Taiwan, degrees are flooding in society. A general depreciation of locally produced degrees has been observed. Many holders of PhD, master's and bachelor's degrees are trapped. Apart from those from a handful of prestigious universities, most have difficulty finding a job and eventually become a social burden.

Graduates not from the few top universities end up idle and become a social liability. For example, over 1,000 people who applied for 300 temporary cleaning jobs at a 2018 recruitment session in Taichung, a major city in Taiwan, possessed bachelor's or even master's degrees even though the advertised positions stated that only six years of elementary school were required.

Between 2009 and 2010, the Ministry of Education in Taiwan allocated a special budget to encourage those who had just finished school and started working as interns, bringing their monthly salary up to NT$22,000. Over the years, the 22K, as the group became known, has become synonymous with low wages for young workers. According to a 1111 Power Bank survey, the average monthly salary of college graduates in 2021 has increased only 31% in the past 12 years, to NT$28,838, equivalent to around US$11,000 per year, about one-third of Taiwan's GDP per capita.

It seems a bit exaggerated to say that Taiwan's college graduates earn NT$22K per month, but it's not far from the truth. The consequences of an ill-considered policy in democratized Taiwan appear to follow the Philippines' example, creating a gap between educational output and employment opportunities. The quality of those with university degrees in the Philippines varies: sometimes graduates from professional disciplines who speak fluent English have to go abroad as domestic helpers working for a meager income. Another extreme phenomenon caused by the low 22K starting salary is that some young people become NEETs (see Chapter 3) after completing their studies. They are content to rely on their parents for food and lodging.

Low salary? The common justification is that Taiwan's commodity prices are lower and so low salaries are not an exaggeration. In that case, can tuition fees at Taiwan, Hong Kong and Mainland universities, as well as the salaries of their professors and graduates, be objectively compared? Governments have introduced education reforms. Have they considered improving teachers' salaries?

Salary Comparisons of Fresh University Graduates

Graduates are important human resources contributing to society and deserving proper remuneration. Alumni salaries are important performance indicators when evaluating the performance of universities and education systems.

As described in Chapter 3, Taiwan was flooded with graduates right after the economic boom of the late 1990s. The overproduction of underqualified graduates caused societal instability, with too many feeling unhappy. So how does the salary for Taiwan's graduates compare with those from the US and developed regions in Asia, in addition to the above-mentioned 22K phenomenon? The average starting salary for university graduates in the US is more than double that in Hong Kong, five times that in Taiwan, and seven times that in the Mainland. On both sides of the Strait, the average annual income for university graduates is much lower than that in the US, which might be explained by the cost of living in respective countries and regions and the need to adjust it accordingly.

Instead of comparing the per capita income of college graduates with the cost of living in different communities, let us normalize the comparison by taking into consideration the average salary of fresh university graduates and the GDP per capita of the country/region they come from. With such comparable conditions, Figure 20.1 shows the percentage of starting salaries for university graduates from three places across the Strait, Japan, Singapore, South Korea and the US to the local GDP per capita.

The ratios in Figure 20.1 show the relative salaries paid to fresh graduates and the general population in their own societies. This ratio indicates the extent that society values college graduates, and a high ratio means that the graduates are highly valued by their respective societies.

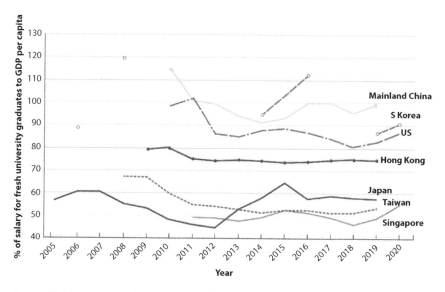

Figure 20.1 Percentage of starting salary of university graduates to GDP per capita.

Figure 3.1 and Figure 20.1 indicate that degrees do not necessarily imply better salaries when comparing these graduates with other employees, regardless of the per capita GDP of their respective societies. With information on the GDP of those countries and regions listed in Figure 3.1, it is obvious that an abundance of degrees does not improve the GDP of these societies, an indirect illustration that the granting of university degrees has failed to increase GDP in individual countries and regions.

Furthermore, an abundance of degrees does not necessarily help fresh university graduates to be better paid than other employees. As shown in Figure 20.1, the low ratio in Taiwan serves as a good example. Taiwan has enrolled almost all high-school graduates in university, but their graduate income is meager; whereas South Korea has admitted many high-school graduates to university, and their graduates are relatively better paid. The underlying reason is renovation, as detailed in Part V of this book.

Apart from low pay, Taiwan's university graduates suffer setbacks from poor career prospects. Some young people with college degrees are reluctant to succumb to lower status but well-paying, down-to-earth jobs, even though their degrees do not reflect their true ability. Under such circumstances, how can we expect university education to train a crop of students to become experts in different trades? Young people are supposed to be the hope for the future. But furnished only with depreciated degrees, they may not necessarily feel hopeful.

Figure 20.1 shows that Taiwan clearly has not been mindful of the well-being of young people when promoting higher education. Yet universities and the government should shoulder the responsibility of exploring how the workplace should treat graduates. Figure 20.1 also points out that the starting salaries as a percentage of GDP per capita for fresh university graduates are low in Singapore, but the impact of the low ratio is less severe comparatively speaking because Singapore's GDP per capita is twice that of Taiwan.

Student Tuition and Faculty Salary

In Chapters 2 and 3, I mentioned student tuition's role in higher education and discussed the low tuition charged to university students across the Strait. In order to understand the levels of student tuition in different countries and regions and their impact on faculty salary, instead of comparing tuition in terms of absolute values, we may want to normalize tuition further according to GDP per capita. In this regard, tuition fees in Mainland China and Taiwan, especially those in public universities, are still the lowest among those across the Strait. They are also lower than the tuition fees in Japan, Singapore, South Korea and the US. A low tuition policy is exercised in several developed European countries, such as France and Germany, with significant government subsidies, which can be considered an alternative system.

For convenience and clarity, let us compare the salaries of assistant professors in universities. Also, for comparability, GDP normalizes the salaries of assistant professors per capita. After adjusting according to GDP per capita, Figure 20.2 shows the relationship between the average annual salary of assistant professors in Hong Kong, Japan, Mainland China, South Korea, Singapore, Taiwan, the UK and the US after being normalized according to GDP per capita. Figure 20.3 shows university tuition fees as a percentage of GDP per capita in the above places.

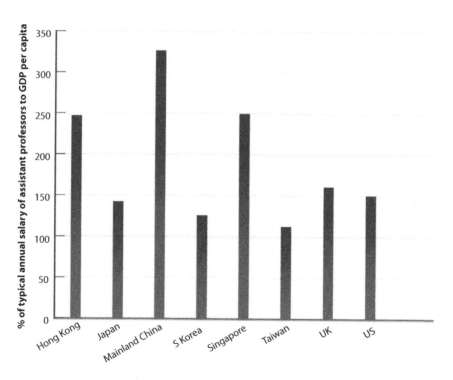

Figure 20.2 Percentage of the typical annual salary of assistant professors to GDP per capita.

Note: Faculty salaries, including Assistant Professors, in the US are for 9 months.

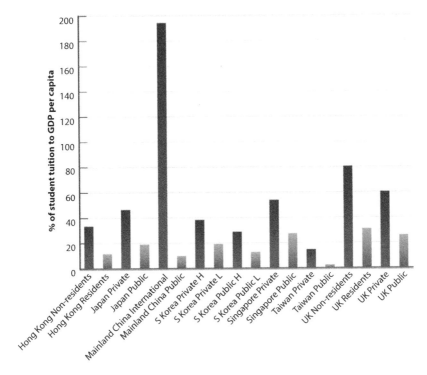

Figure 20.3 Percentage of student tuition to GDP per capita.

Notes: 1. H denotes the high end and L the low end of the tuition range at private and public universities in South Korea. 2. The exchange rate is as of February 7, 2022; https://www.xe.com/zh-HK/currencyconverter/

As can be seen in Figure 20.2 and Figure 20.3, tuition and faculty salary are correlated, except for the Mainland, where public universities are heavily subsidized, and hence the faculty are highly paid in relation to GDP per capita. And yet tuition fees remain low. Private universities on the Mainland are usually joint ventures with foreign partners. Students pay extremely high tuition fees in terms of GDP per capita.

For Taiwan, both student tuition and faculty salaries are low, relative to GDP per capita, because student tuition and faculty salary haven't changed much over many years, relative to inflation. Similar conclusions can be drawn if we consider other academic ranks. The salaries of assistant professors in Hong Kong and Singapore are high, while tuition fees for local students in Hong Kong are relatively low. Information on average student tuition in South Korea is unavailable, and I only use H to denote the high end and L for the low end of tuition ranges at private and public universities.

There are three points worth pointing out here. First, because the salaries for those above the rank of assistant professor, especially at full professor level, fluctuate greatly, we are not comparing salaries above the rank of assistant professors. Otherwise, salaries for some individual professors in the US are expected to be several times or even at least ten times higher than professors of the same grade in Taiwan, Hong Kong, Mainland China, South Korea and Japan. When we examine faculty salary in these communities normalized by GDP per capita, Taiwan' professors are paid the least because the salary difference between professors at all levels, from assistant to full professor, in Taiwan is limited.

Secondly, the annual salary of assistant professors in various academic disciplines varies greatly in different countries and regions. For example, the annual salary of an assistant professor in a business school in the US may be several times that of an assistant professor in a liberal arts school; the annual salary of an assistant professor in a business school in Hong Kong is 20 to 30% higher that of an assistant professor in a liberal arts school; while the annual salary of an assistant professor in a business school in Taiwan is comparable to those in a liberal arts school. What's more, the annual salaries of assistant professors in business schools in the Mainland and the salaries of assistant professors in liberal arts schools vary due to the different practices adopted by each university. Some are like those in the US, with a significant gap, while most are similar to those in Taiwan. In this regard, the Mainland is closer to American capitalism than Hong Kong and Taiwan.

Thirdly, as shown in Figure 20.3, tuition fees at public and private universities can vary widely across countries and regions. However, Figure 20.2 does not differentiate the salary difference between public and private universities since there is no data on the salaries of professors at distinct levels of public and private universities. Based on years of experience, the salaries of professors at all levels in the US do not differ between public and private universities, while professors at all levels in public universities in Taiwan generally have higher salaries and better benefits than those in private universities. Unlike the US, the academic rankings of public universities in Taiwan and Hong Kong are much higher than those of private universities.

Taiwan has produced an abundance of doctoral graduates but hasn't provided them with enough career opportunities. One consequence is that National Chung Hsing University posted advertisements for PhD holders for part-time lecturer positions but with no pay under the pretense of providing training (September 27, 2018, *United Daily*). This is no different from some universities demanding that new hires donate a portion of their salaries back to the university as if encouraging them to work for the next life as well. Low enrollment affects tuition income. Universities that are economically stretched could only resort to cutting salaries. According to statistics from the Ministry of Education, the average monthly salary for full professors is slightly more than NT$60,000 (close to US$2,000) at some private tertiary institutions (September 18, 2022, *United Daily*), far below the monthly stipend for PhD students at Hong Kong universities.

Taiwan's higher education is lifeless, constantly setting off alarm bells, hemorrhaging over 2,000 teaching staff in the past five years, especially young and prime-age professors whose numbers are declining year by year. Again, Figure 20.2 points out that the 1990s' education reforms that took place in Taiwan owing to political populism have been disastrous! Higher education is at a stalemate, and the related issues have not been resolved for many years. As shown in Table 18.1, it is not surprising that Taiwan's universities are not ranked high, or even dropped significantly.

Driven by politics, the motto that "people learn asynchronously and specialize in different fields" is often ignored and hence causes laypeople to disrupt higher education, particularly in Taiwan. Flowers may fade and bloom again, but people once old cannot regain their youth. Yet higher education policies across the Strait are repeatedly led by bureaucracy. Chinese societies worship the prestige of Nobel laureates, regarding them as omnipotent, and prefer relying on renowned people in even areas beyond their expertise, just as they tend to overemphasize college degrees and overvalue graduates from famous universities. Many people across the Strait have a self-inflated ego to their past glory, and with the help of society, some even use that to boost political influence. In the US, universities only reward an individual's performance in specialized areas of expertise and only recognize the current academic performance. This offers a lesson worth learning.

Higher Education is Costly

Higher education should reflect the actual cost of research and learning to a certain degree. It is only right and proper that education beneficiaries pay according to the quality of their education. Appropriate financial support can be considered for people with proper interest and aptitude but who cannot afford it. However noble it may sound, equality in everything can mean inequality. Underfed horses cannot run fast; underfunded universities suffer a shortage of staff and lack of research. Quality is bound to be poor if one depends only on using gimmicks to attract funding.

More specifically, higher education should not thoughtlessly offer what turns out to be high-level but low-quality general education that deviates from societal needs, creating a fast-growing number of undergraduates and squeezing vocational school-leavers out of jobs. This results in a drop in the employment rate of college graduates in their own disciplines and a low starting salary (at times even lower than that of skilled technicians). Graduates from vocational institutes also lack practical experience, and what they have learned is not useful; so they cannot be qualified for the work of senior technicians.

I cannot help but wonder whether higher education in Hong Kong, which has improved by retaining good faculty with the offer of decent benefits, can sustain its development now that Mainland China, Singapore and South Korea are rapidly enhancing the quality of their higher education and strategically increasing faculty pay. How will Taiwan's higher education, which is suffering crises due to insufficient funds and the low-grade democratic movement, deal with the aftermath?

Running a university is nothing like setting up a street stall where one just comes and goes without spending much, nor do teaching and research operate like social welfare activities where participants are rarely subjected to performance evaluation, and everyone is entitled to claim an equal share of resources.

The Driving Force behind Progress

No society is perfect. Any progress is based on a drive to improve the status quo.

To improve, we must recognize the status quo and systematically understand our shortcomings. The starting point for quality control is identifying problems and highlighting assignable causes for defects or errors. Similarly, what we first need to do to enhance higher education is ascertain shortcomings and strive for improvement rather than only focusing on extolling glories and singing praises.

Pride goes before a fall because we are so used to shortcomings that we hardly notice them anymore; hence, there is an inevitable decline. Out of the depths of misfortune comes bliss because there are too many flaws unmatched by anyone else. Therefore, only after we have realized what needs to be improved can we see the light at the end of the tunnel. Although governments and societies on either side of the Strait have not prospered yet, they sometimes see what is worthy of praise and then brag about themselves, exaggerating their advantages and hiding their shortcomings. It is especially true when the government strongly supports time-honored universities. There are too many exaggerated, superficial reports in the media and too few factual analyses.

Based on the information in Table 18.1, Table 20.1 lists the comparison of higher education among the Four Asian Tigers. The performance of the universities in the Four Asian Tigers is directly proportional to the per capita GDP of each region and inversely proportional to the number of universities per capita in each region. Specifically, they run from high to low as Singapore, Hong Kong, South Korea and Taiwan. If we look more closely at the current educational attainment per capita, we can clearly see that Taiwan has the highest education attainment per capita, and its GDP per capita and university performance are the lowest. Taiwan claims to be with the highest popularization of higher education. However, among the Four Asian Tigers, Taiwan has the lowest GDP per capita, the lowest starting salaries for college graduates (Figure 20.1) and professors' salaries (Figure 20.2). Of course, morale cannot be too good, either. What kind of niche areas of academia has democratization brought to Taiwan's higher education? Have those in power conducted any soul-searching or self-reflection on these "equally poor" phenomena?

A Hairdresser's Story

There is a hairdresser whose guiding principle is to use the shortest strand of hair as the benchmark for cutting. If the hairdresser accidentally cuts a strand shorter than the one used as the benchmark, the shorter strand becomes the new benchmark, and the rest of the hair will have to be cut accordingly. But because the hairdresser keeps accidentally making mistakes, the benchmark has to be continuously revised until, eventually, the customer has no hair left. Of course, the customer is not happy, but the aims of the hairdresser are fulfilled.

This story bears some resemblance to salary cuts for every trade, including those for college graduates. Just as the hairdresser has used the shortest strand of hair as the benchmark, the lowest salary point has become the benchmark for adjusting pay for everyone. This is an example of self-contradicting populism. While everyone is complaining about their low wages, at the same time, they expect tasty food in sizeable portions at bargain prices, begrudging the shop proprietors the profits they make. There are so many cases like this that it has become the norm. Therefore, to keep prices down, the proprietor of a beef noodle restaurant picked out the leftover meat from a previous customer's bowl and served it to the next diner.

Table 20.1 Comparison of four Asian Tigers.

Country/region	Population (millions)	2022 GDP per capita (US$)	Number of Universities[a]	Number of universities per million	Ratio of no. of universities in top 100 of QS, THE, ARWU[b] to total no. of universities
Singapore	5.7	66K	6	1.1	0.35
South Korea	51.7	38K	190	3.7	0.01
Hong Kong	7.5	50K	11	1.5	0.09
Taiwan	23.7	39K	137	5.8	0

[a] Estimated number, based on those universities with graduate schools.
[b] From Table 18.1.

By reusing uneaten meat, the price could be lowered (May 23, 2012, TVBS News Network).

For the same reason, others do not like to see you enjoying a high salary. This kind of spiteful jealousy leads to the phenomenon of "equal poverty", bringing to mind the customer whose head is shorn clean under the hairdresser's razor, the dishonesty of the manager of the beef noodle shop and university professors' low salaries. It might be possible, during private moments, to take comfort in the thought that everyone is paid the same low salary, but this does not mean that poverty is a pleasure.

Strangely, many people criticize professors' salaries as too high. Oddly, many comment that the gap between the rich and poor has widened in Taiwan. An increasing wealth gap is indeed a global challenge, but in Taiwan, on the contrary, the wealth gap is relatively small. Throughout history, the Chinese have been less concerned about poverty than equity. Therefore, it is puzzling why today's 22K Taiwanese society is concerned about poverty on the one hand but worried about inequity on the other.

Isn't it perplexing that an independent state, the Republic of China, founded on the *Three Principles of the People*, namely nationalism, livelihood and democracy, should find itself turning into a stalwart of communism 100 years later?

21
Course Design and Choice of Majors

Before I assumed my position as CityU president, I had already had exchanges with Mainland Chinese colleagues for over 30 years. I devoted a lot of thought to the gap between Mainland Chinese universities and top universities around the world. Recently published international university rankings indicate that a few of their outstanding universities have surpassed Hong Kong universities and are far ahead of those in Taiwan, as indicated in Table 18.1. Measured by the output of university professors' research papers, Mainland universities do not necessarily perform well, while Taiwanese universities are even at the bottom across the Strait (see Table 18.2). While universities in Hong Kong may be more advanced than their counterparts in Taiwan and Mainland China, they still lag behind the more advanced Western higher education institutions.

Other than the deficiency in soulware as outlined in Chapter 1, in what ways are universities across the Strait falling behind first-rate universities elsewhere?

Evaluation-Rankings-Job Market

Subjective evaluations by professors and those in leadership positions within the higher education sector across the Strait are not convincing. Objective standards must be set to persuade smart customers in higher education, i.e., a series of measurable benchmarks and criteria to be formulated as the basis for evaluation.

Setting such benchmarks is a method as well as a philosophy. The process motivates universities to aim for an established goal and highlights information that usually receives little attention. They need to face the reality that high school students and counselors, university students and administrators, company recruiters and the public attach importance to publicly acknowledged standards. These rankings influence high school students applying for university and graduates choosing graduate schools.

Way Kuo. *The Absence of Soulware in Higher Education*, (293–302) © 2023 Scrivener Publishing LLC

Publicly acknowledged rankings are effective benchmarks and criteria for measuring the quality of higher education and reflect employees' salaries and benefits in the job market. If a university's undergraduate programs rank high, and the performance of its graduate programs is equally impressive, alumni are more likely to donate generously; and students are more willing to pay higher tuition fees for a high-quality learning experience and opportunities to engage in quality research. As a result, faculty salaries will rise accordingly. The rankings for higher education institutions and their performance in different domains are positively correlated and closely interrelated, constituting a dynamic interacting system.

Quality management experience tells us that it is easier to do the right thing and difficult to do the wrong thing in a sound system (see Chapter 4). Using benchmarks and criteria for objective assessment helps build a sound system. With the higher education sector across the Strait today, there is some distance between the status quo and the ideal situation. In addition to the tangible ranking indicators, course design and selection of majors are two important indicators. These two indicators, which are usually manipulated by social mindset, have no obvious relationship with rankings, but they affect academic development.

Evaluation of University Curricula

University students in Hong Kong and Taiwan take more or less the same number of credits as US students. An undergraduate student in the US, for example, must take 120 semester credits before he/she can graduate. Mainland Chinese undergraduates, however, have to take at least 150 semester credits. In addition, as mentioned in Chapter 3, a semester in Mainland China is 21 to 22 weeks long, obviously much heavier when compared with 18 to 19 weeks in Taiwan, 14 to 16 weeks in Hong Kong, and 13 to 15 weeks per semester in a two-semester academic year in the US.

In the US, only 56% of undergraduates graduate. Across the Strait, university students must deal with various kinds of exams, but the graduation rate is almost 100%. Just as farmers are hurt by falling grain prices in the event of overproduction, the increase in the number of graduates devalues the degree. Even when they find jobs, the starting salaries for university graduates decrease significantly. Taking GDP per capita into consideration, as shown in Figure 20.1, the starting salaries of university graduates in Taiwan still lag far behind. In addition to low salaries, the quality of their degrees is frequently questioned, which is often a source of personal discontent and leads to a sense of social inequality. In the absence of objective evaluation for differentiating between the strong and the weak, people will again indulge in aggrandizement.

Most college students on both sides of the Strait are accustomed to learning passively from textbooks. In fact, they should read on their own to learn most of the content from books before coming to class and will lag behind if they rely only on the teacher for knowledge. Likewise, if professors repeat only what is in the book and are unable to make use of contemporary academic research to extend knowledge and deepen learning, their teaching is not useful to students.

A thorough understanding of a small part of what one learns is far better than taking in a great deal of undigested materials without understanding. AI relies on a large amount of data to provide fast computing and decision-making functions to help with our lives. Despite its strong impact, AI has low analytical capabilities and does not possess such important soft skills as original ideas and creativity. For someone who reads a vast number of books but doesn't do research, doesn't know right from wrong and has little common sense, the most he/she can be is AI, with the computing power and execution speed of a robot. After all, no one has the computing power to execute instructions as fast as AI.

Whether we see AI as a boon or a threat, it will have profound implications for individuals and society. In spite of its numerous benefits, AI poses risks such as displacing occupations, increasing unemployment, making humans lazy and increasing socioeconomic inequality, to name just a few. A much-talked about AI product is ChatGPT, an AI dialogue platform able to generate content, understand a user's intentions, answer follow-up questions and reject inappropriate requests.

While on the topic of AI, we need to remember that professional ethics is fundamental to all of us. In using AI, we need to pay special emphasis on ethics; otherwise, society will get messy and uncontrollable.

Ideally, university students should frequently engage in discussions that nurture independent thinking and lead to better credits. Of course, mediocre performance in such activities leads to low scores, and too many low scores might mean not graduating.

Many students across the Strait still follow the tradition of getting their credits by passing examinations based on textbook knowledge. They are much less involved in projects or presentations and are not required to pursue research. To initiate an inspiring discussion, a good teacher must have some command of scholarship anchored in their own explorations and research. If a teacher is unable to integrate their research into teaching, even when they are engaged in research, they will not succeed in inspiring students to move to a higher level of inquiry or to innovate.

Different learning modes exert different demands on students to meet academic requirements. Graduates from US universities are equipped with greater independent thinking, stronger professional analytical skills, and a more creative and innovative mindset. Many academic subjects nowadays are highly cross-disciplinary in nature. If university teachers have little involvement in interdisciplinary research on such topics, how can they supervise their students, and how can we expect them to contribute proactively to innovation and knowledge creation in the globalized 21st century?

Trivially Divided Disciplines and Sloppy Decisions

Universities across the Strait like to fragment academic disciplines into discrete subject areas, resulting in a proliferation of departments and majors that bear all kinds of titles or names, many of which are awkward and senseless.

For example, an automobile department set up a major in the automobile; a nano degree was created because nanotechnology happened to be a fad; a tourism department was established to promote the leisure industry; majors in creative writing and cultural learning were founded to accede to societal demands. I have even heard of such titles as a funeral management department, a vegetarian food department, a make-up department, etc. These majors are sub-divisions of the broader disciplines of mechanical engineering, electrical engineering, history, marketing or food science. Such a narrowly focused naming will inevitably need to be changed frequently to meet changing social needs, which is against the spirit of education. It is also unfavorable for students studying these subjects to face future employment challenges. Setting up certain majors and programs arbitrarily gives students the wrong impression that it is acceptable to pursue their frivolous fancies. Now, new AI department is being developed.

The fragmentation of disciplines to create a proliferation of discrete academic programs can appeal only to a small group for a fleeting moment and bucks universities' long-term missions. In American universities, academic programs are broadly based, while curricula are constantly updated through research to enhance academic departments. New departments or colleges are set up infrequently and the titles of academic degrees are limited; they would never create bizarre new majors to court public favor.

University education is based on quality, not quantity. Yet in Taiwan, the number of universities has ballooned in recent years under democratic politics. In Hong Kong and Mainland China, strange and seemingly useful, but short-sighted, programs have been introduced. There are no stringent requirements for admitting students or graduation.

On October 13, 2021, tremendous fanfare in Taiwan greeted news that Harvard Beijing Academy, a long-term collaboration between Harvard University and Beijing Language and Culture University, would be renamed Harvard Taipei Academy since it would now partner with NTU instead. From 2022, the renamed academy was expected to send Harvard students to NTU for an 8-week Chinese course every summer. Cultural activities include visiting the National Palace Museum, Shilin Night Market, Yangmingshan National Park and learning calligraphy, chess, paper-cutting, and making dumplings. Such extracurricular activities are hardly worthy of high-profile publicity at regular universities.

Science may save the world in the proverbial sense, but it is actually more technological innovation. The transfer of science to technology is a process, as is the transfer of knowledge to practical skills. If the education sector is concerned only with the unilateral transmission and imparting of received knowledge but neglects application and ignores research, students will not have the capability to add value to the overall environment through innovation.

Children in the US receive practical, logical and analytical thinking training from primary school. Classwork focuses on originality, teamwork, professional ethics, communication, social responsibility and often creative thinking and entrepreneurship. Universities advocate, though with hardship, internship experience. Through stringent quality control and accreditation of programs, even graduates from an average university in the US are guaranteed to be of excellent quality and can "hit the ground running", starting to work independently from day one. It is known that the semester- or year-long internship opportunities that American companies provide help students become professionally mature and more likely to be retained by the host companies after graduation.

In Japan, on the other hand, businesses do not have the expectation that graduates will have learned everything in college. Hence, they offer on-the-job training. A Sony CEO once told me that under the mainstream practice of life-long employment in Japanese enterprises, new graduates receive a great deal of vigorous training to turn them into tailor-made employees. Japanese enterprises do not want universities to assume that they know what talent the business sector requires. They are worried that students might be misled, making it difficult to meet their needs. Even in my interview with Hideo Ohno, the President of Tohoku University, he explained that Japan's university education focuses on substance teaching.

American and Japanese education philosophies have unique features, each with their own forte. Societies across the Strait place undue emphasis on degrees while university graduates, particularly in Hong Kong, favor stable government jobs, unlike their counterparts in the US and Japan.

Learning and Selection of Majors

A few summers ago, a Hong Kong high school graduate died through suicide after failing to be admitted to college.

In fact, failure to get into college may have opened up more possibilities for the student concerned. Many accomplished people today have not been to college. It is wrong to think that death is the only way out if admission is denied. It is harmful to emphasize degrees, especially those awarded by renowned universities, and fail to acknowledge the importance of substantive learning for its own sake.

Another bizarre phenomenon in recent years is that very few top high school students in Hong Kong select science and technology, which is far different from 30 to 40 years ago and different from the current situation in other parts of the world. In selecting their future professions, Hong Kong students invariably choose medicine, law and business as their top choices, while science, technology, engineering and liberal arts are lower down the list, even though science and technology are increasingly dominant in the current international environment. In fact, science and engineering graduates will be the mainstay in the employment market, according to a recent US employment market survey. There will be broader, rather than narrower, prospects for people engaging in science and technology. Besides, the development of science and technology will strengthen the middle class and reduce the gap between the rich and the poor.

One may distinguish oneself in any profession or trade. When excellent high school students choose university majors in a healthy society, there should be a normal distribution. That is, there should be outstanding students selecting different majors, liberal arts, science, business, engineering, medicine, law, agriculture, and so forth. Why do people in Hong Kong, who are said to have the highest average IQ in the world, deviate from this world trend?

The provision of a universal college education that guarantees graduation may seem to improve the average level of education, but in fact, it wastes social talent and prevents some people from attaining their full potential, receiving a watered-down university degree instead. Some hills are suitable for growing oranges, others only for planting guava. If we expand universities with no limitations and interfere with a few specific disciplines without constraint, it will be like growing quantities of low-quality apples, much of which we can't bear to throw away.

Associate Degrees and Community Colleges

Since 1997, Hong Kong has produced many associate degree holders. The initial purpose may have been based on good intentions to replicate the US community college system, creating a multitude of ill-positioned courses that provide little general knowledge and lack special expertise. However, in an environment that values degrees, many Hong Kong students still want to earn a bachelor's degree after obtaining an associate degree.

In order to accommodate associate degree awardees, the UGC created additional senior intake places so that quality students can enter the third year of a four-year program after completing a recognized sub-degree program. Several universities are required to admit about 5,000 more students who have completed the two-year associate degree program into the four-year top-up program. But this requirement is extremely difficult to achieve. Most associate degree graduates can choose only soft subjects that do not require prerequisite courses because they do not have a solid academic foundation. Such two-phase bachelor's degree programs are not coherent with each other and can hardly be satisfactory to either teaching or student learning.

Initially, the government had no clear arrangements for how to deal with high school students after graduation. Instead, it pursued a piecemeal approach that treats the head when the head aches and treats the foot when the foot hurts. Although such hasty approaches have resulted in temporary solutions, it simply delays tackling today's problems until tomorrow, causing misery for everyone. That being the case, why not simply increase the number of places for a four-year undergraduate program?

In the US, community college students are usually more mature and greatly treasure their hard-to-acquire learning opportunities if they manage to get admitted to a four-year university. Many perform outstandingly and become mainstays of society. But in Hong Kong, few incoming associate degree students gain admission to the limited number of degree places offered by local universities. Since associate degree programs focus mainly on low-quality general knowledge rather than career-oriented skills, the students will not know what to do next and will probably stay unemployed if they fail to enroll in a four-year university program after two years of study. However, if universities feel obliged to enroll large numbers of sub-degree holders, social problems like high unemployment rates will likely follow.

It is understood that associate degree holders in Hong Kong are the most frustrated group in the city. These consequences, unintended as they might be, hinder social stability and progress and waste social resources, individual talent and two years of the students' lives. Because of a suboptimal education system, community colleges unexpectedly burden society.

In addition, students at Hong Kong community colleges pay higher tuition fees than those who attend a UGC-funded university, but students at a US community college pay much less than those who attend a regular four-year US university, which is an important reason for US students from less privileged family backgrounds to choose to study at a community college. If a Hong Kong student from a low-income family cannot enter a four-year university, they may have to pay a higher tuition fee to study for a two-year associate degree. Who can explain why this is fair?

Bachelor's degrees may not be the best choice for certain young people, nor an effective way to make effective use of social resources, just as general education may not be appropriate for every university student. The development of "post-90s" and "post-00s" universities highlights the importance of upholding excellence in higher education. To make the best use of talents, universities should seriously consider offering high-level skills-based and career-oriented education in line with social developments. They should replace associate degree programs that have produced graduates who are not competitive in the job market and cannot easily get admitted to a four-year degree program, and which do not provide a promising pathway for high school graduates.

However, after more than 20 years, the Hong Kong government realized its mistake: in 2021, it announced that associate degree programs would be adjusted, reduced or even canceled. Since the education policy was set by non-professionals without any simulation before implementation, we have witnessed a government U-turn that allows universities to reduce senior intake places. That decision was again led by laypeople.

Drunk Man Reported Missing Joins Search Party for Himself

In August 2022, the media across the Taiwan Strait reported that several hundred young people looking for jobs, and some unemployed middle-aged people from Taiwan, Hong Kong and Macau had been lured to Cambodia, Myanmar and other places where they engaged in fraudulent activities. Their freedom of movement was restricted by criminal groups, and they were even resold into forced labor as "piggies", according to some appalling stories circulating in the media. Also, as reported, a man among a group of victims rescued and returned to Taiwan was suspected of being a member of a fraud ring. He was arrested after he disembarked. As the Chinese idiom goes, fish eyes (a sham) are passed off as pearls (genuine treasure). A swindler is hidden among the swindled. Can this be considered a sophisticated or dumb scam? Or are we uninformed or too often exposed to such scams?

On the other hand, according to a story in a Turkish newspaper *Daily Sabah* on September 28, 2021, a rescue team was dispatched to find a man named Beyhan Mutlu, 50, from the town of Inegol in the Bursa province in northwest Turkey. He had been reported missing by his family, but it transpired that Mutlu had wandered off into a forest after drinking with friends. There, he came across a search party. Not realizing he was the objective of the search party, he joined in!

When he realized that the rescuers were calling out his name, he responded, "I'm here!" After listening to Mutlu's statement, the police drove him home. Doesn't Mutlu's story sound similar to what often happens in our life?

Time judges all. Even after just a rough evaluation, don't you think our government could be the biggest scam syndicate?

22

Accomplished Hermits behind Unprepossessing Gates

Universities across the Strait are full of vitality, but their academic culture needs to be enhanced. For example, universities in Hong Kong achieve high rankings in UK-based ranking agencies partly because the total number of universities in Hong Kong is small, allowing for a better concentration of resources. Hong Kong is where money dominates and where English and utility are emphasized at the expense of history and culture. In addition, the interaction between teachers and students is still inhibited by hierarchical thinking. This in turn hinders students from developing to their full potential because of the aloof teacher-student relationship and the lack of a decent model to learn from.

This is why I advocate that academics must return to basics and not lose sight of the core mission. "Just as a real hermit remains at peace amid the din of a city/ So a great scholar remains well-accomplished through research based on practical teaching, without being distracted by what seems to dazzle." I drafted this two-line poem to remind everyone of the essentials embedded in our grand academic task. Since then, CityU has been positioned to provide student-centered and innovation-based professional education, committed to the continuous improvement of university administration.

Israel's Culture

Jews are known for their intelligence. Although the Jewish population accounts for less than 0.25% of the world's population, Jews have won 22% of the world's Nobel Prizes. Numerous diligent Jews, such as Einstein, provide philosophical and innovative ideas for others to follow!

Surrounded by whom they regarded as their enemies, the Jewish diaspora established Israel in 1948 on the west bank of the Judaean Desert to the east of the Mediterranean Sea. "Dried vines, old trees, drowsy crows when the day's done / Short bridge, trickling stream, long sands and dunes / Ancient trails, cold west wind, a gaunt horse / In the west, the dying sun – / At Land's End, just the heart-torn, homesick one!" (Adapted from the translation by Frank C. Yue). This Chinese poem from the Yuan dynasty thoroughly expresses the feelings of homecoming wanderers in the early days of the founding of the State of Israel and accurately depicts the desolate desert wilderness. On top of that, Israel must face perpetual foreign pressure.

Since the founding of Israel, Israelis have worked through all kinds of hardships to transform the barren desert within their country into an oasis of fertile land where they could contribute to the world's scientific and technological civilization. Universities in Israel are fully autonomous with no supervising bodies, and they operate smoothly, a sharp contrast to how governments across the Strait regularly interfere in universities' affairs.

They adopt sound advice from all quarters, seek peace and equality, and speak for and practice justice. For example, the Technion-Israel Institute of Technology, a university for the professions, has allocated 20% of its approximately 14,000 precious student places to Arab students. Tel Aviv University also has a policy that aims to increase the ratio of female to male students in science and engineering to 50%.

"Two men may be born as dear brothers, even though they do not come from the same family." Such empathy and broadmindedness are by no means conceivable in cultures where narrowmindedness is the heritage. There are 12 universities in Israel, all of which are excellent even though they are young. Several Israelis have been awarded Nobel Prizes in physics, chemistry and economics. The Technion-Israel Institute of Technology alone has produced three Nobel Prize winners. None of the universities on either side of the Strait can match that accomplishment.

"Song to a Crude Hut" composed by the poet Liu Yuxi during the Tang dynasty is a widely read essay. "It matters not the height; a mountain becomes famous if a deity resides in it. It matters not the depth; a body of water becomes magical if a dragon lives in it." These lines voiced the author's aspiration that, if he cultivated his morality, he would not be affected by the crude living environment; instead, he would feel content living in poverty and appreciating the environs of his humble hut. Nothing looks ostentatious in Israel. Restaurants and universities have simple facades, nothing luxurious or extravagant. "Moss ascends the steps, turning them green, and the grass color enters the blinds, turning them light green. In talk and laughter there are scholars with profound knowledge, and among those coming and going there are no illiterate men." (Translation is adapted from the translation by Feng Xin-ming.) These are my favorite lines in the "Song of Crude Hut", perfect for describing Israel today, where we see positive green energy wherever we turn and where the most educated people on Earth reside with the highest rates of literacy and the highest percentage of people among its citizens to have received higher education.

Israel may not be as prosperous as Hong Kong, but it has a deep-rooted culture. While the international rankings of its universities are only above average, their accomplishments are commendable. I asked Professor Ariel Porat, President of Tel Aviv University, about these achievements, and he replied that their success is due to a sense of belonging within Israel's educational culture. After searching high and low, we conclude there is no match for a sense of belonging!

In the past 100 years, other than empty rhetoric, have the smart Chinese people on either side of the Strait contributed anything truly remarkable to the world? Are there any philosophies worth cherishing?

Ukrainian Persistence

Ukraine is known as the breadbasket of Europe, but for over 1,000 years, this part of Eastern Europe has been engulfed by war, carved up by imperialist powers and repeatedly turned over to others. The Chernobyl nuclear disaster in 1986 brought Ukraine to the attention of the world. I have visited the Chernobyl nuclear power plant and Crimea twice. Reading Ukrainian history makes one want to cry!

Ever since my youth, I have had an inexplicable fondness for the selfless contributions rendered by nurses. Florence Nightingale was such a figure. She came from a wealthy family and was well-educated. During the Crimean War in the 1850s, despite her family's opposition, she responded to the call from the British government to become a field nurse. She trained other nurses and nursed wounded soldiers in Constantinople, gaining a reputation for greatly reducing hospital death rates. She analyzed casualty records and used a simple polar area diagram to demonstrate that more British soldiers died from infectious diseases or lack of care than battle injuries. Therefore, improving sanitation was paramount. The chart she used in her analysis was a sketch of the pie chart or the circular histogram, commonly used in all walks of life today. So, Nightingale not only laid the foundation for the nursing profession, but was also a pioneer in statistical graphics and left a historical footprint in Ukraine. Her birthday, May 12, is designated as International Nurses Day.

In the spring of 2022, when Russia invaded Ukraine, I became naturally concerned about the safety of the Chernobyl Nuclear Power Plant.

I also thought about Nightingale's contributions to Crimea. What's more, Tu King Ning from CityU has maintained a long-term academic relationship with Andriy Gusak from Cherkasy National University in Ukraine. Therefore, I thought about visiting Ukraine again. However, the fierce fighting and travel logistics made an in-person visit impossible. In the end, a Zoom meeting was arranged with Rector Oleksandr Cherevko of Cherkasy National University in which I expressed support for the faculty and staff, students and researchers and tried to understand the huge damage that the Russia-inflicted conflict had caused. Ukraine is facing an invasion by a foreign power, which may not be over for a while. I sincerely hope peace will come soon and that life, teaching and research will return to normal.

The war has caused great suffering in Ukraine. Almost all the overseas students have left. "In the shade grows ancient moss green/ Its color turning the autumn clouds and mist cyan-blue." (Li Bai) Ukrainian universities are as indomitable as Ukraine the nation. University faculty and staff, who are already low-paid and war-torn, accepted a 25% pay cut. Despite adversity, morale is high, and the university continues to conduct teaching and research, just like the everlasting green moss turning the ambient clouds and mist cyan blue.

Innovation in Japan

Online companies in Japan conducted an interesting survey on what had been the most important invention in Japan since World War II. The answer was not mobile phones, sound systems, the Lexus, heavy industry, Japanese manga, democracy, or fashion products. It was instant noodles.

This fast-food item was invented by an ethnic Taiwanese residing in Japan and has become so popular that it is now marketed all over the world under different names. It can be eaten raw, cooked, boiled, steamed or fried. It can be a snack or a meal and commands the same status as burgers on many occasions, exerting considerable influence on our everyday lives.

Japan attaches foremost importance to science and technology and is known for its innovations. At one time, there was an exhibition of toilets at Narita International Airport. Many Chinese tourists were so enthralled by the Japanese electric toilet seats that they purchased them in a frenzy, only to find out later that they were manufactured in China.

The Japanese pay attention to toilet etiquette and special attention to hygiene and cleanliness. One of the hit songs in Japan in 2010, *God in the*

Toilet (*Toilet no Kamisama*), is just one illustration. In 2015, a government award for the best toilets was set up to recognize public toilets that were clean and convenient. They also considered putting dry toilets in elevators for people trapped during an earthquake. Other Japanese innovations and technological advancements have contributed enormously to the development of toilets and toilet diplomacy.

Speaking of toilets, a common phenomenon in Taiwan, Hong Kong and the Mainland is dirty toilets. Except for a ridiculously small number of high-end hotels and restaurants, many toilets at universities and high and elementary schools invariably stink. Yet no one seems to care.

Hermits of This World

On a rainy afternoon in July 2013, during my second invited visit to the Fukushima Nuclear Power Plant in Japan, I noticed something interesting as I left the campus of Kyoto University. Even though professors and alumni at this distinguished university have won eight Nobel Prizes, three Fields Medals, and three Kyoto Prizes, I saw through the rain that the gateway was small and plain but elegant. All the buildings were simple but functional, and the professors were erudite, humble and reticent, like hermits out of this world. And the campus was wholly immersed in academic pursuits, free from political interference. These characteristics exemplify what I hold dear in my heart regarding universities. We can find many highly accomplished hermits despite unprepossessing gates.

On another rainy, chilly day in mid-March 2023, I led a 12-person team to examine the ruptured Fukushima Nuclear Power Plant. We witnessed how well the staff at the plant had treated the wastewater coming from the polluting plant. In addition, engineers and workers meticulously followed the clear and simple instructions erected around the plant and the surrounding areas.

Sentiments Regarding University Names

Part II of this book contains a brief analysis of four diverse types of universities. Each type has its own individual forte, and all have teaching and research as their components.

Academic achievements have nothing to do with whether an institution carries "university" in its name. Ecole Polytechnique Fédérale de Lausanne (EPFL) in Switzerland is a good example. MIT, which ranked first in the QS Global University Rankings for many years, is often referred to as the "Massachusetts University of Technology" by many Mainland Chinese websites. What kind of psychology is at play here?

Regardless of the type of university, academic achievements have nothing to do with the size of the institution. Caltech is among the best examples, with only about 300 faculty members and over 2,100 students. It doesn't carry "university" in its name and doesn't value general education like those across the Strait. At a time when everyone is pursuing grandeur and comprehensiveness, Caltech seems to be swimming against the current, and yet its academic reputation remains unaffected. École normale supérieure in Paris also doesn't carry "university" in its name and is even smaller than Caltech, and yet its academic reputation ranks among the top in the world.

American higher education is world-leading, firmly established and forward-looking. But its universities rarely add new degree courses, and new universities are not easily established. Cornell Tech in New York is an exception. Established by Cornell University in partnership with the Technion-Israel Institute of Technology, Cornell Tech is a science and technology-focused campus modeled after Caltech, small but of high quality.

Israel's higher education is outstanding, and yet the university campuses and gates are not at all ostentatious. The campus of Cherkasy National University in Ukraine is not very extensive, either. Even though the university suffered during the war, its professors were calm and undisturbed, like old monks in meditation, performing their academic duties and research as usual. Similarly, Japan is known for its down-to-earth attitude, as reflected in its clean airports and universities that are functional without paying too much attention to the facade. The excellence of a university, therefore, depends not on its name or size but on its quality and distinctiveness and sense of belonging.

Campuses and Gates

Societies across the Strait attach great importance to higher education; Mainland invests the most. A substantial number of universities on the Mainland possess huge new campuses, some as large as several thousand *mu* (1,000 *mu* = 165 acres), which is hardly negotiable on foot. The buildings are massive, looking more like palatial halls in ancient China and consuming a great deal of energy due to poor lighting systems and lack of energy saving or environmental protection. In addition, many buildings and facilities are dilapidated. Paint is peeling off buildings that are only about 10 years old, while walls and windows look gray and dirty, covered with dust and cobwebs as if abandoned. Yet no one seems to care.

While university campuses in Taiwan and Mainland China may vary in size, they lack proper management and regular maintenance, as indicated by stinking toilets and campus lawns overgrown with weeds. Universities in Hong Kong rarely have spacious campuses or towering grand appearances. Instead, facilities are thronging with bustling people going about daily business, but the campus environment is clean and neat.

Perhaps influenced by a popular but misleading notion that fine clothing makes a person, universities across the Strait emphasize decorating their outward appearance rather than improving their inner substance, and they spend a hefty sum on elaborately designed gates, logos, names and flags. In some cases, enlarged university names and logos are erected at every entrance, decorated with neon lights that look like lanterns at night. It is really a paradoxical combination of paying so much attention to ornamentation and, at the same time, a puzzling neglect of keeping campus clean, functional and sustainable.

In the summer of 2015, I re-visited Princeton University, this time paying special attention to the university environment. While the campus has beautiful green surroundings with well-groomed lawns and lush trees and shrubs, it is exceedingly difficult to find the name of the university. Not only are the gates inconspicuous, but the building names are equally hard to locate. In fact, some of the academic buildings did not seem to have a name at all.

Americans are not known for their modesty and are even considered arrogant. In spite of that, American universities behave like humble Chinese gentlemen from the old days, whereas universities across the Strait veer in the opposite direction. Scholarships of the universities may lack grandeur, but their scene is not small at all.

We ought to concentrate on promoting scholarship instead of outward appearance. We should be pragmatic and not waste time pursuing an unproductive life, only eating and drinking. Faculty today must adhere to modern standards for nurturing students while students must respect teachers and not yell pointlessly behind the gates. They should cherish academic freedom, just like the professors at Kyoto University. We can learn a lot about advancing innovation by considering instant noodles, which only seem ordinary, or by examining toilet culture, which may not appear to be exalted but is inherently creative.

The scale of a university is not important, the history of a university is not important, campus size is not important, and the display of the university name and logo is not important. It is not important whether or not the word "university" appears in the institution's name. The culture of academic freedom and the quality of education stand paramount.

There will surely be many accomplished hermits, notwithstanding the unprepossessing gates.

Dedication to Work, both Fair and Unselfish

It is public knowledge at CityU that Dean C of a particular college is at odds with Dr. D, the general manager of a university enterprise. They constantly argue for the interests of their respective units, sometimes heatedly. During the 2021 annual assessment exercise, Dean C served as a member of the university assessment committee. When Dr. D's case was being discussed, I noticed that Dean C gave Dr. D a high score, advocating that Dr. D's salary increase should be 4.5% based on the average salary increase of 4% for the whole university. This could be seen as a modern version of the unselfish story about Qi Huangyang, a noble official of the State of Jin, recorded in *The Annals of Lu Buwei*, who always recommended others for higher positions with an objective eye rather than for vested interest.

Part V
CREATIVITY AND INNOVATION

Waves behind drive those before them,
As the beauty reapplies her power.
Rain and dew nurture the grass and trees,
Giving the landscape a fresh countenance.

At the invitation of the General Administration of Quality Supervision, Inspection and Quarantine of China, I delivered a speech titled "Quality and Innovation" at the First Conference of Quality on September 15, 2014. Other speakers included Zhou Ji, President of the Chinese Academy of Engineering, and Carlos Gutiérrez, former US Secretary of Commerce. More than 700 experts, including senior corporate members from more than 40 countries, leaders of quality at the State Council and those at the provincial and city levels, as well as heads of enterprises, attended.

Because of the special status of some attendees, the venue, the Great Hall of the People, was heavily guarded. Unexpectedly, just before my presentation, I discovered that because of a persistent technical problem, I could not fully use the materials I had prepared. I wanted to demonstrate that every improvement in quality over the last 100 years initiates the next level of innovation, and every innovation is an actualization of that which the last quality standard embodies. Ironically, such an important concept could not be presented because of a technical glitch. At a well-publicized, national-level conference about quality held at the Great Hall of the People in front of international experts, the display monitor on the computer broke down due to negligence. Although such an error could have happened at any conference, this incident gave me the opportunity to underline my main point: Quality is the prerequisite for innovation. I developed my point further with reference to higher education and energy safety, showing that innovation would be meaningful only after product safety and reliability have been well established.

Soulware, Innovation, Research and Development

A journey of a thousand miles begins with the first step. As a visual aid to Part V, Figure V.1 below shows data on R&D involvement in the US, Mainland China, Taiwan, Hong Kong, Singapore, South Korea and Japan from 1996 to 2019, represented in a percentage of GDP invested in R&D in these countries and regions.

Looking at the ratio of total domestic R&D expenditure to GDP, the US was 2.8% between 2009 and 2018 and exceeded 3% for the first time in 2019; Taiwan grew gradually over the years since 1999 to 3.5% in 2019; and Hong Kong started to grow slightly in recent years, and was still lower than 1% in 2021. For Mainland China, the figure was 0.56% in 1996, reached 2.2% in 2018 and grew to 2.4% in 2020. South Korea has the highest R&D expenditure, reaching 4.6%.

As shown in Figure V.1, a large R&D investment has been generated in Taiwan over the years, but when soulware is not developed, the potential returns are severely compromised. The mistakes in higher education have led to social problems. Even though the investment in higher education is extremely low in Hong Kong, it is able to sustain the low admission rate shown in Figure 3.1.

In other words, the situation in Hong Kong and Taiwan is not ideal. Compared to South Korea, the admission rate for universities in Taiwan

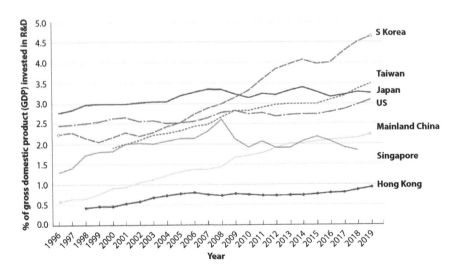

Figure V.1 R&D investment in the US, Mainland China, Taiwan, Hong Kong, Singapore, South Korea and Japan.

(Figure 3.1) is extremely high because of poor management, comparable to the situation in Hong Kong with its excessively low admission rate and conservative approach. South Korea admits an appropriate number of university students but maintains a significant investment in R&D and performs the best. The success of hi-tech corporations in South Korea is obvious. In recent years, South Korea has repeatedly demonstrated its creativity, while the Mainland has made remarkable progress, whereas Hong Kong and Taiwan have remained static.

Without healthy soulware, little can be done well. Shortcomings brought forth by poor leadership harm higher education and innovation.

Knowledge Transfer

When examining the quality of higher education, we tend to pay attention to the performance of universities, the studies of the students, the employability of graduates, the productivity of faculty, the contributions of alumni to society, and other similar criteria. However, these factors represent only the conditions necessary for excellence at a university. There are other intangible responsibilities that a university must shoulder, for example, promoting creativity and innovation, cultivating talent, creating knowledge and stimulating thought.

In order to play a role in society, modern universities have to insist that knowledge creation and transfer is an important part of their mission. Knowledge transfer adds value and ensures availability for all. The dissemination of new knowledge through R&D investment can provide possible solutions to pressing global issues, which is the main point of the process of knowledge transfer. For universities to stay competitive, knowledge transfer must be articulated to faculty and students and embedded in teaching, learning, research and outreach.

In recent years, I have learned after interviewing dozens of university presidents around the world that many universities have set up specific mechanisms to promote knowledge transfer as an indicator of performance. For example, the University of Stuttgart in the German motor city has established university committees to plan and promote knowledge transfer regularly. The University of British Columbia, which has produced eight Nobel laureates, is committed to knowledge transfer while conducting basic research and has assisted in establishing 245 spin-off companies, some of which have become industry leaders. STEMCELL Technologies Canada, founded by university researchers, is one of the largest companies of its kind in the world.

Cornell Tech is perhaps the most creative institution for innovation and knowledge transfer. This pioneering new model campus established in 2012 fuses teaching with entrepreneurship on campus to incubate science-tech companies directly. Its goal is to create 28,000 jobs and 600 companies in the first three decades with $23 billion in economic benefits. As of 2022, its current crop of students and postdoctoral scholars have launched more than 70 tech start-ups in New York, attracting $75 million in investment.

Successful innovative knowledge transfer is crucial to the rise and fall of a country or region. Israel is a useful example. A country of nine million people and lacking natural resources, Israel has fought several wars against its neighbors since its founding in 1948. It has grown obstinately to become the world's leading "Start-up Nation". The Technion-Israel Institute of Technology, established in 1924, has made great contributions by training 70% of the founders and administrators of high-tech companies across the country. Its graduates have founded 792 companies, of which 19 are unicorns.

The future is here; only change remains the same. Who will promote creativity and innovation? Who will perform knowledge transfer? The bottleneck is the utilization of people's talents, and the mentality of those in power is the bottleneck of innovation.

23
Creativity Depends on Asking Questions

Chinese culture attaches importance to commonality, encouraging people to go with the flow rather than stand out from the crowd. Following the pace of the times, young people across the Strait are now told to be creative. The prerequisite for creativity is curiosity, a state of mind that inspires discovery and exploration. So, older people cannot be innovative?

In Chapter 11, we spoke of the story of a middle-aged official who graduated from a prestigious high school and did well at university but never realized his aspirations after his career ran into trouble. This is by no means an uncommon occurrence, and it is a phenomenon worth examining. A lack of innovation might leave us ruminating only on past glories.

Ask More Questions

Einstein points out the need to "learn from yesterday, live for today, hope for tomorrow," reminding us that "the important thing is not to stop questioning." Many problems and issues need to be solved, and so we have to be prepared for tomorrow by using technologies that have yet to be invented, planning for jobs that do not yet exist and solving problems that we are not yet aware of.

An abundance of examples can validate these words. Not long ago, we were still using airmail and surface mail to communicate, but today many people transmit messages and pictures by email, WeChat, microblogs, WhatsApp, blogs, Facebook, Flickr, Instagram and video conferencing. The telephone has developed from 3G to 4G, then 5G; and 6G is just around the corner. The iPhone and iPad and other electronic tools have become hugely popular. Television has changed from black and white to color, from high definition to high dimension. Traditional cars have evolved into electric cars from gasoline or diesel and then a hybrid of different power sources. Sensors are used extensively to enhance product safety, and airborne vehicles are now being developed. Although these new means of transportation

---

Way Kuo. *The Absence of Soulware in Higher Education*, (315–322) © 2023 Scrivener Publishing LLC

can render our lives more convenient and comfortable, they also create new problems and opportunities, all of which need to be addressed.

Think More

A few stories below will illustrate the importance of discovery and innovation.

The first is about clean water. According to a report by the US National Academy of Science, clean drinking water can extend human life by 10 years, but one-tenth of the world's population still has no access to clean drinking water. After seeing how so many African children have no potable water, Theresa Dankovich, a civil and environmental engineering researcher at Carnegie Mellon University, developed a low-priced "drinkable book" whose paper pages were embedded with nanoparticles with each sheet able to filter 100 liters of water. This innovation can supply drinkable water for an individual for up to four years and was named by *Time* as one of the top 25 inventions of 2015.

Another story is about cars and bicycles. Many years ago, owning a car was regarded as a symbol of culture and wealth. At that time, people in villages and small towns in Mainland China depended mainly on bicycles and public transport. However, with the development of its economy, China has surpassed the US in car sales. By the end of 2020, according to China's Traffic Management Bureau, the number of registered vehicles reached 281 million. Today, China is the world's largest market for self-driving cars on highways. The trend today is to design and manufacture self-driving ground vehicles, electric cars and hydrogen-powered cars instead of traditional gasoline-burning automobiles.

However, bicycles are back in vogue in advanced economies in the West as a response to pollution. In July 2007, the Paris municipal government launched a scheme called Vélib (a portmanteau of the French word *vélo*, meaning bicycle, and *liberté*, meaning liberty) that rented out bicycles at a low rate. Cyclists can access over 10,000 bicycles in 750 bicycle parks throughout the city. The first year of operation saw more than 200 million rentals, and the scheme has expanded to over 40 suburbs of the capital.

A similar plan launched in the summer of 2010 in London provided more than 5,000 bicycles at over 300 rental spots, while Taipei rolled out a popular program called Ubike in 2009, and in November 2012, a full-scale bicycle rental system was officially launched and enjoyed great popularity. Hong Kong has experimented with a bicycle-sharing system in recent years and opened an 82-km cycling track.

Many of us have seen how tires on bicycles, motorcycles, cars, trucks, buses and even planes can go flat. Almost all vehicles use air-filled tires, but manufacturers are beginning to develop non-air-filled tires because of their inherent shortcoming.

For our next example, let's consider the reduction of carbon dioxide, which in high concentrations causes dizziness, suffocation and death, and contributes to the greenhouse effect, which in turn impacts the global climate. The bicycle rental and sharing programs described above are some alternative measures deployed worldwide to reduce carbon emissions.

Reducing carbon emissions was a key topic that the Kyoto Protocol attempted to tackle by proposing a carbon emission trading system, with the unit of trading set as the tonnage of carbon dioxide. The system allowed countries with spare emission units to sell their excess capacity to countries that were over their targets. Another effective way of reducing emissions is inspired by the working of the sand clock. We can install such a clock in the desert and use the thermal energy stored in the sand during the day to generate electricity at night. The energy conversion rate is as high as 60% in part because the energy can be stored and used in a variety of ways.

There are many industrial uses of carbon dioxide. It can be used to extinguish a fire and add bubbles to soft drinks. My cooking secret is enhancing the flavor of beef, pork and chicken at a barbeque by adding carbon dioxide. How to do that? Perhaps give this culinary puzzle some thought.

It is also possible to immerse grapes in carbon dioxide for anaerobic fermentation. In an oxygen-free state, the sugar in the grapes turns into alcohol and yields a full-textured wine with a mild flavor under the right conditions. Coffee beans can be similarly put through anaerobic fermentation. Place ripe coffee beans into a tightly sealed metal container and then inject carbon dioxide to allow the beans to ferment and break down in an oxygen-free environment. The result is a mouth-wateringly sweet aroma.

Solidified carbon dioxide (dry ice) can be used, for example, to enhance the atmosphere. Most interestingly, scientists are investigating ways to turn carbon dioxide into energy. By adding catalytic agents or through photosynthesis, carbon dioxide can be turned into fuel for automobiles. Isn't this how plants generate energy? For trees, carbon dioxide is useful gas, indispensable for photosynthesis.

Scientists can already extract carbon dioxide from waste gas produced by power plants, and they may be able to extract carbon dioxide directly from the air in the future, in which case the amount of carbon dioxide in the air will be reduced dramatically, improving the quality of the environment, and relieving the energy shortage. When this technology becomes a reality, will we continue to consider carbon dioxide harmful? Who knows, we may even start to sell carbon dioxide for a profit!

Limited knowledge, an outdated mode of thinking, a refusal to raise questions and an inability to make connections—all these will hinder our capacity to understand the workings of the world. So how can we hope to innovate then?

New Technology, New Challenges

Thanks to cloud computing, we now enjoy the convenience of information brought straight to us via the internet, wherever we may be. At the same time, society is plagued by internet-related crimes: attacks on hardware and software, financial crimes, internet abuse and bullying. In recent years, Taiwanese politicians have used the "cyber army" to rule the country and malign political enemies.

As an example, cybercrime in the US has risen from 16,838 cases in 2000 to 791,790 cases in 2020. It was estimated that in 2021, internet crime accounted for a total global losses of US$6 trillion. In addition how secure and reliable is cloud computing? This question appears all the more pressing, especially when the crime involved presents a threat to national security. If it is not a serious issue, why did Xi Jinping take the trouble to fly across the Pacific Ocean to Washington, D. C. on June 27, 2015, to establish a hotline with President Obama on internet hacking? And why did Biden accuse Russia of being the source of internet crime threatening US security? According to the report "Worldwide Threat Assessment" issued by the National Intelligence Committee, which comprises the FBI, Homeland Security and the CIA, the Director of National Intelligence considers internet crime the highest threat to US national security.

In the face of new technological challenges, there is a need to assess risk, ascertain the reason for the emergence of undesirable incidents, formulate policies for relief, reduce opportunities for their emergence and minimize their impact. For example, drones prove useful in agriculture, transportation, entertainment, photography, the preservation of the natural environment and other matters related to people's livelihoods. They constitute, however, a double-edged sword. When they are misused, they can produce a lot of harm. On January 26, 2015, a 2-foot drone crashed on the White House lawn. The unmanned device was discovered to be purely recreational, and President Obama and his family faced no danger as they were traveling in India at the time. But it was unnerving to think that such a drone could penetrate White House security. If terrorists used drones to carry explosives, military cameras, telecommunication and surveillance and other devices, the consequences would be unthinkable. Indeed, drones are already used as military weapons in places such as the Middle East and Ukraine.

Social media technology has developed rapidly in recent years and is particularly welcomed among young people. Take, for example, TikTok (the overseas version of China's Douyin), a mobile-sharing app specializing in video and music that has grown exponentially in Europe, the Americas and India, with a worldwide download rate of 2 billion. It has attracted 100 million users in the US in a short time. Most users are young, the group targeted by major technology industries and advertisers. It is the only social media app that has succeeded in making a name for itself in the US internet market monopolized by major technology corporations.

Close on the heels of the convenience of social media was the concern over privacy and national security in 2020 when TikTok, originating from China, became a target for crackdown amid the worsening Sino-American relationship, while the Indian government banned TikTok following the conflict at the China-India border. In July of that year, the US and Australia also declared their intention to ban TikTok on the grounds of privacy and national security. In an interview aired on Fox News, former US Secretary of State Mike Pompeo said, "These Chinese software companies doing business in the US, whether it's TikTok or WeChat – there are countless more – are feeding data directly to the Chinese Communist Party, their national security apparatus." Trump said if TikTok did not sell its business to an American corporation within a designated time, it would have to close and that a major part of the proceeds would be handed over to the US Treasury.

Concerns over facial recognition and other technologies in personal messages certainly apply to most social media programs. The strict monitoring of the internet, anti-monopoly and privacy protection laws around the world make it more difficult to obtain personal information. However, as virtue raises one foot, vice raises ten; internet fraud is rampant, and the number of people defrauded yearly is skyrocketing.

In *War and Anti-War: Making Sense of Today's Global Chaos*, published in 1995, futurists Alvin and Heidi Toffler imagined what cutting-edge weapons would be like, a fearful undertaking because new technology made it possible for humans to create more problems for themselves. Air pollution is one such issue. We should understand that problems that can arise will arise. After all, the cause for success as well as failure is "human", which is why our highly myopic governments should perhaps don a pair of spectacles so that they can see beyond the trivial details in front of their noses. Their short-sightedness is our greatest handicap.

One Health

On June 26, 2019, the day after my interview with Sabine Kunst, Rector of Humboldt University, my colleagues and I visited the site where the Berlin Wall had stood. That day was a heat wave, registering high of 36° C, but we discovered that there was no air-conditioning at the McDonald's where we planned to eat. I was not particularly shocked by this because ever since the German government ordered the cessation of nuclear energy, there has been a power shortage and a jump in electricity prices. In the outlying areas of Germany, power outages are frequent. Coupled with Russia's controlled import of natural gas, the poor bear the brunt, and society is unsettled.

Technology should promote our well-being. Just as we have become slaves to technology, how can large-sized Germans turn their backs on technology and submit themselves to the sweltering heat? A lose-lose for all, and so why bother?

Strait-jacketed by binary thinking and with an emphasis on situating humans at the center, some hold the view that stressing scientific and technological development means negligence of the importance of humanity. But what do they mean by human-centeredness? What is the point of upholding that idea while losing the world? With the help of creativity, we shall have innovation, which not only allows us to discover problems but also provides solutions. The ecosystem of the Earth can then be preserved. Take the energy issues we are facing today. There should be many solutions; it is just that we do not know what they are yet. The government should take the lead in innovative technology, but aren't many practices that violate innovation and technology also led by the government?

In short, these are results of innovation generated without due consideration to the concept of One Health premised on the co-existence and co-prosperity of humans, animals, and the environment (see Figure 23.1). The new coronavirus pandemic that swept through the world in 2020 has presented us with an embarrassing real-life example. To Buddhists, humans, animals, and nature are inseparable initially. There is a saying in ancient books that things that do not conform to nature will be despised while co-existence is preferred. Taoists believe that humans exist in harmony with nature, holding to the thought that "all things and I are one." Under the influence of Western industrialization, One Health has been brushed aside despite the fact that the world is already seriously polluted and the Earth and its creatures are suffering.

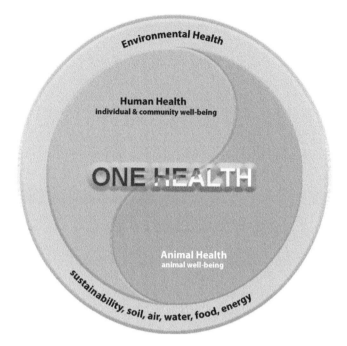

Figure 23.1 The One Health concept.

A Composition from a Small Child

A primary school teacher asked students to compose an essay about the hot weather. One child wrote about thanking two people for making life possible. The first person was the mythological archer Hou Yi who shot down nine of the ten suns originally hanging in the sky, and the second was the American engineer Wills H. Carrier who invented the air-conditioner. In this child's mind, we would have died from heat if not for these two. He also viewed that basking in happiness is not a reflection of ability; if one has the ability, one can bask in the sun. It is not naivety that defeats people, but the real heat! This creative writing from a child's unsullied mind reaches beyond the imagination of erudite but rigid thinkers.

Taking in the sordid air, half down my throat, half dissipated into the breeze. While the external world is not constant, our internal enlightening should be (香港慈山寺, Tsz Shan Monastery). To innovate, we should have the pure heart of an innocent newborn baby.

24

How to Promote Innovative Technology?

One must get down to brass tacks and formulate plans to push for economic restructuring. Paying lip service is inefficient; we must commit thought to action. For example, Iowa is an agricultural state in the US, but at one time, it was where high-end electromechanical products by John Deere, Amana, Pella Windows, and others were manufactured. In the early 20th century, the state government wanted to convert Iowa from an agricultural into an industrial base. Yet it failed to invest adequately, and the state remains primarily agricultural today, which shows that having only good wishes and taking inadequate action does not lead to success.

When I was a child, negative comments were commonplace whenever the subject of Japan arose. Today one hears similar expressions of doubt when people talk about South Korea. Yet a lot can be learned from South Korea and Japan in terms of creativity and innovation. Both are known for their emphasis on the humanities. Japan's tea ceremony and its Tang-style architecture march hand in hand with its technological culture. This is but one obvious example. We can also consider the airline business. In the 1970s, Korean Air was considered one of the worst airlines for safety. Today, the carrier's record and quality of service compare favorably with others.

Although innovation originates from the free roaming of the mind and the unshackled exploration that transcends the limitations of the environment, investment is still important. In 2019, Japan spent 3.28% of its GDP on research (Figure V.1). That Japan is ahead of the world in science and technology is closely related to its investment in research. Not only is its research funding ahead of the world in proportion to its GDP, but the R&D expenses provided by its enterprises are significant. If we take another look at South Korea, Singapore, Taiwan and Hong Kong, i.e., the Four Tigers, it should not be difficult to see that the development of the technology industry requires investment and other measures to promote economic development and the growth of the middle class.

Way Kuo. The Absence of Soulware in Higher Education, (323–338) © 2023 Scrivener Publishing LLC

South Korea

South Korea has adopted a centrally planned, top-down model for its science and technology policies. The industrial structure is vertically integrated, encompassing almost all upstream, middle and downstream areas. The government has set a grand vision for the auto industry to surpass the US, the electronics industry to surpass Japan, and Chinese medicine research to surpass China.

In 1961, South Korea established its Economic Planning Board. In 1967, the Technology Bureau affiliated with the Board was expanded to become the Department of Science and Technology and was upgraded to the Ministry of Science and Technology in 1988. In 1999, the National Science and Technology Council, presided over by the President, was created. In 2001, the role of the Korea Institute of Science and Technology Evaluation and Planning, which was responsible for planning, forecasting, evaluating and studying science and technology development, was expanded to include formulating future strategies for science and technology, coordinating government R&D programs and budget allocation, and evaluating the performance of national R&D programs and government-funded research plans.

In 2008, the then-president of South Korea, Lee Myung-bak, presided over the formulation of the Science and Technology Basic Plan. Key industries were developed, and the percentage of GDP spent on R&D was raised in 2012. Samsung became the world's leading producer of mobile phones, and South Korea is now the world's third-largest shipbuilding nation and will possibly become the world's third-largest exporter of nuclear power reactors within 20 years, all of which have been possible through a super high percentage of R&D investment, as seen in Figure V.1 above.

The scope of innovation is very broad, venturing beyond science and technology to encompass the arts, drama, education, fashion, new media, blockchain, supply chain management and cyberculture. I have paid close attention to the development of South Korea for more than 30 years, a nation that has revamped its image many times during this period. In addition to the outstanding achievements of technological enterprises such as Samsung, the export of South Korean culture, such as the popularity of learning the Korean language, has attracted the world's attention. In May 2021, the government announced its strategic plan for developing the semiconductor industry, intending to inject US$450 billion to turn South Korea into the world's largest production base for wafers.

South Korea has the ambition to become the semiconductor empire in the world. In 2021, the global semiconductor market sales was worth

US$594.96 billion, according to Gartner, a global leading IT research firm and consultancy. South Korea's semiconductor industry made up about 19.3% of the global market, propelled by its memory market. In 2022, the government announced that it would provide tax incentives and subsidies to build a semiconductor engineering training center to help South Korean companies raise their market share in the non-memory chip market to 10% by 2030. But the US government's move to block South Korean chip firms from exporting advanced semiconductor equipment and high-powered chips to China in a bid to cripple China's access to critical technologies are complicating the operations of such Korean companies as Samsung Electronics and SK Hynix in China. The latter had planned to install some of its new extreme ultraviolet lithography (EUV) machines produced by the Dutch firm ASML in its factory in Wuxi, Jiangsu province. South Korea has an export-oriented economy, accounting for 50 percent of its total GDP. And China and the US are its two largest trading partners. Its ambition to become the semiconductor empire is facing obstacles because of the China-US trade war.

In South Korea, culture, science and technology advance in unison. Broadband technology has given impetus to the creative industries, where entertainment combined with the fashion industry to power up the global flow of South Korean culture, known as the "Korean Wave". The momentum for this phenomenon is closely tied to government policies. Aiming to develop South Korean cuisine into one of the top five in the world is another example.

South Korea has much to show for its investment in science and technology, and the causal link between effort and return is evident.

Singapore

Singapore formulated its first five-year National Technology Plan in 1991. Its Agency for Science, Technology and Research studies industry needs and provides support. At the same time, it forms policies for recruiting talent from all over the world and trains pre-tertiary, undergraduate and graduate students, ensuring a sufficient supply of R&D expertise. It is noteworthy that to attract overseas enterprises and global talent, Singapore built up its first-class infrastructure by constructing Biopolis (on biomedicine) and Fusionopolis (on information and communication). In addition, the GET-Up plan launched in 2003 aimed to boost Singapore's global competitiveness by providing local technology-intensive enterprises with technical, human and financial support as well as helping to open overseas markets, encouraging small and medium-sized companies to absorb and apply new technologies.

Singapore Management University was established in 2000 in line with the government's science and technology policy to provide degree courses in management. It quickly attracted global attention with its outstanding performance. Singapore's decision-making is decisive, and its execution of those decisions is effective.

Currently, Singapore's information technology ranks among the top in the world. Its biotechnology and pharmaceutical industries are developing rapidly, and a number of the world's leading biomedical science companies, including Pfizer, Novartis and Wyeth, have set up production bases in Singapore.

Although Singapore is relatively small, its overall development is impressive, largely due to its investment in science and technology, making it an interesting model for transnational cooperation. That Rolls Royce picked Singapore as the manufacturing base for its aircraft engines is a case in point.

In 2021 and 2022, Singapore replaced Hong Kong as the largest foreign exchange trading center and the largest financial center in Asia, respectively. Sixty years ago, Singapore's GDP was comparable with that of Taiwan, Hong Kong and South Korea, but now it is leading the other three Asian Tigers by a long stretch and even surpasses that of the US, largely due to its success in technological innovation.

Taiwan

Based on a US model, the National Science Council, affiliated with the Executive Yuan, was established in 1959 in Taiwan to promote and fund academic research, the development of science and technology and science parks, putting it well ahead of the other three Asian Tigers. Realizing that traditional industries would lose their advantage with the gradual increase in the cost of land and labor, emerging industries were selected for development with the support of science and technology research. The six selection criteria were market potential, industrial relevance, added value, technology sophistication, pollution, and energy dependence. As a result, the Hsinchu Science Industrial Park was set up in 1980 to promote hi-tech industries, train local talent and recruit skilled overseas professionals. Subsequently, science and industry parks were established in the central and the southern areas.

Taiwan's investment in scientific research kept pace with advanced countries, and the idea of innovation used to be very strong. In the last thirty years, Taiwan's achievements in hi-tech industries such as semiconductors, electronics and information have been remarkable. A white paper on science and technology was formulated to build cluster science parks for a technology corridor in western Taiwan.

Regrettably, internal political strife has drained much of this energy and undermined returns on its early investments in science and technology. People with legal and political backgrounds usually take turns to take charge, especially among legislators and officials in the 2022 administration. Most came to prominence through elections with outstanding wit, eloquence and political performance, but their management of government affairs defies logic. For example, they have completely mismanaged environmental issues.

On top of that, for political reasons, the procurement stagnation of COVID-19 vaccines in 2021 and a shortage of rapid antigen test kits in 2022 showed Taiwan's lagging behind other developed economies in Asia. Only when the overall rate of vaccination became alarmingly low, and the death rate embarrassingly high, did it become clear that Taiwan was medically ill-equipped to fight the pandemic. Yet officials remained unmoved by the criticisms and no one took responsibility for these failures.

Compared with South Korea, which is democratic and successful, Taiwan has made a reasonable investment in R&D, but its higher education, political and economic plans have drifted off course while the incentive to invest is weakening. With a loss of focus on research, Taiwan can only watch neighboring countries and regions make astonishing progress.

Hong Kong

Hong Kong has a narrow industrial base and lacks economic diversification to nurture a strong middle class. It is heavily skewed towards finance, real estate and commerce, causing an imbalance in the industrial structure and undermining diversity and harmony.

About 30 years ago, some dedicated people in Hong Kong held a series of intensive seminars to promote innovation, but they failed to arouse much attention. Over 20 years ago, Tung Chee-hwa, the then Chief Executive of Hong Kong, advocated that science and technology should be the direction forward. However, his initiative was thwarted by the Asian economic crisis. A good start ended poorly. In about 2000, Hong Kong set up the Innovation and Technology Commission and the Hong Kong Applied

Science and Technology Research Institute, and a few discrete projects have been launched over the past dozen years, but they failed to produce substantial results. There is no overall policy for science and technology. The government has been too conservative, and it was not until November 2015 that the Innovation and Technology Bureau was established.

Hong Kong is one of the few places in the world not burdened with a defense budget, nor does it have to hand over its surplus to the central government. Yet its investment in R&D was only 0.93% of GDP. Where did the savings go? Hong Kong's manufacturing is only 1.1% of its gross local product, and its spending on R&D is utterly inadequate, lagging far behind its northern neighbor, Shenzhen. Compared with Shenzhen, with its late start in 2000, Hong Kong has advantages in its academic research, publications and citations. But Hong Kong is grievously inadequate in technology industrialization and commercialization.

Because of its well-run economy and trade, Hong Kong does not feel the urgency to innovate, paying lip service only, which explains why Hong Kong has little to show in this area. Science and technology are indeed the pillars of sustainable development, without which the gap between the poor and the rich in Hong Kong will worsen, and social welfare won't solve the ensuing social unrest. Following my frequent requests and the voices of many industrialists, Carrie Lam finally gave due attention to these long-lasting historical shortfalls, setting a goal at the Internet Economy Summit in 2018 that innovation and technology research funds would reach US$6 billion, or 1.5% of Hong Kong GDP, by 2022. Her successor advocates integrating with the industrial chain of surrounding cities, developing innovation and technology to make Hong Kong an international hub for scientific research. But specific details for implementation have yet to be made.

Mainland China

From the microcosmic point of view, there is no necessary connection between an academic degree and innovation. The degree awarded by universities across the Strait imposes restrictions on innovation in several ways. Macrocosmically, there is no free competition in Mainland China, where people are more interested in short returns, and their approach to recruiting global talent is conservative. All these features stand at odds with innovation and originality.

Under authoritarian direction, Mainland China takes bold steps in developing science and technology. According to the 2020 EU Industrial R&D Investment Scoreboard, since 2000, in terms of substantial R&D

expenditure, China's rate of increase has been 16% per annum. After surpassing the 27 EU members in 2015, it has remained second in the world. In 2019, China's R&D investment was US$514.8 billion and is expected to surpass the US in 2025.

Eager to report their success, officials on the Mainland are only too happy to use their money to support research and education. The problem is that they want quick returns: As soon as they assume office, they advance plans more quickly than flipping the pages of a book. Party and government leaders at the district, county, and even provincial and municipal levels can immediately overthrow their predecessors' plans. This is in sharp contrast to the inertia in Hong Kong and the populist-driven politics in Taiwan. The Mainland and Singapore have similar administrative styles; only Mainland China has better resources but less developed soulware, compromising the effectiveness of its actions.

Mainland China's progress in IT software has been excellent, but it still lags behind in infrastructure for heavy industries. For example, China tops the world in steel production but imports a large quantity of ore. For every unit of steel it produces, China uses more ore, coal and electricity than any other developed country, while consuming these precious resources causes serious pollution. Ironically, the over-production of steel, including the highly priced variety, is dependent on imports to satisfy the needs of hi-tech industries. Compared with high-end steel produced in the US and Japan, China's steel industry yields only low financial gains. This is like the production of Apple products. The lion's share of profits goes to the US, while the Mainland receives a pittance for the work outsourced to its factories.

The Role of the University

In the era of the knowledge economy, South Korea has achieved striking success by adopting a model that allows businesses to support R&D through consultation and patent approval. By comparison, it is not difficult to understand why Hong Kong did not have a science and technology policy in the colonial era. But even today, despite its abundant human resources, science and technology in Hong Kong still wobble and continue to lag behind. Apart from the cognitive and cultural factors within society, it makes one wonder whether Hong Kong bureaucrats, apart from micromanaging in policy implementations, really mean to assist new enterprises and encourage innovation.

Following the expansion of higher education in Taiwan, there are more than one million undergraduates and 200,000 graduate students annually.

It is reasonable to assume that the many graduates would provide a talent pool for branding Taiwan. Yet Taiwan is dwarfed in comparison with South Korea. Since the Brain Korea 21 program in 1999, South Korea has thrown itself wholeheartedly into the integration of industry, academia and research, and it obtained 21,997 US patents in 2020, surpassing Taiwan's 12,141 patents. Why has Taiwan, which led technological industries and possesses an impressive number of university graduates, fallen behind?

The Sino-American trade war will continue and may even escalate to affect international trade and investment opportunities. Does Taiwan wish to increase its manufacturing market share in this context? If Taiwan wants to maintain its momentum, besides its existing advantage in the electronic industry (which will soon become obsolete), are there any niche areas or products over which it may wield a competitive advantage? Energy, biotechnology, cloud computing, and information service are all areas with potential. Has the government formulated a feasible and effective policy beyond the out-sourcing mode of thinking? Does the Taiwanese government have its own science and technology innovation policy, like South Korea and Singapore? And what role do universities play?

If we care enough about the output of patents at universities, it is certainly worth looking at the distribution of granted US utility patents. Table 24.1 lists the total number of US utility patents granted to individual universities in the US, the UK, Mainland China, Japan, Singapore, South Korea, Taiwan, Hong Kong and others between 2017 and 2021. The numbers shown form a reference index of the innovation performance of higher education in the above countries and regions.

To be precise, the excellent collaboration among America's industry, academia and research depends on its close to 100 universities with extremely high research capabilities and close integration of teaching and research. In the last 50 years, America's higher education has not only been the biggest in scale, with the highest number of international students, but it is also representative of the best higher education system in the world. Their achievements are reflected in their invention of teaching software and the publication of numerous textbooks (Chapters 4 and 8); many Nobel Prize winners (Chapter 13); their respect for academic freedom and campus autonomy (Introduction and Chapter 15) and free competition (Chapter 13); outstanding faculty and high academic rankings (Chapter 18); and patents, inventions and innovations (Chapter 24). The success of their higher education contributions to world civilization is attributed to the separation of politics and education, multiple funding sources, the tradition of freedom under the rule of law, performance culture, market competition, governance by professional experts and other mechanisms.

Table 24.1 Number of US utility patents granted to universities in the US, the UK, Mainland China, Japan, Singapore, South Korea, Hong Kong, Taiwan and others.

Country/region	Number of US utility patents granted to universities				
	2021	2020	2019	2018	2017
US	6785	7336	7208	6329	6406
UK	170	212	215	195	187
Mainland China	2098	1665	1391	1003	1017
Japan	701	788	814	701	788
Singapore	100	108	106	100	105
South Korea	1008	1351	1340	1187	1163
Hong Kong	185	163	167	132	139
Taiwan	355	407	452	430	466
Others	1295	1193	1339	1111	1028

There are many notable examples of integrating industry, academia and research. Leveraging support from universities, science parks have enhanced the development of hi-tech industries. On the other hand, the innovation zones that have sprouted in recent years are driven mostly by universities. Currently, there are five innovation zones in the US. The Tech Square at Georgia Institute of Technology is the most successful, housing 45 technology companies. The rising star Cornell Tech is also worth mentioning. Innovation zones provide a convenient and forthright way of expanding the talent pool at universities. CityU's HKTech 300 introduced this American model to its campus, making it a first for Hong Kong, investing HK$600 million (US$80 million) to support 300 start-ups for its students and alumni. The response has been extremely enthusiastic, with at least two companies contributing US$35 million.

It is a common practice to support a particular industry within a designated period of time through policies. In its first 5-year economic plan, South Korea proposed to protect its automobile industry by weeding out the weak and concentrating on supporting the Hyundai Group. Since 1996, the Dutch government has given its full support to the development of agriculture and now the country has become the third largest exporter of agricultural products, netting 94.5 billion euros in 2019. The key industries in both South Korea and the Netherlands have improved the well-being of the middle-class thanks to R&D investment.

Unlike real estate and the stock market, science and technology constitute the lifeline for society in the 21st century for the creation of wealth. They are the pillars of the middle class. A forward-looking science and technology policy and R&D investment-induced innovations not only promote economic growth but also determine the rise and fall of a country or region. The development of medical services and the promotion of sophisticated agriculture and veterinary medicine in places across the Strait can learn from the Dutch practice of creating a thriving environment for their industry through loans rather than depending on political and economic expediency, such as subsidizing farmers.

Not only can the interplay between industry, university and research help raise the level of technology, but it can also promote innovation and maximize the marginal and spill-over advantages. Why do Hong Kong and Taiwanese people ignore such potentials and instead seek self-satisfaction in securing concurrent employment in industry, government and university?

Innovative Technology and Intellectual Property

Europe, the US, and China have established anti-trust laws to prevent major technological corporations from cornering the market. Among those affected by such legislative measures are Facebook, Google and Alibaba, representing a new wave of actions targeting monopolies following the breakup of AT&T in the 1980s. Other corporations are expected to be affected, too. These actions suggest that capitalism is not about the endless expansion of capital, much less about allowing companies to make endless profits. While formulating anti-monopoly market actions, people actively promote innovative technologies and protect intellectual property rights.

Many problems Taiwan and Hong Kong face are attributable to a failure to understand the connection between innovation in higher education, entrepreneurship and people's well-being. Proper investment in related scientific research, forward-looking resources and high-quality culture will improve life, remove obstacles to social advancement, and reduce the uncertainty that engenders social unrest. The question is no longer whether one should invest in innovative research but whether one has done enough to implement the right policies and encourage investment in enterprises. Research in science and technology has to be prioritized. The environment and challenges on the two sides of the Strait are different. Systematic planning is indispensable. Policies regarding scientific and technological research are best left in the hands of professionals, and breakthroughs are only possible by altering the way governments operate.

Successful innovation depends on the ability of the researchers, the subject, and the research team's organization. To realize its dream of "Created in China," Mainland China is more ambitious than Hong Kong and Taiwan in designing innovation plans and surpasses both places through its determination. To its credit, the Mainland attaches great importance to education and learning and respects those with a broad range of knowledge. Its human resources are rich, but a severe shortage of modern management personnel with domineering party and government personnel, is a serious drawback.

Innovative technology has to be protected by IP rights that can provide the necessary incentives for commercializing university research and technology transfer. IP rights and patents impact technology transfer and innovation. IP violations range from copying the brand of a product to copying a product without honoring a registered trademark, ignoring trademark infringements, copying through reverse engineering, translating foreign texts without obtaining consent, and using software products ineligible for patent production. South Korea, Japan, and even the US have had a poor record in stealing intellectual property as well; Taiwan and Hong Kong used to be a haven for copycats, especially for college textbooks. Mainland China has recently taken over as a major copycat, and its acts of alleged IP theft have attracted criticism from overseas companies investing in Mainland China.

While plagiarism in art and fashion is nothing new to the Chinese, complaints about such misdemeanors and related breaches of IP rights will lessen when more Chinese companies become patent holders. According to a Thomson Reuters report in 2011, "China became the world's top patent filer, surpassing the US and Japan as it steps up innovation to improve its IP rights track record." This trend and the ongoing US-China trade war were expected to force China to adopt international standards and encourage better protection and enforcement of IP rights. If Mainland China wakes up to this challenge, China could experience an innovation renaissance.

Removing Political Interference in Industrial Development

While visiting Paris, I saw billboards printed in simplified Chinese characters beside Korean in subway stations. I could sense how China and South Korea were perceived in European metropolises. It reminded me of Taiwanese manufacturers, whose medium and small enterprises tend to compete in the market on their own, which disadvantages them against competitors steered by national policies.

Taiwan launched its "Two Trillion and Twin Star Development Program" in 2002 and the "Branding Taiwan Plan" in 2006. In 2009 and 2010, it rolled out plans for the six core strategic and four major smart industries, respectively. But perhaps because of the Taiwanese culture of prioritizing politics, industrial development has been steered down a path that fails to benefit society. Political slogans multiply, but rather than providing nourishment, they hamper the continued growth of technological innovations.

More prominent cases include the Fourth Nuclear Power Plant and aviation operations. First proposed in the 1980s, the plant experienced delays of up to 30 years and in the end cost over US$10 billion. So far, the plant is still sealed and the nuclear fuel has been shipped out. When time and operational losses are factored in, the total cost the Taiwanese people bear is staggering.

Dreams are the most beautiful. The government vowed to phase out nuclear power right before it began ruling in 2016, promising that the electricity supply would be stable and no substantial bill increases for 10 years. While leaving the completed Fourth Nuclear Power Plant idle, the government began to experience the threat of power shortage and fretted over the low base-load power supply. To cope, the government introduced several initiatives, injecting a total of US$10 billion to develop renewable energy, formulate a forward-looking energy plan and increase the purchase of natural gas and relevant equipment. Nevertheless, these exorbitant expenses did nothing to ensure a steadier electricity supply. In 2021, the Taiwan Power Company handled the crisis by reducing the voltage to stabilize the power supply, unrelated to the power outage. After this expedient measure, another US$3.5 billion investment was made in promoting thermal power generation. The cost of electricity increased by an average of 11% starting from April 2023 following on from similar price rises in 2022 and the decommissioning of the Second Nuclear Power Plant in March 2023.

The cost of the above non-nuclear initiatives has not yet factored in transport costs, the volatility of international oil and gas prices, and the possible national security dilemmas involved, not to mention environmental pollution. The fact that lung cancer, the leading cause of cancer deaths in Taiwan, is caused by air pollution is ignored, and the same for many incalculable economic losses. According to a report from the College of Public Health at the NTU, 6,000 people die from lung cancer caused by air pollution in Taiwan annually. Who is going to bear the cost, and when?

Who really cares about the possible consequences of the outbound migration of scientific and technological enterprises resulting from a low base-load power supply or the deterrence against the inbound migration of new scientific and technological firms? Not to mention the opportunity costs of myriad factors ranging from higher electricity prices, a low base-load supply of electricity, slack investment incentives, the Trump factor, and so forth, in addition to known economic losses and expenditures.

Taiwan has no grid connection to the outside world. It imports 98% of its energy. The average annual consumption ranks top among the Four Asian Tigers, but people enjoy an extremely low energy rate. Pricing is a way to control consumption. Electricity prices should accurately reflect the differential charges for consumption patterns at different times of the day to help save energy and protect the environment. Unfortunately, political ideology rides roughshod over people's well-being. So far, Taiwan still doesn't have a non-partisan energy and environmental protection policy designed by professionals. Nor do people foresee any breakthrough in new energy research and development.

More distantly, while working as a department head at Texas A&M University in 1995, an alumnus working for American Airlines (AA) in Dallas paid a visit. He was looking into the technical feasibility of using Taiwan International Airport as AA's hub in East Asia but finally decided to drop the plan because the Taiwanese government opposed the policy of free direct links for mail, transport and trade across the Strait. AA's decision was reasonable because the airport cannot be a transportation hub without the support of free direct links. Ironically, the free direct links exist today regardless of whether the government approves or opposes them; the reality is Taoyuan lost its opportunity to become a transportation hub. Opportunity knocks but once. Taiwan's loss of opportunities in terms of culture, tourism, trade, international exchange, etc., will make for an interesting case study.

Nowadays, new hi-tech products continuously enter the market, promoting and enhancing global economic development. Singapore is a tiny country with a small population, but it is committed to enterprise development and innovation and seizes every chance to transform itself. In 2010, Singapore formulated a 10-year Strategic Development Plan for developing itself into a globalized metropolis with a highly skilled population and innovative economy. However, some people might think Singapore is not very democratic, and therefore it does not offer a good case for comparison.

Let us, therefore, look at South Korea. Consistency in government policy in South Korea has not suffered despite multiple political changes. Instead, democratic development has boosted economic progress. On the other hand, Taiwan has witnessed tremendous progress in democratization, but has it become a force to help or hinder the improvement of people's welfare? For years, society was trapped in a mire of endless political confrontations while the government lacked any macro policies on science and technology. When in power, neither of the ruling parties could attract the necessary expertise to meet science and technology development. In the promotion of culture in Taiwan, little thought has been given to science and technology. Those in official positions like to impose themselves on those below by acting as the messengers or executors of orders, however trivial those directives may be. In so doing, they lose sight of what is important; consequently, the future appears dimmer.

At a minimum, enterprise development should be free from political interference. Ideally, we need to pay attention to the fundamentals of the manufacturing sector, avoiding reliance on political and economic welfare tactics for short-term solutions. Both Singapore and South Korea are role models for Taiwan. One is smaller in terms of population and land area while the other is larger, but Taiwan likes to consider itself the Switzerland of the Orient, forgetting that this politically neutral European state, with equal wealth, has historical advantages that may not be replicable elsewhere. What Taiwan needs is a common consensus based on people's welfare and then rid itself of constant political wrangling.

The outlook is sad. It is important that we do not delude ourselves. The world we live in is full of contradictions, and our society is neither rich nor benevolent in spite of its social inequality.

Professor Huang vs Professor Singpurwalla

Professor Huang is an outstanding academic at a university in Taiwan. Prior to receiving the letter of appointment from CityU in 2017, he was leading a reasonably successful project with three less senior researchers. Their research proposal had passed the expert review, and they were expecting the government to allocate funding. It turned out that the funding agency had decided not to fund his project after hearing about his imminent departure. The original plan put together by this 4-member team to train Taiwanese students and anchor their scientific research on Taiwanese soil came to nothing.

Singpurwalla, who joined CityU from a distinguished US university in 2013, is a different story. After he resigned from his position in the US, news came through that his research project had received funding from an American foundation. In his case, however, the university in the US agreed to let Singpurwalla carry out his research in Hong Kong. Two years after he arrived in CityU, the US Navy injected hundreds of thousands of US dollars into his research. For convenience, he was encouraged to conduct his research in Hong Kong.

Professors do not conduct their research for profit. From a macro-perspective, learning exists in a world undivided by national boundaries. Let the person who can contribute to human society take charge. From a narrower perspective, in the eyes of common sense, the point of research is to invest in the future, injecting life and energy into the locality and promoting welfare. Again, let the person who can do it take charge. From an even narrower perspective, even if we think only of our own benefit and do not care about the world, support for academic endeavors is not an act of charity or social welfare payment. We should offer our deepest thanks to professors who obtain funding through their ability and after a rigorous review process.

We should treat people professionally. For example, those in charge should do all they can to retain an outstanding talent who intends to leave the job. If those efforts fail, heads of units should reflect on the matter but never shoot themselves in the foot.

From these two incidents above, we can see the difference between the US and Taiwan. The American approach is to think of talented people as their own, regardless of skin color, origin, gender, culture, region, political and economic background. The point is to ensure that the research project will benefit humankind. Although it has taken some exclusory measures against Chinese scholars living in America due to some anti-China sentiment, the US has enabled an adjustable system to admit talent (See Chapter 15). In Taiwan, "Hokkien culture in southeastern China / Welcomes blossoming flowers in the spring and autumn. / Thick-headed politicians who pretend to be sharp / Tell me where I can find my old home?" Personnel matters override all other considerations, and promising research projects are suspended. Once again, politics interferes with education, resulting in both talent and research emigrating to more accommodating locations, worsening the situation. What is to be done?

Huang and Singpurwalla were both engaged in research projects approved before arriving at CityU. Whether their research is successful or not has nothing to do with the university. While they use CityU's time and resources, their success or failure may benefit or harm Taiwan and the US. It does not matter where a research project is performed. In response to the 31 measures from the Mainland aiming to attract talent from Taiwan, the government in Taiwan put forward four major directives and eight major strategies. On the surface, it seems the government is trying to create an environment congenial to local talent, but the stories of Huang and Singpurwalla suggest otherwise. Why is it that Taiwan chooses to obstruct its way to progress?

25

Where Is the Innovative Talent?

I gave a talk in 2018 at a seminar for high school students in Hong Kong organized by InnoTech, a committee on innovation, technology and re-industrialization established by the Hong Kong government. I asked the audience two questions. The first concerned how many in the audience were interested in studying modern science and technology. To my surprise, not a single one of the 200 or more students raised their hands. I was hoping at least a few would be interested; so I persisted. Finally, several members of the audience said that careers in science and technology were not very promising: salaries too low, jobs not stable, working hours too long. Others said jobs in science and technology were not innovative enough.

My second question to the audience was whether anyone knew anything about Barry Lam or Kai-fu Lee. No one had even heard of them. Such responses are common in Hong Kong.

Barry Lam and Kai-fu Lee

Although Barry Lam and Kai-fu Lee are hugely influential in the IT field, the majority of Hong Kong students have not heard of them. Barry Lam founded Quanta Computer, one of the world's largest notebook manufacturers. He grew up in a working-class area of Tiu Keng Leng in Hong Kong and went to study abroad at the NTU at the age of 18. After graduation, he founded Quanta Computer with his friends, building it into a leading international producer of laptops. Even today, he speaks Mandarin with a Hong Kong accent. People in Hong Kong might be interested to know that *Forbes* named him one of the 500 richest men in the world. According to Hong Kong standards, he is among the richest business and industrial tycoons.

Kai-fu Lee is a superstar pioneer in China's internet sector and an entrepreneur dedicated to education. He resigned from his high salary position in 2009 and set up Innovation Works to help people innovate and start their own businesses. I invited him to deliver a lecture at CityU on December 13, 2015. Most attendees, who were not local, filled two lecture theaters and mobbed him after his talk, a rare sight in Hong Kong. He caused another sensation when he gave online lectures at CityU in July 2021 and July 2022, at the height of the COVID-19 pandemic.

Computers, the internet and cloud computing have become an inseparable part of our daily life amid the explosion of information, and yet many people in Hong Kong have never heard of either of these two IT heavyweights. That makes one wonder what is missing in Hong Kong.

Charles Kao and Daniel Choi

Two Nobel laureates in physics happen to have connections to Hong Kong. One is Charles Kao, former president of the Chinese University of Hong Kong, and for that reason, slightly better known locally than the other Nobel laureate Daniel Choi, an expert in theories of physics. Choi came to Hong Kong by himself in 1951 when he was only 12. After finishing high school, he went to study in the US. Kao was awarded the Nobel Prize in Physics in 2009, a rarity for an engineer, while Choi won the Nobel Prize in Physics in 1998.

Charles Kao and Daniel Choi should be the pride of Hong Kong, but they enjoy more prestige in Chinese communities outside of Hong Kong. One cannot but wonder why Hong Kong differs from other places. In countries such as South Korea, where science and technology and culture are developed, how the people there would love to produce a Nobel Prize winner in the sciences! And yet here in Hong Kong, we do not know how to cherish these two gems.

In addition to Kao and Choi, other major names in science with strong ties to Hong Kong include Leroy L. Chang, Eugene Wong, Alfred Y. Cho, and Shing-tung Yau. Hong Kong people should probably ask themselves why these eminent scientists did not receive the support in Hong Kong that could have unleashed their talents. How come their work had to take root only in technology-based industries in the West? Every now and then, people are puzzled that so few local scholars, let alone famous ones, work in Hong Kong's universities. Well, the reason is young people have set their sights on making money rather than pursuing innovation in technology and science.

Pride and Regret

The Chinese are not inferior to any other people in terms of natural intelligence. Yet high-caliber higher education and research have yet to germinate in places across the Strait. Take the Chinese Nobel laureates in physics and chemistry as an example. Most undertook undergraduate studies and developed their research careers, including PhDs, in the West.

People in Hong Kong are effective at building a large profit with a small capital outlay, which is why so many top-notch local students attracted by promises of quick returns select finance and business programs at university. But this mindset is hardly in the best interests of young Hong Kongers, although the youth are not to blame: The fault lies with those in influential positions who fail to see science and technology's critical role in today's world.

The optical fiber communication that Charles Kao invented in 1966 has revolutionized life on Earth, in the deep oceans and in outer space. Yet the British Hong Kong government did not support this technology in the 1970s. Just imagine the enormous profits if Hong Kong had supported Kao with, say, US$2 million in funding to help turn his invention into cutting-edge products and related services locally. Hong Kong could have been a world-class hub in communication, earning trillions and trillions of dollars over the past 50-odd years. Taking a further step, if the British Hong Kong government had decided to utilize the newborn optical fiber to lead the development of related hardware and software and peripheral technologies such as medical apparatus, energy, transport, and other industries, we would not still be considering what new technological industries to develop.

Let me conclude with another outrageous story. A newspaper columnist in Hong Kong published an article in 2009 in which he confessed that, when a student at the Chinese University of Hong Kong, he did not think much of Charles Kao as president, but then with the news that Kao had been awarded the Nobel Prize in Physics, he realized his misjudgment. Charles Kao, he recanted, is "such a wonderful university president." What does the Nobel Prize have to do with the ability to serve as a university president? It is unclear why the columnist thought Charles Kao was not a good president. He admitted he was wrong as a student, but it appears that he was wrong again in 2009. To the extent that he had no understanding of the significance of fiber optics or why Charles Kao was awarded the Nobel Prize, he was wrong a third time. This story reveals that Hong Kong people know nothing about university research, and yet they like to pontificate about the future direction universities should take, however irrelevant their remarks may be.

Science and technology are the cornerstones of high productivity, bringing profits, welfare and added value. Charles Kao established the Department of Electronics at the Chinese University of Hong Kong, which was a great accomplishment, but his talent was underused. In comparison, at that time, Singapore had just become an independent country and had yet to take its first steps in developing science and technology. The Hsinchu Science Park in Taiwan was built only ten years later. TSMC, the world's largest semiconductor dedicated IC Foundry business, was founded by the Taiwan Government in 1987. South Korea was taking preliminary steps in science and technology, and Japan was only beginning to roll out its high-quality motor vehicles and semiconductor industries. However, science and technology in these places are now far ahead of Hong Kong.

Reflections

Many people can see the profit in science and technology but may not understand how it advances society. The wealth gap in Hong Kong is significant. While finance and real estate are known to be prosperous, not everyone has gained. A consequence of the growing inequality is that Hong Kong's middle class is shrinking, resulting in a problematic social imbalance. Science and technology can promote diversification in industry and create a healthier and broader economic base while improving the social ecosystem. Take Taiwan, for example, high-end technology boosted other industries and grew the middle class.

The Hong Kong government and the higher education sector are responsible for nurturing future pillars of society. What kind of examples should they set for Hong Kong's Generations Y and Z? What will happen to Hong Kong if, frustrated by the limitations of the structurally homogenous real estate industry, young people become unwilling or unmotivated to avail themselves of opportunities in the Mainland and elsewhere? Hong Kong will be left behind while others enjoy economic prosperity. How come people like Barry Lam (laptop computers), Kai-fu Lee (Chinese internet), Charles Kao (telecommunications and medical care) and Daniel Choi (electronics), whose work is so relevant to everyday life, are unknown in Hong Kong? Whose fault is that?

Technological culture is mainstream today. What kind of culture is now in vogue in Hong Kong? I am reminded of a poem written by the Tang poet Gao Shi showing his commiseration over Fan Shuhan, who, despite his distinguished career, was once looked upon by other people as just a commoner. Talking about commoners, well, I can again think of one other such commoner.

Kin-man Yeung

Few people have heard of Kin-man Yeung. He is neither particularly old nor has had a distinguished academic degree. But through his own exceptional experience and insights, he has managed to carve out a world for himself from scratch.

Yeung was born and raised in Hong Kong. In 2003, Motorola adopted his crystal screen design for the Razr mobile phone. He founded Biel Crystal (HK) Manufactory Limited, an RMB120 billion company that manufactures optical glass and other hi-tech products in Huizhou, Guangdong. In 2022, the company's turnover exceeded RMB100 billion. With a net worth of over US$20 billion, Yeung is known for his generosity, having donated HK$200 million to CityU. Yet Hong Kongers hardly know anything about him, standing as another case of brain drain from Hong Kong.

Barry Lam and Kin-man Yeung do not have degrees beyond a bachelor, which is consistent with what I have discussed in Chapter 11. Academic degrees should not be equated with knowledge and do not guarantee success. For similar reasons, I wonder if you would be interested in finding out which leaders of science and technological corporations, such as CEOs of major companies, are graduates of prestigious universities.

Elite CEO's Academic Background

Innovative technology is developing well in the Mainland in the 21st century. Technological corporations have mushroomed, putting hi-tech Chinese companies among the best in the world. Many distinguished founders of these companies, such as Ma Huateng of Tencent and Ren Zhengfei of Huawei, did not graduate from first-rate universities. Some might think that Kin-man Yeung, Ma Huateng and Ren Zhengfei are exceptions to the rule. Are they, though? My curiosity was piqued; I looked into the background of the CEOs of some major corporations in the US, Mainland China, Hong Kong and Taiwan and produced Table 25.1.

Most CEOs at US corporations graduated from state universities. There are 506 CEOs on the Fortune Global 500 list. Among these, only 96 (35+61), or 19%, graduated from universities that appear on the list of

Table 25.1 Academic background of CEOs in the US, Mainland China, Hong Kong and Taiwan.[a]

Country/region	Number of CEOs of top companies[b]	Average age	Number of CEOs graduated from prestigious universities[c]		Number of CEOs of top companies holding no undergraduate degree record
			Public university	Private university	
US	506	58	35 (260[d])	61 (212[d])	34
Mainland China	499	56	70 (105[e])	1 (0[e])	271[f]
Hong Kong	99	57	24	2	26[f]
Taiwan	49	65	24	1	6

[a] Data recorded as of October 1, 2022.
[b] "Top Companies" refers to those of the Fortune 500 companies in the case of the US; of the top 500 companies in the case of Mainland China; of the top 100 Hong Kong companies in the case of Hong Kong; and of the top 45 companies by market capitalization in the case of Taiwan.
[c] Prestigious universities are defined in the case of the US as the top American universities (see Table 18.1) that are simultaneously ranked in the top 100 by QS 2023, ARWU 2022, and QS Graduate Employability 2022; mainland China, China's universities ranked in the top 200 by QS2023 and THE 2023; Hong Kong, Hong Kong's universities ranked in the top 500 by QS 2023 and THE 2023; and Taiwan, Taiwanese universities ranked in the top 500 by QS 2023 and THE 2023. The criteria for prestigious universities across the Strait are relaxed because only five in the Mainland (see Table 18.1) meet the standards set for US universities. This is particularly true for Hong Kong and Taiwan, hence the standards are further loosened to make the analysis more meaningful.
[d] Indicate all US Fortune 500 CEOs.
[e] As described in Chapter 3, here it refers to graduates from the "Project 985" universities designated by the government. There are 105 CEOs who graduated from 39 such universities.
[f] No university degrees or lack of related information.

the first 100 universities whose graduates are judged to have the highest rankings according to QS, THE, ARWU and QS employability. About 34 CEOs, or 7%, do not have a university degree, and about 42% graduated from private universities. Among the CEOs with a university degree, 55% went to state universities, not any of the private universities known to the Chinese, which completely skewers preconceived ideas among those on the two sides of the Strait who wish to enroll at private US universities.

Fifty-four percent of the CEOs at major corporations in Mainland China do not have a university degree, or information about their education is unavailable. Only 14% graduated from famous universities. There are very few private universities in the Mainland and Hong Kong, and those that exist are very small. Almost no CEO at any company graduated from local private universities.

With only 1 university in Hong Kong and none in Taiwan appearing in the first 100 universities in all four world university ranking lists (See Chapter 18), I will not use the ranking of the universities as a criterion here. Of the CEOs of Hong Kong major corporations, about 26% do not have a university degree, or information about their academic background is not available. In Taiwan, 12% do not have a university degree. Of the CEOs with a university degree, 37% did not graduate from what are considered to be recognized top universities. In other words, 49% of Taiwan's CEOs are not from the top universities.

It is worth noting that only 18% of CEOs graduated from prestigious universities, including in the US. Times have changed. For hi-tech corporations such as Google and Facebook, there is not much demand for traditional university graduates. These companies are more interested in people with technical training, programming skills, and creativity.

This analysis indicates once again that a diploma from a university, prominent or not, across the Strait or in the US or anywhere else, is not a pass to a CEO position in a major corporation, neither is it a guarantee for a successful career. Still, many people in Taiwan, Hong Kong and the Mainland put much weight on a university diploma and not enough on true knowledge. Why?

Crouching Tiger, Hidden Dragon

We should move with the times and look beyond the present. However, just as we ask young people to be more farsighted, have we thought about how our educational and research institutions should embrace the future, transcend language barriers, and seek development in the Asia Pacific region and the world? Have the government and higher education institutions considered how young people can become innovative before they are ever actually encouraged to give full play to their creativity?

The idea for Ang Lee's film *Crouching Tiger, Hidden Dragon* was conceived in Taiwan, but the project was aborted soon after it started. The producers turned to Hong Kong for financial backing, but in its usual bean-counting way, Hong Kong did not see any promise. The Mainland was preoccupied; and did not have much of a creative vision at that time. In the end, *Crouching Tiger, Hidden Dragon* grabbed the attention of an American company. After making the script more appealing to the West, a beautiful Chinese-style martial arts classic was shot, taking advantage of what the Hollywood system has to offer and gaining worldwide fame and winning many awards. Box-office earnings worldwide hit US$800 million.

Like *Crouching Tiger, Hidden Dragon*, the projects of many entrepreneurs across the Strait that did not bloom in Taiwan, Hong Kong or the Mainland found favor elsewhere, thanks to external support. Isn't that a sad case for the three places with hidden talents?

Reporters have asked me why Hong Kong is economically prosperous and yet lacks innovation and an entrepreneurial spirit. Many reasons spring to mind: The relevant authorities, for stability and ease of monitoring, have set rigid rules for higher education so that financial resources can be easily distributed; they have laid down a fixed recruitment target for the number of young people to be admitted to institutions of higher education every year; and they are still hanging on to their long overdue statement on university positioning (Chapters 7 and 8). These are just some examples of their conservatism, which may help to prevent minor administrative mistakes, but it will lead to trouble one day because it stifles creativity and innovation.

Technological development changes every day. Hong Kong has already missed out on the opportunity to develop fiber-optic communication on the strength of Charles Kao's discoveries. There are pressing issues such as energy resources and environmental protection. If we had learned to seize the opportunity, previously unforeseeable new areas might have emerged, bringing prosperity beyond the financial fields. In 2022, CityU took the lead in Asia investing in HKTech 300, a project that enables students and alumni to develop their enterprises. However, the government seems to be slow in response.

Reporters have also asked me how universities in Hong Kong could become more creative. The government and society need to improve the local entrepreneurial environment and respect education and research.

Otherwise, universities will be too busy trying to satisfy government demands rather than thinking about innovation and creativity. Who will recognize the creativity at universities, and who will waste time looking for trouble under such circumstances?

Steve Jobs

Steve Jobs took a leap into the unknown, proposing a new personal computing concept different from the IBM design and Microsoft operation system. When Apple was stuck in a quagmire, he thought up a rescue plan. Thinking out of the box, he did not believe lowering prices would save Apple. But nobody was willing to listen; instead, he was kicked out of the company he had founded. His approach contrasts closely with what we see in places across the Strait.

To quote Confucius, "A virtuous man will not find himself alone." Neither will a capable man like Jobs. Apple creates value. Today, as one of the world's most valued brands, it has entered the Top 10 of the Fortune 500. Jobs was inspired by the miracle of cooperation that characterized the Beatles' music, and he believed deeply that commercial success grew from teamwork.

Besides nurturing outstanding scientists, the Chinese have recorded many accomplishments in science and technology. For example, Min Kao founded GPS Garmin, Yang Zhiyuan created Yahoo and others. They are a testament to the exceptional, innovative capability of the Chinese in industry and commerce. However, almost all of them were educated in the West, conducted research in the West, and started their enterprises and projects to succeed in the West, and then proceeded to win world recognition.

Is this a result of the half-alive, half-dead state of studying at universities in this part of the world, so much so that the talent available does not reach its full potential? Is it because the social structure has yielded the best we can expect? If a university can integrate teaching and research, if society is mature enough, and if governments modernize, we can cultivate talent we can be proud of. As I look toward the prospects of innovation, I see a road with overgrown thorns and thistles. Unless we sweep aside the bad and promote the good, we may even double our efforts but still see only half the results. While most people thoughtlessly pursue an academic degree, let us ask, given the present rigid system we operate under and the exceptional wisdom of the Chinese, why do we not look for alternatives? As the Tang poet Lin Shangyin once wrote, "With all the gold that we have, why do we limit ourselves to building a house rather than a multi-storied mansion?"

Resources are important, but talent is more so.

The Story of Michael Yang

Michael Yang is a chair professor at CityU with a doctorate in chemistry from the University of Toronto. I was told that he was involved in many areas besides teaching, which sparked my interest. I looked at his CV and discovered that in addition to his outstanding research, he had started a few small biotech companies with his students. Then one day, I spoke to him about the need for focus, and I proposed to him: In order to make full use of his talent, he could either choose to conduct his research within the university and put aside his involvement at his companies, or he could leave the university and devote himself wholeheartedly to his other responsibilities. If he chose the former, he could still own shares in his companies and take up positions such as consultant or director. If the latter, he could be appointed as a part-time professor at CityU.

Very often, the best option is not a compromise. He picked the first choice. Incidentally, when I was department head at Texas A&M University, I encountered the same situation. The difference was that Mark chose to leave Texas A&M University and focus on his company, with outstanding accomplishments.

In 2008, CityU's Cabinet integrated disciplines and created frontier specialties. In 2014, in preparing for the future, I divided the pre-existing Chemistry and Biology departments into three, against opposition from moribund conservative voices. The professors in environmental biology were absorbed into the newly established School of Energy and Environment, chemistry teachers were retained and put into the reconfigured Department of Chemistry, while the few professors specializing in biochemistry were assimilated into the newly established Department of Biomedical Sciences. At that time, there were expressions of ridicule and envy within and beyond the university. Amid the hubbub, the general tone was that CityU had taken this step much too late as a university. The government had its attention elsewhere besides. There was not much future for the changes CityU was undertaking.

I approached Yang and asked him to head the Department of Biomedical Sciences with a quota of 30 professors with a brief to create a world-class department. Surprised, he accepted the heavy responsibilities and set out to recruit globally outstanding professors. In five years, he succeeded in building an excellent department.

Later, when we were looking for the Dean of the Jockey Club College of Veterinary Medicine and Life Sciences, I gave Yang a second surprise. I asked him to be the acting dean in the interim period, emphasizing that it was only an acting position because the deanship requires someone with a background in veterinary science. He took up the new responsibilities enthusiastically, giving his best to the job. A year later, he relieved himself of the post and prepared to return to teaching and research at the Department of Biomedical Sciences.

Then, with the support of the Committee, I gave Yang a third unexpected assignment. I invited him to assume the position of Vice-President (Research and Technology). CityU stands out in technology fields. It is ranked among the top universities in Hong Kong. Compared with other higher education institutions in Hong Kong, it has obtained the highest number of utility patents from the US and the most awards at the International Exhibition of Inventions of Geneva. With his expertise in technology promotion, he was the ideal person to lead research and technology at CityU.

In 2020/21, the new coronavirus went rampant. All over the world, people were conducting diagnostic tests. Prenetics, the top brand in new coronavirus and gene test kits, is one of the many companies Yang and his students founded. In the summer of 2021, news came that Prenetics had been recognized as a unicorn company that fulfilled the requirements of the lowest capital of US$1 billion. This is one of the few hi-tech unicorn companies set up by university graduates from Hong Kong.

It is a great turn of events when success is due to help from a benefactor. To be another person's benefactor or witness others succeed is even more welcome. Talented people abound in Hong Kong, and so the question is whether we should pay attention. Resources are also plentiful in Hong Kong. The question is whether they are put to good use. Hong Kong can access the highway of creativity, but the question is whether the people have the heart for it. If the problem with Hong Kong is related to opportunities, it is the same with Taiwan and the Mainland. What other people don't do, universities do.

26

Creativity in Higher Education and Risk-Taking

It was reported that a teacher in a county primary school on the Mainland gave a score of 0 to a pupil for his mathematics assignment. An uproar ensured because the pupil had supplied an unconventional answer.

Here is the mathematical question: "There are 383 pieces of rock candy, 125 marshmallows, and 231 lollipops in Little Judy's pocket. In the morning, she ate 209 pieces of rock candy, 74 marshmallows and 147 lollipops. What is the result?" The pupil's mind worked like a machine. Rather than subtracting, he immediately answered, "She'll have diabetes!" The unimaginative teacher did not give the pupil any points for his answer.

Here is another story. Many years ago, the dean of an engineering school tried to encourage his fellow academics to generate some creative ideas. To show that he was sincere, he solicited proposals. One professor requested a leave of absence for half a year to seek inspiration on Hawaii's beaches. The dean gladly agreed. Word got around, and immediately another professor made the same request, but the dean was less supportive this time. Displeased, the second professor asked for an explanation. The dean said, "But there is nothing creative in your proposal!" Copying is brainless; creativity requires the mind.

It was reported that in the hacker training base in China, a group of teenagers could traverse the world of the internet by relying on a few introductory books, not to mention university studies. They shook off traditional theory's burden and created unimaginable computer viruses and anti-viruses. One cannot but wonder if our formal education has become useless and has gone awry.

Creativity in Education

Technology has brought industrial development, social networks, health and entertainment to the human world. In recent years, smartphones, tablet computers, commercial drones and other advanced electronic products have made us work more efficiently and made our lives easier. However, we must reflect on our behavior to create a livable environment. From the point of view of education, we have to examine the university's role, mission and curriculum design if we want to ensure that technology will bring about transformation.

Salman Khan has turned tradition upside down with his website Khan Academy using modern communication technology. Offering free online math and science courses, the Khan Academy attracts 20,000 regular users from US schools. The schoolteachers are responsible only for answering students' questions after watching the videos. The Academy boasts a monthly clicking rate of 5 million, far more than the 1.5 million clicks on MIT's open online courses. Between 2009, when the website opened, and the end of 2021, more than 1 billion people from more than 3 million subscribers around the world watched Khan's programs via YouTube.

The Khan Academy website does not come via an education department at a university and is not connected with any high school. Yet its striking results might serve as a footnote for the argument to this book and deserve careful consideration at universities and for university education professionals.

Like industrial innovations, the success of higher education depends on investment, the pursuit of excellence and the encouragement of creativity and innovation. Japan's Global COE and South Korea's Brain Korea 21 invest heavily in key disciplines to support excellent teaching and research. In light of this, if the three places across the Strait have indeed taken to heart the concept of balancing investment and return, they will take results from teaching and research seriously. They will not regard themselves as mere consumers of innovative technology, passively looking at universities as a tool to satisfy the present labor market and blindly duplicating outdated teaching and research methods, ignoring the need to make concrete, long-term contributions.

History has shown that no single society or country will lead culture and technology forever. Modern higher education needs to bring together innovative teachers and students to unleash the latter's potential. If we understand the importance of excellence, we will not fall victim to preconceived notions of treating universities as mere servants, brusquely ordering them around.

Online and Off-line

In the early Republican era of the 20th century in China, when mechanical printing was all the rage, some scholars tried to buck the trend by reading only string-bound books and writing only with traditional brushes. Forty years ago, opposition reached sky-high when seeking students' opinions on teaching was first introduced. Twenty years ago, many professors disapproved when distance learning began sending out lecture notes by mail, believing teaching would be compromised. A dozen or so years ago, after PowerPoint arrived, some professors insisted on using a blackboard. Their only concession was using a desk projector as a teaching aid. In retrospect, nostalgia cannot stand the test of time. ChatGPT is now confusing many people and also used by many people.

Now, high-speed internet communication has transformed every aspect of our lives. For some courses, exchanges on the internet proved to be more efficient than the traditional way of teaching. Teachers and students are usually content to interact online, although some insist that face-to-face teaching is the only efficient teaching mode. Therefore, internet teaching falls under suspicion, with more than a few believing without evidence that only small group teaching produces results.

In 2011, Stanford University successfully attracted 160,000 students when it officially launched its MOOCs. Many other universities later offered MOOC courses. For this reason, 2012 was named the Year of the MOOC by *The New York Times*. Based on the concept of distance learning, MOOCs use the internet to deliver learning globally in an instantaneous, multi-faceted, highly efficient and flexible way, representing a revolutionary and creative way of teaching. These courses, prepared and delivered by excellent professors, have proven to be clear and exquisitely designed. And the results are often superb.

Based on available data, many MOOC teachers come from top ranking universities that abide by the philosophy of integrating teaching and research. Currently, an overwhelming number of courses originate from universities (Stanford, Harvard, MIT) that occupy top positions in three international ranking systems. In the Mainland, the first universities to offer MOOCs include Tsinghua University, Peking University and Shanghai Jiaotong University, which happen to be the top universities across the Strait.

It may be true that MOOCs are a trivial matter in course design, but it is an inevitable result of market-oriented evaluations. MOOCs have taken over the education field like a wind sweeping through the grass on the prairie. They are the perfect evolution of the integration of teaching and research and bring a new ethos and opportunities to education. Features such as evaluation among students, large-class instruction and individual learning are all commendable. Equally praiseworthy is that even though the teacher and students are not face-to-face, the format accommodates students from all levels. They can adjust their learning time and style in accordance with their own capabilities on MOOCs and engage in research between studies. Such an approach is hardly possible under traditional theories of teaching. A MOOC at NTU on probability attracted more than 100,000 students. Who says large classes can't be held? And how can some maintain the argument that there is no teacher-student communication in large classes?

At the beginning of 2020, the new coronavirus raged across the planet. Factories, shops and schools were closed, and some countries closed their borders and imposed compulsory quarantine. CityU was one of the first universities in the world to switch completely to Zoom-based distance teaching. From February 7, 2020, the university adjusted the traditional face-to-face teaching to distance learning using Zoom to reduce the risk of virus transmission. Students and teachers in 110 countries or regions had real-time, comprehensive and interactive classes in accordance with the original schedule through the online CityU-Learning platform. In September 2020, CityU-Learning 2.0, a hybrid mode of teaching that combined face-to-face and online instruction, was launched. It even managed to allow lab work to be temporarily replaced using virtual reality technology to conduct experiments. The overall results were better than expected.

Online teaching is now widespread in universities, high schools and primary schools. In some ways, the more diligent students may have learned more rapidly during this period than professors who had to acquire new skills as online educators. In this situation, online teaching or reports must use precise language to deal with the audience (viewers) who can check information online at any time.

In Chapter 10, I have emphasized that students need not attend lectures as they can study independently. Why, then, do we need professors for teaching? As instructors, should professors not re-examine the substance and methods of their teaching so that students can learn something that they cannot find online? Teaching depends on research, and universities should think of ways to deal with the challenges the internet presents to teachers. They should work with the internet to enrich the content of education. I do not know if online teaching has reached its highest efficiency, but I firmly believe that professors should ensure that students can feel the worth of a university education though being delivered online.

It was said in ancient China that a scholar could know world affairs without leaving his home. What a modern view, in some way. Staying home does not deprive you of an international outlook. When offline, you can still find what you need to know, and you will still know yourself.

No Risk, No Innovation

Due to the Industrial Revolution, mass production greatly reduced production costs and increased output, benefiting the public. Thanks to the quality innovation concept in the last century, on top of quantity enhancement, product quality was greatly enhanced. Later, to meet the needs of customized production, apart from improving the quality of the average product and reducing the variation of quality among the same kinds of products, the public increased individual demand for product diversification.

During this process, accountability assumed greater prominence. Accountability provides a balance between product quality and advertising promotion to avoid unsubstantiated claims made by exaggerated advertisements. As stated in Chapter 18, the importance of quality has expanded from manufacturing to the service and education sectors, significantly contributing to people's livelihoods and well-being.

The acceptance of responsibility on the part of the institutions is the basic standard and assurance of the effectiveness of teaching and research activities. However, since its adoption in Hong Kong, accountability has become so hugely overstretched that it is now a synonym for close surveillance and control. Even student representatives want to supervise the work of a university. In the name of accountability, the public and the media maintain a close watch over universities while the government seeks to control them, directing attention to monitoring universities and focusing on trivial management issues. Or accountability is often used as justification for turmoil or exercising power. Many outsiders are eager to try to use accountability to shield their interests or for marketing their decrees and restraining others.

If we want to adopt international norms in higher education, people who hold others accountable must follow due process and uphold the facts. If accountability is to be applied in universities, everyone at every level of the organization should be responsible, rather than only those at designated levels, lest teaching, learning and research get bogged down. The path where accountability has degenerated into a blame culture concerned only with consequences and not causation, procedural correctness and not innovativeness will lead us to a risk aversion mentality that will hinder innovation and the development of much-needed soulware. Risk aversion taken too far will confuse society, which will eventually harm innovation.

It is like too many monks in a small temple or people wearing too big hats for their heads. It turns out that, after all, the government itself is the bottleneck for innovation in higher education.

The Cross-Strait Tsing Hua Research Institute set up an office in 2015 to promote innovation on the campus of National Tsing Hua University in Hsinchu, Taiwan, through the Tze Chiang Foundation of Science and Technology, organized by alumni. In November 2021, the government alleged that communists had infiltrated the Foundation, and subsequently, the Ministry of Education was instructed to take speedy punitive action. Under such circumstances, universities and professors risk criticism if they engage in academic exchanges with the Mainland.[1]

One of the characteristics of innovation is the willingness to take risks. Apart from overcoming rigid policies and insufficient investment, the essential component in the modernization of higher education is to face the inherent and socially conservative attitudes encountered in operations, including the high risk of innovation failure.

Creativity and Innovation Help Entrepreneurship

Now comes the most difficult question: what is the use of an academic degree?

Never think of a degree from a prestigious school as a pass to a good job. Similarly, those without a degree should not be marginalized in the labor market. All roads lead to knowledge. Chapter 11 points out that many who withdrew from their studies or did not even pass through university gates have become successful. A university education, therefore, does not necessarily bring you success. Often, a degree might prevent you from becoming successful. People with knowledge may not have a degree. In many situations, degree holders are anything but knowledgeable. Knowledge without practice does not help, either.

That is why universities should emphasize practice for the sake of creativity and never regard their jobs as merely handing out degrees. They should not make the mistake of disconnecting teaching from research. Researchers need to bring their studies into the classroom, just as teachers have to learn about advanced trends, concepts and debating points in their

---

[1] *The Storm Media*,《風傳媒》November 12, 2021.

field. To settle the question of openness is a major issue confronting teaching and research.

As in industry, higher education circles are competitive places where colleagues need to compete for resources, reputation and recognition. We examine the rationale of the division of knowledge by discipline and ask substantive questions. Over the years, many disciplines have been combined or eliminated. If we do not want to be left behind, we need to adjust to the times and decide which disciplines should stay. In response to social needs, a university should not set too narrow a boundary for its curriculum. Some key exploratory and professional education fields—such as energy and environment, creative media, medical engineering and smart city—often cross multiple disciplines. Only through these intersecting explorations can we find development niches and develop new disciplines and domains.

A university can be seen as a laboratory for cross-disciplinary inquiries. Students can obtain the expert guidance they need, pursue their interests and realize their ideals. Students who are intrinsically motivated, creative and strong at expressing themselves have the highest chance of becoming key leaders in their profession. Universities and teachers do not often give their students sufficient opportunities to realize their full potential.

As Arden L. Bement, former National Science Foundation director and National Institute of Standard and Technology (NIST) director, pointed out, we live in a closely connected world. If one person catches a cold, others will sneeze, which is, unfortunately, an apt description of the potentially deadly COVID-19 experienced at the time of writing. Creativity and entrepreneurship are core themes of the 21st century. Bement believes that it is possible to teach creativity and entrepreneurship, especially in times of crisis. He pointed to wartime transportation systems, rockets, missiles, and night-vision technology as examples.

If you are completely ignorant about these issues' social and cultural backgrounds, then having just the technology and theories at your disposal is not enough. Without innovation, there is no entrepreneurship. Higher education can fall behind the times, just as products can become quickly obsolete. The rise and fall of Wang An's computer business in the 1980s and the decline of AT&T and Ericsson, both leaders in the mobile phone market at one point, are lessons to bear in mind.

Entrepreneurs must dare to dream and reflect on pre-existing cultural values. After determining the right direction by considering what lies beyond received social values, one can execute the plan. People who only stick to the rules will not understand these elements. Unfortunately, despite numerous calculations, the governments are too content with outdated practices, emphasizing the distribution of "human resources" and ignoring the "talent mining" plan. This is reminiscent of traditional bookkeepers who only focus on balancing the books but are unaware that the way to innovation and success can only be accessed by adhering to "activity-base" accounting in entrepreneurship.

It is estimated that AI will contribute US$17.5 trillion to the global economy in 2023. Nowadays, everyone talks about AI and tries to predict future applications, but how many of us know that AI has been a subject of study and research for over 40 years? People engaged in the robust and fast-developing industries of AI and IT cannot but be exposed to high risk. The lack of tolerance for failure in Japan's culture is the main reason that venture capital activities are not highly developed there. Hiroshi Mikitani and Tanaka Yoshikazu, who turned themselves into well-known billionaires in Japan on account of their IT businesses, are rare exceptions.

Americans think of founding businesses as fulfilling their dreams and satisfying their interests. The Chinese tend to think of owning a degree as a way to gratify their sense of vanity. The difference between the two is that Americans can accept failure with equanimity. While the Japanese are solid and the Chinese clever, they are alike in that both societies fear failure. Once an entrepreneur fails, it is rare for him or her to make a comeback. Systematic innovation can pave the way to innovate and start a business. The returns can be huge, but the risk remains just as high. There must be perseverance and constant striving to start a business.

Challenges in Higher Education in Taiwan, Hong Kong and Mainland

Compared with neighboring countries and regions, the number of universities in Hong Kong is by no means high. By scale, the universities are not large, and the number of enrolled students is low. For that reason, although the government's investment in education only takes up a rather low percentage of the revenue (about one-third that of the Mainland, two-fifths that of Singapore, one-fourth that of Taiwan and one-fifth that of South Korea), the per capita amount of resources is still relatively significant. High salaries and excellent benefits have attracted many specialists and scholars to Hong Kong, if neglecting political considerations.

At one point, Hong Kong was the leader of the Four Asian Tigers. It started earlier than Taiwan, South Korea and Singapore. Hong Kong's prosperity was not unrelated to its special political, economic and geographical situation. Hong Kong did not draw up its own educational policies. No thought was given to making education take root; nor was it considered necessary to innovate in education. Innovation was not encouraged, and naturally, it was never an item to be assessed.

Before 1997, thanks to the changing relationship between the Mainland and the international community and other political factors, Hong Kong was a blessed place insulated from the influences of external forces. Lacking natural resources, it was lucky enough to maintain an affluent way of life. National defense was never an issue, nor was a national defense budget. Nobody thought of exploiting Hong Kong for their own interests; rather, Hong Kong seemed to enjoy special considerations from all parties concerned.

After 1997, the old protective umbrella was gone. However, people's livelihoods were just as well-provided for. The Mainland shouldered defense costs, saving Hong Kong an exorbitant expenditure. In that regard, Hong Kong is far luckier than an overwhelming number of places. But when Hong Kong was ruled by the British, the people were not given the opportunity to think independently or to play the role of socially involved citizens. Now operating under the one-country two-systems principle, Hong Kong people can control the direction of their educational development. Ironically, they are bewildered, as if lost in a dream.

With such a high degree of freedom, Hong Kong is like an unbridled horse galloping freely across the steppes. Accustomed to the old ways, the city has become completely disoriented in the highly competitive field of higher education. The rallying call of internationalization is heard often enough, but nobody seems to appreciate the need to be innovative.

While other people are finding ways to expand and diversify the employment market, Hong Kong still uses traditional bookkeeping methods to handle educational problems. Though Hong Kong proclaims to support entrepreneurship, its hands are tied. The city cannot think its way out of the situation and only can watch competitors sail away to success.

Apart from the superficial change to the curriculum from 3 to 4 years in 2012, Hong Kong's higher education field has inherited the old British management structure and has never rethought those lingering problems that stem from careless thinking, such as those mentioned in the early chapters of this book: complex administrative practices, the entanglement of interests and the lack of direction. But Hong Kong has a surplus of revenue, and so it does not have to obsess about short-term returns. Society has to be prepared for crises and plans the intangible as part of the medium- and long-term plan. There is no need to treat university innovation as a normal expense item on a balance sheet. In looking for new possibilities, one has to be willing to stray off the beaten track. If teaching and research innovation cannot take root in Hong Kong and contribute to the world, how can we be in a position to speak about internationalization?

What, then, is the situation in Taiwan and the Mainland?

In Hong Kong where the population is one-third that of Taiwan, there are only eight UGC-funded universities and a small number of non-government-funded universities. The population of South Korea and the UK is more than double that of Taiwan, but each has more than 100 universities. In Singapore whose population is only one-fifth that of Taiwan, there are only five, while both Hong Kong and Singapore are stronger in their finances than Taiwan. Now Taiwan's higher education has reached a bottleneck caused by having more than 160 under-resourced universities at one stage. Even by the spring of 2022, after a considerable number had been forced to close or merge, there was still a surplus of 137 universities. The number of students applying for university education plummeted, and a total of 51 universities, including top national universities, failed to meet their enrollment targets in fall 2022, with more than 14,000 places unfilled. The situation of not being able to enroll enough students to fill the quota is embarrassing. Clearly, the problem of higher education in Taiwan is being compounded.

For many years, I have called for sustainable development in higher education. The authorities should guide those who need help and support those who excel. It should emphasize quality and set up a system to strategically regroup key universities that distinguish themselves in both teaching and research and help reorient those who are weak. It should open a new world that provides students with professional training that will likely lead to innovation and entrepreneurship. Even if the remaining 137 universities are halved, there are still too many. Taiwan used to achieve impressive economic growth with limited resources before 2000. Today, resources are scarce, politics still seem to be taking command of the situation in Taiwan, and higher education has not progressed. In terms of the medical profession, there are currently 12 universities in Taiwan that award degrees in medicine, but enrollment is far from ideal. In 2022, there were proposals from three more universities to establish medical departments. Have they given any thought to the cost of setting up such a department, hiring qualified teachers and acquiring the necessary equipment? How about the question of quality assurance? Why don't they consider strengthening the existing medical departments to maximize the marginal effect of medical teaching and research?

In the development of modern education, nothing is more important than investment in operational funding and human resources. The allocation to universities in Taiwan was NTD$50 billion (US$1.7 billion), representing only a small portion of what is needed. Using operating funds to repair the sewage system or build student dormitories precisely reflects how university infrastructure in Taiwan is lagging behind. One blushes to think about it. In past years, the populism-driven educational reforms in Taiwan have run contrary to the principles of higher education discussed in Chapter 13. They have put Taiwan's higher education in a quandary, making education reform akin to a luxury item to be reserved for discussion at a less harried time.

With the development of the market economy in the Mainland, competition, fairness, efficiency and quality have become problems at hand. Other issues associated with higher education, such as research ethics, potential problems of unequal treatment, and a pervasive sense of restlessness, also need to be addressed. The growth of universities on the Mainland and the widening scope of student recruitment have highlighted the excessive expansion of quantity. If a solution cannot be found immediately to control the loss of quality caused by the expansion of university education, the Mainland is going to duplicate the mistakes caused by education reform in Taiwan. The hands of the talented will be tied, and the pace of social progress will slow down.

Higher education is growing at an unprecedented pace on the Mainland, but its execution, as well as the result of its efforts, do not measure up to the ambition and the lofty rhetoric of the authorities. It is heartening to see China's government formulating a national higher education agenda and investing significant sums. However, innovation in education inevitably stalls because of the authoritarian political operations led by party and government personnel.

Innovation in education policy needs to be guided by specialists. Going to university with no clear goal is a common problem. Another is the failure to equip students who fail to get into the university with useful skills. Both result from an educational policy lacking foresight.

Distance between the US and Taiwan, Hong Kong and Mainland China

Innovation is a hot topic all over the world, the focus of attention for governments at all levels. Innovation has to be based on science to make creativity serve the people's welfare and the sustainability goal. The point is not to use it as a routine driving force for scientific study or industrial reform, and definitely not as a tool for making money and grabbing power.

Advanced enterprises invest in the future, not in low labor costs but in production quality, reliability, innovation ability and the industry cluster effect. Innovation has a very serious implication for society, politics, law, environmental protection, public welfare, international cooperation and other areas. Innovation should not ignore moral, legal and humanitarian issues. In order to support social advancement, higher education should take the lead in embracing diversity in terms of age, sex, religion, ethnicity and perceptions. People in power must attach importance to talents and recognize that a diversified society is conducive to academic innovation. In Chapters 6, 9 and 19, I have alluded to instances of flawed understanding that result from accepting what one hears without due verification.

Under the impetus of innovation, society has high expectations of universities' scientific and technological research output. We should choose economic growth as a key theme in accepting higher education's role in providing the labor market with the necessary skills and knowledge. Students with innovative abilities will become leaders and entrepreneurs of tomorrow. Innovations that do not lead to the betterment of human welfare are meaningless. In this regard, while the problems facing higher education in the three communities across the Strait may be different, their goal is the same, and there is room for improvement for all.

The impressive results of the collaboration between industry, university and research in Europe and North America are due to the generous support for universities from the corporate world. That is how universities can contribute more to society. However, collaborations between industry and universities across the Strait have little to boast about. Without the involvement of industry, it is unsurprising that universities cannot produce the required human resources in a timely way. The industry has little hope when teaching and research are not integrated.

Hong Kong prides itself on a developed economic system governed by the rule of law, with the unique advantage of enjoying an ample supply of natural resources even though it has none. It also has a few good universities. However, even though Hong Kong has been affluent and possesses a good looking science park, its effectiveness is impeded by the lack of a science and technology policy while the government is unable to make good use of professional management experts.

Under the democratic system now in place, Taiwan has yet to learn to "do things right," let alone "do the right things." The former emphasizes the procedures of action to uphold justice, and the latter the essence of the action and the scope of innovation. In the current circumstances, as shown in Figures 20.1 and 20.2, innovation is no match for the control that is put upon it. It is not surprising that society is at a standstill. Is the well-being of the people in the hearts of those in power?

As a matter of fact, competition and cooperation are compatible. Competition promotes progress as long as it is fair. In competition, we may find collaborative partners. However, when some people talk about innovation in Hong Kong and Taiwan, what they have in mind is the pathways set for higher education, and they are unaware of the soulware needed and how crafty words can derail the noblest ideal! Scientific and technological collaborations between Mainland China and South Korea started as early as 1992 after they had established diplomatic relations. China imported advanced technologies from the European Union as well and now possesses advanced technological skills for high-speed trains, computers and satellite research and development. The Long March series of launch vehicles has been judged reliable, and following the US, the Zhurong Rover has been sent to explore Mars. Why couldn't societies across the Strait take advantage of their same culture and same language to cooperate with and complement each other to broaden the path for sustainable development together?

China set a goal of surpassing the US in R&D investment by 2022, according to information provided by Credit Suisse at the 2016 Shenzhen Investment Forum. Some top American universities have China Studies programs on their curriculum. Insightfully, all have taken time to send out feelers to the Mainland for possible areas of collaboration. Even with the ongoing conflict between China and the US, both sides are still trying to understand each other better. Hong Kong and Taiwan are comparatively much closer to the Mainland. How do they look at the present situation? What do they plan to do?

Hong Kong and Taiwan are geographically close, but there is no Hong Kong expert on Taiwan or Taiwanese expert on Hong Kong. Feng Mingchu, a Hong Konger, studied in Taiwan. An accomplished individual, she served as director of the Palace Museum in Taipei until she stepped down in May 2016. I have asked hundreds of Hong Kongers, but only a few have heard of her. Similarly, most Taiwanese know nothing about Taiwanese scholars working in Hong Kong. For that matter, is there an academic unit or authoritative scholar in Hong Kong or Taiwan specializing in the study of the Mainland? And is there any noted research center or scholar in Hong Kong specializing in the study of Hong Kong? What about Taiwan or the Mainland? There is a lack of understanding between Taiwan, Hong Kong and the Mainland. Perhaps they do not even know too much about themselves.

Hong Kong is physically closer to Mainland China than Taiwan, and Taiwan's physical distance from Mainland China is closer than its distance to the US. But the psychological gap between the US and Mainland China seems narrower than between Taiwan and Mainland China, and the psychological distance between Taiwan and Mainland China seems closer than that between Hong Kong and Mainland China.

The distance between mountains is the clouds; the distance between trees is the wind; the distance between people is the heart, and that which is between the hearts determines the soulware of higher education across the Strait. A state of mental confusion seems to pervade Hong Kong and Taiwan in spite of their proximity to Mainland China, and the same seems true with the Mainland in relation to Hong Kong and Taiwan.

27
Setting Policy Direction and Avoiding Nano-Management

Universities in Asia attach great importance to the teaching and research of science and technology but rarely devote much effort to discussing science and technology policies, particularly in Hong Kong where there is no science and technology policy. Hong Kong education institutions are administered meticulously, with an emphasis on regulations and not breakthroughs. Thinking out of the box and changing the management are imperative.

The American Higher Education Experience

The US does not have a unified nationwide higher education system. The federal government provides individual universities with peer-reviewed and merit-based funding through designated strategic development projects. Universities operate with academic autonomy in an environment mostly independent of political interference and are free to pursue promising academic and research programs. American students may not be as intelligent as students from Taiwan, Hong Kong or the Mainland, but a degree granted by an American university is an assurance of quality. In general, a graduate from an American university tends to be forthright in terms of creativity, originality, independence of thought, respect for others, involvement in society and interactions with people.

After World War II, the US government increased its investment in basic research and managed to keep its leading position in science and technology. Between 1958 and 1968, funding for universities increased five times, encouraging research activities in universities where innovation took the lead and industry played a secondary role, greatly strengthening the overall future competitiveness of American universities in academic areas of humanities, social sciences, medicine, agriculture, law, business, science and engineering.

American universities and national laboratories are two forces for transforming the world. From DNA to genetic engineering and oncogenes research; from AI to 3D printing and modern communication; from semi-conductors to computer and quantum calculations; from medical appliances to organ transplants and prenatal care; from the invention of the Salk vaccine for polio to the discovery of prions and the coronavirus vaccines; from stem cells to HIV/AIDS treatment and other improvements in the cultivation, storage and transportation of crops and innovative development in culture and arts, environmental protection, new energies to veterinary medicine, the new media and so forth—the university has a role to play.

The development of technology cannot be separated from investment in research and development. According to a report published by *Battelle R&D Magazine* in December 2010 on the prospect of global expenses for research and development, US investment in research and development between 2009 and 2011 represented around one-third of the global total. US corporate participation is even higher than that of the federal government. Of the total national investment of US$465 billion in 2014, US$307.5 billion came from the corporate world.

In recent years, even though overall investment from the federal government in research and development has dwindled, the American corporate world is still very active, coming to the top in terms of the number of participating corporations and the amount of investment. According to the Industrial R&D Investment Scoreboard 2020 released by the EU, the US was ranked 1st with 775 among the top 2,500 corporations that invested in research and development in 2019. China came second with 536, followed by the EU with 421, Japan with 309, and other regions of the world with 459. At his point, the US still has the greatest investment in research and development in the world. In 2019, the total reached US$612.7 billion. In response to the competition posed by China and other countries, despite the new coronavirus and the unclear economic prospects, the House of Representatives passed the US Innovation and Competition Act proposed by the Biden administration with an investment of US$250 billion in June 2021. Later, on August 10, a massive $1 trillion infrastructure bill was passed.

The six major US government departments (Department of Health and Human Services, National Science Foundation, Department of Defense, Department of Energy, National Aeronautics and Space Administration, and Department of Agriculture) provide over 90% of the total competitive funds for scientific research. In addition, national laboratories indirectly subsidize scientific research activities at universities. The federal government has played an important role in funding university research for a long time. At the end of the 1960s, federal funding for university research was as high as 73%. At present, the percentage is approximately 60%, with an amount of US$30 billion.

At the same time, corporate support for university research and development has jumped from the 3% of total funding in the 1960s to today's 6%. In the 2022 fiscal year, the Biden administration invested over US$10 billion in the research budget of the National Science Foundation in order to provide funding for basic scientific research in American universities. Even during periods of economic recession and fiscal contraction, the US does not suspend interactions between industry, university and research. No other factor can better account for the strength of the US.

The cost of high-quality higher education is inevitably expensive. State universities in the US receive only 10 to 20% of their annual budget from state governments. The balance is made up of tuition fees, research funding and donations. For their support of scientific research and teaching in universities, the industry has to be recognized for its great service to American society. Take, for example, the Georgia Institute of Technology. For its income in 2021, the state government contributed about 15%, tuition fees about 19%, while 51% came from scientific programs and the competitive grants and contracts from the federal and state governments, the military and major corporations. Accordingly, each professor must compete to win US$600,000 in research funding.

According to the investigation report "Voluntary Support of Education" published by the Council for Advancement and Support of Education in the fiscal year of 2020, all universities and colleges in the US raised a total amount of non-deliverable donations of US$49.5 billion. According to US higher education institutions, university endowments total more than US$600 billion. The US lead in science and technology, and the progressiveness of American higher education are strongly tied to government and industry investment.

Policy and Market Orientation

Success in higher education and science and technology depends on policy direction. In the field of education, once policies are set, governments should let educational institutions have a free hand to work out individual development strategies following market forces. Insistence on micromanagement goes against the basic principles of modern management, and governance is bound to be ineffective.

Regarding science and technology, the US's leading edge stems from its forward-looking policies. Lewis M. Branscomb, former director of the National Bureau of Standards (later changed to NIST), once pointed out that American science and technology policies are based on four fundamental principles:

1. Basic research will eventually generate new technology and new industries.
2. The federal government must proactively discover and develop new technologies to meet special national targets.
3. The government is not supposed to develop specific business technologies or help specific enterprises through direct investment.
4. It is the role of the federal government to create an effective market environment and, when necessary, point out where enterprises should devote their resources.

These principles, which have been instrumental in making the US a giant in global innovation and higher education, are applicable to societies across the Strait. In formulating higher education policies, governments can channel parts of the defense budgets to support collaborations between education, research, and industry to guide the development of society and enterprises. With such strategic investments, society or enterprises will develop naturally according to the policy directions. We should act according to progressive soulware, respect university governance by professional experts, and foster an atmosphere conducive to academic excellence. In this way, academics can fully concentrate on their academic work just as researchers can fully attend to their research projects.

Cure Thy Absence, Sanctify Thy Soul

In an education ecosystem where outstanding universities are engaged in the pursuit of excellence, resource allocation is based on the criterion of excellence. For example, if two people or two universities have each applied for research funds, the submission will be evaluated based on merit, which is not necessarily exercised in Hong Kong. Funding will be allocated only to the submissions judged to have higher merit and should never be based on preconceived ideas that would keep us far removed from excellence in higher education and undermine the ideal of academic meritocracy. However, in our society, this kind of advocacy for developing an ideal educational ecosystem or implementing fair and objective evaluation in higher education is not used out of fear of causing displeasure of those in authority.

Stones from the US may serve to polish the jade of those across the Strait. If higher education can accomplish the following three suggestions, many of the perplexing problems that people face today can be solved:

1. Increase investment in teaching and research and promote free competition. Liberate ourselves from the outdated conservative mindset that has been obstructing higher education advancement.
2. Review the existing higher education practice with reference to US higher education. Eliminate conflicts of interest and rectify the skewed practice of funding allocation.
3. Set a clear policy direction. Put professional experts at the helm and innovation at the center. Stay far away from micro- and nano-management, which many government leaders are particularly good at.

Let the fallen petals flow down the stream. The fisherman will then find his way to the land of bliss. May politics stay away from the universities, cure thy absence, and sanctify thy soul!

This is what Xun Zi (荀子) believes in, as stated in his "On Kings and Lords":

> *The main way is to rule the near but not the far, the bright but not the dark, and the one but not the two. If a lord can rule the near, the far will be governed. If he can rule the bright, the dark will be transformed. If he can rule one, all the hundred others will be set right. If he listens broadly, he will have more than enough time to manage things that require his attention. In this way, he will attain the highest state of governing. If he is able to rule the near but also wants to rule the far; able to rule the bright but also wants to rule the dark; able to rule one but also wants to rule the hundred, he is trying to do too much. The result of doing too much is the same as not doing enough. It is similar to putting up a straight rod and hoping to find a crooked shadow.*
>
> *If a lord is not able to rule the near and yet wants to rule the far; not able to see the bright and yet wants to detect the dark; not able to take care of one thing and yet wants to handle one*

hundred of them, he is acting against all reasons. It is similar to putting up a crooked rod and hoping to find a straight shadow. Therefore, a wise lord seizes upon the principle, while a muddle-headed lord seizes upon the details. When a lord seizes upon the principal, everything will be taken care of to the finest detail. When he seizes upon the details, everything will be overlooked. A ruler should pick one minister, announce one law and expound on one order. In this way, he will have everything covered and taken care of and see his state prosper. The minister should put a hundred officials in order and manage a hundred affairs so that he can decide on the officials' positions and titles, assess their contribution and determine what rewards they deserve. At the end of the year, he will report to the ruler their successes. Things that are done well will be affirmed, and things that were done poorly will be abandoned. Therefore, a ruler should be diligent in identifying the right people but be relaxed in using their talent.[1]

It is not a good idea to micro-manage and is radically wrong to nano-manage.

---

[1] Translated by Eddie Tam.

Epilogue: How Does a University Set the Trend?

As the place where knowledge is created, a university should set the trend for the rest to follow. Yet, in the eyes of the common people across the Strait, universities have deteriorated into a kind of degree-granting machine. For some students, a degree is all they hope to get from universities, but of course, the better known the university is, or the more degrees they get, the better. Many universities seem quite anxious about the function they are asked to perform and go out of their way to cooperate, giving those in power another way of controlling the universities. They know that the resources for teaching and research are in the hands of the government, which can arbitrarily impose rules on them as it pleases.

Besides, when people in Taiwan, Hong Kong and the Mainland regard concurrent appointments in industry, the government and academia as a badge of honor, it is only natural that there is a considerable amount of mutual backscratching among those in these three domains. Students copy adults and soon learn to follow the smell of power and money. Isn't this how many student movements start? As matters deteriorate, the media, politicians, and outsiders from commercial circles get drawn in. They pick on universities for the most trivial reasons to gain something for themselves.

Whether they are democratic or not, or what type of democracy they may be practicing, the three governments in Taiwan, Hong Kong and the Mainland all come from the same breed. Accustomed to their high position, they look for opportunities to consolidate their power, setting up policies that demand universities to serve the government. Looking at it positively, one can say that the universities do their best to endow their degrees with value. They set down requirements for their students so that they learn skills that will enable them to find an ideal job or develop a career. Universities with a conscience even encourage research and systematically nurture their students. Unfortunately, most universities are at the beck and call of governments and are ready to bend to populist demands. They are incapable of operating independently and carrying out any forward-looking plans. They play no instrumental social function; the most they can hope to do is to make some level of delta difference.

To set the trend for society, a university has to be open-minded. It should embark on a journey of free exploration and independent operation. Teaching and research need to be integrated, as politics and education should be kept apart. Do not allow academic credentials to be commodified or swept away by the currents and bow to politics.

If universities cannot set the trend, who can?

Tu Youyou – a Breath of Fresh Air

If not for the Lasker Award that she won for her work in clinical medicine in 2011, I fear that very few people would know about To Youyou. In 2015, she won another recognition for her work, a Nobel Prize in Medicine. Yet substantive discussion about her is still a rarity. There is formulaic praise, just as there are many who remain unconvinced by her contributions and wonder why it is so easy to win awards these days. They must be asking: What is all the fuss about?

The news of the Nobel Prize came like a bolt of lightning, clearing the air in the higher education circles in the Mainland and even Hong Kong and Taiwan, dispelling the ostentatious behavior and shallowness that pervades society. The spiritual meaning of her accomplishment is much more significant than the historical record she set when she became the first Chinese Mainlander to be awarded a Nobel Prize in the sciences. The magnitude of her contributions, along with her lack of recognition across the Strait, the absence of boastfulness and the heavy Chinese flavor in her work, form such an incongruent picture that accords with the spirit behind this book.

It came to me as a big surprise that the universities across the Strait had not heard anything about her, let alone her work. Some still hold on to the outdated belief that quinine extracted from the bark of the chinchona is the best cure for malaria and that malaria has already been wiped from the surface of the world, and so is not worth looking into. Little do they know that since the 1950s, the malaria parasite has gotten drug resistant. The drug synthesized in imitation of the structure of quinine has been rendered ineffective, causing approximately a million deaths per year. Thanks to To Youyou, a new way of curing the disease has been found, saving thousands and thousands of lives.

People would not have been surprised and can understand my point if they had taken the time to read the poem "Song To the Daoist Master Liu of White Dragon Cave" written by Zhang Boduan (張伯端) during the Song dynasty:

> Those who want fish should better weave a net first
> Than exclaiming in vain, standing near the pond.
> I heard you have known medicine for years.
> Why don't you try your hand in alchemy?
> Keep the candles from being blown out by the wind,
> Complain not about the cycles of life.
> Lately the world is filled with fraud,
> With many commoners claiming great knowledge.
> But when asked what the five elements are
> All become tongue-tied as if they were mute.
> In addition to breathing and fasting,
> There are many other ways.
> Haven't we all heard in classic literature
> the ultimate Yang of Dao is the best?
> Blame not how frivolous and absurd preaching
> blinds and perplexes our contemporaries.
> As you and I share the same insight,
> I venture to open my heart to you.[1]

Tu Youyou is like a true Daoist sage, there to transport common souls like us to a nobler world. When soulware is absent, higher education across the Strait will have to wait for a transporter like Tu Youyou.

If we bring quality benchmarks and evaluation into full play to cultivate soulware, universities will hopefully become a necessity rather than an ornament for academics.

After all, which is more important: delicious cooking or a chef's license?

Why do many people value credentials more than learning? To put it differently, what should universities do to practice the ideal of integrating teaching and research and realize the goal of providing our students with the highest marginal effect of learning? What should a university do to not to have to regret when individuals rise to prominence without the help of a university degree, which can be seen as unwitting contempt for the existence of universities?

Taking a step further, what is the point of transmitting knowledge and techniques without imparting the right ideals? Nowadays, young people stay informed via mobile phones. How are we going to distinguish a university education from what they learn from their phones and computers?

---

[1] Translated by Longgen Chen.

A Philosophy of One's Own

At the mention of philosophy and sages, I think of Confucius, Mencius and the pre-Qin philosophers from China. From the West, I think of Socrates (470–399 B.C.E.), Plato (427–347 B.C.E.) and Aristotle (384–322 B.C.E.), the forefathers of western political philosophy; Rene Descartes (1596–1650), who put doubt before faith, epitomizing his thinking in the phrase "I think. Therefore I am"; Voltaire (1694–1778), the father of French thought who critiqued Catholicism but admired Confucianism; and Jean-Jacques Rousseau (1712–1778), who discourses on democratic political philosophy.

Later, Immanuel Kant (1724–1804), at the vanguard of the idealism school, is regarded as one of the most influential thinkers after Socrates, Plato and Aristotle. On the other hand, Georg W. F. Hegel (1770–1831) is considered the representative thinker of objective idealism.

In the 19th century, Europe took the lead in philosophical inquiry. Important thinkers include Søren Kierkegaard (1813–1855), the existentialist, Arthur Schopenhauer (1788–1860), the pessimist, Friedrich Nietzsche (1844–1900), the metaphysicist, and Karl Marx (1818–1883) and Friedrich Engels (1820–1895), best known for their views on historical materialism, dialectics as well as their critique of capitalism, as encapsulated by the term Marxism.

Stepping into the 20th century, Edmund Husserl (1859–1938) broadened the field of philosophical inquiry with phenomenology, while the logician Bertrand Russell (1872–1970) exerted great influence on thinkers from China. By the middle of the 20th century, philosophy became an academic specialty, although post-modernist thinkers Martin Heidegger (1889–1976) and Michel Foucault (1926–1984) are barely worth mentioning. They have done little to broaden our thinking.

It is said that "time" serves to embellish the writing of literary giants. The Tang dynasty poet Li Bai's lines, "People of our times have never set eyes on the moon from yesteryear, but the moon of today has shone on our forefathers," are an ingenious way of capturing the mystery of time. Similarly, the military leader Yue Fei from the Song dynasty wrote, "The flowers will come to blossom at another time, but our youth, once passed, will never come again." The poet Tao Yuanming from the Jin dynasty writes in his Miscellaneous Poems, "Without roots/ We drift like dust on the road/…We'd better depart on time/ As the Sun and Moon never cease their motion." These lines suggest that mortal beings don't have command over themselves because they are dominated and constrained by time and space.

Time is an important theme in philosophy and science. Time enchants philosophers. Confucius sighed over its passage, and the *Shizi* text written during the Warring States period defined the universe as encompassing a spatial and temporal dimension that envelops us. The *Shizi* is considered the first to propose a philosophical view that integrates time and space. China, as it turned out, was imprisoned in the frame of time for several thousand years.

Buddhist saints seek emancipation from time and space so that they can mentally visit the Pure Land, or Dharmadhatu, without any restrictions. Time flies; ten years pass like a split second as they spend time cultivating themselves in mountain caves. Yet their mind is pure, and their will is constant, attached to nothing.

Modern philosophers hold two different views of time. Isaac Newton (1642–1727) believed that time is the basic structure of the universe, a dimension that follows a set sequence. Other philosophers, including Kant, thought that time is a mental concept. Acting together with space and mathematics, time allows people to order and compare events.

The mathematician Hermann Minkowski (1864–1909) expounded on his understanding of time as the fourth dimension outside space, a concept known as Minkowski space. The concept of time and space propounded in the *Shizi* is a purely abstract concept of the cosmos, finally finding verification with Einstein, who understood the relativity of time and space. James Maxwell (1831–1879), of the same period as Minkowski, formulated laws of electromagnetism, Werner Karl Heisenberg (1901–1976) devised the uncertainty principle, and Max Planck (1858–1947) proposed the study of quantum mechanics. The philosophical expositions that they and other mathematicians offered exercised incomparable influence. Their epoch-making contributions far outweigh the philosophers outside of the likes of Marx and Newton.

Yet there is a blank in the philosophical circles for nearly a century afterward. The world of thought has grown lifeless.

Owl and Phoenix

Logically, the more one studies, the richer one's thinking should be. The more educated people there are, the more diverse the world of thought and the more vibrant the exchanges should be. But as we peer back into history, periods characterized by a proliferation of thinkers and a blossoming of thought were not peaceful; they were chaotic. Consider the Spring and Autumn and the Warring States periods in China or World War I and World War II in the 20th century when the interference of politics was absent.

Many thinkers are not all that well educated. Where do they acquire the knowledge that fuels their thinking? After careful consideration of the details, it would seem that only when politics is kept from interfering with the pursuit of learning can we hope to see the blossoming of different schools of thought.

Strictly speaking, while education has become widespread across the Strait, it is by no means developed. Many have earned an academic degree, but few are truly learned. Those who can formulate a school of thought of their own are nowhere to be found. Democracy is cheapened when authoritarianism goes unchallenged. Heresies dominate, and universities go mute when outsiders and governments intrude into campuses. Politics continues to meddle with universities. Some may agree privately on the need to separate politics and education, but no one dares to acknowledge their opinions publicly. After all, if Mainland China is not a gentleman, Taiwan is phony.

Universities should set the trend and not be led by politics. It should not follow the vulgar or be led by politicians. Otherwise, how can we hope to see the birth of great thinkers and philosophers? Hegel, Schopenhauer, Marx, Engels, Planck and Einstein all came from Humboldt University before the Soviet forces occupied East Germany in 1949. Ever since that, apart from taking an occasional walk down memory lane, Humboldt University has made little contribution whatsoever.

The myriad dharmas are created from our minds (souls) alone. In the "Autumn Waters" by Zhuang Zi, "An owl that had captured a half-rotten rat let out a screech when a *fenghuang*, an immortal bird in ancient Chinese culture, flew by overhead." The owl feared that the *fenghuang*, akin to a phoenix in Western culture, might steal its meal. The analogy suggests some people consider "half-rotten rats to be gourmet food and worry unnecessarily that others might fight even over something putrid" as expressed in a poem by Li Shangyin in the late Tang dynasty. Western democracy has shown signs of cracks in the 21st century. The half-baked Taiwanese style of democracy is teetering on its feet. Then there are those in power behaving dictatorially like the communists. Yet the communist society in the Mainland is continually revising itself toward capitalism, with money and profit-making being the single target for some in power.

Too often, there is a lack of integrated teaching and research and seldom a distinct separation of politics and education. Many such owls exist today, and too few Chinese phoenixes across the Taiwan Strait. When will universities shake off the shackles and start acting as a midwife for the birth of beneficial ways of thinking about the world?

References to Tables and Figures

1. Table 0.1: Students from Mainland China studying in the U.S. during 2009–2020
   https://opendoorsdata.org/fact_sheets/china *The Open Doors Report on International Educational Exchange is a comprehensive information resource on international students in the US and US students studying abroad. It is sponsored by the U.S. Department of State with funding provided by the U.S. Government and is published by IIE. For more information, visit www.opendoorsdata.org*
2. Figure 3.1: University enrollment rate in the US, Mainland China, Japan, Singapore, South Korea, Taiwan and Hong Kong
   Hong Kong: University Grants Committee https://cdcf.ugc.edu.hk/cdcf/statEntry.action?lang=EN *(First Year Student Intakes (headcount))*. Prior to 2012, a 13-year primary and secondary school system was adopted in Hong Kong and it was difficult to record the university enrollment rate.
   Education Bureau https://www.edb.gov.hk/attachment/en/about-edb/publications-stat/figures/Enrol_2020.pdf (no. of high school students = S6+S7+repeaters);
   Mainland China: Ministry of Education https://www.statista.com/statistics/1113954/china-tertiary-education-college-university-enrollment-rate/;
   US: National Center for Education Statistics https://nces.ed.gov/programs/digest/d20/tables/dt20_302.10.asp *(% of recent high school completers enrolled in 4-yr university or college)*;
   Singapore: Statistics Singapore https://tablebuilder.singstat.gov.sg/table/TS/M850261 *(no. of secondary students)*; https://www.statista.com/statistics/624429/enrollment-in-universities-in-singapore/

(Full-time Enrollment in Universities in Singapore 2012-2021)
Japan: Ministry of Education, Culture, Sports, Science and Technology https://www.statista.com/statistics/1198580/japan-higher-education-enrollment-rate-by-gender/
South Korea: Statistics Korea; Korean Educational Development Institute: https://www.statista.com/statistics/629032/south-korea-university-enrollment-rate/
Taiwan: Ministry of Education https://stats.moe.gov.tw/files/important/OVERVIEW_U10.pdf
Data before 2010 are unavailable for most of the selected countries.

3. Figure 3.2: Number of newborn babies in Taiwan, Hong Kong and Mainland China (1950 to 2021)
   United Nations – World Population Prospects (https://population.un.org/wpp/)

4. Figure 3.3: Birth rates in Taiwan, Hong Kong and Mainland China (1950 to 2021)
   United Nations – World Population Prospects (https://population.un.org/wpp/)

5. Table 17.1: Annual fatalities in Taiwan, Hong Kong, Mainland China and the US over the indicated years
   Nuclear accidents
   　Sovacool, B. K. (2010). A Critical Evaluation of Nuclear Power and Renewable Electricity in Asia. Journal of Contemporary Asia. 40(3). 369-400.
   　https://www.tandfonline.com/doi/full/10.1080/00472331003798350
   Earthquakes
   　https://zh.m.wikipedia.org/zh-hk/%E8%87%BA%E7%81%A3%E5%9C%B0%E9%9C%87%E5%88%97%E8%A1%A8
   　https://zh.wikipedia.org/zh-mo/%E4%B8%AD%E5%9C%8B%E5%A4%A7%E9%99%B8%E5%9C%B0%E9%9C%87%E5%88%97%E8%A1%A8
   　https://en.wikipedia.org/wiki/List_of_disasters_in_the_United_States_by_death_toll
   　https://scweb.cwb.gov.tw/zh-tw/page/disaster/6
   　https://www.emdat.be/database
   　https://data.earthquake.cn/datashare/report.shtml?PAGEID=disastershow

REFERENCES TO TABLES AND FIGURES   379

   Auto accidents
      https://roadsafety.tw/Dashboard/Custom?type=%E7%B5%B1%E8%A8%88%E5%BF%AB%E8%A6%BD%E5%9C%96%E8%A1%A8#dash_item_1876
      https://www.td.gov.hk/tc/road_safety/road_traffic_accident_statistics/accident_trend_since_1953/index.html
      https://www.statista.com/statistics/276260/number-of-fatalities-in-traffic-accidents-in-china/
      https://www.chyxx.com/industry/202202/996611.html
      https://en.wikipedia.org/wiki/Motor_vehicle_fatality_rate_in_U.S._by_year
      https://crashstats.nhtsa.dot.gov/#!/PublicationList/38
   COVID-19
      https://covid19.who.int/WHO-COVID-19-global-data.csv
      https://chp-dashboard.geodata.gov.hk/covid-19/zh.html
      https://nidss.cdc.gov.tw/nndss/deadmap?id=19CoV&type=3
      http://www.nhc.gov.cn/xcs/yqtb/202209/16883ba1a5004ad994d10eab1cd2555e.shtml
   Lung cancer
      https://www.stat.gov.tw/lp.asp?CtNode=1829&CtUnit=690&BaseDSD=7&xq_xCat=05
      https://dep.mohw.gov.tw/DOS/lp-5069-113.html
      https://www3.ha.org.hk/cancereg/topten.html
      https://www.censtatd.gov.hk/en/EIndexbySubject.html?pcode=FA100094&scode=160
      https://www.hk01.com/article/294399?utm_source=01articlecopy&utm_medium=referral
      https://www.sciencedirect.com/science/article/pii/S2667005422000047
      https://gco.iarc.fr/today/data/factsheets/populations/160-china-fact-sheets.pdf
      https://gis.cdc.gov/Cancer/USCS/#/Trends/
      https://www.cdc.gov/cancer/dcpc/research/update-on-cancer-deaths/index.htm
6. Figure 20.1: Percentage of starting salary of university graduates to GDP per capita
   Mainland China: MyCOS Human Resources Surveys https://www.statista.com/statistics/252912/monthly-salary-of-university-graduates-in-china/

Hong Kong: University Grants Committee https://data.gov.hk/en-data/dataset/hk-ugc-ugc-average-annual-salaries-graduates

Taiwan: International Monetary Fund (IMF) https://www.statista.com/statistics/727592/gross-domestic-product-gdp-per-capita-in-taiwan/

(2008-2016) https://kknews.cc/zh-hk/education/q25gm3y.html

(2017-2019) https://yoursalary.taiwanjobs.gov.tw/Salary/SalaryHome#

Singapore: Ministry of Manpower https://www.statista.com/statistics/975552/median-monthly-starting-salary-local-university-graduates-singapore/

    (2020 data) https://blog.seedly.sg/graduate-starting-salary-nus-ntu-smu-sutd-sit/#nus

Japan: Ministry of Health, Labour and Welfare "Wage Structure Basic Statistics Survey Results" https://www.mhlw.go.jp/toukei/itiran/roudou/chingin/kouzou/19/index.html

US: National Center for Education Statistics

    (2010 & 2011) https://www.forbes.com/sites/jennagoudreau/2011/06/01/best-entry-level-jobs/?sh=6fb27e824942

    (2012) https://money.cnn.com/2013/01/10/pf/college/graduate-salaries/index.html

    (2013) https://directemployers.org/2013/04/25/salaries-climb-for-the-class-of-2013/

    (2014) https://www.naceweb.org/job-market/compensation/overall-starting-salary-for-class-of-2015-graduates-up-4-3-percent/

    (2015 & 2016) https://ecc.uic.edu/wp-content/uploads/sites/78/2017/10/nace-salary-survey-spring-2017.pdf

    (2016 & 2017) https://www.naceweb.org/job-market/compensation/class-of-2017s-overall-starting-salary-shows-little-gain/

    (2018 & 2019) https://www.naceweb.org/uploadedfiles/files/2021/publication/executive-summary/2021-nace-salary-survey-summer-executive-summary.pdf

    (2020) https://www.naceweb.org/job-market/compensation/average-salary-for-class-of-2019-up-almost-6-percent-over-class-of-2018s/

South Korea:
    South Korea Employers Federation, Towers Watson
    Data unavailable for most years

References to Tables and Figures 381

GDP per capita for all countries: https://data.worldbank.org/indicator/NY.GDP.PCAP.CD

7. Figure 20.2: Percentage of the typical annual salary of assistant professors to GDP per capita

GDP per capita of all countries: International Monetary Fund, World Economic Outlook Database, April 2021
https://www.imf.org/en/Publications/WEO/weo-database/2021/April/weo-report?c=512,914,612,614,311,213, 911,314,193,122,912,313,419,513,316,913,124,339,63 8,514,218,963,616,223,516,918,748,618,624,522,622,1 56,626,628,228,924,233,632,636,634,238,662,960,423, 935,128,611,321,243,248,469,253,642,643,939,734,64 4,819,172,132,646,648,915,134,652,174,328,258,656,6 54,336,263,268,532,944,176,534,536,429,433,178,436, 136,343,158,439,916,664,826,542,967,443,917,544,941, 446,666,668,672,946,137,546,674,676,548,556,678,181, 867,682,684,273,868,921,948,943,686,688,518,728,83 6,558,138,196,278,692,694,962,142,449,564,565,283,8 53,288,293,566,964,182,359,453,968,922,714,862,135, 716,456,722,942,718,724,576,936,961,813,726,199,73 3,184,524,361,362,364,732,366,144,146,463,528,923,7 38,578,537,742,866,369,744,186,925,869,746,926,466, 112,111,298,927,846,299,582,487,474,754,698,&s=NGDP-DPC,&sy=1993&ey=2023&ssm=0&scsm=1&scc=0&ssd=1&ssc=0&sic=0&sort=country&ds=.&br=1

Salary of assistant professors:

https://www.glassdoor.com.hk/Salaries/us-assistant-professor-salary-SRCH_IL.0,2_IN1_KO3,22.htm?clickSource=searchBtn

https://www.glassdoor.com.hk/Salaries/japan-assistant-professor-salary-SRCH_IL.0,5_IN123_KO6,25.htm?clickSource=searchBtn

https://www.glassdoor.com.hk/Salaries/singapore-assistant-professor-salary-SRCH_IL.0,9_IM1123_KO10,29.htm?clickSource=searchBtn

https://www.glassdoor.com.hk/Salaries/taiwan-assistant-professor-salary-SRCH_IL.0,6_IN240_KO7,26.htm?clickSource=searchBtn

https://www.glassdoor.com.hk/Salaries/uk-assistant-professor-salary-SRCH_IL.0,2_IN2_KO3,22.htm?clickSource=searchBtn

382 REFERENCES TO TABLES AND FIGURES

> https://www.glassdoor.com.hk/Salaries/china-assistant-professor-salary-SRCH_IL.0,5_IN48_KO6,25.htm?clickSource=searchBtn
> https://www.salaryexpert.com/salary/job/assistant-professor/china (second source for China)
> https://www.glassdoor.com.hk/Salaries/hong-kong-assistant-professor-salary-SRCH_IL.0,9_IN106_KO10,29.htm?clickSource=searchBtn
> https://www.glassdoor.com.hk/Salaries/south-korea-assistant-professor-salary-SRCH_IL.0,11_IN135_KO12,31.htm?clickSource=searchBtn

8. Figure 20.3: Percentage of student tuition to GDP per capita
GDP per capita of all countries: International Monetary Fund, World Economic Outlook Database, April 2021
https://www.imf.org/en/Publications/WEO/weo-database/2021/April/weo-report?c=512,914,612,614,311,213,911,314,193,122,912,313,419,513,316,913,124,339,638,514,218,963,616,223,516,918,748,618,624,522,622,156,626,628,228,924,233,632,636,634,238,662,960,423,935,128,611,321,243,248,469,253,642,643,939,734,644,819,172,132,646,648,915,134,652,174,328,258,656,654,336,263,268,532,944,176,534,536,429,433,178,436,136,343,158,439,916,664,826,542,967,443,917,544,941,446,666,668,672,946,137,546,674,676,548,556,678,181,867,682,684,273,868,921,948,943,686,688,518,728,836,558,138,196,278,692,694,962,142,449,564,565,283,853,288,293,566,964,182,359,453,968,922,714,862,135,716,456,722,942,718,724,576,936,961,813,726,199,733,184,524,361,362,364,732,366,144,146,463,528,923,738,578,537,742,866,369,744,186,925,869,746,926,466,112,111,298,927,846,299,582,487,474,754,698,&s=NGDPDPC,&sy=1993&ey=2023&ssm=0&scsm=1&scc=0&ssd=1&ssc=0&sic=0&sort=country&ds=.&br=1
US: https://www.usnews.com/education/best-colleges/paying-for-college/articles/paying-for-college-infographic
Japan: https://www.studyinjapan.go.jp/en/planning/academic-fees
Singapore: Public https://smartwealth.sg/cost-of-university-fees-singapore
> Private https://www.income.com.sg/blog/cost-of-university-in-singapore
Taiwan: Public https://ntuinfo.ntu.edu.tw/pdf/fee_ba109.pdf

References to Tables and Figures 383

   Private https://enroll.kmu.edu.tw/tuition-fee
   United Kingdom: https://www.topuniversities.com/student-info/student-finance/how-much-does-it-cost-study-uk
   Mainland China: Public https://www.sohu.com/a/322304703_120023972
   International: (Average from the following 6 data sources)
      https://www.xjtlu.edu.cn/en/admissions/domestic/fees-and-scholarships
      https://wku.edu.cn/en/admissions/international-students-admission
      https://www.sicas.cn/School/98/Contents/110828103710360.shtml
      https://m.cucas.cn/fees?sid=1299
      https://www.nottingham.edu.cn/en/study-with-us/undergraduate/tuition-fees-and-finance.aspx
      https://shanghai.nyu.edu/undergraduate-admissions/cost-and-financial-aid/cost-of-attendance
   Hong Kong: University Grants Committee ($42,100), Private Hang Seng University of Hong Kong (both local and non-local)
   South Korea: https://studylink.com/countries/south-korea
9. Table 20.1: Comparison of Four Asian Tigers
   https://zh.wikipedia.org/zh-tw/%E4%BA%9A%E6%B4%B2%E5%9B%9B%E5%B0%8F%E9%BE%99
10. Figure V.1: R&D investment in the US, Mainland China, Taiwan, Hong Kong, Singapore, South Korea and Japan
    Before 2000, World Bank: https://data.worldbank.org/indicator/GB.XPD.RSDV.GD.ZS?end=2018&start=1996&view=chart
    From 2000, OECD: https://data.oecd.org/rd/gross-domestic-spending-on-r-d.htm
    Hong Kong: Census and Statistics Department https://www.statista.com/statistics/632546/hong-kong-research-development-expenditure-ratio-to-gdp/
    Countries and regions other than Taiwan: https://data.worldbank.org/indicator/GB.XPD.RSDV.GD.ZS?locations=HK-SG-KR-CN-DE-US-IL-DK-SE-CH
    Taiwan: (2009-2014) http://www.chinatimes.com/cn/newspapers/20160216000054-260202
       (2015) http://www.epochtimes.com/gb/17/3/15/n8926759.htm

(2016) https://udn.com/news/ story/7238/2813191
11. Table 24.1: Number of US utility patents granted to universities in the US, the UK, Mainland China, Japan, Singapore, South Korea, Hong Kong and Taiwan
PatentsView (https://patentsview.org), *a platform from the Office of the Chief Economist at USPTO* (https://patentsview.org/what-is-patentsview)
12. Table 25.1: Academic background of CEOs in the US, Mainland China, Hong Kong and Taiwan
US: List of Fortune 500 https://fortune.com/fortune500/2021/search
Mainland China: https://www.fortunechina.com/fortune500/c/2021-07/20/content_392708.htm
Hong Kong: (https://www.top100hk.com/result/2019-%e7%b6%9c%e5%90%88%e5%af%a6%e5%8a%9b100%e5%bc%b7/)
Taiwan: https://zh.wikipedia.org/zh-hk/%E8%87%BA%E7%81%A350%E6%8C%87%E6%95%B8

Appendix: Basic Principle of Academic Governance

While the University remains committed to engaging with the society, since 2008 it has consistently argued for the separation of politics and education to ensure that CityU's academic mission can be fully achieved to become a leading global university.

External parties should not interfere with or disrupt the academic governance of a university, and asserting political neutrality ensures we maintain academic freedom and campus autonomy. Students, faculty, staff and alumni should not use CityU for the promotion of personal political viewpoints or individual agendas outside our core missions of teaching, research and knowledge transfer. To consolidate our global excellence in research and professional education, we will sustain a teaching and research environment in which the principles of neutrality and autonomy are strictly observed. We support, on a law-abiding basis, rational discussion and we accommodate a range of views in the spirit of mutual respect and collegiality. Academic freedom and campus autonomy stand among our core values and must be respected.

The separation of politics and education is fundamental to academic freedom and campus autonomy.

About the Author

Way Kuo, President Emeritus and Senior Fellow at the Hong Kong Institute for Advanced Study, was President and University Distinguished Professor at CityU from 2008 to 2023. During his tenure, CityU was recognized as one of the most progressive universities in the world.

The President of France and the President of Italy bestowed on him the title and rank of the Chevalier de l'Ordre National de la Legion d' Honneur de France and the Cavaliere dell'Ordine della Stella d'Italia in 2019 and 2021, respectively. In 2021, he was elected International Fellow of the Canadian Academy of Engineering because "he strongly advocates campus autonomy and academic freedom" and "combines an unflagging dedication to academia and professional service to the international community."

He is a member of the US National Academy of Engineering, Academia Sinica in Taiwan, and a foreign member of the Chinese Academy of Engineering in recognition of his contributions to systems reliability.

Eight academic books co-authored by him are considered classics, and some for establishing standards for electronics reliability. In addition, following the 2011 earthquakes in Japan, he was the first invited foreign expert to assess the safety of the First Nuclear Power Plant in Fukushima. His popular science book *Critical Reflections on Nuclear and Renewable Energy* was published in Chinese and English in 2013 and 2014, respectively, and translated into Japanese, French and Russian.

He was a member of the senior management team at Oak Ridge National Laboratory, and University Distinguished Professor and Dean of Engineering at the University of Tennessee. He held the endowed Wisenbaker Chair of Engineering in Innovation and was Head of the Department of Industrial Engineering at Texas A&M University. Before launching academic career, he worked at Bell Laboratories.

Index

1,000 *li* horses, x
2023 Hong Kong Diploma of Secondary Education (HKDSE), 29
2030 Agenda for Sustainable Development, xxxiii
22K phenomenon, 282-283
360-degree evaluation of institutions, 252

A farmer's advice, 159
A third type of error, 57
Absence of soulware,
　entanglement of industry, government and university, 185
　failure to understand the contemporary mission for a university, 186
　misplaced mindset, 186-187
Academic,
　ethics, 28, 195, 197-199, 228
　freedom, definition, 194-195
　freedom, vi, xii, xvi, xxxvii-xxxviii, 14, 35, 47, 110, 169, 171-175, 183, 189-190, 193-195, 197-199, 201-203, 205-209, 221, 225, 242, 246, 309, 330, 385, 387
　governance, vi, xvi, 36, 169, 207, 242, 385
Accountability, xii, xvi, xxxvii, 5, 11, 13, 180-181, 221, 252, 256, 258, 355
Accreditation(s), 114, 143, 145, 258, 260-261, 297

AI (artificial intelligence), 25, 105, 208, 295-296, 358, 366
Amalgamation and reorganization of universities (in France), 46
Andrew Wakefield, 198
Anonymous,
　allegations, 12-13
　letter, xxxvi, 12, 13, 167, 202
Anthony Fauci, 248-249
Apartheid (in South Africa), 47, 224, 229
Arden L. Bement, 357
ARWU (Academic Ranking of World Universities), 262-264, 266, 276-277, 291, 344-345
Associate degree (programs), 40, 299-300
Autonomy,
　campus, xii, xvi, xxviii, 14, 49, 169, 171-174, 181-182, 189, 193, 199-200, 202, 208, 238, 241, 330, 385, 387
　university, 25, 174, 197, 200
　academic, xv, 21, 28, 279, 365

Baguwen (or 8-legged essay), 93
Bai Juyi (白居易), 121
Baron de Montesquieu, 104
Barry Lam, 339, 342-343
Bayh-Dole Act, 114
Bell Laboratories, 387
Berkeley Free Speech Movement, 221
Bernard Shaw's Stephen, 123
Beyond Boundaries, xvii, xix, xxi, 179

Biden, 209
Biel Crystal, 91, 343
Bildung, xi, xiv, 132
Birth rate, xxi, 49-53, 63-67, 93, 378
Black powder, 104-105
Blind spot, v, 4, 12, 17, 69, 71, 73, 75, 77, 125, 128, 130, 132, 201-202, 247
  for adults, 130, 132
  for youths, 128, 132
Blindness of the soul, xxxiv, 3, 13, 198, 247-248
Bo Le (伯樂), x
Bob Woodward, 179
Boshi (博士), 137, 138-139
Botu (博土), 138
Brain drain, 71-73, 209, 343
Brain Korea 21, 330, 352
Branch campuses (international), 6-8
Brexit, 22
Bush, 206-207

C9 League, 33, 42, 216
Cai Yuanpei (蔡元培), 202, 215, 225, 255
Cantonese, 135
Cecil Rhodes, 224
Ch'ien Mu (錢穆), 142, 147
Charles Kao, 76, 91, 108, 340, 341-342, 346
ChatGPT, 295, 353
Chernobyl, 305
Chen Peizhe, 248
Changjiang Scholars, 209
Chief Executive of Hong Kong, 216, 241, 321
China Initiative, 208, 213
China Modernization Report 2015, 256
China Times, 195, 201, 249
China: An Analysis, 273
Chinese returnees from overseas, 209
Citations, 74, 76, 199, 265, 328
CityU-Learning (platform), 130, 354

Clarifying Some Myths of Teaching and Research, 87, 259, 269
Clear positioning, 119
Collège de France, xviii, 46, 146
Committee(s), xxxv, 11-12, 28, 59, 127, 181, 207, 240, 243-244, 248, 310, 313, 318, 339, 349, 377, 380, 383
Confucius, 2, 86, 95, 116, 124, 125, 131-133, 149, 154, 162, 186, 194, 347, 374-375
The Analects of Confucius, 100, 104
Cornerstone of creativity and innovation, 190
Coronavirus, 3-4, 63, 130, 212-213, 249, 320, 349, 354, 366
COVID-19 (pandemic), xvii, xix, xxix, xxxi, 3, 40, 43, 65, 80, 85, 130, 161, 210, 211, 213, 217, 236-237, 243, 246-247, 327, 340, 357, 379
COVID-19 Hate Crimes Act, 213
Creativity, vi, xiii, xvi, xxxiv, xl, 35, 74, 91, 104, 119, 156, 187-188, 190, 193, 200-201, 206, 264, 295, 311, 313-315, 317, 319-321, 323, 345-347, 349, 351-353, 355-357, 359, 361, 363, 365
Crouching Tiger, Hidden Dragon, 89, 345, 346
Cultural Revolution, xiii, 33, 41, 155, 201, 261

Daniel Choi, 340, 342
Dante Alighieri, 173
David Baltimore, 196
Data science, 9, 118, 144, 266
Deming's 14 points, 257
Disputes over teaching versus research universities, 107
Diversified college enrollment scheme, 30
Do the right things, 362
Do things right, 362
Double First Class (initiative or plan), 34, 37

INDEX   391

Drinkable book, 316
Dual emphasis on teaching and
    research, 116, 118
Dujiangyan irrigation system, 157
Dynamic zero-case, 3

Education efficiency, x
Education Reforms in Taiwan, 29,
    281
Elements of university composition,
    xi, xxi
Elite higher education, 19, 31
Emergency Response Unit, 242
Enrollment drop, xxix
Enrollment ratio(s) (or rate), xxi, 29,
    44-45, 52-53, 64, 377-378
Enrollment (student), xxix, 30, 42, 51,
    53, 60, 64, 97, 274, 276
Entanglement, xiv, xxxvi, xl, 36, 105,
    170, 183, 185, 189, 197, 224, 248,
    359
Equal poverty, 292
Ethnic groups in Taiwan, 51
Essence of learning, xl, 106
Evaluation of research, 259
Excellence of American higher
    education, 180

Father of success, vi, 255
Fetishize academic degrees, xiii
Fields medals, 307
Financial turmoil in the US, 2
Florence Nightingale, 305
Forbes, 62, 92, 339
Four Asian Tigers, xxii, 250, 264,
    290-291, 335, 358
Four major American initiatives for
    reinvigorating universities, 118
Four types of universities, 113, 116,
    120-121
Fourth nuclear power plant, 232, 334
Fragmentation of disciplines, 296
Frank Goodnow, 273
Free direct links, 335

Fukushima Daiichi Nuclear Power
    Plant, 62
Further and Higher Education Act, 20

GDP (Gross Domestic Product), xxi,
    25, 27, 98, 282-287, 290-291, 294,
    312, 323-326, 328, 379, 381, 382
Ge zhi (格致) (short for *ge wu zhi zhi*),
    xl, 106
Gene modification, 199
General education, xiv, xxv, 128, 131,
    141-146, 248, 289, 300, 308
General Scholastic Ability Test, 40
Generation(s) Y, 19, 342
Generation(s) Z, 19, 342
Genichi Taguchi, 77, 88
Genome editing, 199
Global COE, 352
Goodnow, 273-274, 280
Grandmasters, x, 14
Gregory Mankiw, 86
Greta Thunberg, 223
Guglielmo Marconi, 23
Gwangju Students Movement in 1929,
    223

H-factor (h-index factor), 76-77, 265
Hardware, x, xi, xxxix, 10-11, 14, 35,
    73-74, 101, 105, 117, 119, 166,
    180, 252, 277, 278, 318, 341
Haruko Obokata, 196
Harvard Business Review, 206
Hermit in Between, 121
Higher Education Funding Council for
    England, 22
*Higher Education: Students at the Heart
    of the System* (white paper), 21
Hiroshi Mikitani, 358
Hong Kong Coalition, 243
Hong Kong Form Six, 41
Hong Kong Institute for Advanced
    Study, iii, xix, 387
Hong Kong Special Administration
    Region (HKSAR), 29, 65, 162, 216

HKTech 300, 331, 346
Horizon 2020, 22
Huang Kuan, 39
Human resources, x, 36, 65, 67, 72, 120, 282, 329, 333, 358, 360, 362, 379
Humboldt brothers, 177-178

International atomic energy agency, 62
IEEE Transactions on Reliability, ix, xxv, 55, 77
Impact of pandemic on higher education, 210
Importance of discovery and innovation, 316
Impression score, 267, 270
Inbreeding, 14
Individualized production, 2
Industrial revolution, 2, 95, 106, 273, 355
Industry-university-research collaboration, xii, 5
Ingesting without digesting, 190
Innovation, vi, ix, xi-xiii, xvi, xxxiii-xxxiv, xxxvii, xl, 8, 10, 14, 22, 31-32, 34, 36, 48, 56, 59, 73-74, 77, 97, 101-102, 104-105, 108, 114, 116, 133, 135, 150, 169, 173, 176, 183, 185, 188, 190, 193, 201, 203, 205, 209, 237, 238, 242, 253, 256-257, 264, 274, 277-278, 296, 297, 303, 306, 307, 309, 311-316, 320, 323, 324, 326-335, 339-340, 346-347, 352, 355-363, 365-366, 368-369, 387
Innovation zones in the US, 331
Integrating industry, academia and research, 331
Integrating industry, education and research, xii
Integration of politics and education, 171

Integration of religion and education, 171, 176
Integration of religion and the state, 171
Integration of teaching and research (教研合一), v, xv-xvii, xix, xxxvi, 28, 35, 101, 114, 116-117, 119, 176-178, 180, 248, 252, 330, 353
Integration of the church and the state (宗統合一), 170, 176
Intellectual Property, 194, 208, 332-333
Internationalization, v, x-xi, xv-xvi, xxxiv-xxxvi, xl, 1-5, 7, 9-11, 13-15, 17, 53, 58, 70, 72, 75, 77, 80, 82-83, 87, 93-97, 102, 160, 173, 189, 202, 216, 359-360
Internationalization of higher education, v, xvi, xxxiv-xxxvi, 1-2, 5, 9, 13, 70, 72, 173
Ioannidis, 265, 266
IT, 325, 329, 339-340, 352-353, 358

Japan, xiii, xvi, xxi-xxiv, xxxiii, 4, 6, 29, 32, 34, 44-45, 48, 52, 64, 86, 96, 106, 113, 134, 136, 173, 177, 196, 216, 223, 225, 229, 235, 246, 250, 256-257, 262-263, 266, 273, 277, 283, 285-287, 297-298, 306-308, 312, 323-324, 329-331, 333, 342, 358, 366, 377-378, 380-384, 387
Japanese occupation, 29, 32, 42, 223
John Henry Newman, 107
John Locke, 104
Joint College Entrance Examination, 30, 269
Joseph Needham, 105

Kai Lai Chung, 90
Kai-fu Lee, 339, 342
Kalven Report, 172, 190
Ke Qihua, 89
Khan Academy, 352
Kin-man Yeung, 343

Knowledge transfer, xxxix, 313-314, 385
Kominka policy, 32
Korean Wave, 325

Land-grant university, 115, 118, 274
Lao zi (老子), 147
Lewis M. Branscomb, 368
Li Bai (李白), 88, 145, 306, 374
Liberal arts, vi, 19, 104, 114-115, 118, 120, 141-143, 145, 150, 239, 265, 273-274, 277, 279-280, 287, 298
Liu yuxi (劉禹錫), 176, 237, 304
Localization policy, 52
Low base-load power supply, 334
Low birth rate, 51, 63-67, 93
Low tuition (policy), 21, 37-39, 285
Lusheng, 41

Macau (Macao), xxiv, xxxii, 3, 6, 27, 32, 165, 272, 300
Malala Yousafzai, 223
Marconi, 23
Marine Corps, 78, 228
McDonald's, 67, 90, 245, 320
Mandarin, 5, 41, 84, 86, 91, 93, 339
Mark S. Wrighton, xviii, 179
Mass customization, 2
Mass higher education, 19
May 4 massacre, 222
May fourth movement, 14, 225-226
Medical conscience, 249
Meiji restoration, 32, 48, 256, 273
Michael M. Crow's three governance factors, 181, 183
Michael Sandel, 86
Michael Yang, 348-349
Micro-management, xxxv, xxxix, 119, 251, 370
Mindset (of higher education), xxxvii, 10, 11, 167, 191, 369
Ming Pao, xxiv, 90

Minkowski space, 375
Modeling and simulations, 62
MOOC(s), 143, 353-354
Morningside Park Protest, 221

Nano-management, vi, 251, 365, 369-370
National Academy, xxxii, 316, 387
National Research Council, 257
National Science Foundation, 109, 277, 357, 366-367
National Security Law (National Security Act), 214, 244
NEETs, 38, 282
Neidisheng, 41
New Culture Movement, 225
New York Times, xxv, 179, 353
Nicolaus Copernicus, 173
Night of Broken Glass, 177
NIST, 357, 368
Nobel Prize, 23, 32, 46-47, 76-77, 91, 108, 110, 139, 141, 146, 154, 157, 164, 179-180, 256, 279, 303-304, 307, 330, 340-341, 372
Nuclear Power Plant, 62, 232-233, 235, 247, 305, 307, 334, 387

Obama, 134, 207, 318
Occupy Wall Street, 222
Office for Students and UK Research and Innovation, 22
On Kings and Lords, 369
One Health, xxi, 110, 161, 241, 320-321
Open letter (calling for Sino-American cooperation), 211
Open Letter to the People of the United States From 100 Chinese Scholar, 212
Outline Development Plan for the Guangdong-Hong Kong-Macao Greater Bay Area, 6

Pearl river delta, 7
Peer-reviewed (academic) papers, 74, 261, 365
Personalized development, 2
Plate glass universities, 20
Populism, vi, x, xxxv, 56, 66, 69, 106, 174, 197, 219, 231-233, 235-237, 239-241, 243, 245-247, 249-250, 256, 288, 290, 361
Populist policy, 232
Power outage(s), 233-235, 320, 334
President's Lecture Series: Excellence in Academia, 110
Professionalism, 13, 133-135, 152, 167, 186-187, 190, 233, 256, 270
Professional,
  accreditation, 114, 258, 261
  education, xiv, 114, 144, 303, 357, 385
Project 985, 33, 37, 344
Pui Ching Middle School, xviii, 91

QS Global University Graduate Employability Rankings, 262, 264
QS World University Rankings, 20, 46, 47, 262, 276
Quality assurance, xxviii, xxxviii-xxxix, 10, 14, 53, 88, 251, 257-258, 262, 360
Quality is the prerequisite for innovation, 311

Rainbow energies, 234
Red Scare, 206, 209
Research Assessment Exercise (RAE), 187
Research universities, xxxvi, 77, 107, 109, 113, 116-117
Restrictions on higher education, 119
Rhodes Must Fall campaign, 224
Richard Florida, 206
Ridhima Pandey, 223
Robbins Report, 20

Robert M. Hutchins, 206
Robert M. Rosenzweig, 117
Ron Miller, 124
Rong Hong, 39
Roosevelt, xxix-xxxii

Salman Khan, 352
Sand clock, 317
SAT, 274-275
Science and technology policies, 324, 365, 368
Secularism, 171
Segregation of teaching and research, xxxvii
Self-driving cars, 316
Separation of church and state (宗統分割), 170-171
Separation of politics and education (政教分離), v-vi, xi-xii, xv-xvii, xix, xxxvii-xxxviii, 169-170, 172-174, 176, 178, 180-189, 193, 199, 202, 205, 215-216, 225, 241-242, 244, 252, 330, 376, 385
Separation of powers, 104, 126
Separation of teaching and research, xxxv
Social sciences, 29, 35, 87, 104, 109, 118, 146, 150, 239, 274, 276-279, 365
Thesis-gate Scandal, 179, 246
Shimonoseki Treaty (Treaty of Shimonoseki), 29, 32
Shizi, 375
Simplicity, v, 26, 55-57
Singapore, xviii, xxi-xxii, 3, 8, 37, 44-45, 52, 133, 154, 216, 262-264, 266, 270, 283-286, 289-291, 312, 323, 325-326, 329-331, 335-336, 342, 358, 360, 377-378, 380-384
Sister Xi, 135-136
Six Arts, 79, 124, 131
Social Movement(s), vi, 98, 143-144, 174, 219-220, 226-227, 232, 244

Song to a Crude Hut, 304-305
Soulware of higher education, xxxiv, 10, 364
Soulware of internationalization, xl
Soulware, x-xii, xiv-xvi, xix, xxxiv, xxxix, 10-12, 14, 17, 167, 180-181, 183, 185, 190, 196, 198, 201, 252-254, 264, 278
South China Morning Post, xxiv, 9, 194
South Korea, xiii, xxi, xxii-xxxiii, 4, 15, 31, 37, 44-45, 52, 64, 66, 78, 85, 89, 95, 96-97, 134, 196, 216, 223-224, 227, 229, 262-264, 266, 283-287, 289-291, 312-313, 323-327, 329-333, 335-336, 340, 342, 352, 358, 360, 363, 377-378, 380, 382-384
Specialist versus (and) generalist, v, 137, 142
Start-up Nation, 314
Steve Jobs, 347
Street politics, x, xxxv, xxxvi, 169, 183, 189, 191, 200, 242-244
Student movement(s), 223-225, 371
Student movements in the US, 221-222
Su shi (蘇軾), xi, xiv
Subcontracting of academic papers, 75
Subjects take priority, 275
Substance rather than language matters, 278

Tanaka Yoshikazu, 358
Tang Poetry, 84
Tangling politics with education, x
Taoyuan International Airport, 62, 96, 335
Teachers' union, 183-184, 238
Teaching and research universities, 107, 113, 116
Teaching evaluation, 259
Teaching universities, xxxvi, 101, 109, 114, 117
Team spirit, 125, 133-135, 161, 246

Thatcherism, 19-20
The (right) Way, xix, 65, 80, 237
The Boxer Indemnity Scholarship Program, xxx, 39
The Oblivion of Zhongyong, 158
The Strait, 5, 10, 12-15, 17, 23-24, 28, 31, 34, 36-37, 39, 44-45, 47, 51, 53- 56, 59, 67- 69, 71, 73, 75, 77- 81, 83, 85-87, 89-91, 93, 95, 98, 100, 105-107, 113, 115, 117, 124-126, 128, 132, 135, 138-140, 142, 148-149, 152-153, 156, 158, 162, 166, 169-171, 173-177, 180, 182-185, 187, 194-195, 208-209, 214, 216, 222-228, 230-232, 239, 242, 245, 247, 256-257, 265, 268, 282-284, 287, 289-290, 293-297, 302, 306, 307, 309, 312, 314, 316-317, 320-321, 325-327, 330-331, 335-338, 340, 345-347, 350-351, 357, 370, 374, 377, 383, 386-389, 394-395, 404-406, 410-411, 413-415, 418
Times Higher Education (The), xvii, xxv, 276
The World University Rankings, 262-264, 266, 268, 276-277, 291, 344-345
Third-world inferiority syndrome, 187
Thousand Talents Program, 209
Three components of an ideal higher education, 189
Three layers (of academic freedom), 193
Three parallels, 34
Three (wisdom) pillars, xii, xxi
Thun-Hohenstein education reform, 177
Top Industrial Managers for Europe network, 46
Total quality management, 257-258
Trade war against China, 2
Transnational education, 7

Triphibian involvement, 185
Trump, xxix, xxxii-xxxiii, xxxviii, 134, 207-208, 210, 212-213, 222, 249, 319, 335
Tsinghua College (tsinghua xuetang), xxx
Tsz shan monastery (香港慈山寺), 321
Tu youyou, 77, 139, 151, 372-373
Tuhao (newly rich hillbillies), 149-151
Tuition fees (increase of), 21-22
Two different views of time, 375
Two types of errors, 57

Ukraine, 48, 65, 305-306, 308, 319
United Daily, xxv, 61, 174, 287-288
University's governance, vi, xvi, 36, 169, 171, 194, 207, 242, 368, 385
University,
    California Institute of Technology, Caltech, 37, 308
    California State Universities, 109
    Carnegie Mellow University, 316
    Catholic University of Leuven, KU Leuven, xviii, 6, 176
    Chinese University of Hong Kong, CUHK, xiv, xxiii, 267, 340-342
    City University of Hong Kong, CityU, iii, ix, xiv, xviii, xix
    City University of New York, 179, 206
    Columbia University, 37, 89, 221, 268
    Cornell Tech in New York, xviii, 308, 314, 331
    Cornell University, xxiii, 58, 123, 188, 194, 241, 308
    École Normale Supérieure, 46, 308
    École Polytechnique Fédérale de Lausanne (EPFL), 307
    George Washington University, xviii, 178, 179
    Georgia Institute of Technology, Georgia Tech, xxiii, 117, 331, 367
    Harvard University, 86, 211, 212, 266, 297
    Hong Kong University of Science and Technology, HKUST, xxiii, 22
    Humboldt University of Berlin, xviii, 108, 172, 177
    Imperial College, 20, 23, 46
    Indian Institute of Technology, xviii, xxiv
    Institut Polytechnique de Paris, xviii, 47, 133
    Iowa State University, xxiv, 82, 157, 168
    Johns Hopkins University, 108, 177, 194, 273, 277
    Juilliard School, 115
    Karolinska Institutet, 115
    Kent State University, 222
    Korea Advanced Institute of Science and Technology, xix
    Kyoto University, 33, 307, 309
    Ludwig Maximilian University of Munich, xviii, 47
    McGill University, xix
    Massachusetts Institute of Technology, MIT, xxix, xxxviii, 47-48, 80, 114-115, 198, 208, 212-213, 277, 307, 353
    Mayo Clinic College of Medicine, 115
    Nanjing University, 269
    National Chiao Tung University, xxiii
    National Taiwan University, NTU, xix, xxiii, 29, 34, 58-59, 195, 198, 201, 232, 249, 255, 264-265, 267, 297, 334, 339, 354
    National Tsing Hua University, xxiii, 87, 127, 269, 356
    National University of Singapore, xviii, 8, 37
    New York University, 6, 9
    Old University of Leuven, 176

Paris Sciences et Lettres University, PSL, xviii, 46
Peking University, xxiii, 7, 9, 33, 166, 216, 255-256, 267, 353
Princeton University, 309
Renmin University of China, 194, 269
Rockefeller University, 196, 198
Shanghai Jiao Tong University, xviii, 6, 198, 267, 271, 277
Seoul National University, xix, 37, 198
Saint Petersburg State University, 48
Stanford University, xxix, 37, 124, 266, 353
Technical University of Munich, 47
Texas A&M University, ix, xxiv, 89, 115, 274, 281, 335, 348, 387
Tel Aviv University, xviii, 37, 304-305
Tsinghua University, xix, xxiii-xxiv, 7, 33, 58, 124, 216, 256, 267, 353
Université Catholique de Louvain, UC Louvain, xviii, 176
Washington University in St. Louis, xviii, 178-179
University Grants Committee (UGC), 28, 37, 39-40, 43-44, 71, 94, 187, 214, 219, 238, 241, 245, 299, 300, 360, 377, 380, 383
University of,
  Bologna, xviii, 23, 173
  British Columbia, xviii, 313
  California, 222
    UC Berkeley, 108, 114, 207, 221, 277
    UC Davis, 222
    UC San Diego, 117-118
  Cambridge, 19
  Cape Town, xviii, 47, 224, 229
  Chicago, 6, 108, 172, 206
  Edinburgh, 39
  Helsinki, xix
  Hong Kong (HKU), xiv, 9, 91, 267
  Illinois, xviii, xxx
  Malaya, 268-269
  Manchester, 20, 23
  Michigan, 6, 222
  Missouri, 221
  New South Wales, 175
  North Carolina, Chapel Hill, 222
  Nottingham, 6
  Oxford, 19, 224
  Southern California, 268-269
  Sydney, xix, xxiv, 175
  Tennessee, xxiii, 13, 124, 387
  Texas, Austin, 222
  Tokyo, 33, 177, 198
  Toronto, 348
  Vienna, xviii, 171, 176-177, 181
  Washington in Seattle, 158, 266, 277
  Wisconsin-Madison, 115
University Organization Acts, 177
University system in Germany, 47
US Innovation and Competition Act, 366
US investment in research and development, 366
US News & World Report, 261, 268, 276
US-China confrontation, xxxii-xxxiii, 3
US-China Trade War, xxix, 65, 333
USA Today, 253, 261
USA Patriot Act, 206

Voluntary Support of Education (report), 367

Wall Street, 222
Wall Street Journal, xxxi
Wang Chuanshan (王船山), xv
W. Edwards Deming, 257
WHO, 140
Whole person education, v, 120-121, 123-125, 127-129, 131-133, 136, 142, 164, 166-168, 248
Win-win relationship, 140
Wong tsu, 48

Xun zi (荀子), 369

Yang jinshi (洋進士), 138
Yardsticks (or benchmark) for evaluating research, 259-260
Yoshiki Sasai, 196
Yushan Talents scheme, xxx

Zero case(s), 3, 237
Zero-COVID policy, 3-4, 63
Zhang Zhidong (張之洞), 48, 256
Zhu Xi (朱熹), xl, 100, 137, 193
Zhuang Zi (莊子), 89, 146, 376
Zhuge Liang (諸葛亮), 227